Cryptography in C and C++

MICHAEL WELSCHENBACH
Translated by DAVID KRAMER

ISBN 978-1-4302-5098-2

ISBN 978-1-4302-5099-9 (eBook)

President and Publisher: Paul Manning
Lead Editor: Dominic Shakeshaft
Technical Reviewer: David Putnam
Editorial Board: Steve Anglin, Mark Beckner, Ewan Buckingham, Gary Cornell, Louise Corrigan, Morgan Ertel, Jonathan Gennick, Jonathan Hassell, Robert Hutchinson, Michelle Lowman, James Markham, Matthew Moodie, Jeff Olson, Jeffrey Pepper, Douglas Pundick, Ben Renow-Clarke, Dominic Shakeshaft, Gwenan Spearing, Matt Wade, Tom Welsh
Coordinating Editor: Kathleen Sullivan
Copy Editor: Nicole LeClerc
Compositor: David Kramer
Artist: Kurt Krames
Cover Designer: Anna Ishchenko

Translated from German by David Kramer

Distributed to the book trade worldwide by Springer Science+Business Media New York, 233 Spring Street, 6th Floor, New York, NY 10013. Phone 1-800-SPRINGER, fax (201) 348-4505, e-mail `orders-ny@springer-sbm.com`, or visit `www.springeronline.com`. Apress Media, LLC is a California LLC and the sole member (owner) is Springer Science + Business Media Finance Inc (SSBM Finance Inc). SSBM Finance Inc is a Delaware corporation.

For information on translations, please e-mail `rights@apress.com`, or visit `www.apress.com`.

Apress and friends of ED books may be purchased in bulk for academic, corporate, or promotional use. eBook versions and licenses are also available for most titles. For more information, reference our Special Bulk Sales–eBook Licensing web page at `www.apress.com/bulk-sales`.

Any source code or other supplementary materials referenced by the author in this text is available to readers at `www.apress.com`. For detailed information about how to locate your book's source code, go to `www.apress.com/source-code/`.

To my family, as always

Contents

List of Figures

List of Tables

Foreword

CRYPTOGRAPHY IS AN ANCIENT ART, well over two thousand years old. The need to keep certain information secret has always existed, and attempts to preserve secrets have therefore existed as well. But it is only in the last thirty years that cryptography has developed into a science that has offered us needed security in our daily lives. Whether we are talking about automated teller machines, cellular telephones, Internet commerce, or computerized ignition locks on automobiles, there is cryptography hidden within. And what is more, none of these applications would work without cryptography!

The history of cryptography over the past thirty years is a unique success story. The most important event was surely the discovery of public key cryptography in the mid 1970s. It was truly a revolution: We know today that things are possible that previously we hadn't even dared to think about. Diffie and Hellman were the first to formulate publicly the vision that secure communication must be able to take place spontaneously. Earlier, it was the case that sender and receiver had first to engage in secret communication to establish a common key. Diffie and Hellman asked, with the naivety of youth, whether one could communicate secretly without sharing a common secret. Their idea was that one could encrypt information without a secret key, that is, one that no one else could know. This idea signaled the birth of public key cryptography. That this vision was more than just wild surmise was shown a few years later with the advent of the RSA algorithm.

Modern cryptography has been made possible through the extraordinarily fruitful collaboration between mathematics and computer science. Mathematics provided the basis for the creation and analysis of algorithms. Without mathematics, and number theory in particular, public key cryptography would be impossible. Mathematics provides the results on the basis of which the algorithms operate.

If the cryptographic algorithms are to be realized, then one needs procedures that enable computation with large integers: The algorithms must not function only in theory; they must perform to real-world specifications. That is the task of computer science.

This book distinguishes itself from all other books on the subject in that it makes clear this relationship between mathematics and computing. I know of no book on cryptography that presents the mathematical basis so thoroughly while providing such extensive practical applications, and all of this in an eminently readable style.

What we have here is a master writing about his subject. He knows the theory, and he presents it clearly. He knows the applications, and he presents a host of procedures for realizing them. He knows much, but he doesn't write like a know-it-all. He presents his arguments clearly, so that the reader obtains a clear understanding. In short, this is a remarkable book.

So best wishes to the author! And above all, best wishes to you, the reader!

Albrecht Beutelspacher

About the Author

MICHAEL WELSCHENBACH CURRENTLY WORKS FOR SRC Security Research & Consulting GmbH in Bonn, Germany. He graduated with a master's degree in mathematics from the University of Cologne and has gained extensive experience in cryptological research over the years. Currently, his favorite programming languages are C and C++. When not working, he enjoys spending time with his wife and two sons, programming, reading, music, photography, and digital imaging.

About the Translator

DAVID KRAMER EARNED HIS PH.D. in mathematics at the University of Maryland, and his M.A. in music at Smith College. For many years he worked in higher education, first as a professor of mathematics and computer science, and later as a director of academic computing. Since 1995 he has worked as an independent editor and translator. He has edited hundreds of books in mathematics and the sciences and has translated a number of books in a variety of fields, including *The Definitive Guide to Excel VBA* and *The Definitive Guide to MySQL*, both by Michael Kofler; and *Enterprise JavaBeans 2.1*, by Stefan Denninger and Ingo Peters; all published by Apress. Other translations include *Luck, Logic, and White Lies*, by Jörg Bewersdorff; *The Game's Afoot! Game Theory in Myth and Paradox*, by Alexander Mehlmann; the children's musical *Red Riding! Red Riding!* by Ernst Ekker with music by Sergei Dreznin; *In Quest of Tomorrow's Medicines*, by Jürgen Drews; and the novel *To Err Is Divine*, by Ágota Bozai.

Preface to the Second American Edition

When I have to wrestle with figures, I feel I'd like to stuff myself into a hole in the ground, so I can't see anything. If I raise my eyes and see the sea, or a tree, or a woman—even if she's an old 'un—damme if all the sums and figures don't go to blazes. They grow wings and I have to chase 'em.

—Nikos Kazanzakis, *Zorba the Greek*

THE SECOND AMERICAN EDITION OF this book has again been revised and enlarged. The chapter on random number generators has been completely rewritten, and the section on primality testing was substantially revised. The new results of Agrawal, Kayal, and Saxena on primality tests, whose discovery in 2002 that "PRIMES is in P" caused a sensation, are covered. The chapter on Rijndael/AES has been relocated for a better presentation, and it is pointed out that the standardization of Rijndael as the Advanced Encryption Standard has meanwhile been made official by the U.S. National Institute of Standards and Technology (NIST).

Unlike previous editions of the book, the second American edition does not contain a CD-ROM with the source code for the programs presented. Instead, the source code is available for download at www.apress.com in the Downloads section.

I wish to thank the publishers and translators who have meanwhile made this book available in Chinese, Korean, Polish, and Russian and through their careful reading have contributed to the quality of this edition.

I again thank David Kramer for his engaging and painstaking English translation, and Gary Cornell, of Apress, for his willingness to bring out the second American edition.

Finally, I wish to thank Springer Science publishers, and in particular once again Hermann Engesser, Dorothea Glausinger, and Ulrike Sricker, for their pleasant collaboration.

Preface to the First American Edition

Mathematics is a misunderstood and even maligned discipline. It's not the brute computations they drilled into us in grade school. It's not the science of reckoning. Mathematicians do not spend their time thinking up cleverer ways of multiplying, faster methods of adding, better schemes for extracting cube roots.

—Paul Hoffman, *The Man Who Loved Only Numbers*

THE FIRST AMERICAN EDITION IS A TRANSLATION OF the second German edition, which has been revised and expanded from the first German edition in a number of ways. Additional examples of cryptographic algorithms have been added, such as the procedures of Rabin and El Gamal, and in the realization of the RSA procedure the hash function RIPEMD-160 and formatting according to PKCS #1 have been adopted. There is also a discussion of possible sources of error that could lead to a weakening of the procedure. The text has been expanded or clarified at a number of points, and errors have been corrected. Additionally, certain didactic strategies have been strengthened, with the result that some of the programs in the source code differ in certain details from those presented in the book. Not all technical details are of equal importance, and the desire for fast and efficient code is not always compatible with attractive and easy-to-read programs.

And speaking of efficiency, in Appendix D running times are compared to those for certain functions in the GNU Multiprecision Library. In this comparison the FLINT/C exponentiation routine did not do at all badly. As a further extension, Appendix F provides references to some arithmetic and number-theoretic packages.

The software has been expanded by several functions and in places has been significantly overhauled, and in the process a number of errors and points of imprecision were removed. Additional test functions were developed and existing test functions expanded. A security mode was implemented, whereby security-critical variables in the individual functions are deleted by being overwritten. All C and C++ functions are now clearly cited and annotated in the appendices.

Since current compilers represent varying stages of development of the C++ standard, the C++ modules of the FLINT/C package have been set up in such a way that both traditional C++ header files of the form xxxxx.h and the new

ANSI header files can be used. For the same reason the use of the operator new( ) has been checked, as always, as to whether the null pointer is returned. This type of error handling does not make use of the ANSI standard *exceptions*, but it nonetheless functions with current compilers, while the method that conforms to the standard, by which new( ) generates an error via throw( ), is not universally available.

Although the focus of this book is the fundamentals of asymmetric cryptography, the recent nomination of *Rijndael* by the American National Institute of Standards and Technology (NIST) to be the advanced encryption standard (AES) encouraged me to include a final chapter (Chapter 11) with an extensive description of this algorithm. I am indebted to Gary Cornell, at Apress, for bringing up the subject and convincing me that this would be a worthwhile complement to the topics of this book. I would like to thank Vincent Rijmen, Antoon Bosselaers, Paulo Barreto, and Brian Gladman for their kind permission to include the source code for their Rijndael implementations in the source code that accompanies this book.

I wish to thank all the readers of the first edition, particularly those who called errors to my attention, made comments, or suggested improvements. All their communications were most welcome. As always, the author assumes all responsibility for errors that may yet remain in the text or the software, as well as for any new errors that may have crept in.

I offer my heartfelt thanks to Gary Cornell, at Apress, and again to Hermann Engesser, Dorothea Glaunsinger, and Ulrike Stricker, at Springer-Verlag, for their unstinting commitment and friendly collaboration.

I am deeply grateful to my translator, David Kramer, who has contributed with distinguished expertise and indefatigable dedication many valuable hints, which have been incorporated into the German edition of this book as well.

Warning

Before making use of the programs contained in this book please refer to the manuals and technical introductions for the relevant software and computers. Neither the author nor the publisher accepts any responsibility for losses due to improper execution of the instructions and programs contained in this book or due to errors in the text or in the programs that despite careful checking may remain. The programs in the downloadable source code are protected by copyright and may not be reproduced without permission of the publisher.

Disclaimer

In this book frequent use is made of the term "leading zeros." The use of this term is in no way to be construed as alluding to any person or persons, in public or private life, living or dead, and any such correspondence is entirely coincidental.

Preface to the First German Edition

Mathematics is the queen of the sciences, and number theory is the queen of mathematics. Frequently, she deigns to assist astronomy and other of the natural sciences, but primacy is due her under all circumstances.
—Carl Friedrich Gauss

WHY DO WE NEED A book on cryptography whose principal focus is the arithmetic of whole numbers—the integers—and its application to computer programming? Is this not a rather insignificant subject in comparison to the important problems with which computer science generally involves itself? So long as one confines oneself to the range of numbers that can be represented by the standard numerical types of a programming language, arithmetic is a rather simple affair, and the familiar arithmetic operations make their traditional appearances in programs accompanied by the familiar symbols $+$, $-$, $/$, $*$.

But if one requires results whose length far exceeds what can be expressed in 16 or 32 bits, then the situation begins to get interesting. Even the basic arithmetic operations are no longer available for such numbers, and one gets nowhere without first investing considerable effort in solving problems that never even seemed like problems before. Anyone who investigates problems in number theory, whether professionally or as a hobby, in particular the topic of contemporary cryptography, is familiar with such issues: The techniques of doing arithmetic that we learned in school now demand renewed attention, and we find ourselves sometimes dealing with incredibly involved processes.

The reader who wishes to develop programs in these areas and is not inclined to reinvent the wheel will find included with this book a suite of functions that will serve as an extension of C and C++ for calculating with large integers. We are not talking about "toy" examples that say, "this is how it works in principle," but a complete collection of functions and methods that satisfy the professional requirements of stability, performance, and a sound theoretical basis.

Making the connection between theory and practice is the goal of this book, that is, to close the gap between the theoretical literature and practical programming problems. In the chapters ahead we shall develop step by step the fundamental calculational principles for large natural numbers, arithmetic in finite rings and fields, and the more complex functions of elementary number theory, and we shall elucidate the many and various possibilities for applying these principles to modern cryptography. The mathematical fundamentals will be explained to the extent necessary for understanding the programs that are presented here, and for those interested in pursuing these matters further there are extensive references to the literature. The functions that we develop will then be brought together and extensively tested, resulting in a useful and comprehensive programming interface.

Beginning with the representation of large numbers, in the following chapters we shall first deal with the fundamentals of computation. For addition, subtraction, multiplication, and division of large numbers we shall create powerful basic functions. Building on these, we shall explain modular arithmetic in residue classes and implement the relevant operations in library functions. A separate chapter is devoted to the time-intensive process of exponentiation, where we develop and program various specialized algorithms for a number of applications in modular arithmetic.

After extensive preparation, which includes input and output of large numbers and their conversion into various bases, we study algorithms of elementary number theory using the basic arithmetic functions, and we then develop programs, beginning with the calculation of the greatest common divisor of large numbers. We shall then move on to such problems as calculating the Legendre and Jacobi symbols, and inverses and square roots in finite rings, and we shall also become familiar with the Chinese remainder theorem and its applications.

In connection with this we shall go into some detail about the principles of identifying large prime numbers, and we shall program a powerful multistage primality test.

A further chapter is devoted to the generation of large random numbers, in which a cryptographically useful bit generator is developed and tested with respect to its statistical properties.

To end the first part we shall concern ourselves with testing arithmetic and other functions. To do this we shall derive special test methods from the mathematical rules of arithmetic, and we shall consider the implementation of efficient external tools.

The subject of the second part is the step-by-step construction of the C++ class LINT (Large INTegers), in the course of which we shall embed the C functions of the first part into the syntax and semantics of the object-oriented programming language C++. We shall put particular weight on formatted input and output of LINT objects with flexible stream functions and manipulators, as well as error handling with exceptions. The elegance with which algorithms can be formulated in C++ is particularly impressive when the boundaries between standard types and large numbers as LINT objects begin to dissolve, resulting in the syntactic closeness to the implemented algorithms and in great clarity and transparency.

Finally, we shall demonstrate the application of the methods we have developed by implementing an extensive RSA cryptosystem for encryption and the creation of digital signatures. In the process we shall explain the theory of the RSA procedure and its operation as the most prominent representative of asymmetric cryptosystems, and in a self-contained example we shall develop an extensible kernel for applications of this ultramodern cryptographic process according to the object-oriented principles of the programming language C++.

We shall round all of this off with a glimpse of further possible extensions of the software library. As a small highlight at the end we shall present four functions in 80x86 assembly language for multiplication and division, which will improve the performance of our software. Appendix D contains a table of typical calculation times with and without the assembler supplement.

All readers of this book are heartily invited to join me on this path, or perhaps—depending on individual interest—to focus on particular sections or chapters and try out the functions presented there. The author hopes that it will not be taken amiss that he refers to his readers, together with himself, as "we." He hopes thereby to encourage them to take an active role in this journey through a cutting-edge area of mathematics and computer science, to figure things out for themselves and take from this book what is of greatest benefit. As for the software, let the reader not be lacking in ambition to extend the scope or speed of one or more functions through new implementations.

I wish to thank Springer-Verlag and particularly Hermann Engesser, Dorothea Glaunsinger, and Ulrike Stricker for their interest in the publication of this book and for their friendly and active collaboration. The manuscript was reviewed by Jörn Garbers, Josef von Helden, Brigitte Nebelung, Johannes Ueberberg, and Helga Welschenbach. I offer them my heartfelt thanks for their critical suggestions and improvements, and above all for their care and patience. If despite all of our efforts some errors remain in the text or in the software, the author alone bears the responsibility. I am extremely grateful to my friends and colleagues Robert Hammelrath, Franz-Peter Heider, Detlef Kraus, and Brigitte Nebelung for their insights into the connections between mathematics and computer science over many years of collaboration that have meant a great deal to me.

Part I

Arithmetic and Number Theory in C

How necessary arithmetic and the entire art of mathematics are can be easily measured, in that nothing can be created that is not connected with precise number and measurement, and no independent art can exist without its measures and proportions.

—Adam Ries: *Book of Calculation*, 1574

Typographical rules for manipulating numerals are actually arithmetical rules for operating on numbers.

—D. R. Hofstadter: *Gödel, Escher, Bach: An Eternal Golden Braid*

The human brain would no longer be burdened with anything that needed to be calculated! Gifted people would again be able to think instead of scribbling numbers.

—Sten Nadolny: *The Discovery of Slowness*, trans. Ralph Freedman

CHAPTER 1

Introduction

God created the integers. All the rest is the work of man.
  —Leopold Kronecker

If you look at zero you see nothing; but look through it and you will see the world.
  —Robert Kaplan, *The Nothing That Is: A Natural History of Zero*

TO BE INVOLVED WITH MODERN cryptography is to dive willy-nilly into number theory, that is, the study of the natural numbers, one of the most beautiful areas of mathematics. However, we have no intention of becoming deep-sea divers who raise sunken treasure from the mathematical ocean floor, which in any case is unnecessary for cryptographic applications. Our goals are much more modest. On the other hand, there is no limit to the depth of involvement of number theory with cryptography, and many significant mathematicians have made important contributions to this area.

The roots of number theory reach back to antiquity. The Pythagoreans—the Greek mathematician and philosopher Pythagoras and his school—were already deeply involved in the sixth century B.C.E. with relations among the integers, and they achieved significant mathematical results, for example the famed Pythagorean theorem, which is a part of every school child's education. With religious zeal they took the position that all numbers should be commensurate with the natural numbers, and they found themselves on the horns of a serious dilemma when they discovered the existence of "irrational" numbers such as $\sqrt{2}$, which cannot be expressed as the quotient of two integers. This discovery threw the world view of the Pythagoreans into disarray, to the extent that they sought to suppress knowledge of the irrational numbers, a futile form of behavior oft repeated throughout human history.

Two of the oldest number-theoretic algorithms, which have been passed down to us from the Greek mathematicians Euclid (third century B.C.E.) and Eratosthenes (276–195 B.C.E.), are closely related to the most contemporary encryption algorithms that we use every day to secure communication across the Internet. The "Euclidean algorithm" and the "sieve of Eratosthenes" are both quite up-to-date for our work, and we shall discuss their theory and application in Sections 10.1 and 10.5 of this book.

Among the most important founders of modern number theory are to be counted Pierre de Fermat (1601–1665), Leonhard Euler (1707–1783), Adrien Marie Legendre (1752–1833), Carl Friedrich Gauss (1777–1855), and Ernst Eduard Kummer (1810–1893). Their work forms the basis for the modern development of this area of mathematics and in particular the interesting application areas such as cryptography, with its asymmetric procedures for encryption and the generation of digital signatures (cf. Chapter 17). We could mention many more names of important contributors to this field, who continue to this day to be involved in often dramatic developments in number theory, and to those interested in a thrilling account of the history of number theory and its protagonists, I heartily recommend the book *Fermat's Last Theorem*, by Simon Singh.

Considering that already as children we learned counting as something to be taken for granted and that we were readily convinced of such facts as that two plus two equals four, we must turn to surprisingly abstract thought constructs to derive the theoretical justification for such assertions. For example, set theory allows us to derive the existence and arithmetic of the natural numbers from (almost) nothing. This "almost nothing" is the empty (or null) set $\varnothing := \{\ \}$, that is, the set that has no elements. If we consider the empty set to correspond to the number 0, then we are able to construct additional sets as follows. The successor 0^+ of 0 is associated with the set $0^+ := \{\,0\,\} = \{\,\varnothing\,\}$, which contains a single element, namely the null set. We give the successor of 0 the name 1, and for this set as well we can determine a successor, namely $1^+ := \{\,\varnothing, \{\,\varnothing\,\}\,\}$. The successor of 1, which contains 0 and 1 as its elements, is given the name 2. The sets thus constructed, which we have rashly given the names 0, 1, and 2, we identify—not surprisingly—with the well-known natural numbers 0, 1, and 2.

This principle of construction, which to every number x associates a successor $x^+ := x \cup \{\,x\,\}$ by adjoining x to the previous set, can be continued to produce additional numbers. Each number thus constructed, with the exception of 0, is itself a set whose elements constitute its *predecessors*. Only 0 has no predecessor. To ensure that this process continues ad infinitum, set theory formulates a special rule, called the *axiom of infinity:* There exists a set that contains 0 as well as the successor of every element that it contains.

From this postulated existence of (at least) one so-called *successor set*, which, beginning with 0, contains all successors, set theory derives the existence of a minimal successor set $\mathbb{N}$, which is itself a subset of every successor set. This minimal and thus uniquely determined successor set $\mathbb{N}$ is called the set of *natural numbers*, in which we expressly include zero as an element.[1]

---

[1] It was not decisive for this choice that according to standard DIN 5473 zero belongs to the natural numbers. From the point of view of computer science, however, it is practical to begin counting at zero instead of 1, which is indicative of the important role played by zero as the neutral element for addition (additive identity).

The natural numbers can be characterized by means of the axioms of Giuseppe Peano (1858–1932), which coincide with our intuitive understanding of the natural numbers:

(I) The successors of two unequal natural numbers are unequal: From $n \neq m$ it follows that $n^+ \neq m^+$, for all $n, m \in \mathbb{N}$.

(II) Every natural number, with the exception of 0, has a predecessor: $\mathbb{N}^+ = \mathbb{N} \setminus \{\, 0 \,\}$.

(III) The principle of *complete induction:* If $S \subset \mathbb{N}$, $0 \in S$, and $n \in S$ always imply $n^+ \in S$, then $S = \mathbb{N}$.

The principle of complete induction makes it possible to derive the arithmetic operations with natural numbers in which we are interested. The fundamental operations of addition and multiplication can be defined recursively as follows. We begin with **addition**:

For every natural number $n \in \mathbb{N}$ there exists a function s_n from $\mathbb{N}$ to $\mathbb{N}$ such that

(i) $s_n(0) = n$,

(ii) $s_n\left(x^+\right) = (s_n(x))^+$ for all natural numbers $x \in \mathbb{N}$.

The value of the function $s_n(x)$ is called the *sum $n + x$* of n and x.

The existence of such functions s_n for all natural numbers $n \in \mathbb{N}$ must, however, be proved, since the infinitude of natural numbers does not a priori justify such an assumption. The existence proof goes back to the principle of complete induction, corresponding to Peano's third axiom above (see [Halm], Chapters 11–13). For **multiplication** one proceeds analogously:

For every natural number $n \in \mathbb{N}$ there exists a function p_n from $\mathbb{N}$ to $\mathbb{N}$ such that

(i) $p_n(0) = 0$,

(ii) $p_n\left(x^+\right) = p_n(x) + n$ for all natural numbers $x \in \mathbb{N}$.

The value of the function $p_n(x)$ is called the *product $n \cdot x$* of n and x.

As expected, multiplication is defined in terms of addition. For the arithmetic operations thus defined one can prove, through repeated application of complete induction on x in accordance with Axiom III, such well-known arithmetic laws as associativity, commutativity, and distributivity (cf. [Halm], Chapter 13). Although we usually use these laws without further ado, we shall help ourselves to them as much as we please in testing our FLINT functions (see Chapters 13 and 18).

In a similar way we obtain a definition of **exponentiation**, which we give here in view of the importance of this operation in what follows.

For every natural number $n \in \mathbb{N}$ there exists a function e_n from $\mathbb{N}$ to $\mathbb{N}$ such that

(i) $e_n(0) = 1$,

(ii) $e_n\left(x^+\right) = e_n(x) \cdot n$ for every natural number $x \in \mathbb{N}$.

The value of the function $e_n(x)$ is called the xth *power* n^x of n. With complete induction we can prove the *power law*

$$n^x n^y = n^{x+y}, \quad n^x \cdot m^x = (n \cdot m)^x, \quad (n^x)^y = n^{xy},$$

to which we shall return in Chapter 6.

In addition to the calculational operations, the set $\mathbb{N}$ of natural numbers has defined on it an order relation "$<$" that makes it possible to compare two elements $n, m \in \mathbb{N}$. Although this fact is worthy of our great attention from a set-theoretic point of view, here we shall content ourselves with noting that the order relation has precisely those properties that we know about and use in our everyday lives.

Now that we have begun with establishing the empty set as the sole fundamental building block of the natural numbers, we now proceed to consider the materials with which we shall be concerned in what follows. Although number theory generally considers the natural numbers and the integers as given and goes on to consider their properties without excessive beating about the bush, it is nonetheless of interest to us to have at least once taken a glance at a process of "mathematical cell division," a process that produces not only the natural numbers, but also the arithmetic operations and rules with which we shall be deeply involved from here on.

About the Software

The software described in this book constitutes in its entirety a package, a so-called function library, to which frequent reference will be made. This library has been given the name FLINT/C, which is an acronym for "functions for large integers in number theory and cryptography."

The FLINT/C library contains, among other items, the modules shown in Tables 1-1 through 1-5, which can be found as source code at www.apress.com.

Table 1-1. Arithmetic and number theory in C in directory flint/src

`flint.h`	header file for using functions from `flint.c`
`flint.c`	arithmetic and number-theoretic functions in C
`kmul.{h,c}`	functions for Karatsuba multiplication and squaring
`ripemd.{h,c}`	implementation of the hash function RIPEMD-160
`sha{1,256}.{h,c}`	implementations of the hash functions SHA-1, SHA-256
`entropy.c`	generation of entropy as start value for pseudorandom sequences
`random.{h,c}`	generation of pseudorandom numbers
`aes.{h,c}`	implementation of the Advanced Encryption Standard

Table 1-2. Arithmetic modules in 80x86 assembler (see Chapter 19) in directory flint/src/asm

`mult.{s,asm}`	multiplication, replaces the C function `mult()` in `flint.c`
`umul.{s,asm}`	multiplication, replaces the C function `umul()`
`sqr.{s,asm}`	squaring, replaces the C function `sqr()`
`div.{s,asm}`	division, replaces the C function `div_l()`

Table 1-3. Tests (see Section 13.2 and Chapter 18) in directories flint/test and flint/test/testvals

`testxxx.c[pp]`	test programs in C and C++
`xxx.txt`	test vectors for AES

Table 1-4. Libraries in 80x86 assembler (see Chapter 19) in directories flint/lib and flint/lib/dll

`flinta.lib`	library with assembler functions in OMF (object module format)
`flintavc.lib`	library with assembler functions in COFF (common object file format)
`flinta.a`	archive with assembler functions for emx/gcc under OS/2
`libflint.a`	archive with assembler functions for use under LINUX
`flint.dll`	DLL with the FLINT/C functions for use with MS VC/C++
`flint.lib`	link library for `flint.dll`

Table 1-5. RSA implementation (see Chapter 17) in directory flint/rsa

`rsakey.h`	header file for the RSA classes
`rsakey.cpp`	implementation of the RSA classes `RSAkey` and `RSApub`
`rsademo.cpp`	example application of the RSA classes and their functions

A list of the individual components of the FLINT/C software can be found in the file `readme.doc` is the source code. The software has been tested with the indicated development tools on the following platforms:

- GNU gcc under Linux, SunOS 4.1, and Sun Solaris

- GNU/EMX gcc under OS/2 Warp, DOS, and Windows (9x, NT)

- Borland BCC32 under Windows (9x, NT, 2000, XP)

- lcc-win32 under Windows (9x, NT, 2000, XP)

- Cygnus cygwin B20 under Windows (9x, NT, 2000, XP)

- IBM VisualAge under OS/2 Warp and Windows (9x, NT, 2000, XP)

- Microsoft C under DOS, OS/2 Warp, and Windows (9x, NT)

- Microsoft Visual C/C++ under Windows (9x, NT, 2000, XP)

- Watcom C/C++ under DOS, OS/2 Warp, and Windows (3.1, 9x, NT, XP)

- OpenWatcom C/C++ under Windows (2000, XP)

The assembler programs can be translated with Microsoft MASM,[2] with Watcom WASM, or with the GNU assembler GAS. They are contained in the downloadable source code in translated form as libraries in OMF (object module

---

[2] Call: `ml /Cx /c /Gd ⟨filename⟩`.

format) and COFF (common object file format), respectively, as well as in the form of a LINUX archive, and are used instead of the corresponding C functions when in translating C programs the macro FLINT_ASM is defined and the assembler object modules from the libraries, respectively archives, are linked.

A typical compiler call, here for the GNU compiler gcc, looks something like the following (with the paths to the source directories suppressed):

```
gcc -O2 -o rsademo rsademo.cpp rsakey.cpp flintpp.cpp
    randompp.cpp flint.c aes.c ripemd.c sha256.c entropy.c
    random.c -lstdc++
```

The C++ header files following the ANSI standard are used when in compilation the macro FLINTPP_ANSI is defined; otherwise, the traditional header files xxxxx.h are used.

Depending on the computer platform, there may be deviations with regard to the compiler switches; but to achieve maximum performance the options for speed optimization should always be turned on. Because of the demands on the *stack*, in many environments and applications it will have to be adjusted.[3] Regarding the necessary stack size for particular applications, one should note the suggestion about the exponentiation functions in Chapter 6 and in the overview on page 117. The stack requirements can be lessened by using the exponentiation function with dynamic stack allocation as well as by the implementation of dynamic registers (see Chapter 9).

The C functions and constants have been provided with the macros

__FLINT_API	Qualifier for C functions
__FLINT_API_A	Qualifier for assembler functions
__FLINT_API_DATA	Qualifier for constants

as in

```
extern int __FLINT_API add_l(CLINT, CLINT, CLINT);
extern USHORT __FLINT_API_DATA smallprimes[];
```

or, respectively, in the use of the assembler functions

```
extern int __FLINT_API_A div_l (CLINT, CLINT, CLINT, CLINT);
```

These macros are generally defined as empty comments /**/. With their aid, using the appropriate definitions, compiler- and linker-specific instructions to functions and data can be made. If the assembler modules are used and not

---

[3] With modern computers with virtual memory, except in the case of DOS, one usually does not have to worry about this point, in particular with Unix or Linux systems.

the GNU compiler gcc, the macro __FLINT_API_A is defined by __cdecl, and some compilers understand this as an instruction that the assembler functions corresponding to the C name and calling conventions are to be called.

For modules that import FLINT/C functions and constants from a dynamic link library (DLL) under Microsoft Visual C/C++, in translation the macros -D__FLINT_API=__cdecl and -D__FLINT_API_DATA= __declspec (dllimport) must be defined. This has already been taken into account in flint.h, and it suffices in this case to define the macro FLINT_USEDLL for compilation. For other development environments analogous definitions should be employed.

The small amount of work involved in initializing a FLINT/C DLL is taken care of by the function FLINTInit_l(), which provides initial values for the random number generator[4] and generates a set of dynamic registers (see Chapter 9). The complementary function FLINTExit_l() deallocates the dynamic registers. Sensibly enough, the initialization is not handed over to every individual process that uses the DLL, but is executed once at the start of the DLL. As a rule, a function with creator-specific signature and calling convention should be used, which is executed automatically when the DLL is loaded by the run-time system. This function can take over the FLINT/C initialization and use the two functions mentioned above. All of this should be considered when a DLL is created.

Some effort was made to make the software usable in security-critical applications. To this end, in *security mode* local variables in functions, in particular CLINT and LINT objects, are deleted after use by being overwritten with zeros. For the C functions this is accomplished with the help of the macro PURGEVARS_L() and the associated function purgevars_l(). For the C++ functions the destructor ~LINT() is similarly equipped. The assembler functions overwrite their working memory. The deletion of variables that are passed as arguments to functions is the responsibility of the calling functions.

If the deletion of variables, which requires a certain additional expenditure of time, is to be omitted, then in compilation the macro FLINT_UNSECURE must be defined. At run time the function char* verstr_l() gives information about the modes set at compile time, in which additionally to the version label X.x, the letters "a" for assembler support and "s" for security mode are output in a character string if these modes have been turned on.

---

[4]   The initial values are made up of 32-bit numbers taken from the system clock. For applications in which security is critical it is advisable to use suitable random values from a sufficiently large interval as initial values.

Legal Conditions for Using the Software

The software is exclusively for private use. For such purposes the software may be used, altered, and distributed under the following conditions:

1. The copyright notice may not be altered or deleted.

2. All changes must be annotated by means of comment lines. Any other use, in particular the use of the software for commercial purposes, requires written permission from the publisher or the author.

The software has been created and tested with the greatest possible care. Since errors can never be completely eliminated, neither the author nor the publisher can take responsibility for direct or indirect damages that may arise from the use or unusability of the software, regardless of the purpose to which it has been put.

Contacting the Author

The author would be glad to receive information about errors or any other helpful criticism or comment. Please write to him at `cryptography@welschenbach.com`.

CHAPTER 2

Number Formats: The Representation of Large Numbers in C

So I have made up my own system for writing large numbers and I am going to use this chapter as a chance to explain it
—Isaac Asimov, *Adding a Dimension*

The process that has led to the higher organization of this form could also be imagined differently
—J. Weber, *Form, Motion, Color*

ONE OF THE FIRST STEPS in creating a function library for calculating with large numbers is to determine how large numbers are to represented in the computer's main memory. It is necessary to plan carefully, since decisions made at this point will be difficult to revise at a later time. Changes to the internal structure of a software library are always possible, but the user interface should be kept as stable as possible in the sense of "upward compatibility."

It is necessary to determine the order of magnitude of the numbers to be processed and the data type to be used for coding these numerical values.

The basic function of all routines in the FLINT/C library is the processing of natural numbers of several hundred digits, which far exceeds the capacity of standard data types. We thus require a logical ordering of a computer's memory units by means of which large numbers can be expressed and operated on. In this regard one might imagine structures that automatically create sufficient space for the values to be represented, but no more than is actually needed. One would like to maintain such economically organized housekeeping with respect to main memory by means of dynamic memory management for large numbers that allocates or releases memory according to need in the course of arithmetic operations. Although such can certainly be realized (see, for example, [Skal]), memory management has a price in computation time, for which reason the representation of integers in the FLINT/C package gives preference to the simpler definition of static length.

For representing large natural numbers one might use vectors whose elements are a standard data type. For reasons of efficiency an unsigned data type is to be preferred, which allows the results of arithmetic operations to be stored in this type without loss as unsigned long (defined in flint.h as ULONG), which is the largest arithmetic standard C data type (see [Harb], Section 5.1.1). A ULONG variable can usually be represented exactly with a complete register word of the CPU.

Our goal is that operations on large numbers be reducible by the compiler as directly as possible to the register arithmetic of the CPU, for those are the parts that the computer calculates "in its head," so to speak. For the FLINT/C package the representation of large integers is therefore by means of the type unsigned short int (in the sequel USHORT). We assume that the type USHORT is represented by 16 bits and that the type ULONG can fully accept results of arithmetic operations with USHORT types, which is to say that the informally formulated size relationship USHORT $\times$ USHORT $\leq$ ULONG holds.

Whether these assumptions hold for a particular compiler can be deduced from the ISO header file limits.h (cf. [Harb], Sections 2.7.1 and 5.1). For example, in the file limits.h for the GNU C/C++ compiler (cf. [Stlm]) the following appears:

```
#define UCHAR_MAX 0xffU
#define USHRT_MAX 0xffffU
#define UINT_MAX 0xffffffffU
#define ULONG_MAX 0xffffffffUL
```

One should note that with respect to the number of binary places there are actually only three sizes that are distinguished. The type USHRT (respectively USHORT in our notation) can be represented in a 16-bit register; the type ULONG fills the word length of a CPU with 32-bit registers. The type ULONG_MAX determines the value of the largest unsigned whole numbers representable by scalar types (cf. [Harb], page 110).[1] The value of the product of two numbers of type USHRT is at most 0xffff * 0xffff = 0xfffe0001 and is thus representable by a ULONG type, where the least-significant 16 bits, in our example the value 0x0001, can be isolated by a cast operation into the type USHRT. The implementation of the basic arithmetic functions of the FLINT/C package is based on the above-discussed size relationship between the types USHORT and ULONG.

An analogous approach, one that used data types with 32-bit and 64-bit lengths in the role of USHORT and ULONG in the present implementation, would reduce the calculation time for multiplication, division, and exponentiation

---

[1] Without taking into account such practical nonstandard types as unsigned long long in GNU C/C++ and certain other C compilers.

by about 25 percent. Such possibilities are realizable with functions written in assembler with direct access to 64-bit results of machine instructions for multiplication and division or with processors with 64-bit registers that would also allow to C implementations the lossless storage of such results in a ULONG type. The FLINT/C package contains some examples whose gain in speed results from the use of arithmetic assembler functions (see Chapter 19).

The next question is that of the ordering of the USHORT digits within a vector. We can imagine two possibilities: from left to right, with a descending evaluation of digits from lower to higher memory addresses, or the other way round, with an ascending evaluation of digits from lower to higher memory addresses. The latter arrangement, which is the reverse of our usual notation, has the advantage that changes in the size of numbers at constant addresses can take place with the simple allocation of additional digits, without the numbers having to be relocated in memory. Thus the choice is clear: The evaluation of digits of our numerical representation increases with increasing memory address or vector index.

As a further element of the representation the number of digits will be appended and stored in the first element of the vector. The representation of long numbers in memory thus has the format

$$n = (l n_1 n_2 \ldots n_l)_B, \quad 0 \leq l \leq \text{CLINTMAXDIGIT}, \quad 0 \leq n_i < B, \ i = 1, \ldots, l,$$

where B denotes the base of the numerical representation; for the FLINT/C package we have $B := 2^{16} = 65536$. The value of B will be our companion from here on and will appear continually in what follows. The constant CLINTMAXDIGIT represents the maximal number of digits of a CLINT object.

Zero is represented by the length $l = 0$. The value n of a number that is represented by a FLINT/C variable n_l is calculated as

$$n = \begin{cases} \sum_{i=1}^{n\_l[0]} n\_l[i] B^{i-1}, & \text{if } n\_l[0] > 0, \\ 0, & \text{otherwise.} \end{cases}$$

If $n > 0$, then the least-significant digit of n to the base B is given by n_l[1], and the most-significant digit by n_l[n_l[0]]. The number of digits of n_l[0] will be read in what follows by the macro DIGITS_L (n_l) and set to 1 by the macro SETDIGITS_L (n_l, 1). Likewise, access to the least-significant and most-significant digits of n_l will be conveyed by LSDPTR_L(n_l) and MSDPTR_L(n_l), each of which returns a pointer to the digit in question. The use of the macros defined in flint.h yields independence from the actual representation of the number.

Since we have no need of a sign for natural numbers, we now have all the required elements for the representation of such numbers. We define the corresponding data type by

```
typedef unsigned short clint;
typedef clint CLINT[CLINTMAXDIGIT + 1];
```

In accordance with this, a large number will be declared by

```
CLINT n_l;
```

The declaration of function parameters of type CLINT can follow from the instruction CLINT n_l in the function header.[2] The definition of a pointer myptr_l to a CLINT object occurs via CLINTPTR myptr_l or clint *myptr_l.

FLINT/C functions can, depending on the setting of the constant CLINTMAXDIGIT in flint.h, process numbers up to 4096 bits in length, which corresponds to 1233 decimal digits or 256 digits to the base 2^{16}. By changing CLINTMAXDIGIT the maximal length can be adjusted as required. The definitions of other constants depend on this parameter; for example, the number of USHORTs in a CLINT object is specified by

```
#define CLINTMAXSHORT CLINTMAXDIGIT + 1
```

and the maximal number of processable binary digits is defined by

```
#define CLINTMAXBIT CLINTMAXDIGIT << 4
```

Since the constants CLINTMAXDIGIT and CLINTMAXBIT are used frequently, yet are rather unwieldy from a typographical point of view, we shall denote these constants by abbreviations MAX_B and MAX_2 (with the exception of program code, where the constants will appear in their normal form).

With this definition it follows that CLINT objects can assume whole-number values in the interval $\left[0, B^{\text{MAX}_B} - 1\right]$, respectively $\left[0, 2^{\text{MAX}_2} - 1\right]$. We denote the value $B^{\text{MAX}_B} - 1 = 2^{\text{MAX}_2} - 1$, the largest natural number that can be represented by a CLINT object, by $N_{\max}$.

---

[2] In this regard compare Chapters 4 and 9 of the extremely readable book [Lind], where there is an extensive explanation of when vectors and pointers in C are equivalent, and above all, when this is not the case and what types of errors can arise from a misunderstanding of these issues.

For some functions it is necessary to process numbers that have more digits than can be accommodated by a CLINT object. For these cases the variants of the CLINT type are defined by

```
typedef unsigned short CLINTD[1+(CLINTMAXDIGIT<<1)];
```

and

```
typedef unsigned short CLINTQ[1+(CLINTMAXDIGIT<<2)];
```

which can hold double, respectively four times, the number of digits.

As support personnel to aid in programming, the module flint.c defines the constants nul_l, one_l, and two_l, which represent the numbers 0, 1, and 2 in CLINT format; and in flint.h there are corresponding macros SETZERO_L(), SETONE_L(), and SETTWO_L(), which set CLINT objects to the corresponding values.

CHAPTER 3

Interface Semantics

> When people hear some words, they normally believe
> that there's some thought behind them.
>
> —Goethe, *Faust*, Part 1

IN THE FOLLOWING WE SHALL set some fundamental properties that relate to the behavior of the interface and the use of FLINT/C functions. First we shall consider the textual representation of CLINT objects and FLINT/C functions, but primarily we wish to clarify some fundamentals of the implementation that are important to the use of the functions.

The functions of the FLINT/C package are identified with the convention that their names end with "_l"; for example, add_l denotes the addition function. Designators of CLINT objects likewise end with an underscore and an appended l. For the sake of simplicity we shall equate from now on, when conditions permit, a CLINT object n_l with the value that it represents.

The representation of a FLINT/C function begins with a header, which contains the syntactic and semantic description of the function interface. Such function headers typically look something like the following.

Function:	a brief description of the function
Syntax:	int f_l (CLINT a_l, CLINT b_l, CLINT c_l);
Input:	a_l, b_l (operands)
Output:	c_l (result)
Return:	0 if all is ok
	otherwise, a warning or error message

Here we distinguish, among other things, between **output** and **return** value: While **output** refers to the values that are stored by the function in the passed arguments, by **return** we mean the values that the function returns via a return command. Except for a few cases (for example, the functions ld_l(), Section 10.3, and twofact_l(), Section 10.4.1), the return value consists of status information or error messages.

Parameters other than those involved with **output** are not changed by the function. Calls of the form f_l(a_l, b_l, a_l), where a_l and b_l are used as arguments and a_l is overwritten with the return value at the end of the computation, are always possible, since the return variable is written to with the return value only after the complete execution of the operation. From assembler programming one says in this case that the variable a_l is used as an *accumulator*. This modus operandi is supported by all FLINT/C functions.

A CLINT object n_l possesses *leading zeros* if for a value l one has

```
(DIGITS_L (n_l) == l) && (l > 0) && (n_l[l] == 0);
```

Leading zeros are redundant, since although they lengthen the representation of a number, they have no effect on its value. However, leading zeros are allowed in the notation of a number, for which reason we should not simply ignore this option. The acceptance of leading zeros is, to be sure, a burdensome implementation detail, but it leads to increased tolerance of input from external sources and thus contributes to the stability of all the functions. CLINT numbers with leading zeros are thus accepted by all FLINT/C functions, but they are not generated by them.

A further setting is related to the behavior of arithmetic functions in the case of *overflow*, which occurs when the result of an arithmetic operation is too large to be represented in the result type. Although in some publications on C the behavior of a program in the case of arithmetic overflow is said to be implementation-dependent, the C standard nonetheless governs precisely the case of overflow in arithmetic operations with unsigned integer types: There it is stated that arithmetic modulo 2^n should be executed when the data type can represent integers of n-bit length (see [Harb], Section 5.1.2). Accordingly, in the case of overflow the basic arithmetic functions described below reduce their results modulo $(N_{max} + 1)$, which means that the remainder after whole-number division by $N_{max} + 1$ is output as the result (see Section 4.3 and Chapter 5). In the case of *underflow*, which occurs when the result of an operation is negative, a positive residue modulo $(N_{max} + 1)$ is output. The FLINT/C functions thus behave in conformity with arithmetic according to the C standard.

If an overflow or underflow is detected, the arithmetic functions return the appropriate error code. This and all other error codes in Table 3-1 are defined in the header file flint.h.

Table 3-1. FLINT/C error codes

Error Code	Interpretation
E_CLINT_BOR	invalid basis in str2clint_l() (see Chapter 8)
E_CLINT_DBZ	division by zero
E_CLINT_MAL	error in memory allocation
E_CLINT_MOD	nonodd (even) modulus in Montgomery multiplication
E_CLINT_NOR	register unavailable (see Chapter 9)
E_CLINT_NPT	null pointer passed as argument
E_CLINT_OFL	overflow
E_CLINT_UFL	underflow

The Fundamental Operations

Thus calculation can be seen as the basis and foundation of all the arts.
— Adam Ries, *Book of Calculation*

And you, poor creature, you are completely useless. Look at me. Everyone needs me.
— Aesop, "The Fir and the Blackberry Bush"

There is one small prerequisite for mastering the mathemagic tricks in this chapter—you need to know the multiplication tables through 10 . . . backward and forward.
— Arthur Benjamin, Michael B. Shermer, *Mathemagics*

THE FUNDAMENTAL BUILDING BLOCKS OF any software package for computer arithmetic are the functions that carry out the basic operations of addition, subtraction, multiplication, and division. The efficiency of the entire package hangs on the last two of these, and for that reason great care must be taken in the selection and implementation of the associated algorithms. Fortunately, volume 2 of Donald Knuth's classic *The Art of Computer Programming* contains most of what we need for this portion of the FLINT/C functions.

In anticipation of their representation to come, the functions developed in the following sections use the operations cpy_l(), which copies one CLINT object to another in the sense of an allocation, and cmp_l(), which makes a comparison of the sizes of two CLINT values. For a more precise description see Section 7.4 and Chapter 8.

Let us mention at this point that for the sake of clarity, in this chapter the functions for the fundamental arithmetic operations are developed all of a piece, while in Chapter 5 it will prove practical to split some of the functions into their respective "core" operations and from there develop additional steps such as the elimination of leading zeros and the handling of overflow and underflow, where, however, the syntax and semantics of the functions are kept intact. For an understanding of the relations described in this chapter this is irrelevant, so that for now we can forget about these more difficult issues.

4.1 Addition and Subtraction

> This notion of "further counting" means, "to the integer n_1 add the integer n_2," and the integer s at which one arrives by this further counting is called "the result of addition" or the "sum of n_1 and n_2" and is represented by $n_1 + n_2$.
>
> —Leopold Kronecker, *On the Idea of Number*

Since addition and subtraction are in principle the same operation with differing signs, the underlying algorithms are equivalent, and we can deal with them together in this section. We consider operands a and b with representations

$$a := (a_{m-1}a_{m-2}\ldots a_0)_B = \sum_{i=0}^{m-1} a_i B^i, \qquad 0 \le a_i < B,$$

$$b := (b_{n-1}b_{n-2}\ldots b_0)_B = \sum_{i=0}^{n-1} b_i B^i, \qquad 0 \le b_i < B,$$

where we assume $a \ge b$. For addition this condition represents no restriction, since it can always be achieved by interchanging the two summands. For subtraction it means that the difference is positive or zero and therefore can be represented as a CLINT object without reduction modulo $(N_{\max} + 1)$.

Addition consists essentially of the following steps.

Algorithm for the addition $a + b$

1. Set $i \leftarrow 0$ and $c \leftarrow 0$.

2. Set $t \leftarrow a_i + b_i + c$, $s_i \leftarrow t \bmod B$, and $c \leftarrow \lfloor t/B \rfloor$.

3. Set $i \leftarrow i + 1$; if $i \le n - 1$, go to step 2.

4. Set $t \leftarrow a_i + c$, $s_i \leftarrow t \bmod B$, and $c \leftarrow \lfloor t/B \rfloor$.

5. Set $i \leftarrow i + 1$; if $i \le m - 1$, go to step 4.

6. Set $s_m \leftarrow c$.

7. Output $s = (s_m s_{m-1} \ldots s_0)_B$.

The digits of the summands, together with the carry, are added in step 2, with the less-significant part stored as a digit of the sum, while the more-significant part is carried to the next digit. If the most-significant digit of one of the summands is reached, then in step 4 any remaining digits of the other summand are added to any remaining carries one after the other. Until the last summand digit is processed, the less-significant part is stored as a digit of the sum, and the more-significant part is used as a carry to the next digit. Finally, if there is a leftover carry at the end, it is stored as the most-significant digit of the sum. The output of this digit is suppressed if it has the value zero.

Steps 2 and 4 of the algorithm appear in a similar form in the case of subtraction, multiplication, and division. The associated code, which is illustrated by the following lines, is typical for arithmetic functions:[1]

```
s = (USHORT)(carry = (ULONG)a + (ULONG)b + (ULONG)(USHORT)(carry >> BITPERDGT));
```

The intermediate value t that appears in the algorithm is represented by the variable carry, of type ULONG, which holds the sum of the digits a_i and b_i as well as the carry of the previous operation. The new summation digit s_i is stored in the less-significant part of carry, from where it is taken by means of a cast as a USHORT. The resulting carry from this operation is held in the more-significant part of carry for the next operation.

The implementation of this algorithm by our function add_l() deals with a possible overflow of the sum, where in this case a reduction of the sum modulo $(N_{\max} + 1)$ is carried out.

Function:	addition
Syntax:	int add_l (CLINT a_l, CLINT b_l, CLINT s_l);
Input:	a_l, b_l (summands)
Output:	s_l (sum)
Return:	E_CLINT_OK if all is ok
	E_CLINT_OFL in the case of overflow

```
int
add_l (CLINT a_l, CLINT b_l, CLINT s_l)
{
  clint ss_l[CLINTMAXSHORT + 1];
  clint *msdptra_l, *msdptrb_l;
  clint *aptr_l, *bptr_l, *sptr_l = LSDPTR_L (ss_l);
  ULONG carry = 0L;
  int OFL = E_CLINT_OK;
```

---

[1]   The C expression in this compact form is due to my colleague Robert Hammelrath.

The pointers for the addition loop are set. Here it is checked which of the two summands has the greater number of digits. The pointers aptr_l and msdaptr_l are initialized such that they point respectively to the least-significant and most-significant digits of the summand that has the most digits, or to those digits of a_l if both summands are of the same length. This holds analogously for the pointers bptr_l and msdbptr_l, which point to the least-significant and most-significant digits of the shorter summand, or to those digits of b_l. The initialization is carried out with the help of the macro LSDPTR_L() for the least-significant digits and MSDPTR_L() for the most-significant digits of a CLINT object. The macro DIGITS_L (a_l) specifies the number of digits of the CLINT object a_l, and with SETDIGITS_L(a_l, n) the number of digits of a_l is set to the value n.

```
if (DIGITS_L (a_l) < DIGITS_L (b_l))
 {
  aptr_l = LSDPTR_L (b_l);
  bptr_l = LSDPTR_L (a_l);
  msdptra_l = MSDPTR_L (b_l);
  msdptrb_l = MSDPTR_L (a_l);
  SETDIGITS_L (ss_l, DIGITS_L (b_l));
 }
else
 {
  aptr_l = LSDPTR_L (a_l);
  bptr_l = LSDPTR_L (b_l);
  msdptra_l = MSDPTR_L (a_l);
  msdptrb_l = MSDPTR_L (b_l);
  SETDIGITS_L (ss_l, DIGITS_L (a_l));
 }
```

In the first loop of add_l the digits of a_l and b_l are added and stored in the result variable ss_l. Any leading zeros cause no problem, and they are simply used in the calculation and filtered out when the result is copied to s_l. The loop runs from the least-significant digit of b_l to the most-significant digit. This corresponds exactly to the process of pencil-and-paper addition as learned at school. As promised, here is the implementation of the carry.

```
while (bptr_l <= msdptrb_l)
 {
  *sptr_l++ = (USHORT)(carry = (ULONG)*aptr_l++
                   + (ULONG)*bptr_l++ + (ULONG)(USHORT)(carry >> BITPERDGT));
 }
```

> The two USHORT values *aptr and *bptr are copied via a *cast* to ULONG representation and added. To this the carry from the last interation is added. The result is a ULONG value that contains the carry from the addition step in its higher-valued word. This value is allocated to the variable carry and there reserved for the next iteration. The value of the resulting digit is taken from the lower-valued word of the addition result via a cast to the type USHORT. The carry saved in the higher-valued word of carry is included in the next iteration by a shift to the right by the number BITPERDGT of bits used for the representation of USHORT and a cast to USHORT.
>
> In the second loop only the remaining digits of a_l are added to a possible existing carry and stored in s_l.

```
while (aptr_l <= msdptra_l)
  {
   *sptr_l++ = (USHORT)(carry = (ULONG)*aptr_l++
                        + (ULONG)(USHORT)(carry >> BITPERDGT));
  }
```

> If after the second loop there is a carry, the result is one digit longer than a_l. If it is determined that the result exceeds the maximal value N_{max} representable by the CLINT type, then the result is reduced modulo $(N_{max} + 1)$ (see Chapter 5), analogously to the treatment of standard unsigned types. In this case the status announcement of the error code E_CLINT_OFL is returned.

```
if (carry & BASE)
  {
   *sptr_l = 1;
   SETDIGITS_L (ss_l, DIGITS_L (ss_l) + 1);
  }
if (DIGITS_L (ss_l) > (USHORT)CLINTMAXDIGIT)      /* overflow? */
  {
   ANDMAX_L (ss_l);       /* reduce modulo (Nmax + 1) */
   OFL = E_CLINT_OFL;
  }
cpy_l (s_l, ss_l);

return OFL;
}
```

The run time t of all the procedures given here for addition and subtraction is $t = O(n)$, and thus proportional to the number of digits of the larger of the two operands.

Now that we have seen addition, we shall present the algorithm for subtraction of two numbers a and b with representations

$$a = (a_{m-1}a_{m-2}\ldots a_0)_B \geq b = (b_{n-1}b_{n-2}\ldots b_0)_B$$

to base B.

Algorithm for the subtraction $a - b$

1. Set $i \leftarrow 0$ and $c \leftarrow 1$.

2. If $c = 1$, set $t \leftarrow B + a_i - b_i$; otherwise, set $t \leftarrow B - 1 + a_i - b_i$.

3. Set $d_i \leftarrow t \bmod B$ and $c \leftarrow \lfloor t/B \rfloor$.

4. Set $i \leftarrow i + 1$; if $i \leq n - 1$, go to step 2.

5. If $c = 1$, set $t \leftarrow B + a_i$; otherwise, set $t \leftarrow B - 1 + a_i$.

6. Set $d_i \leftarrow t \bmod B$ and $c \leftarrow \lfloor t/B \rfloor$.

7. Set $i \leftarrow i + 1$; if $i \leq m - 1$, go to step 5.

8. Output $d = (d_{m-1}d_{m-2}\ldots d_0)_B$.

The implementation of subtraction is identical to that of addition, with the following exceptions:

- The `ULONG` variable `carry` is used to "borrow" from the next-higher digit of the minuend if a digit of the minuend is smaller than the corresponding digit of the subtrahend.

- Instead of an overflow one must be on the lookout for a possible underflow, in which case the result of the subtraction would actually be negative; however, since `CLINT` is an `unsigned` type, there will be a reduction modulo $(N_{\max} + 1)$ (see Chapter 5). The function returns the error code `E_CLINT_UFL` to indicate this situation.

- Finally, any existing leading zeros are eliminated.

Thus we obtain the following function, which subtracts a `CLINT` number `b_l` from a number `a_l`.

Function:	subtraction
Syntax:	int sub_l (CLINT aa_l, CLINT bb_l, CLINT d_l);
Input:	aa_l (minuend), bb_l (subtrahend)
Output:	d_l (difference)
Return:	E_CLINT_OK if all is ok.
	E_CLINT_UFL in the case of underflow

```
int
sub_l (CLINT aa_l, CLINT bb_l, CLINT d_l)
{
CLINT b_l;
clint a_l[CLINTMAXSHORT + 1]; /* allow 1 additional digit in a_l */
clint *msdptra_l, *msdptrb_l;
clint *aptr_l = LSDPTR_L (a_l);
clint *bptr_l = LSDPTR_L (b_l);
clint *dptr_l = LSDPTR_L (d_l);
ULONG carry = 0L;
int UFL = E_CLINT_OK;

cpy_l (a_l, aa_l);
cpy_l (b_l, bb_l);
msdptra_l = MSDPTR_L (a_l);
msdptrb_l = MSDPTR_L (b_l);
```

In the following the case a_l < b_l is considered, in which b_l is subtracted not from a_l, but from the largest possible value, N_{max}. Later, the value (minuend+1) is added to this difference, so that altogether the calculation is carried out modulo $(N_{max} + 1)$. To generate the value N_{max} the auxiliary function setmax_l() is used.

```
   if (LT_L (a_l, b_l))
    {
     setmax_l (a_l);
     msdptra_l = a_l + CLINTMAXDIGIT;
     SETDIGITS_L (d_l, CLINTMAXDIGIT);
     UFL = E_CLINT_UFL;
    } else
    {
     SETDIGITS_L (d_l, DIGITS_L (a_l));
    }
   while (bptr_l <= msdptrb_l)
    {
     *dptr_l++ = (USHORT)(carry = (ULONG)*aptr_l++
                    - (ULONG)*bptr_l++ - ((carry & BASE) >> BITPERDGT));
    }
   while (aptr_l <= msdptra_l)
    {
     *dptr_l++ = (USHORT)(carry = (ULONG)*aptr_l++
           - ((carry & BASE) >> BITPERDGT));
    }
   RMLDZRS_L (d_l);
```

The required addition of $(\text{minuend} + 1)$ to the difference $N_{\max} - \text{b\_l}$ stored in
d_l is carried out before the output of d_l.

```
 if (UFL)
  {
   add_l (d_l, aa_l, d_l);
   inc_l (d_l);
  }
 return UFL;
}
```

In addition to the functions add_l() and sub_l() two special functions for
addition and subtraction are available, which operate on a USHORT as the second
argument instead of a CLINT. These are called *mixed functions* and identified by a
function name with a prefixed "u," as in the functions uadd_l() and usub_l() to
follow. The use of the function u2clint_l() for converting a USHORT value into a
CLINT object follows in anticipation of its discussion in Chapter 8.

Function:	mixed addition of a CLINT type and a USHORT type
Syntax:	int uadd_l (CLINT a_l, USHORT b, CLINT s_l);
Input:	a_l, b (summands)
Output:	s_l (sum)
Return:	E_CLINT_OK if all is ok
	E_CLINT_OFL if overflow

```
int
uadd_l (CLINT a_l, USHORT b, CLINT s_l)
{
 int err;
 CLINT tmp_l;

 u2clint_l (tmp_l, b);
 err = add_l (a_l, tmp_l, s_l);
 return err;
}
```

Function:	subtraction of a USHORT type from a CLINT type
Syntax:	int usub_l (CLINT a_l, USHORT b, CLINT d_l);
Input:	a_l (minuend), b (subtrahend)
Output:	d_l (difference)
Return:	E_CLINT_OK if all is ok
	E_CLINT_UFL if underflow

```
int
usub_l (CLINT a_l, USHORT b, CLINT d_l)
{
 int err;
 CLINT tmp_l;  u2clint_l (tmp_l, b);
 err = sub_l (a_l, tmp_l, d_l);
 return err;
}
```

Two further useful special cases of addition and subtraction are realized in the functions inc_1() and dec_1(), which increase or decrease a CLINT value by 1. These functions are designed as accumulator routines: The operand is overwritten with the return value, which has proved practical in the implementation of many algorithms.

It is not surprising that the implementations of inc_1() and dec_1() are similar to those of the functions add_1() and sub_1(). They test for overflow and underflow, respectively, and return the corresponding error codes E_CLINT_OFL and E_CLINT_UFL.

Function:	increment a CLINT object by 1
Syntax:	int inc_l (CLINT a_l);
Input:	a_l (summand)
Output:	a_l (sum)
Return:	E_CLINT_OK if all is ok
	E_CLINT_OFL if overflow

```
int
inc_l (CLINT a_l)
{
 clint *msdptra_l, *aptr_l = LSDPTR_L (a_l);
 ULONG carry = BASE;
 int OFL = E_CLINT_OK;
 msdptra_l = MSDPTR_L (a_l);
 while ((aptr_l <= msdptra_l) && (carry & BASE))
  {
   *aptr_l = (USHORT)(carry = 1UL + (ULONG)*aptr_l);
   aptr_l++;
  }
 if ((aptr_l > msdptra_l) && (carry & BASE))
  {
   *aptr_l = 1;
   SETDIGITS_L (a_l, DIGITS_L (a_l) + 1);
   if (DIGITS_L (a_l) > (USHORT) CLINTMAXDIGIT)   /* overflow ? */
    {
     SETZERO_L (a_l);        /* reduce modulo (Nmax + 1) */
     OFL = E_CLINT_OFL;
    }
  }
 return OFL;
}
```

Function:	decrement a `CLINT` object by 1
Syntax:	int dec_l (CLINT a_l);
Input:	a_l (minuend)
Output:	a_l (difference)
Return:	E_CLINT_OK if all is ok
	E_CLINT_UFL if underflow

```
int
dec_l (CLINT a_l)
{
 clint *msdptra_l, *aptr_l = LSDPTR_L (a_l);
 ULONG carry = DBASEMINONE;

 if (EQZ_L (a_l))      /* underflow ? */
  {
   setmax_l (a_l);       /* reduce modulo max_l */
   return E_CLINT_UFL;
  }
 msdptra_l = MSDPTR_L (a_l);

 while ((aptr_l <= msdptra_l) && (carry & (BASEMINONEL << BITPERDGT)))
  {
   *aptr_l = (USHORT)(carry = (ULONG)*aptr_l - 1L);
   aptr_l++;
  }
 RMLDZRS_L (a_l);
 return E_CLINT_OK;
}
```

4.2 Multiplication

If the individual summands $n_1, n_2, n_3, \ldots, n_r$ are all equal to one and the same integer n, then one calls the addition "multiplication of the integer n by the multiplier r" and sets $n_1 + n_2 + n_3 + \cdots + n_r = rn$.

—Leopold Kronecker, *On the Idea of Number*

Multiplication is one of the most critical functions of the entire FLINT/C package due to the computation time required for its execution, since together with division it determines the execution time of many algorithms. In contrast to our experience heretofore with addition and subtraction, the classical algorithms for multiplication and division have execution times that are quadratic in the number of digits of the arguments, and it is not for nothing that Donald Knuth asks in one of his chapter headings, "How fast can we multiply?"

In the literature there have been published various procedures for rapid multiplication of large and very large integers, among which are some rather difficult methods. An example of this is the procedure developed by A. Schönhage and V. Strassen for multiplying large numbers by application of fast Fourier transforms over finite fields. The running time in terms of the number of digits n in the arguments is bounded above by $O(n \log n \log \log n)$ (see [Knut], Section 4.3.3). These techniques encompass the fastest known multiplication algorithms, but their advantage in speed over the classical $O\left(n^2\right)$ methods comes into play only when the number of binary digits is in the range 8,000–10,000. Based on the demands of cryptographic systems, such numbers, at least for the present, are far beyond the range envisioned in the application domain of our functions.

For our realization of multiplication for the FLINT/C package we would like first to use as a basis the grade school method based on "Algorithm M" given by Knuth (see [Knut], Section 4.3.1), and we shall make an effort to achieve as efficient an implementation of this procedure as possible. Then we shall occupy ourselves in a close examination of the calculation of squares, which offers great potential for savings, and for both cases we shall finally look at the multiplication procedure of Karatsuba, which is asymptotically better than $O\left(n^2\right)$.[2] The Karatsuba multiplication arouses our curiosity, since it seems simple, and one could pleasantly occupy a (preferably rainy) Sunday afternoon trying it out. We shall see whether this procedure has anything to contribute to the FLINT/C library.

4.2.1 The Grade School Method

We are considering multiplication of two numbers a and b with representations

$$a = (a_{m-1}a_{m-2}\ldots a_0)_B = \sum_{i=0}^{m-1} a_i B^i, \quad 0 \le a_i < B,$$

$$b = (b_{n-1}b_{n-2}\ldots b_0)_B = \sum_{i=0}^{n-1} b_i B^i, \qquad 0 \le b_i < B,$$

to the base B. According to the procedure that we learned in school, the product ab can be computed for $m = n = 3$ as shown in Figure 4-1.

---

[2] When we say that the calculation time is asymptotically better, we mean that the larger the numbers in question, the greater the effect. One should not fall victim to premature euphoria, and for our purposes such an improvement may have no significance whatsoever.

$$(a_2a_1a_0)_B \cdot (b_2b_2b_0)_B$$

			c_{20}	p_{20}	p_{10}	p_{00}
+		c_{21}	p_{21}	p_{11}	p_{01}	
+	c_{22}	p_{22}	p_{12}	p_{02}		
	$(p_5$	p_4	p_3	p_2	p_1	$p_0)_B$

Figure 4-1. Calculations for multiplication

First, the partial products $(a_2a_1a_0)_B \cdot b_j$ for $j = 0, 1, 2$, are calculated: The values a_ib_j are the least-significant digits of the terms $(a_ib_j + \text{carry})$ with the *inner products* a_ib_j, and the c_{2j} are the more-significant digits of the p_{2j}. The partial products are summed at the end to form the product $p = (p_5p_4p_3p_2p_1p_0)_B$.

In the general case the product $p = ab$ has the value

$$p = \sum_{j=0}^{n-1} \sum_{i=0}^{m-1} a_ib_j B^{i+j}.$$

The result of a multiplication of two operands with m and n digits has at least $m + n - 1$ and at most $m + n$ digits. The number of elementary multiplication steps (that is, multiplications by factors smaller than the base B) is mn.

A multiplication function that followed exactly the schema outlined above would first calculate all partial products, store these values, and then sum them up, each provided with the appropriate scaling factor. This school method is quite suitable for calculating with pencil and paper, but for the possibilities of a computer program it is somewhat cumbersome. A more efficient alternative consists in adding the inner products a_ib_j at once to the accumulated values in the result digit p_{i+j}, to which are added the carries c from previous steps. The resulting value for each pair (i, j) is assigned to a variable t:

$$t \leftarrow p_{i+j} + a_ib_j + c,$$

where t can be represented as

$$t = kB + l, \quad 0 \le k, \quad l < B,$$

and we then have

$$p_{i+j} + a_ib_j + c \le B - 1 + (B - 1)(B - 1) + B - 1$$
$$= (B - 1)B + B - 1 = B^2 - 1 < B^2.$$

The current value of the result digit is taken by the assignment $p_{i+j} \leftarrow l$ from this representation of t. As the new carry we set $c \leftarrow k$.

The multiplication algorithm thus consists entirely of an outer loop for calculating the partial products $a_i \, (b_{n-1} b_{n-2} \ldots b_0)_B$ and an inner loop for calculating the inner products $a_i b_j, j = 0, \ldots, n-1$, and the values t and $p_i + j$. The algorithm then appears as follows.

Algorithm for multiplication

1. Set $p_i \leftarrow 0$ for $i = 0, \ldots, n-1$.

2. Set $i \leftarrow 0$.

3. Set $j \leftarrow 0$ and $c \leftarrow 0$.

4. Set $t \leftarrow p_{i+j} + a_i b_j + c, p_{i+j} \leftarrow t \bmod B$, and $c \leftarrow \lfloor t/B \rfloor$.

5. Set $j \leftarrow j + 1$; if $j \leq n-1$, go to step 4.

6. Set $p_{i+n} \leftarrow c$.

7. Set $i \leftarrow i + 1$; if $i \leq m-1$, go to step 3.

8. Output $p = (p_{m+n-1} p_{m+n-2} \ldots p_0)_B$.

The following implementation of multiplication contains at its core this main loop. Corresponding to the above estimate, in step 4 the lossless representation of a value less than B^2 in the variable t is required. Analogously to how we proceeded in the case of addition, the inner products t are thus represented as ULONG types. The variable t is nonetheless not used explicitly, and the setting of the result digits p_{i+j} and the carry c occurs rather within a single expression, analogous to the process already mentioned in connection with the addition function (see page 25). For initialization a more efficient procedure will be chosen than the one shown in step 1 of the algorithm.

Function:	multiplication
Syntax:	int mul_l (CLINT f1_l, CLINT f2_l, CLINT pp_l);
Input:	f1_l, f2_l (factors)
Output:	pp_l (product)
Return:	E_CLINT_OK if all is ok
	E_CLINT_OFL if overflow

```
int
mul_l (CLINT f1_l, CLINT f2_l, CLINT pp_l)
{
 register clint *pptr_l, *bptr_l;
 CLINT aa_l, bb_l;
 CLINTD p_l;
 clint *a_l, *b_l, *aptr_l, *csptr_l, *msdptra_l, *msdptrb_l;
 USHORT av;
 ULONG carry;
 int OFL = E_CLINT_OK;
```

> First the variables are declared; p_l will hold the result and thus is of double length. The ULONG variable carry will hold the carry. In the first step the case is dealt with in which one of the factors, and therefore the product, is zero. Then the factors are copied into the workspaces aa_l and bb_l, and leading zeros are purged.

```
if (EQZ_L (f1_l) || EQZ_L (f2_l))
  {
   SETZERO_L (pp_l);
   return E_CLINT_OK;
  }
cpy_l (aa_l, f1_l);
cpy_l (bb_l, f2_l);
```

> According to the declarations the pointers a_l and b_l are given the addresses of aa_l and bb_l, where a logical transposition occurs if the number of digits of aa_l is smaller than that of bb_l. The pointer a_l always points to the operand with the larger number of digits.

```
 if (DIGITS_L (aa_l) < DIGITS_L (bb_l))
   {
    a_l = bb_l;
    b_l = aa_l;
   }
 else
   {
    a_l = aa_l;
    b_l = bb_l;
   }
 msdptra_l = a_l + *a_l;
 msdptrb_l = b_l + *b_l;
```

> To save time in the computation, instead of the initialization required above, the partial product $(b_{n-1}b_{n-2}\ldots b_0)_B \cdot a_0$ is calculated in a loop and stored in $p_n, p_{n-1}, \ldots, p_0$.

```
carry = 0;
av = *LSDPTR_L (a_l);
for (bptr_l = LSDPTR_L (b_l), pptr_l = LSDPTR_L (p_l);
              bptr_l <= msdptrb_l; bptr_l++, pptr_l++)
 {
   *pptr_l = (USHORT)(carry = (ULONG)av * (ULONG)*bptr_l +
                     (ULONG)(USHORT)(carry >> BITPERDGT));
 }
*pptr_l = (USHORT)(carry >> BITPERDGT);
```

> Next follows the nested multiplication loop, beginning with the digit a_l[2] of a_l.

```
 for (csptr_l = LSDPTR_L (p_l) + 1, aptr_l = LSDPTR_L (a_l) + 1;
              aptr_l <= msdptra_l; csptr_l++, aptr_l++)
  {
   carry = 0;
   av = *aptr_l;
   for (bptr_l = LSDPTR_L (b_l), pptr_l = csptr_l;
              bptr_l <= msdptrb_l; bptr_l++, pptr_l++)           {
     *pptr_l = (USHORT)(carry = (ULONG)av * (ULONG)*bptr_l +
        (ULONG)*pptr_l + (ULONG)(USHORT)(carry >> BITPERDGT));
    }
   *pptr_l = (USHORT)(carry >> BITPERDGT);
  }
```

> The largest possible length of the result is the sum of the numbers of digits of a_l and b_l. If the result has one digit fewer, this is determined by the macro RMLDZRS_L.

```
SETDIGITS_L (p_l, DIGITS_L (a_l) + DIGITS_L (b_l));
RMLDZRS_L (p_l);
```

> If the result is larger than can be accommodated in a CLINT object, it is reduced, and the error flag OFL is set to the value E_CLINT_OFL. Then the reduced result is assigned to the object pp_l.

```
if (DIGITS_L (p_l) > (USHORT)CLINTMAXDIGIT)    /* overflow ? */
 {
  ANDMAX_L (p_l);    /* reduce modulo (Nmax + 1) */
  OFL = E_CLINT_OFL;
 }
cpy_l (pp_l, p_l);
return OFL;
}
```

With $t = O(mn)$ the run time t for the multiplication is proportional to the product of the numbers of digits m and n of the operands. For multiplication, too, the analogous mixed function is implemented, which processes a CLINT type and as second argument a USHORT type. This short version of CLINT multiplication requires $O(n)$ CPU multiplications, which is the result not of any particular refinement of the algorithm, but of the shortness of the USHORT argument. Later, we shall set this function implicitly within a special exponentiation routine for USHORT bases (see Chapter 6, the function wmexp_l()).

For the implementation of the umul_l() function we return primarily to a code segment of the mul_l() function and reuse it with a few modifications.

Function:	multiplication of a CLINT type by a USHORT
Syntax:	int umul_l (CLINT aa_l, USHORT b, CLINT pp_l);
Input:	aa_l, b (factors)
Output:	pp_l (product)
Return:	E_CLINT_OK if all is ok
	E_CLINT_OFL if overflow

```
int
umul_l (CLINT aa_l, USHORT b, CLINT pp_l)
{
 register clint *aptr_l, *pptr_l;
 CLINT a_l;
 clint p_l[CLINTMAXSHORT + 1];
 clint *msdptra_l;
 ULONG carry;
 int OFL = E_CLINT_OK;
```

```
cpy_l (a_l, aa_l);
if (EQZ_L (a_l) || 0 == b)
 {
  SETZERO_L (pp_l);
  return E_CLINT_OK;
 }
```

> After these preliminaries, the CLINT factor is multiplied in a pass through a loop by the USHORT factor, and at the end the carry is stored in the most-significant USHORT digit of the CLINT value.

```
msdptra_l = MSDPTR_L (a_l);
carry = 0;
for (aptr_l = LSDPTR_L (a_l), pptr_l = LSDPTR_l (p_l);
                 aptr_l <= msdptra_l; aptr_l++, pptr_l++)
 {
  *pptr_l = (USHORT)(carry = (ULONG)b * (ULONG)*aptr_l +
       (ULONG)(USHORT)(carry >> BITPERDGT));
 }
*pptr_l = (USHORT)(carry >> BITPERDGT);
SETDIGITS_L (p_l, DIGITS_L (a_l) + 1);
RMLDZRS_L (p_l);
if (DIGITS_L (p_l) > (USHORT)CLINTMAXDIGIT)   /* overflow ? */
 {
  ANDMAX_L (p_l);      /* reduce modulo (Nmax + 1) */
  OFL = E_CLINT_OFL;
 }
cpy_l (pp_l, p_l);
return OFL;
}
```

4.2.2 Squaring Is Faster

The calculation of a large square is accomplished with significantly fewer multiplications than in the case of the multiplication of large numbers. This is a result of the symmetry in the multiplication of identical operands. This observation is very important, since when it comes to exponentiation, which involves not one, but hundreds, of squarings, we shall be able to achieve considerable savings in speed. We again look at the well-known multiplication schema, this time with two identical factors $(a_2 a_1 a_0)_B$ (see Figure 4-2).

$$(a_2a_1a_0)_B \cdot (a_2a_1a_0)_B$$

				a_2a_0	a_1a_0	$\boldsymbol{a_0\,a_0}$
$+$			a_2a_1	$\boldsymbol{a_1\,a_1}$	$\boxed{a_0a_1}$	
$+$		$\boldsymbol{a_2\,a_2}$	$\boxed{a_1a_2}$	$\boxed{a_0a_2}$		
$\big(p_5$	p_4	p_3	p_2	p_1	$p_0\big)_B$	

Figure 4-2. Calculations for squaring

We recognize that the inner products a_ia_j for $i = j$ appear once (in boldface in Figure 4-2) and twice for $i \neq j$ (in boxes in the figure). Thus we can save three out of nine multiplications by multiplying the sum $a_ia_jB^{i+j}$ for $i < j$ by 2. The sum of the inner products of a square can then be written as

$$p = \sum_{i,j=0}^{n-1} a_ia_jB^{i+j} = 2\sum_{i=0}^{n-2}\sum_{j=i+1}^{n-1} a_ia_jB^{i+j} + \sum_{j=0}^{n-1} a_i^2 B^{2i}.$$

The number of required elementary multiplications is thus reduced with respect to the school method from n^2 to $n(n+1)/2$.

A natural algorithmic representation of squaring calculates the above expression with the two summands in two nested loops.

Algorithm 1 for squaring

1. Set $p_i \leftarrow 0$ for $i = 0, \ldots, n-1$.

2. Set $i \leftarrow 0$.

3. Set $t \leftarrow p_{2i} + a_i^2$, $p_{2i} \leftarrow t \bmod B$, and $c \leftarrow \lfloor t/B \rfloor$.

4. Set $j \leftarrow i + 1$. If $j = n$, go to step 7.

5. Set $t \leftarrow p_{i+j} + 2a_ia_j + c$, $p_{i+j} \leftarrow t \pmod B$, and $c \leftarrow \lfloor t/B \rfloor$.

6. Set $j \leftarrow j + 1$; if $j \leq n - 1$, go to step 5.

7. Set $p_{i+n} \leftarrow c$.

8. Set $j \leftarrow i + 1$; if $i = n - 1$, go to step 7.

9. Output $p = (p_{2n-1}p_{2n-2} \ldots p_0)_B$.

In selecting the necessary data types for the representation of the variables we must note that t can assume the value

$$(B - 1) + 2(B - 1)^2 + (B - 1) = 2B^2 - 2B$$

(in step 5 of the algorithm). But this means that for representing t to base B more than two digits to base B will be needed, since we also have $B^2 - 1 < 2B^2 - 2B <$

$2B^2 - 1$, and so a ULONG will not suffice for representing t (the inequality above is derived from the fact that one additional binary digit is needed). While this poses no problem for an assembler implementation, in which one has access to the carry bit of the CPU, it is difficult in C to handle the additional binary digit. To get around this dilemma, we alter the algorithm in such a way that in step 5 the required multiplication by 2 is carried out in a separate loop. It is then required that step 3 be carried out in its own loop, whereby for a slight extra expenditure of effort in loop management we are spared the additional binary digit. The altered algorithm is as follows.

Algorithm 2 for squaring

1. Initialization: Set $p_i \leftarrow 0$ for $i = 0, \ldots, n - 1$.

2. Calculate the product of digits of unequal index: Set $i \leftarrow 0$.

3. Set $j \leftarrow i + 1$ and $c \leftarrow 0$.

4. Set $t \leftarrow p_{i+j} + a_i a_j + c$, $p_{i+j} \leftarrow t \bmod B$, and $c \leftarrow \lfloor t/B \rfloor$.

5. Set $j \leftarrow j + 1$; if $j \leq n - 1$, go to step 4.

6. Set $p_{i+n} \leftarrow c$.

7. Set $i \leftarrow i + 1$; if $i \leq n - 2$, go to step 3.

8. Multiplication of inner products by 2: Set $i \leftarrow 1$ and $c \leftarrow 0$.

9. Set $t \leftarrow 2p_i + c$, $p_i \leftarrow t \bmod B$, and $c \leftarrow \lfloor t/B \rfloor$.

10. Set $i \leftarrow i + 1$; if $i \leq 2n - 2$, go to step 9.

11. Set $p_{2n-1} \leftarrow c$.

12. Addition of the inner squares: Set $i \leftarrow 0$ and $c \leftarrow 0$.

13. Set $t \leftarrow p_{2i} + a_i^2 + c$, $p_{2i} \leftarrow t \bmod B$, and $c \leftarrow \lfloor t/B \rfloor$.

14. Set $t \leftarrow p_{2i+1} + c$, $p_{2i+1} \leftarrow t \bmod B$, and $c \leftarrow \lfloor t/B \rfloor$.

15. Set $i \leftarrow i + 1$; if $i \leq n - 1$, go to step 13.

16. Set $p_{2n-1} \leftarrow p_{2n-1} + c$; output $p = (p_{2n-1}p_{2n-2} \ldots p_0)_B$.

In the C function for squaring the initialization in step 1 is likewise, in analogy to multiplication, replaced by the calculation and storing of the first partial product $a_0 \left(a_{n-1}a_{n-2} \ldots a_1 \right)_B$.

Function:	squaring
Syntax:	int sqr_l (CLINT f_l, CLINT pp_l);
Input:	f_l (factor)
Output:	pp_l (square)
Return:	E_CLINT_OK if all is ok
	E_CLINT_OFL if overflow

```
int
sqr_l (CLINT f_l, CLINT pp_l)
{
 register clint *pptr_l, *bptr_l;
 CLINT a_l;
 CLINTD p_l;
 clint *aptr_l, *csptr_l, *msdptra_l, *msdptrb_l, *msdptrc_l;
 USHORT av;
 ULONG carry;
 int OFL = E_CLINT_OK;

 cpy_l (a_l, f_l);
 if (EQZ_L (a_l))
  {
   SETZERO_L (pp_l);
   return E_CLINT_OK;
  }
 msdptrb_l = MSDPTR_L (a_l);
 msdptra_l = msdptrb_l - 1;
```

The initialization of the result vector addressed by pptr_l is carried out by means of the partial product $a_0 \left(a_{n-1} a_{n-2} \ldots a_1\right)_B$, in analogy with multiplication. The digit p_0 is here not assigned; it must be set to zero.

```
*LSDPTR_L (p_l) = 0;
carry = 0;
av = *LSDPTR_L (a_l);
for (bptr_l = LSDPTR_L (a_l) + 1, pptr_l = LSDPTR_L (p_l) + 1;
                bptr_l <= msdptrb_l; bptr_l++, pptr_l++)
```

```
  {
   *pptr_l = (USHORT)(carry = (ULONG)av * (ULONG)*bptr_l +
           (ULONG)(USHORT)(carry >> BITPERDGT));
  }
 *pptr_l = (USHORT)(carry >> BITPERDGT);
```

The loop for summing the inner products $a_i a_j$.

```
for (aptr_l = LSDPTR_L (a_l) + 1, csptr_l = LSDPTR_L (p_l) + 3;
                        aptr_l <= msdptra_l; aptr_l++, csptr_l += 2)
  {
   carry = 0;
   av = *aptr_l;
   for (bptr_l = aptr_l + 1, pptr_l = csptr_l; bptr_l <= msdptrb_l;
              bptr_l++, pptr_l++)
    {
     *pptr_l = (USHORT)(carry = (ULONG)av * (ULONG)*bptr_l +
        (ULONG)*pptr_l + (ULONG)(USHORT)(carry >> BITPERDGT));
    }
   *pptr_l = (USHORT)(carry >> BITPERDGT);
  }
msdptrc_l = pptr_l;
```

Then comes multiplication of the intermediate result in `pptr_l` by 2 via shift operations (see also Section 7.1).

```
carry = 0;
for (pptr_l = LSDPTR_L (p_l); pptr_l <= msdptrc_l; pptr_l++)
 {
  *pptr_l = (USHORT)(carry = (((ULONG)*pptr_l) << 1) +
                        (ULONG)(USHORT)(carry >> BITPERDGT));
 }
*pptr_l = (USHORT)(carry >> BITPERDGT);
```

Now we compute the "main diagonal."

```
 carry = 0;
 for (bptr_l = LSDPTR_L (a_l), pptr_l = LSDPTR_L (p_l);
             bptr_l <= msdptrb_l; bptr_l++, pptr_l++)
```

```
{
  *pptr_l = (USHORT)(carry = (ULONG)*bptr_l * (ULONG)*bptr_l +
                  (ULONG)*pptr_l + (ULONG)(USHORT)(carry >> BITPERDGT));
  pptr_l++;
  *pptr_l = (USHORT)(carry = (ULONG)*pptr_l + (carry >> BITPERDGT));
}
```

All the rest follows in analogy to multiplication.

```
SETDIGITS_L (p_l, DIGITS_L (a_l) << 1);
RMLDZRS_L (p_l);
if (DIGITS_L (p_l) > (USHORT)CLINTMAXDIGIT)   /* overflow ? */
 {
  ANDMAX_L (p_l);    /* reduce modulo (Nmax + 1) */
  OFL = E_CLINT_OFL;
 }
cpy_l (pp_l, p_l);
return OFL;
}
```

The run time for squaring is, with $O\left(n^2\right)$, likewise quadratic in the number of digits of the operators, but with $n(n + 1)/2$ elementary multiplications it is about twice as fast as multiplication.

4.2.3 Do Things Go Better with Karatsuba?

> The antispirit of multiplication and division deconstructed everything and then focused only on a specific part of the whole.
>
> —Sten Nadolny (trans. Breon Mitchell), *God of Impertinence*

As announced, we shall now consider a method of multiplication named for the Russian mathematician A. Karatsuba, who has published several variants of it (See [Knut], Section 4.3.3). We assume that a and b are natural numbers with $n = 2k$ digits to base B, so that we can write $a = (a_1 a_0)_{B^k}$ and $b = (b_1 b_0)_{B^k}$ with digits a_0 and a_1, respectively b_0 and b_1, to base B^k. Were we to multiply a and b in the traditional manner, then we would obtain the expression

$$ab = B^{2k} a_1 b_1 + B^k \left(a_0 b_1 + a_1 b_0\right) + a_0 b_0,$$

with four multiplications to base B^k and thus $n^2 = 4k^2$ elementary multiplications to base B. However, if we set

$$c_0 := a_0 b_0,$$
$$c1 := a_1 b_1,$$
$$c2 := (a_0 + a_1)(b_0 + b_1) - c_0 - c_1,$$

then we have

$$ab = B^k \left(B^k c_1 + c_2 \right) + c_0.$$

For calculating ab it now appears that only three more multiplications by numbers to base B^k, or $3k^2$ multiplications to base B, are necessary, in addition to some additions and shifting operations (multiplication by B^k can be accomplished by left shifting by k digits to base B; see Section 7.1). Let us assume that the number of digits n of our factors a and b is a power of 2, with the result that by recursive application of the procedure on the remaining partial products we can end with having to carry out only elementary multiplications to base B, and this yields a total of $3^{\log_2 n} = n^{\log_2 3} \approx n^{1.585}$ elementary multiplications, as opposed to n^2 in the classical procedure, in addition to the time for additions and shift operations.

For squaring, this process can be simplified somewhat: With

$$c_0 := a_0^2,$$
$$c_1 := a_1^2,$$
$$c_2 := (a_0 + a_1)^2 - c_0 - c_1,$$

we have

$$a^2 = B^k \left(B^k c_1 + c_2 \right) + c_0.$$

Furthermore, to our advantage, the factors in the squaring always have the same number of digits, which is not generally the case in multiplication. With all these advantages, we should, however, mention that recursion within a program function always costs something, so that we may hope to experience a savings in time over the classical method, which manages without the added burden of recursion, only when the numbers get large.

To obtain information on the actual time performance of the Karatsuba procedure the functions kmul() and ksqr() are provided. The division of the factors into two halves takes place in situ, and so a copying of the halves is unnecessary. But it is necessary that the functions be passed pointers to the least-significant digits of the factors and that the numbers of digits be passed separately.

The functions presented below in experimental form use the recursive procedure for factors having more than a certain number of digits determined by a macro, while for smaller factors we turn to conventional multiplication or squaring. For the case of nonrecursive multiplication the functions kmul() and ksqr() use the auxiliary functions mult() and sqr(), in which multiplication and squaring are implemented as *kernel functions* without the support of identical argument addresses (accumulator mode) or reduction in the case of overflow.

Function: Karatsuba multiplication of two numbers a_l and b_l with $2k$ digits each to base B

Syntax: void kmul (clint *aptr_l, clint *bptr_l,
int len_a, int len_b, CLINT p_l);

Input: aptr_l (pointer to the least-significant digit of the factor a_l)
bptr_l (pointer to the least-significant digit of the factor b_l)
len_a (number of digits of a_l)
len_b (number of digits of b_l)

Output: p_l (product)

```
void
kmul (clint *aptr_l, clint *bptr_l, int len_a, int len_b, CLINT p_l)
{
CLINT c01_l, c10_l;
clint c0_l[CLINTMAXSHORT + 2];
clint c1_l[CLINTMAXSHORT + 2];
clint c2_l[CLINTMAXSHORT + 2];
CLINTD tmp_l;
clint *a1ptr_l, *b1ptr_l;
int l2;

if ((len_a == len_b) && (len_a >= MUL_THRESHOLD)
                && (0 == (len_a & 1)) )

   {
```

If both factors possess the same even number of digits above the value MUL_THRESHOLD, then recursion is entered with the splitting of the factors into two halves. The pointers aptr_l, a1ptr_l, bptr_l, b1ptr_l are passed to the corresponding least-significant digits of one of the halves. By not copying the halves, we save valuable time. The values c_0 and c_1 are calculated by recursively calling kmul() and then stored in the CLINT variables c0_l and c1_l.

```
l2 = len_a/2;

a1ptr_l = aptr_l + l2;
b1ptr_l = bptr_l + l2;

kmul (aptr_l, bptr_l, l2, l2, c0_l);
kmul (a1ptr_l, b1ptr_l, l2, l2, c1_l);
```

The value $c_2 := (a_0 + a_1)(b_0 + b_1) - c_0 - c_1$ is computed with two additions, a call to kmul(), and two subtractions. The auxiliary function addkar() takes pointers to the least-significant digits of two equally long summands together with their number of digits, and outputs the sum of the two as a CLINT value.

```
addkar (a1ptr_l, aptr_l, l2, c01_l);
addkar (b1ptr_l, bptr_l, l2, c10_l);
kmul (LSDPTR_L (c01_l), LSDPTR_L (c10_l),
                DIGITS_L (c01_l), DIGITS_L (c10_l), c2_l);
sub (c2_l, c1_l, tmp_l);
sub (tmp_l, c0_l, c2_l);
```

The function branch ends with the calculation of $B^k\left(B^k c_1 + c_2\right) + c_0$, which used the auxiliary function shiftadd(), which during the addition left shifts the first of the two CLINT summands by a given number of places to base B.

```
shiftadd (c1_l, c2_l, l2, tmp_l);
shiftadd (tmp_l, c0_l, l2, p_l);
}
```

If one of the input conditions is not fulfilled, the recursion is interrupted and the nonrecursive multiplication mult() is called. As a requirement for calling mult() the two factor halves in aptr_l and bptr_l are brought into CLINT format.

```
else
 {
  memcpy (LSDPTR_L (c1_l), aptr_l, len_a * sizeof (clint));
  memcpy (LSDPTR_L (c2_l), bptr_l, len_b * sizeof (clint));

  SETDIGITS_L (c1_l, len_a);
  SETDIGITS_L (c2_l, len_b);
  mult (c1_l, c2_l, p_l);
  RMLDZRS_L (p_l);
 }
}
```

The Karatsuba squaring process proceeds analogously to this and will not be described in detail. For calling kmul() and ksqr() we make use of the functions kmul_l() and ksqr_l(), which are equipped with the standard interface.

Function:	Karatsuba multiplication and squaring
Syntax:	int kmul_l (CLINT a_l, CLINT b_l, CLINT p_l); int ksqr_l (CLINT a_l, CLINT p_l);
Input:	a_l, b_l (factors)
Output:	p_l (product or square)
Return:	E_CLINT_OK if all is ok E_CLINT_OFL if overflow

The implementation of the Karatsuba functions are contained in the source file kmul.c in the downloadable source code (www.apress.com).

Extensive tests with these functions (on a Pentium III processor at 500 MHz under Linux) have given best results when the nonrecursive multiplication routine is called for a digit count under 40 (corresponding to 640 binary digits). The computation time of our implementation appears in Figure 4-3.

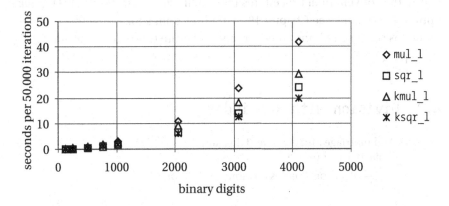

Figure 4-3. CPU time for Karatsuba multiplication

We conclude from this overview what we expected, that between standard multiplication and squaring there is a difference in performance of about 40 percent, and that for numbers of over 2000 binary digits a pronounced spread of the measured times becomes noticeable, with the Karatsuba routine in the lead. It is interesting to note that "normal" squaring sqr_l() is noticeably faster than Karatsuba multiplication, and Karatsuba squaring ksqr_l() takes the lead only above 3000 binary digits.

The large drop in performance of the Karatsuba functions for smaller numbers that was remarked on in the first edition of this book has in the meantime been eliminated. Yet there is still potential for improvement. The observable discontinuity in the calculation times of kmul_l() indicates that the recursion breaks off earlier than specified by the threshold value if the factors of a recursion step do not have an even number of digits. In the worst case this occurs right at the beginning of the multiplication, and even for very large numbers we are no better off than we were in the standard case. It would seem worthwhile, then, to extend the Karatsuba functions to be able to process arguments with differing numbers of digits and odd numbers of digits.

At the Max Planck Institute in Saarbrücken, J. Ziegler [Zieg] developed a portable implementation of Karatsuba multiplication and squaring for a 64-bit CPU (Sun Ultra-1) that overtakes the conventional method at 640 binary digits. With squaring an improvement in performance of 10% occurred at 1024 binary digits and 23% at 2048 binary digits.

C. Burnikel and J. Ziegler [BuZi] have developed an interesting recursive division procedure based on Karatsuba multiplication that from about 250 decimal digits on is increasingly faster than the school method.

Once again, however, the Karatsuba functions have no particular advantage for our cryptographic applications without considerable optimization, for which reason we shall prefer to fall back on the functions mul_l() and sqr_l(), which realize the conventional procedures (and their variants in assembly language optimized by hand; see Chapter 19). For applications for which the Karatsuba functions seem suited one could simply substitute those functions for mul_l() and sqr_l().

4.3 Division with Remainder

> And marriage and death and division
> Make barren our lives.
>
> —Algernon Charles Swinburne, "Dolores"

We still need to place the last stone in our edifice of the fundamental arithmetic processes on large numbers, namely, division, which is the most complex of them all. Since we are calculating with natural numbers, we have only natural numbers at our disposal to express the results of a division. The principle of division that we are about to expound will be called *division with remainder*. It is based on the following relation. Given $a, b \in \mathbb{Z}$, $b > 0$, there are unique integers q and r that satisfy $a = qb + r$ with $0 \leq r < b$. We call q the *quotient* and r the *remainder* of the division of a by b.

Frequently, we are interested only in the remainder and couldn't care less about the quotient. In Chapter 5 we shall see the importance of the operation of calculating remainders, since it is used in many algorithms, always in conjunction with addition, subtraction, multiplication, and exponentiation. Thus it will be worth our while to have at our disposal as efficient a division algorithm as possible.

For natural numbers a and b the simplest way of executing a division with remainder consists in subtracting the divisor b from the dividend a continually until the remaining quantity r is smaller than the divisor. By counting how often we have carried out the subtraction we will have calculated the quotient. The quotient q and the remainder r have the values $q = \lfloor a/b \rfloor$ and $r = a - \lfloor a/b \rfloor b$.[3]

This process of division by means of repeated subtraction is, of course, terribly boring. Even the grade school method of long division uses a significantly more efficient algorithm, in which the digits of the quotient are determined one by one and are in turn used as factors by which the divisor is multiplied. The partial products are subtracted in turn from the dividend. As an example consider the division exercise depicted in Figure 4-4.

```
  354938 : 427 = 831, remainder 101
-  3416↓↓
= 01333↓
 -  1281↓
 = 00528
   -  427
   =  101
```

Figure 4-4. Calculational schema for division

Already at the determination of the first digit, 8, of the quotient we are required to make an estimate or else discover it by trial and error. If one makes an error, then one discovers either that the product (quotient digit times divisor) is too large (in the example, larger than 3549), or that the remainder after subtraction of the partial product from the digits of the dividend is larger than the divisor. In the first case the chosen quotient digit is too large, while in the second it is too small, and in either case it must be corrected.

This heuristic modus operandi must be replaced in an implementation of a division algorithm by a more precise process. In [Knut], Section 4.3.1, Donald Knuth has described how such rough calculations can be made precise. Let us look more closely at our example.

---

[3]   Note that for $a < 0$ with $q = -\lceil |a|/b \rceil$ and $r = b - (|a| + qb)$ if $a \nmid b$, respectively $r = 0$ if $a \mid b$, division with remainder is reduced to the case $a, b \in \mathbb{N}$.

Let $a = (a_{m+n-1}a_{m+n-2} \ldots a_0)_B$ and $b = (b_{n-1}b_{n-2} \ldots b_0)_B$ be two natural numbers, represented to the base B, and for b_{n-1}, the most-significant digit of b, we have $b_{n-1} > 0$. We are looking for the quotient q and remainder r such that $a = qb + r, 0 \leq r < b$.

Following the long division above, for the calculation of q and r a quotient digit $q_j := \lfloor R/b \rfloor < B$ is returned in each step, where in the first step $R = (a_{m+n-1}a_{m+n-2} \ldots a_k)_B$ is formed from the most-significant digit of the dividend with the largest k for which $1 \leq \lfloor R/b \rfloor < B$ holds (in the above example at the start we have $m + n - 1 = 3 + 3 - 1 = 5, k = 2$, and $R = 3549$). Then we will set $R := R - q_j b$, where as a control for the correctness of the quotient digit q_j the condition $0 \leq R < b$ must be satisfied. Then R is replaced by the value $RB + $ (next digit of the dividend), and the next quotient digit is again $\lfloor R/b \rfloor$. The division is complete when all digits of the dividend have been processed. The remainder of the division is the last calculated value of R.

For programming this procedure we must repeatedly determine, for two large numbers $R = (r_n r_{n-1} \ldots r_0)_B$ and $b = (b_{n-1}b_{n-2} \ldots b_0)_B$ with $\lfloor R/b \rfloor < B$, the quotient $Q := \lfloor R/b \rfloor$ ($r_n = 0$ is a possibility). Here we take from Knuth the given approximation $\hat{q}$ of Q, which is computed from the leading digits of R and b.

Let

$$\hat{q} := \min \left\{ \left\lfloor \frac{r_n B + r_{n-1}}{b_{n-1}} \right\rfloor, B - 1 \right\}. \tag{4.1}$$

If $b_{n-1} \geq \lfloor R/b \rfloor$, then for $\hat{q}$ (see [Knut], Section 4.3.1, Theorems A and B), we have $\hat{q} - 2 \leq Q \leq \hat{q}$. Under the favorable assumption that the leading digit of the divisor is sufficiently large in comparison to B, then as an approximation to $Q, \hat{q}$ is at most too large by 2 and is never too small.

By scaling the operands a and b this can always be achieved. We choose $d > 0$ such that $db_{n-1} \geq \lfloor B/2 \rfloor$, set $\hat{a} := ad = (\hat{a}_{m+n}\hat{a}_{m+n-1} \ldots \hat{a}_0)_B$, and set $\hat{b} := bd = (\hat{b}_{n-1}\hat{b}_{n-2} \ldots \hat{b}_0)_B$. The choice of d is then made in such a way that the number of digits of $\hat{b}$ never increases in comparison to that of b. In the above notation it is taken into account that $\hat{a}$ possibly contains one more digit than a (if this is not the case, then we set $\hat{a}_{m+n} = 0$). In any case, it is practical to choose d as a power of 2, since then the scaling of the operands can be carried out with simple shift operations. Since both operands are multiplied by a common factor, the quotient is unchanged; we have $\lfloor \hat{a}/\hat{b} \rfloor = \lfloor a/b \rfloor$.

The choice of $\hat{q}$ in (4.1), which we want to apply to the scaled operators $\hat{a}$, respectively $\hat{r}$, and $\hat{b}$, can be improved with the following test to the extent that $\hat{q} = Q$ or $\hat{q} = Q + 1$: If from the choice of $\hat{q}$ we have $\hat{b}_{n-2}\hat{q} > \left(\hat{r}_n B + \hat{r}_{n-1} - \hat{q}\hat{b}_{n-1}\right) B + \hat{r}_{n-2}$, then $\hat{q}$ is reduced by 1 and the test is repeated. In this way we have taken care of all cases in which $\hat{q}$ is too large by 2 at the outset, and only in very rare cases is $\hat{q}$ still too large by 1 (see [Knut], Section 4.3.1, Exercises 19, 20). The latter is determined from the subtraction of the partial product "divisor times quotient digit" from what is left of the dividend. Then for the last time $\hat{q}$ must be reduced by 1 and the remainder updated. The algorithm for division with remainder is now essentially the following procedure.

Algorithm for division with remainder of $a = (a_{m+n-1}a_{m+n-2}\ldots a_0)_B \geq 0$
by $b = (b_{n-1}b_{n-2}\ldots b_0)_B > 0$

1. Determine the scaling factor d as given above.

2. Set $r := (r_{m+n}r_{n+m-1}r_{m+n-2}\ldots r_0)_B \leftarrow (0a_{m+n-1}a_{m+n-2}\ldots a_0)_B$.

3. Set $i \leftarrow m + n, j \leftarrow m$.

4. Set $\hat{q} \leftarrow \min\left\{\left\lfloor\frac{\hat{r}_iB+\hat{r}_{i-1}}{\hat{b}_{n-1}}\right\rfloor, B - 1\right\}$ with the digits $\hat{r}_i$, $\hat{r}_i - 1$, and $\hat{b}_{n-1}$ obtained from scaling by d (see above). If $\hat{b}_{n-2}\hat{q} > \left(\hat{r}_iB + \hat{r}_{i-1} - \hat{q}\hat{b}_{n-1}\right)B + \hat{r}_{i-2}$, set $\hat{q} \leftarrow \hat{q} - 1$ and repeat this test.

5. If $r - b\hat{q} < 0$, set $\hat{q} \leftarrow \hat{q} - 1$.

6. Set $r := (r_ir_{i-1}\ldots r_{i-n})_B \leftarrow (r_ir_{i-1}\ldots r_{i-n})_B - b\hat{q}$ and $q_j \leftarrow \hat{q}$.

7. Set $i \leftarrow i - 1$ and $j \leftarrow j - 1$; if $i \geq n$, go to step 4.

8. Output $q = (q_mq_{m-1}\ldots q_0)_B$ and $r = (r_{n-1}r_{n-2}\ldots r_0)_B$.

If the divisor has only a single digit b_0, then the process can be shortened by initializing r with $r \leftarrow 0$ and dividing the two digits $(ra_i)_B$ by b_0 with remainder. Here r is overwritten by the remainder, $r \leftarrow (ra_i)_B - q_ib_0$, and a_i runs through all the digits of the dividend. At the end, r contains the remainder and $q = (q_mq_{m-1}\ldots q_0)_B$ forms the quotient.

Now that we have at hand all the requisite processes for implementing division, we present the C function for the above algorithm.

Function:	division with remainder
Syntax:	int div_l (CLINT d1_l, CLINT d2_l, CLINT quot_l, CLINT rem_l);
Input:	d1_l (dividend), d2_l (divisor)
Output:	quot_l (quotient), rem_l (remainder)
Return:	E_CLINT_OK if all is ok
	E_CLINT_DBZ if division by 0

```
int
div_l (CLINT d1_l, CLINT d2_l, CLINT quot_l, CLINT rem_l)
{
 register clint *rptr_l, *bptr_l;
 CLINT b_l;

 /* Allow double-length dividend plus 1 digit */

 clint r_l[2 + (CLINTMAXDIGIT << 1)];
 clint *qptr_l, *msdptrb_l, *lsdptrr_l, *msdptrr_l;
 USHORT bv, rv, qhat, ri, ri_1, ri_2, bn_1, bn_2;
 ULONG right, left, rhat, borrow, carry, sbitsminusd;
 unsigned int d = 0;
 int i;
```

The dividend $a = \left(a_{m+n-1}a_{m+n-2}\ldots a_0\right)_B$ and divisor $b\left(b_{n-1}b_{n-2}\ldots b_0\right)_B$ are copied into the CLINT variables r_l and b_l. Any leading zeros are purged. If the divisor has the value zero, the function is terminated with the error code E_CLINT_DBZ.

We allow the dividend to possess up to double the number of digits determined in MAX_B. This makes possible the later use of division in the functions of modular arithmetic. The storage allotment for a doubly long quotient must always be available to the calling function.

```
 cpy_l (r_l, d1_l);
 cpy_l (b_l, d2_l);

 if (EQZ_L (b_l))
  return E_CLINT_DBZ;
```

A test is made as to whether one of the simple cases is at hand: dividend $= 0$, dividend $<$ divisor, or dividend $=$ divisor. In these cases we are done.

```
 if (EQZ_L (r_l))
  {
   SETZERO_L (quot_l);
   SETZERO_L (rem_l);
   return E_CLINT_OK ;
  }
 i = cmp_l (r_l, b_l);
```

```
if (i == -1)
  {
    cpy_l (rem_l, r_l);
    SETZERO_L (quot_l);
    return E_CLINT_OK ;
  }
else if (i == 0)
  {
    SETONE_L (quot_l);
    SETZERO_L (rem_l);
    return E_CLINT_OK ;
  }
```

> In the next step we check whether the divisor has only one digit. In this case a branch is made to a faster variant of division, which we shall discuss further below.

```
if (DIGITS_L (b_l) == 1)
  goto shortdiv;
```

> Now begins the actual division. First the scaling factor d is determined as the exponent of a power of two. As long as $b_{n-1} \geq$ BASEDIV2 $:= \lfloor B/2 \rfloor$, the most-significant digit b_{n-1} of the divisor is shifted left by one bit, where d, beginning with $d = 0$, is incremented by 1. Furthermore, the pointer msdptrb_l is set to the most-significant digit of the divisor. The value BITPERDGT $- d$ will be used frequently in the sequel, and therefore it is saved in the variable sbitsminusd.

```
msdptrb_l = MSDPTR_L (b_l);
bn_1 = *msdptrb_l;
while (bn_1 < BASEDIV2)
  {
    d++;
    bn_1 <<= 1;
  }
sbitsminusd = (int)(BITPERDGT - d);
```

> If $d > 0$, then the two most-significant digits $\hat{b}_{n-1}\hat{b}_{n-2}$ of db are computed and stored in bn_1 and bn_2. In this we must distinguish the two cases that the divisor b has exactly two, or more than two, digits. In the first case, binary zeros are inserted into $\hat{b}_{n-2}$ from the right, while in the second case the least-significant digits of $\hat{b}_{n-2}$ come from b_{n-3}.

```
if (d > 0)
 {
  bn_1 += *(msdptrb_l - 1) >> sbitsminusd;
  if (DIGITS_L (b_l) > 2)
   {
    bn_2 = (USHORT)(*(msdptrb_l - 1) << d) + (*(msdptrb_l - 2) >> sbitsminusd);
   }
  else
   {
    bn_2 = (USHORT)(*(msdptrb_l - 1) << d);
   }
 }
else
 {
  bn_2 = (USHORT)(*(msdptrb_l - 1));
 }
```

> Now the pointers msdptrr_l and lsdptrr_l are set to the most-significant, respectively least-significant, digit of $(a_{m+n}a_{m+n-1} \ldots a_{m+1})_B$ in the CLINT vector r_l, which will represent the remainder of the division. At the digit a_{m+n} the variable r_l is initialized to 0. The pointer qptr_l is set to the highest quotient digit.

```
msdptrb_l = MSDPTR_L (b_l);

msdptrr_l = MSDPTR_L (r_l) + 1;
lsdptrr_l = MSDPTR_L (r_l) - DIGITS_L (b_l) + 1;
*msdptrr_l = 0;

qptr_l = quot_l + DIGITS_L (r_l) - DIGITS_L (b_l) + 1;
```

> We now enter the main loop. The pointer lsdptrr_l runs over the digits $a_m, a_{m-2}, \ldots, a_0$ of the dividend in r_l, and the (implicit) index i over the values $i = m + n, \ldots, n$.

```
while (lsdptrr_l >= LSDPTR_L (r_l))
 {
```

As preparation for determining $\hat{q}$ the three most-significant digits of part $(a_i a_{i-1} \ldots a_{i-n})_B$ of the dividend multiplied by the scaling factor d are calculated and stored in the variables ri, ri_1, and ri_2. The case where the part of the dividend under consideration has only three digits is handled as a special case. In the first pass through the loop there are at least three digits present: On the assumption that the divisor b itself has at least two digits, there exist the most-significant digits a_{m+n-1} and a_{m+n-2} of the dividend, and the digit a_{m+n} was set to zero during the initialization of r_1.

```
ri = (USHORT)((*msdptrr_1 << d) + (*(msdptrr_1 - 1) >> sbitsminusd));
ri_1 = (USHORT)((*(msdptrr_1 - 1) << d) + (*(msdptrr_1 - 2) >> sbitsminusd));
if (msdptrr_1 - 3 > r_1)     /* there are four dividend digits */
  {
   ri_2 = (USHORT)((*(msdptrr_1 - 2) << d) +
                                  (*(msdptrr_1 - 3) >> sbitsminusd));
  }
else /* there are only three dividend digits */
  {
   ri_2 = (USHORT)(*(msdptrr_1 - 2) << d);
  }
```

Now comes the determination of $\hat{q}$, stored in the variable qhat. Corresponding to step 4 of the algorithm, we distinguish the cases ri $\neq$ bn_1 (frequent) and ri $=$ bn_1 (rare). The case ri $>$ bn_1 is excluded, on account of $r/b < B$. Therefore, $\hat{q}$ is set to the minimum of $\left\lfloor (\hat{r}_i B + \hat{r}_{i-1}) / \hat{b}_{n-1} \right\rfloor$ and $B - 1$.

```
if (ri != bn_1)     /* almost always */
  {
   qhat = (USHORT)((rhat = ((ULONG)ri << BITPERDGT) + (ULONG)ri_1) / bn_1);
   right = ((rhat = (rhat - (ULONG)bn_1 * qhat)) << BITPERDGT) + ri_2;
```

If bn_2 * qhat > right, then qhat is too large by at least 1 and by at most 2.

```
if ((left = (ULONG)bn_2 * qhat) > right)
  {
   qhat--;
```

The test is now repeated only if we have rhat = rhat + bn_1 < BASE due to the decrementing of qhat (otherwise, we already have bn_2 * qhat < BASE^2 ≤ rhat * BASE).

```
      if ((rhat + bn_1) < BASE)
        {
          if ((left - bn_2) > (right + ((ULONG)bn_1 << BITPERDGT)))
            {
              qhat--;
            }
        }
    }
}
else
```

In the second, rare, case, ri = bn_1, first $\hat{q}$ is set to the value BASE $- 1 = 2^{16} - 1 =$ BASEMINONE. In this case for rhat we have rhat = ri * BASE + ri_1 - qhat * bn_1 = ri_1 + bn_1. Only in the case that rhat < BASE is a test made as to whether qhat is too large. Otherwise, we have already bn_2 * qhat < BASE^2 ≤ rhat * BASE. Under the same condition as above the test of qhat is repeated.

```
  {
    qhat = BASEMINONE;
    right = ((ULONG)(rhat = (ULONG)bn_1 + (ULONG)ri_1) << BITPERDGT) + ri_2;
    if (rhat < BASE)
      {
        if ((left = (ULONG)bn_2 * qhat) > right)
          {
            qhat--;
            if ((rhat + bn_1) < BASE)
              {
                if ((left - bn_2) > (right + ((ULONG)bn_1 << BITPERDGT)))
                  {
                    qhat--;
                  }
              }
          }
      }
  }
```

Then comes the subtraction of qhat $\cdot\ b$ from the part $u := (a_i a_{i-1} \ldots a_{i-n})_B$ of the dividend, which is replaced by the difference thus calculated. There are two things to note:

- The products qhat $\cdot\ b_j$ can have two digits. Both digits are saved for the time being in the ULONG variable carry. The more-significant word of carry is dealt with as a carry in the subtraction of the next-higher digit.

- For the case that qhat is still too large by 1 and the difference $u - \text{qhat} \cdot b$ is negative, as a precaution the value $u' := B^{n+1} + u - \text{qhat} \cdot b$ is calculated and the result considered modulo B^{n+1} as the B complement $\hat{u}$ of u. After the subtraction the highest digit u'_{i+1} of u' is located in the most-significant word of the ULONG variable borrow. Finally, that qhat is here too large by 1 is recognized in that $u'_{i+1} \neq 0$. In this case the result is corrected in the following by the addition $u \leftarrow u' + b$ modulo B^{n+1}.

```
borrow = BASE;
carry = 0;
for (bptr_l = LSDPTR_L (b_l), rptr_l = lsdptrr_l;
                bptr_l <= msdptrb_l; bptr_l++, rptr_l++)
 {
  if (borrow >= BASE)
   {
    *rptr_l = (USHORT)(borrow = ((ULONG)*rptr_l + BASE -
        (ULONG)(USHORT)(carry = (ULONG)*bptr_l *
           qhat + (ULONG)(USHORT)(carry >> BITPERDGT))));
   }
  else
   {
    *rptr_l = (USHORT)(borrow = ((ULONG)*rptr_l + BASEMINONEL -
        (ULONG)(USHORT)(carry = (ULONG)*bptr_l * qhat +
           (ULONG)(USHORT)(carry >> BITPERDGT))));
   }
 }
if (borrow >= BASE)    {
  *rptr_l = (USHORT)(borrow = ((ULONG)*rptr_l + BASE -
                (ULONG)(USHORT)(carry >> BITPERDGT)));
 }
else
 {
  *rptr_l = (USHORT)(borrow = ((ULONG)*rptr_l + BASEMINONEL -
                (ULONG)(USHORT)(carry >> BITPERDGT)));
 }
```

> The quotient digit is stored, subject to a possible necessary correction.

```
*qptr_l = qhat;
```

> As promised, now a test is made as to whether the quotient digit is too large by 1. This is extremely seldom the case (further below, special test data will be presented) and is indicated by the high-valued word of the ULONG variable borrow being equal to zero; that is, that borrow < BASE. If this is the case, then $u \leftarrow u' + b$ modulo B^{n+1} is calculated (notation as above).

```
if (borrow < BASE)
  {
  carry = 0;
  for (bptr_l = LSDPTR_L (b_l), rptr_l = lsdptrr_l;
              bptr_l <= msdptrb_l; bptr_l++, rptr_l++)
    {
    *rptr_l = (USHORT)(carry = ((ULONG)*rptr_l + (ULONG)(*bptr_l) +
              (ULONG)(USHORT)(carry >> BITPERDGT)));
    }
  *rptr_l += (USHORT)(carry >> BITPERDGT);
  (*qptr_l)--;
  }
```

> Now the pointers are set to the remainder and the quotient, and we return to the beginning of the main loop.

```
  msdptrr_l--;
  lsdptrr_l--;
  qptr_l--;
  }
```

The length of the remainder and that of the quotient are determined. The number of digits is at most 1 more than the number of digits of the dividend minus the number of digits of the divisor. The remainder possesses at most the number of digits of the divisor. In both cases the exact length is set by the removal of leading zeros.

```
SETDIGITS_L (quot_l, DIGITS_L (r_l) - DIGITS_L (b_l) + 1);
RMLDZRS_L (quot_l);

SETDIGITS_L (r_l, DIGITS_L (b_l));
cpy_l (rem_l, r_l);

return E_CLINT_OK;
```

> In the case of "short division" the divisor possesses only the digit b_0, by which the two digits $(ra_i)_B$ are to be divided, where a_i runs through all digits of the dividend; r is initialized with $r \leftarrow 0$ and assumes the difference $r \leftarrow (ra_i)_B - qb_0$. The value r is represented by the USHORT variable rv. The value of $(ra_i)_B$ is stored in the ULONG variable rhat.

```
shortdiv:
  rv = 0;
  bv = *LSDPTR_L (b_l);
  for (rptr_l = MSDPTR_L (r_l), qptr_l = quot_l + DIGITS_L (r_l);
                   rptr_l >= LSDPTR_L (r_l); rptr_l--, qptr_l--)
   {
    *qptr_l = (USHORT)((rhat = ((((ULONG)rv) << BITPERDGT) + (ULONG)*rptr_l)) / bv);
    rv = (USHORT)(rhat - (ULONG)bv * (ULONG)*qptr_l);
   }
  SETDIGITS_L (quot_l, DIGITS_L (r_l));
  RMLDZRS_L (quot_l);

  u2clint_l (rem_l, rv);

  return E_CLINT_OK;
}
```

With $t = O(mn)$, the run time t of the division is analogous to that for multiplication, where m and n are the numbers of digits of the dividend and divisor, respectively, to the base B.

In the sequel we shall describe a number of variants of division with remainder, all of which are based on the general division function. First we have the mixed version of the division of a CLINT type by a USHORT type. For this we return once again to the routine for small divisors of the function div_l(), where it is placed almost without alteration into its own function. We thus present only the interface of the function.

Function:	division of a CLINT type by a USHORT type
Syntax:	int udiv_l (CLINT dv_l, USHORT uds, CLINT q_l, CLINT r_l);
Input:	dv_l (dividend), uds (divisor)
Output:	q_l (quotient), r_l (remainder)
Return:	E_CLINT_OK if all is ok
	E_CLINT_DBZ if division by 0

We have already indicated that for a given calculation the quotient of a division is not required, and only the remainder is of interest. This will not result in a great savings of time, but in such cases, at least the passing of a pointer to the storage location of the quotient is burdensome. It is therefore worthwhile to create an independent function for computing remainders, or "residues." The mathematical background of the use of this function is discussed more fully in Chapter 5.

Function:	Remainders (reduction modulo n)
Syntax:	int mod_l (CLINT d_l, CLINT n_l, CLINT r_l);
Input:	d_l (dividend), n_l (divisor or modulus)
Output:	r_l (remainder)
Return:	E_CLINT_OK if all is ok
	E_CLINT_DBZ if division by 0

Simpler than the general case is the construction of the remainder modulo a power of 2, namely 2^k, which is worth implementing in its own function. The remainder of the dividend in a division by 2^k results from truncating its binary digits after the kth bit, where counting begins with 0. This truncation corresponds to a bitwise joining of the dividend to $2^k - 1 = (111111\ldots1)_2$, the value of k binary ones, by a logical AND (cf. Section 7.2). The operation is concentrated on the digit of the dividend in its representation to base B that contains the kth bit; all higher-valued dividend digits are irrelevant. For specifying the divisor the following function mod_l() is passed only the exponent k.

Function:	remainder modulo a power of 2 (reduction modulo 2^k)
Syntax:	int mod2_l (CLINT d_l, ULONG k, CLINT r_l);
Input:	d_l (dividend), k (exponent of the divisor or modulus)
Return:	r_l (remainder)

```
int
mod2_l (CLINT d_l, ULONG k, CLINT r_l)
{
 int i;
```

Since $2^k > 0$, there is no test for division by 0. First d_l is copied to r_l and a test is made as to whether k exceeds the maximal binary length of a CLINT number, in which case the function is terminated.

```
cpy_l (r_l, d_l);
if (k > CLINTMAXBIT)
 return E_CLINT_OK;
```

The digit in r_l in which something changes is determined and is stored as an index in i. If i is greater than the number of digits of r_l, then we are done.

```
i = 1 + (k >> LDBITPERDGT);
if (i > DIGITS_L (r_l))
 return E_CLINT_OK;
```

Now the determined digit of r_l (counting from 1) is joined by a logical AND to the value $2^{k \bmod \text{BITPERDGT}} - 1 (= 2^{k \bmod 16} - 1$ in this implementation). The new length i of r_l is stored in r_l[0]. After the removal of leading zeros the function is terminated.

```
r_l[i] &= (1U << (k & (BITPERDGT - 1))) - 1U;
SETDIGITS_L (r_l, i);
RMLDZRS_L (r_l);

return E_CLINT_OK;
}
```

The mixed variant of calculating residues employs a USHORT type as divisor and represents the remainder again as a USHORT type, where here again only the interface is given, and we refer the reader to the FLINT/C source code for the short functions.

Function:	remainders, division of a CLINT type by a USHORT type
Syntax:	USHORT umod_l (CLINT dv_l, USHORT uds);
Input:	dv_l (dividend), uds (divisor)
Return:	nonnegative remainder if all is ok
	OxFFFF if division by 0

For testing the division there are—as for all other functions as well—some considerations to be taken into account (see Chapter 13). In particular, it is important that step 5 be tested explicitly, though in randomly selected test cases it will appear with a probability of only about $2/B$ $(= 2^{-15}$ in our implementation) (see [Knut], Section 4.3.1, Exercise 21).

In the following the given dividend a and divisor b with associated quotient q and remainder r have the effect that the program sequence associated to step 5 of the division algorithm is run through twice, and can therefore be used as test data for this particular case. Additional values with this property are contained in the test program testdiv.c.

The display of test numbers below shows the digits in hexadecimal, running from right to left in ascending order, without specifying the length:

Test values for step 5 of the division

$a =$ e3 7d 3a bc 90 4b ab a7 a2 ac 4b 6d 8f 78 2b 2b f8 49 19

d2 91 73 47 69 0d 9e 93 dc dd 2b 91 ce e9 98 3c 56 4c f1

31 22 06 c9 1e 74 d8 0b a4 79 06 4c 8f 42 bd 70 aa aa 68

9f 80 d4 35 af c9 97 ce 85 3b 46 57 03 c8 ed ca

$b =$ 08 0b 09 87 b7 2c 16 67 c3 0c 91 56 a6 67 4c 2e 73 e6 1a

1f d5 27 d4 e7 8b 3f 15 05 60 3c 56 66 58 45 9b 83 cc fd

58 7b a9 b5 fc bd c0 ad 09 15 2e 0a c2 65

$q =$ 1c 48 a1 c7 98 54 1a e0 b9 eb 2c 63 27 b1 ff ff f4 fe 5c

0e 27 23

$r =$ ca 23 12 fb b3 f4 c2 3a dd 76 55 e9 4c 34 10 b1 5c 60 64

bd 48 a4 e5 fc c3 3d df 55 3e 7c b8 29 bf 66 fb fd 61 b4

66 7f 5e d6 b3 87 ec 47 c5 27 2c f6 fb

CHAPTER 5

Modular Arithmetic: Calculating with Residue Classes

Every fine story must leave in the mind of the sensitive reader an intangible residuum of pleasure . . .

—Willa Cather, *Not Under Forty*, "Miss Jewett"

WE BEGIN THIS CHAPTER WITH a discussion of the principle of division with remainder. In relation to this we shall explain the significance of these remainders, their possible applications, and how one calculates with them. In order for the functions to be introduced later to be understandable, we begin with a bit of algebra.

We have seen that in division with remainder of an integer $a \in \mathbb{Z}$ by a natural number $0 < m \in \mathbb{N}$ one has the unique representation

$$a = qm + r, \qquad 0 \leq r < m.$$

Here r is called the *remainder after division of a by m* or the *residue of a modulo m*, and it holds that m divides $a - r$ without remainder, or in mathematical notation,

$$m \mid (a - r).$$

This statement about divisibility was given a new notation by Gauss, in analogy to the equal sign:[1]

$$a \equiv r \bmod m$$

(say "a is *congruent* to r modulo m").

Congruence modulo a natural number m is an *equivalence relation* on the set of natural numbers. This means that the set $R := \{ (a, b) \mid a \equiv b \bmod m \}$

---

[1] Carl Friedrich Gauss, 1777–1855, is to be counted among the greatest mathematicians of all time. He made many significant discoveries in mathematics as well as in the natural sciences, and in particular, at the age of 24 he published his famous *Disquisitiones Arithmeticae*, which is the foundation upon which modern number theory has been built.

of integer pairs satisfying $m \mid (a - b)$ has the following properties, which result immediately from division with remainder:

(i) R is *reflexive:* For all integers a it holds that (a, a) is an element of R, that is, we have $a \equiv a \bmod m$.

(ii) R is *symmetric:* If (a, b) is in R, then so is (b, a); that is, $a \equiv b \bmod m$ implies $b \equiv a \bmod m$.

(iii) R is *transitive:* If (a, b) and (b, c) are in R, then so is (a, c); that is, $a \equiv b \bmod m$ and $b \equiv c \bmod m$ implies $a \equiv c \bmod m$.

The equivalence relation R partitions the set of integers into disjoint sets, called *equivalence classes:* Given a remainder r and a natural number $m > 0$ the set

$$\overline{r} := \{\, a \mid a \equiv r \bmod m \,\},$$

or, in other notation, $r + m\mathbb{Z}$, is called the *residue class* of r *modulo* m. This class contains all integers that upon division by m yield the remainder r.

Here is an example: Let $m = 7$, $r = 5$; then the set of integers that upon division by 7 yield the remainder 5 is the residue class

$$\overline{5} = 5 + 7 \cdot \mathbb{Z} = \{\, \ldots, -9, -2, 5, 12, 19, 26, 33, \ldots \,\}.$$

Two residue classes modulo a fixed number m are either the same or disjoint.[2] Therefore, a residue class can be uniquely identified by any of its elements. Thus the elements of a residue class are called *representatives*, and any element can serve as representative of the class. Equality of residue classes is thus equivalent to the congruence of their representatives with respect to the given modulus. Since upon division with remainder the remainder is always smaller than the divisor, for any integer m there can exist only finitely many residue classes modulo m.

Now we come to the reason for this extensive discussion: Residue classes are objects with which one can do arithmetic, and in fact, by employing their representatives. Calculating with residue classes has great significance for algebra and number theory and thus for coding theory and modern cryptography. In what follows we shall attempt to clarify the algebraic aspects of modular arithmetic.

Let a, b, and m be integers, $m > 0$. For residue classes $\overline{a}$ and $\overline{b}$ modulo m we define the relations "$+$" and "$\cdot$", which we call addition and multiplication (of residue classes), since they are based on the like-named operations on the integers:

$\overline{a} + \overline{b} := \overline{a + b}$ (the sum of classes is equal to the class of the sum);

$\overline{a} \cdot \overline{b} := \overline{a \cdot b}$ (the product of classes is equal to the class of the product).

---

[2]   Two sets are said to be *disjoint* if they have no elements in common, or put another way, if their intersection is the empty set.

Both relations are well-defined, since in each case the result is a residue class modulo m. The set $\mathbb{Z}_m := \{\, \bar{r} \mid r \text{ is a residue modulo } m \,\}$ of residue classes modulo m together with these relations forms a *finite commutative ring* $(\mathbb{Z}_m, +, \cdot)$ with unit, which in particular means that the following axioms are satisfied:

1. *Closure with respect to addition:*
   The sum of two elements of $\mathbb{Z}_m$ is again in $\mathbb{Z}_m$.

2. *Associativity of addition:*
   For every $\bar{a}, \bar{b}, \bar{c}$ in $\mathbb{Z}_m$ one has $\bar{a} + \left(\bar{b} + \bar{c}\right) = \left(\bar{a} + \bar{b}\right) + \bar{c}$.

3. *Existence of an additive identity:*
   For every $\bar{a}$ in $\mathbb{Z}_m$ one has $\bar{a} + \bar{0} = \bar{a}$.

4. *Existence of an additive inverse:*
   For each element $\bar{a}$ in $\mathbb{Z}_m$ there exists a unique element $\bar{b}$ in $\mathbb{Z}_m$ such that $\bar{a} + \bar{b} = \bar{0}$.

5. *Commutativity of addition:*
   For every $\bar{a}, \bar{b}$ in $\mathbb{Z}_m$ one has $\bar{a} + \bar{b} = \bar{b} + \bar{a}$.

6. *Closure with respect to multiplication:*
   The product of two elements of $\mathbb{Z}_m$ is again an element of $\mathbb{Z}_m$.

7. *Associativity of multiplication:*
   For every $\bar{a}, \bar{b}, \bar{c}$ in $\mathbb{Z}_m$ one has $\bar{a} \cdot \left(\bar{b} \cdot \bar{c}\right) = \left(\bar{a} \cdot \bar{b}\right) \cdot \bar{c}$.

8. *Existence of a multiplicative identity:* For every $\bar{a}$ in $\mathbb{Z}_m$ one has $\bar{a} \cdot \bar{1} = \bar{a}$.

9. *Commutativity of multiplication:* For each $\bar{a}, \bar{b}$ in $\mathbb{Z}_m$ one has $\bar{a} \cdot \bar{b} = \bar{b} \cdot \bar{a}$.

10. In $(\mathbb{Z}_m, +, \cdot)$ the *distributive law* holds: $\bar{a} \cdot \left(\bar{b} + \bar{c}\right) = \bar{a} \cdot \bar{b} + \bar{a} \cdot \bar{c}$.

On account of properties 1 through 5 we have that $(\mathbb{Z}_m, +)$ is an *abelian group*, where the term *abelian* refers to the commutativity of addition. From property 4 we can define subtraction in $\mathbb{Z}_m$ as usual, namely, as addition of the inverse element: If $\bar{c}$ is the additive inverse of $\bar{b}$, then $\bar{b} + \bar{c} = \bar{0}$, and so for each $\bar{a} \in \mathbb{Z}_m$ we may define

$$\bar{a} - \bar{b} := \bar{a} + \bar{c}.$$

In $(\mathbb{Z}_m, \cdot)$ the group laws 6, 7, 8, and 9 hold for multiplication, where the multiplicative identity is $\bar{1}$. However, in $\mathbb{Z}_m$ it does not necessarily hold that each element possesses a multiplicative inverse, and thus in general, $(\mathbb{Z}_m, \cdot)$ is not a group, but merely a commutative *semigroup* with unit.[3] However, if we remove from $\mathbb{Z}_m$ all the elements that have a common divisor with m greater than 1, we

---

[3] A semigroup $(H, *)$ exists merely by virtue of there existing on the set H an associative relation $*$.

then obtain a structure that forms an abelian group with respect to multiplication (see Section 10.2). This structure, which in particular does not contain $\bar{0}$, is called a *reduced residue system* and is denoted by $(\mathbb{Z}_m^\times, \cdot)$.

The significance of an algebraic structure like $(\mathbb{Z}_m^\times, \cdot)$, in view of the results we have obtained thus far, can be illustrated by looking at some other well-known commutative rings: The set of integers $\mathbb{Z}$, the set of rational numbers $\mathbb{Q}$, and the set of real numbers $\mathbb{R}$ are commutative rings with unit (in fact, the real numbers form a field, indicating additional internal structure), with the difference that these rings are not finite. The rules for computation that we have outlined above for our finite ring are well known to us because we use them every day. We shall return to these laws in Chapter 13. There they will prove to be trusty allies when it comes to testing arithmetic functions. In this chapter we have collected some important prerequisites.

For calculating with residue classes we rely completely on the classes' representatives. For each residue class modulo m we select precisely one representative and thereby form a *complete residue system*, in terms of which all of our calculations modulo m can be carried out. The smallest nonnegative complete residue system modulo m is the set $R_m := \{\,0, 1, \ldots, m-1\,\}$. The set of numbers r satisfying $-\frac{1}{2}m < r \leq \frac{1}{2}m$ will be called the *smallest absolute complete residue system modulo* m.

As an example we consider $\mathbb{Z}_{26} = \{\,\bar{0}, \bar{1}, \ldots, \overline{25}\,\}$. The smallest nonnegative residue system modulo 26 is $R_{26} = \{0, 1, \ldots, 25\}$, and the smallest absolute residue system modulo 26 is the set $\{-12, -11, \ldots, 0, 1, \ldots, 13\,\}$. The relation between arithmetic with residue classes and modular arithmetic with residue systems can be clarified as follows:

$$\overline{18} + \overline{24} = \overline{18 + 24} = \overline{16}$$

is equivalent to

$$18 + 24 \equiv 42 \equiv 16 \bmod 26,$$

while

$$\bar{9} - \overline{15} = \overline{9 + 11} = \overline{20}$$

is equivalent to

$$9 - 15 \equiv 9 + 11 \equiv 20 \bmod 26.$$

By identifying the alphabet with the residue class ring $\mathbb{Z}_{26}$ or the set of ASCII characters with $\mathbb{Z}_{256}$ we can calculate with characters. A simple encoding system that adds a constant from $\mathbb{Z}_{26}$ to each letter of a text is ascribed to Julius Caesar, who is said to have preferred the constant $\bar{3}$. Each letter of the alphabet would thereby be shifted one position to the right, with X moving to A, Y to B, and Z to C.[4]

---

[4] See Aulus Gellius, XII, 9 and Suetonius, Caes. LVI.

Calculation in residue class rings can be made clearer by employing *composition tables*, which we present in Tables 5-1 and 5-2 for the operations "+" and "·" in $\mathbb{Z}_5$.

Table 5-1. Composition table for addition modulo 5

+	0	1	2	3	4
0	0	1	2	3	4
1	1	2	3	4	0
2	2	3	4	0	1
3	3	4	0	1	2
4	4	0	1	2	3

Table 5-2. Composition table for multiplication modulo 5

·	0	1	2	3	4
0	0	0	0	0	0
1	0	1	2	3	4
2	0	2	4	1	3
3	0	3	1	4	2
4	0	4	3	2	1

The fact that the set of residue classes is finite gives the nice advantage over infinite structures, such as the ring of integers, that the representation of the results of arithmetic expressions within a computer program will not cause overflow if in forming residues a suitable class representative is chosen. This operation, as executed for example by the function mod_l(), is called *reduction* (modulo m). We can thus calculate to our hearts' content with the bounded representation of numbers and the functions of the FLINT/C package within a complete residue system modulo m, so long as we have $m \leq N_{\max}$. We always choose positive representatives and rely on nonnegative residue systems. Because of these properties of residue classes the FLINT/C package does very well with the CLINT representation of large numbers, except for a few situations, which we shall discuss in some detail.

So much for the theory of the arithmetic of residue classes. Now we shall develop our functions for modular arithmetic. We first recall the functions mod_l() and mod2_l() from Section 4.3, which return the remainder of a reduction modulo m, respectively modulo 2^k, and we shall deal in turn with modular addition and subtraction, as well as modular multiplication and squaring. Because of its particular complexity, we devote a separate chapter to modular exponentiation.

We shall avoid the notation $\bar{a}$ for a residue class by simply omitting the bar and letting the representative a denote the class of a, provided that there is no chance of confusion.

The process by which the functions for modular arithmetic operate consists essentially in carrying out the corresponding nonmodular function on the operands and then using division with remainder to carry out a modular reduction. However, one must note that intermediate results can grow to a size of $2\mathrm{MAX}_B$ digits, which due to their size or, in the case of subtraction, on account of a negative sign, cannot be represented in a CLINT object. We have previously called these situations respectively overflow and underflow. The basic arithmetic functions possess mechanisms for dealing with situations of overflow and underflow that reduce these intermediate results modulo $(N_{\max} + 1)$ (see Chapters 3 and 4). These would be effective here if the result of the complete modular operation were representable by a CLINT type. In order to obtain correct results in these cases, we shall extract from the functions that we already have for the basic operations, as announced in Chapter 4, kernel functions

```
void add (CLINT, CLINT, CLINT);
void sub (CLINT, CLINT, CLINT);
void mult (CLINT, CLINT, CLINT);
void umul (CLINT, USHORT, CLINT);
void sqr (CLINT, CLINT);
```

The kernel functions comprise the arithmetic operations that have been removed from the functions add_l(), sub_l(), mul_l(), and sqr_l(), which we have met earlier. What remains in these functions are simply the processes of removing leading zeros, supporting the accumulator operation, and handling possible overflow or underflow, while for the actual arithmetic operations the kernel functions are invoked. The syntax and semantics of these earlier functions are not altered, and the functions can be used as described.

As an example of multiplication mul_l(), this process leads to the following function (see in this regard the implementation of the function mul_l() on page 36).

Function:	multiplication
Syntax:	int mul_l (CLINT f1_l, CLINT f2_l, CLINT pp_l);
Input:	f1_l, f2_l (factors)
Output:	pp_l (product)
Return:	E_CLINT_OK if all is ok
	E_CLINT_OFL if overflow

```
int
mul_l (CLINT f1_l, CLINT f2_l, CLINT pp_l)
{
  CLINT aa_l, bb_l;
  CLINTD p_l;
  int OFL = E_CLINT_OK;
```

Purging of leading zeros and support of the accumulator operation.

```
  cpy_l (aa_l, f1_l);
  cpy_l (bb_l, f2_l);
```

Call the kernel function for multiplication.

```
  mult (aa_l, bb_l, p_l);
```

Check for and deal with overflow.

```
  if (DIGITS_L (p_l) > (USHORT)CLINTMAXDIGIT)      /* overflow ? */
    {
      ANDMAX_L (p_l);      /* reduce modulo (Nmax + 1) */
      OFL = E_CLINT_OFL;
    }
  cpy_l (pp_l, p_l);
  return OFL;
}
```

For the remaining functions add_l(), sub_l(), and sqr_l() the changes are similar. The arithmetic kernel functions themselves contain no new components and therefore do not need to be given here. For details look at the implementation in flint.c.

The kernel functions do not allow overflow, and they execute no reduction modulo $(N_{max} + 1)$. They are intended for internal use by the FLINT/C functions and therefore are declared as static. In using them, however, one must note that they are not equipped for dealing with leading zeros and that they cannot be used in accumulator mode (see Chapter 3).

The use of sub() presupposes that the difference is positive. Otherwise, the result is undefined; there is no control in sub() in this regard. Finally, the calling functions must make available enough space for the result of oversized intermediate results. In particular, sub() requires that the result variable have available at least enough storage space as for the representation of the minuend.

We are now equipped to develop the functions madd_l(), msub_l(), mmul_l(), and msqr_l() for modular arithmetic.

Function:	modular addition
Syntax:	int madd_l (CLINT aa_l, CLINT bb_l, CLINT c_l, CLINT m_l);
Input:	aa_l, bb_l (summands), m_l (modulus)
Output:	c_l (remainder)
Return:	E_CLINT_OK if all is ok
	E_CLINT_DBZ if division by 0

```
int
madd_l (CLINT aa_l, CLINT bb_l, CLINT c_l, CLINT m_l)
{
  CLINT a_l, b_l;
  clint tmp_l[CLINTMAXSHORT + 1];

  if (EQZ_L (m_l))
    {
      return E_CLINT_DBZ;
    }
  cpy_l (a_l, aa_l);
  cpy_l (b_l, bb_l);
  if (GE_L (a_l, m_l) || GE_L (b_l, m_l))
    {
      add (a_l, b_l, tmp_l);
      mod_l (tmp_l, m_l, c_l);
    }
  else
```

If a_l and b_l both lie below m_l, then we are spared a division.

```
    {
      add (a_l, b_l, tmp_l);
      if (GE_L (tmp_l, m_l))
        {
          sub_l (tmp_l, m_l, tmp_l);    /* underflow excluded */
        }
```

> In the preceding call by sub_l() some care was taken: We supply sub_l() with the argument tmp_l, which here as the sum of a_l and b_l is possibly one digit larger than allowed by the constant MAX_B. Within the function sub_l() nothing can go awry as long as we provide storage space for an additional digit in the result. Therefore, we let the result be stored in tmp_l and not immediately in c_l, as one might suppose. Because of these conditions, at the end of sub_l() we have that tmp_l has at most MAX_B digits.

```
    cpy_l (c_l, tmp_l);
  }
  return E_CLINT_OK;
}
```

The function for modular subtraction msub_l() uses only the positive intermediate results of the functions add_l(), sub_l(), and mod_l(), in order to remain within a positive residue system.

Function:	modular subtraction
Syntax:	int msub_l (CLINT aa_l, CLINT bb_l, CLINT c_l, CLINT m_l);
Input:	aa_l (minuend), bb_l (subtrahend), m_l (modulus)
Output:	c_l (remainder)
Return:	E_CLINT_OK if all is ok
	E_CLINT_DBZ if division by 0

```
int
msub_l (CLINT aa_l, CLINT bb_l, CLINT c_l, CLINT m_l)
{
  CLINT a_l, b_l, tmp_l;
  if (EQZ_L (m_l))
    {
      return E_CLINT_DBZ;
    }
  cpy_l (a_l, aa_l);
  cpy_l (b_l, bb_l);
```

We distinguish the cases a_l $\geq$ b_l and a_l $<$ b_l. The first case is a standard situation; in the second case we compute (b_l $-$ a_l), reduce modulo m_l, and subtract a positive remainder from m_l.

```
if (GE_L (a_l, b_l))     /* a_l - b_l ≥ 0 */
  {
    sub (a_l, b_l, tmp_l);
    mod_l (tmp_l, m_l, c_l);
  }
else     /* a_l - b_l < 0 */
  {
    sub (b_l, a_l, tmp_l);
    mod_l (tmp_l, m_l, tmp_l);
    if (GTZ_L (tmp_l))
      {
        sub (m_l, tmp_l, c_l);
      }
    else
      {
        SETZERO_L (c_l);
      }
  }
  return E_CLINT_OK;
}
```

Now come the functions mmul_l() and msqr_l() for modular multiplication and squaring, of which we show only that for multiplication.

Function:	modular multiplication
Syntax:	int mmul_l (CLINT aa_l, CLINT bb_l, CLINT c_l, CLINT m_l);
Input:	aa_l, bb_l (factors), m_l (modulus)
Output:	c_l (remainder)
Return:	E_CLINT_OK if all ok
	E_CLINT_DBZ if division by 0

```
int
mmul_l (CLINT aa_l, CLINT bb_l, CLINT c_l, CLINT m_l)
{
  CLINT a_l, b_l;
  CLINTD tmp_l;

  if (EQZ_L (m_l))
    {
       return E_CLINT_DBZ;
    }
  cpy_l (a_l, aa_l);
  cpy_l (b_l, bb_l);
  mult (a_l, b_l, tmp_l);
  mod_l (tmp_l, m_l, c_l);
  return E_CLINT_OK;
}
```

The functions for modular multiplication and squaring are so similar that for modular multiplication we give only the interface of the function.

Function:	modular squaring
Syntax:	int msqr_l (CLINT aa_l, CLINT c_l, CLINT m_l);
Input:	aa_l (factor), m_l (modulus)
Output:	c_l (remainder)
Return:	E_CLINT_OK if all is ok
	E_CLINT_DBZ if division by 0

To each of these functions (of course, with the exception of squaring) there is a corresponding mixed function, which as its second argument takes a USHORT argument. As an example, we demonstrate the function umadd_l(). The functions umsub_l() and ummul_l() follow exactly the same pattern, and so we shall not go into them in detail.

Function:	modular addition of a CLINT type and a USHORT type
Syntax:	int umadd_l (CLINT a_l, USHORT b, CLINT c_l, CLINT m_l);
Input:	a_l, b (summands), m_l (modulus)
Output:	c_l (remainder)
Return:	E_CLINT_OK if all is ok E_CLINT_DBZ if division by 0

```
int
umadd_l (CLINT a_l, USHORT b, CLINT c_l, CLINT m_l)
{
  int err;
  CLINT tmp_l;
  u2clint_l (tmp_l, b);
  err = madd_l (a_l, tmp_l, c_l, m_l);
  return err;
}
```

Our collection of mixed functions with a USHORT argument will be extended in the following chapter to include two further functions. To end this chapter we would like, with the help of modular subtraction, to construct an additional useful auxiliary function that determines whether two CLINT values are equal as representatives of a residue class modulo m. The following function mequ_l() accomplishes this by using the definition of the congruence relationship $a \equiv b \bmod m \iff m \mid (a - b)$.

To determine whether two CLINT objects a_l and b_l are equivalent modulo m_l, we need do nothing further than apply msub_l(a_l, b_l, r_l, m_l) and check whether the remainder r_l of this operation is equal to zero.

Function:	test for equivalence modulo m
Syntax:	int mequ_l (CLINT a_l, CLINT b_l, CLINT m_l);
Input:	a_l, b_l (operands), m_l (modulus)
Return:	1 if (a_l == b_l) modulo m_l 0 otherwise

```
int
mequ_l (CLINT a_l, CLINT b_l, CLINT m_l)
{
  CLINT r_l;
  if (EQZ_L (m_l))
    {
      return E_CLINT_DBZ;
    }
  msub_l (a_l, b_l, r_l, m_l);
  return ((0 == DIGITS_L (r_l))?1:0);
}
```

Where All Roads Meet: Modular Exponentiation

> For a long time on that spot I stood,
> Where two roads converged in the wood and I thought:
> "Someone going the other way
> Might someday stop here for the sake
> Of deciding which path to take."
> But my direction lay where it lay.
> And walking on, I felt a sense
> Of wonder at that difference.
>
> —Ilya Bernstein, *Attention and Man*

IN ADDITION TO THE CALCULATIONAL rules for addition, subtraction, and multiplication in residue classes we can also define an operation of exponentiation, where the exponent specifies how many times the base is to be multiplied by itself. Exponentiation is carried out, as usual, by means of recursive calls to multiplication: For a in $\mathbb{Z}_m$ we have $a^0 := \bar{1}$ and $a^{e+1} := a \cdot a^e$.

It is easy to see that for exponentiation in $\mathbb{Z}_m$ the usual rules apply (cf. Chapter 1):

$$a^e \cdot a^f = a^{e+f}, \qquad a^e \cdot b^e = (a \cdot b)^e, \qquad (a^e)^f = a^{ef}.$$

6.1 First Approaches

The simplest approach to exponentiation consists in following the recursive rule defined above and multiplying the base a by itself e times. This requires $e - 1$ modular multiplications, and for our purposes that is simply too many.

A more efficient way of proceeding is demonstrated in the following examples, in which we consider the binary representation of the exponent:

$$a^{15} = a^{2^3+2^2+2+1} = \left(\left(\left(a^2\right)a\right)^2 a\right)^2 a, \qquad a^{16} = a^{2^4} = \left(\left(\left(a^2\right)^2\right)^2\right)^2.$$

Here raising the base to the fifteenth power requires only six multiplications, as opposed to fourteen in the first method. Half of these are squarings, which, as we know, require only about half as much CPU time as regular multiplications. Exponentiation to the sixteenth power is accomplished with only four squarings.

Algorithms for exponentiation of a^e modulo m that calculate with the binary representation of the exponent are in general much more favorable than the first approach, as we are about to see. But first we must observe that the intermediate results of many integer multiplications one after the other quickly occupy more storage space than can be supplied by all the computer memory in the world, for from $p = a^b$ follows $\log p = b \log a$, and thus the number of digits of the exponentiated a^b is the product of the exponent and the number of digits of the base. However, if we carry out the calculation of a^e in a residue class ring $\mathbb{Z}_m$, that is, by means of *modular* multiplication, then we avoid this problem. In fact, most applications require exponentiation modulo m, so we may as well focus our attention on this case.

Let $e = (e_{n-1}e_{n-2}\ldots e_0)_2$ with $e_{n-1} > 0$ be the binary representation of the exponent e. Then the following *binary algorithm* requires $\lfloor \log_2 e \rfloor = n$ modular squarings and $\delta(e) - 1$ modular multiplications, where

$$\delta(e) := \sum_{i=0}^{n-1} e_i$$

is the number of ones in the binary representation of e. If we assume that each digit takes on the value 0 or 1 with equal probability, then we may conclude that $\delta(e)$ has the expected value $\delta(e) = n/2$, and altogether we have $\frac{3}{2}\lfloor \log_2 e \rfloor$ multiplications for the algorithm.

Binary algorithm for exponentiation of a^e modulo m

1. Set $p \leftarrow a^{e_{n-1}}$ and $i \leftarrow n - 2$.

2. Set $p \leftarrow p^2 \bmod m$.

3. If $e_i = 1$, set $p \leftarrow p \cdot a \bmod m$.

4. Set $i \leftarrow i - 1$; if $i \geq 0$, go to step 2.

5. Output p.

The following implementation of this algorithm gives good results already for small exponents, those that can be represented by the USHORT type.

Function:	mixed modular exponentiation with USHORT exponent
Syntax:	int umexp_l (CLINT bas_l, USHORT e, CLINT p_l, CLINT m_l);
Input:	bas_l (base) e (exponent) m_l (modulus)
Output:	p_l (power residue)
Return:	E_CLINT_OK if all ok E_CLINT_DBZ if division by 0

```
int
umexp_l (CLINT bas_l, USHORT e, CLINT p_l, CLINT m_l)
{
 CLINT tmp_l, tmpbas_l;
 USHORT k = BASEDIV2;
 int err = E_CLINT_OK;

 if (EQZ_L (m_l))
  {
   return E_CLINT_DBZ;     /* division by zero */
  }
 if (EQONE_L (m_l))
  {
   SETZERO_L (p_l);     /* modulus = 1 ==> remainder = 0 */
   return E_CLINT_OK;
  }
 if (e == 0)     /* exponent = 0 ==> remainder = 1 */
  {
   SETONE_L (p_l);
   return E_CLINT_OK;
  }
 if (EQZ_L (bas_l))
  {
   SETZERO_L (p_l);
   return E_CLINT_OK;
  }
 mod_l (bas_l, m_l, tmp_l);
 cpy_l (tmpbas_l, tmp_l);
```

> After various checks the position of the leading 1 of the exponent e is determined. Here the variable k is used to mask the individual binary digits of e. Then k is shifted one more place to the right, corresponding to setting $i \leftarrow n - 2$ in step 1 of the algorithm.

```
while ((e & k) == 0)
  {
   k >>= 1;
  }
 k >>= 1;
```

> For the remaining digits of e we run through steps 2 and 3. The mask k serves as loop counter, which we shift to the right one digit each time. We then multiply by the base reduced modulo m_1.

```
while (k != 0)
  {
   msqr_l (tmp_l, tmp_l, m_l);
   if (e & k)
     {
       mmul_l (tmp_l, tmpbas_l, tmp_l, m_l);
     }
   k >>= 1;
  }
 cpy_l (p_l, tmp_l);
 return err;
}
```

The binary algorithm for exponentiation offers particular advantages when it is used with small bases. If the base is of type USHORT, then all of the multiplications $p \leftarrow pa \bmod m$ in step 3 of the binary algorithm are of the type CLINT * USHORT modulo CLINT, which makes possible a substantial increase in speed in comparison to other algorithms that in this case would also require the multiplication of two CLINT types. The squarings, to be sure, use CLINT objects, but here we are able to use the advantageous squaring function.

Thus in the following we shall implement the exponentiation function wmexp_l(), the dual to umexp_l(), which accepts a base of type USHORT. The masking out of bits of the exponent is a good preparatory exercise in view of the following "large" functions for exponentiation. The way of proceeding consists essentially in testing one after the other each digit e_i of the exponent against a variable b initialized to 1 in the highest-valued bit, and then shifting to the right and repeating the test until b is equal to 0.

The following function wmexp_1() offers for small bases and exponents up to 1000 bits, for example, a speed advantage of about ten percent over the universal procedures that we shall tackle later.

Function:	modular exponentiation of a USHORT base
Syntax:	int wmexp_1 (USHORT bas, CLINT e_1, CLINT rest_1, CLINT m_1);
Input:	bas (base)
	e_1 (exponent)
	m_1 (modulus)
Output:	rest_1 (remainder of bas$^{e\_1}$ mod m_1)
Return:	E_CLINT_OK if all is ok
	E_CLINT_DBZ if division by 0

```
int
wmexp_1 (USHORT bas, CLINT e_1, CLINT rest_1, CLINT m_1)
{
 CLINT p_1, z_1;
 USHORT k, b, w;
 if (EQZ_L (m_1))
  {
   return E_CLINT_DBZ;     /* division by 0 */
  }
 if (EQONE_L (m_1))
  {
   SETZERO_L (rest_1);     /* modulus = 1 ==> remainder = 0 */
   return E_CLINT_OK;
  }
 if (EQZ_L (e_1))
  {
   SETONE_L (rest_1);
   return E_CLINT_OK;
  }
 if (0 == bas)
  {
   SETZERO_L (rest_1);
   return E_CLINT_OK;
  }
 SETONE_L (p_1);
 cpy_1 (z_1, e_1);
```

> Beginning with the highest-valued nonzero bit in the highest-valued word of the exponent z_1 the bits of the exponent are processed, where always we have first a squaring and then, if applicable, a multiplication. The bits of the exponent are tested in the expression if ((w & b) > 0) by masking their value with a bitwise AND.

```
b = 1 << ((ld_l (z_l) - 1) & (BITPERDGT - 1UL));
w = z_l[DIGITS_L (z_l)];
for (; b > 0; b >>= 1)
 {
  msqr_l (p_l, p_l, m_l);
  if ((w & b) > 0)
   {
    ummul_l (p_l, bas, p_l, m_l);
   }
 }
```

> Then follows the processing of the remaining digits of the exponent.

```
for (k = DIGITS_L (z_l) - 1; k > 0; k--)
 {
  w = z_l[k];
  for (b = BASEDIV2; b > 0; b >>= 1)
   {
    msqr_l (p_l, p_l, m_l);
    if ((w & b) > 0)
     {
      ummul_l (p_l, bas, p_l, m_l);
     }
   }
 }
 cpy_l (rest_l, p_l);

 return E_CLINT_OK;
}
```

6.2 M-ary Exponentiation

Through a generalization of the binary algorithm on page 82 the number of modular multiplications for exponentiation can be reduced even further. The idea is to represent the exponent in a base greater than 2 and to replace multiplication by a in step 3 by multiplication by powers of a. Thus let the exponent e be given by $e = (e_{n-1}e_{n-2}\ldots e_0)_M$, to a base M yet to be determined. The following algorithm calculates the powers $a^e \bmod m$.

M-ary algorithm for exponentiation $a^e \bmod m$

1. Calculate and store $a^2 \bmod m, a^3 \bmod m, \ldots, a^{M-1} \bmod m$ as a table.

2. Set $p \leftarrow a^{e_{n-1}} \bmod m$ and $i \leftarrow n - 2$.

3. Set $p \leftarrow p^M \bmod m$.

4. If $e_i \neq 0$, set $p \leftarrow pa^{e_i} \bmod m$.

5. Set $i \leftarrow i - 1$; if $i \geq 0$, go to step 3.

6. Output p.

The number of necessary multiplications evidently depends on the number of digits of the exponent e and thus on the choice of M. Therefore, we would like to determine M such that the exponentiation in step 3 can be computed to the greatest extent possible by means of squaring, as in the example above for 2^{16}, and such that the number of multiplications by the precomputed powers of a be minimized to a justifiable cost of storage space for the table.

The first condition suggests that we choose M as a power of 2: $M = 2^k$. In view of the second condition we consider the number of modular multiplications as a function of M:

We require

$$\lfloor \log_M e \rfloor \log_2 M = \lfloor \log_2 e \rfloor \tag{6.1}$$

squares in step 3 and on average

$$\lfloor \log_M e \rfloor \operatorname{pr}(e_i \neq 0) = \left\lfloor \frac{\log_2 e}{k} \right\rfloor \operatorname{pr}(e_i \neq 0) \tag{6.2}$$

modular multiplications in step 4, where

$$\operatorname{pr}(e_i \neq 0) = \left(1 - \frac{1}{M}\right)$$

is the probability that a digit e_i of e is nonzero. If we include the $M - 2$ multiplications for the computation of the table, then the M-ary algorithm requires on average

$$\mu_1(k) := 2^k - 2 + \lfloor \log_2 e \rfloor + \left\lfloor \frac{\log_2 e}{k} \right\rfloor \left(1 - \frac{1}{2^k}\right) \tag{6.3}$$

$$= 2^k - 2 + \lfloor \log_2 e \rfloor \left(1 + \frac{2^k - 1}{k2^k}\right) \tag{6.4}$$

modular squarings and multiplications.

For exponents e and moduli m of, say, 512 binary places and $M = 2^k$ we obtain the numbers of modular multiplications for the calculation of $a^e \bmod m$ as shown in Table 6-1. The table shows as well the memory requirement for the precomputed powers of $a \bmod m$, which result from the product $(2k - 2)$CLINTMAXSHORT · sizeof(USHORT).

Table 6-1. Requirements for exponentiation

k	Multiplications	Memory (in Bytes)
1	766	0
2	704	1028
3	666	3084
4	644	7196
5	640	15420
6	656	31868

We see from the table that the average number of multiplications reaches a minimum of 640 at $k = 5$, where the required memory for each larger k grows by approximately a factor of 2. But what are the time requirements for other orders of magnitude of the exponents?

Table 6.2 gives information about this. It displays the requirements for modular multiplication for exponentiation with exponents with various numbers of binary digits and various values of $M = 2^k$. The exponent length of 768 digits was included because it is a frequently used key length for the RSA cryptosystem (see Chapter 17). The favorable numbers of multiplications appear in boldface.

Table 6-2. Numbers of multiplications for typical sizes of exponents and various bases 2^k

k	Number of Binary Digits in the Exponent							
	32	64	128	512	768	1024	2048	4096
1	45	93	190	766	1150	1534	3070	6142
2	**44**	88	176	704	1056	1408	2816	5632
3	46	**87**	**170**	666	996	1327	2650	5295
4	52	91	**170**	644	960	1276	2540	5068
5	67	105	181	**640**	**945**	**1251**	2473	4918
6	98	135	209	656	954	1252	**2444**	4828
7	161	197	271	709	1001	1294	2463	**4801**
8	288	324	396	828	1116	1404	2555	4858

In consideration of the ranges of numbers for which the FLINT/C package was developed, it appears that with $k = 5$ we have found the universal base $M = 2^k$, with which, however, there is a rather high memory requirement of 15 kilobytes for the powers $a^2, a^3, \ldots, a^{31}$ to base a that are to be precomputed. The M-ary algorithm can be improved, however, according to [Cohe], Section 1.2, to the extent that we can employ not $M - 2$, but only $M/2$, premultiplications and thus require only half the memory. The task now additionally consists in the calculation of the power $a^e \bmod m$, where $e = (e_{n-1}e_{n-2} \ldots e_0)_M$ is the representation of the exponent to the base $M = 2^k$.

M-ary Algorithm for exponentiation with reduced number of premultiplications

1. Compute and store $a^3 \bmod m$, $a^5 \bmod m$, $a^7 \bmod m$, $\ldots$, $a^{2^k-1} \bmod m$.

2. If $e_{n-1} = 0$, set $p \leftarrow 1$.
   If $e_{n-1} \neq 0$, factor $e_{n-1} = 2^t u$ with odd u. Set $p \leftarrow a^u \bmod m$ and then $p \leftarrow p^{2^t} \bmod m$.
   In each case set $i \leftarrow n - 2$.

3. If $e_i = 0$, set $p \leftarrow p^{2^k} \bmod m$ by calculating $\left(\cdots \left((p^2)^2 \right)^2 \cdots \right)^2 \bmod m$
   (k-fold squaring modulo m).
   If $e_i \neq 0$, factor $e_i = 2^t u$ with odd u; set $p \leftarrow p^{2^{k-t}} \bmod m$ and then $p \leftarrow pa^u \bmod m$; now set $p \leftarrow p^{2^t} \bmod m$.

4. Set $i \leftarrow i - 1$; if $i \geq 0$, go to step 3.

5. Output p.

The trick of this algorithm consists in dividing up the squarings required in step 3 in a clever way, such that the exponentiation of a is taken care of together with the even part 2^t of e_i. Within the squaring process the exponentiation of a by the odd part u of e_i remains. The balance between multiplication and squaring is shifted to the more favorable squaring, and only the powers of a with odd exponent need to be precomputed and stored.

For this splitting one requires the uniquely determined representation $e_i = 2^t u$, u odd, of the exponent digit e_i. For rapid access to t and u a table is used, which, for example, for $k = 5$ is displayed in Table 6-3.

To calculate these values we can use the auxiliary function twofact_l(), which will be introduced in Section 10.4.1. Before we can program the improved M-ary algorithm there remains one problem to be solved: How, beginning with the binary representation of the exponent or the representation to base $B = 2^{16}$, do we efficiently obtain its representation to base $M = 2^k$ for a variable $k > 0$? It will be of use here to do a bit of juggling with the various indices, and we can "mask out" the required digits e_i to base M from the representation of e to base B. For this we set the following: Let $(\varepsilon_{r-1}\varepsilon_{r-2}\ldots\varepsilon_0)_2$ be the representation of the exponent e to base 2 (we need this on account of the number r of binary digits). Let $(e_{u-1}e_{u-2}\ldots e_0)_B$ be the representation of e as a CLINT type to base $B = 2^{16}$, and let $(e'_{n-1}e'_{n-2}\ldots e'_0)_M$ be the representation of e to the base $M = 2^k$, $k \leq 16$ (M should not be greater than our base B). The representation of e in memory as a CLINT object e_l corresponds to the sequence $[u+1], [e_0], [e_1], \ldots, [e_{u-1}], [0]$ of USHORT values e_l[i] for i $= 0, \ldots, u+1$; one should note that we have added a leading zero.

Let $f := \lfloor \frac{r-1}{k} \rfloor$, and for $i = 0, \ldots, f$ let $s_i := \lfloor \frac{ki}{16} \rfloor$ and $d_i := ki \bmod 16$. With these settings the following statements hold:

1. There are $f + 1$ digits in $(e'_{n-1}e'_{n-2}\ldots e'_0)_M$; that is, $n - 1 = f$.

2. e_{s_i} contains the least-significant bit of the digit e'_i.

3. d_i specifies the position of the least-significant bit of e'_i in e_{s_i} (counting of positions begins with 0). If $i < f$ and $d_i > 16 - k$, then not all the binary digits of e'_i are in e_{s_i}; the remaining (higher-valued) bits of e'_i are in e_{s_i+1}. The desired digit e'_i thus corresponds to the k least-significant binary digits of

$$\left\lfloor \frac{e_{s_i+1}B + e_{s_i}}{2^{d_i}} \right\rfloor .$$

Table 6-3. Values for the factorization of the exponent digits into products of a power of 2 and an odd factor

e_i	t	u	e_i	t	u	e_i	t	u
0	0	0	11	0	11	22	1	11
1	0	1	12	2	3	23	0	23
2	1	1	13	0	13	24	3	3
3	0	3	14	1	7	25	0	25
4	2	1	15	0	15	26	1	13
5	0	5	16	4	1	27	0	27
6	1	3	17	0	17	28	2	7
7	0	7	18	1	9	29	0	29
8	3	1	19	0	19	30	1	15
9	0	9	20	2	5	31	0	31
10	1	5	21	0	21			

As a result we have for $i \in \{0, \ldots, f\}$ the following expression for determining e_i':

$$e_i' = ((e\_1[s_i + 1] \mid (e\_1[s_i + 2] << \text{BITPERDGT})) >> d_i) \ \& \ (2^k - 1); \quad (6.5)$$

Since for the sake of simplicity we set $e\_1[s_f + 2] \leftarrow 0$, this expression holds as well for $i = f$.

We have thus found an efficient method for accessing the digits of the exponent in its CLINT representation, which arise from its representation in a power-of-two base 2^k with $k \leq 16$, whereby we are saved an explicit transformation of the exponent. The number of necessary multiplications and squarings for the exponentiation is now

$$\mu_2(k) := 2^{k-1} + \lfloor \log_2 e \rfloor \left(1 + \frac{2^k - 1}{k \cdot 2^k}\right), \quad (6.6)$$

where in comparison to $\mu_1(k)$ (see page 87) the expenditure for the precomputations has been reduced by half. The table for determining the favorable values of k (Table 6-4) now has a somewhat different appearance.

Table 6-4. Numbers of multiplications for typical sizes of exponents and various bases 2^k

k	Number of Binary Digits in the Exponent							
	32	64	128	512	768	1024	2048	4096
1	47	95	191	767	1151	1535	3071	6143
2	44	88	176	704	1056	1408	2816	5632
3	44	85	168	664	994	1325	2648	5293
4	46	85	164	638	954	1270	2534	5066
5	53	91	167	**626**	931	1237	2459	4904
6	68	105	179	**626**	**924**	**1222**	2414	4798
7	99	135	209	647	939	1232	**2401**	4739
8	162	198	270	702	990	1278	2429	**4732**

Starting with 768 binary digits of the exponent, the favorable values of k are larger by 1 than those given in the table for the previous version of the exponentiation algorithm, while the number of required modular multiplications has easily been reduced. It is to be expected that this procedure is on the whole more favorable than the variant considered previously. Nothing now stands in the way of an implementation of the algorithm.

To demonstrate the implementation of these principles we select an adaptive procedure that uses the appropriate optimal value for k. To accomplish this we rely again on [Cohe] and look for, as is specified there, the smallest integer value k that satisfies the inequality

$$\log_2 e \le \frac{k(k+1)2^{2k}}{2^{k+1} - k - 2}, \qquad (6.7)$$

which comes from the formula $\mu_2(k)$ given previously for the number of necessary multiplications based on the condition $\mu_2(k+1) - \mu_2(k) \ge 0$. The constant number of modular squarings $\lfloor \log_2 e \rfloor$ for all algorithms for exponentiation introduced thus far is eliminated; here only the "real" modular multiplications, that is, those that are not squarings, are considered.

The implementation of exponentiation with variable k requires a large amount of main memory for storing the precomputed powers of a; for $k = 8$ we require about 64 Kbyte for 127 CLINT variables (this is arrived at via $(2^7 - 1)$ * sizeof(USHORT) * CLINTMAXSHORT), where two additional automatic CLINT fields were not counted. For applications with processors or memory models with segmented 16-bit architecture this already has reached the limit of what is possible (see in this regard, for example, [Dunc], Chapter 12, or [Petz], Chapter 7).

Depending on the system platform there are thus various strategies appropriate for making memory available. While the necessary memory for the function mexp5_l() is taken from the stack (as automatic CLINT variables), with each call of the following function mexpk_l() memory is allocated from the heap. To save the expenditure associated with this, one may imagine a variant in which the maximum needed memory is reserved during a one-time initialization and is released only at the end of the entire program. In each case it is possible to fit memory management to the concrete requirements and to orient oneself to this in the commentaries on the following code.

One further note for applications: It is recommended always to check whether it suffices to employ the algorithm with the base $M = 2^5$. The savings in time that comes with larger values of k is relatively not so large in comparison to the total calculation time so as to justify in all cases the greater demand on memory and the thereby requisite memory management. Typical calculation times for various exponentiation algorithms, on the basis of which one can decide whether to use them, are given in Appendix D.

The algorithm, implemented with $M = 2^5$, is contained in the FLINT/C package as the function mexp5_l(). With the macro EXP_L() contained in flint.h one can set the exponentiation function to be used: mexp5_l() or the following function mexpk_l() with variable k.

Function:	modular exponentiation
Syntax:	int mexpk_l (CLINT bas_l, CLINT exp_l, CLINT p_l, CLINT m_l);
Input:	bas_l (base) exp_l (exponent) m_l (modulus)
Output:	p_l (power residue)
Return:	E_CLINT_OK if all is ok E_CLINT_DBZ if division by 0 E_CLINT_MAL if malloc() error

We begin with a segment of the table for representing $e_i = 2^t u$, u odd, $0 \le e_i < 2^8$. The table is represented in the form of two vectors. The first, twotab[], contains the exponents t of the two-factor 2^t, while the second, oddtab[], holds the odd part u of a digit $0 \le e_i < 2^5$. The complete table is contained, of course, in the FLINT/C source code.

```
static int twotab[] =
{0,0,1,0,2,0,1,0,3,0,1,0,2,0,1,0,4,0,1,0,2,0,1,0,3,0,1,0,2,0,1,0,5, ...};
static USHORT oddtab[]=
{0,1,1,3,1,5,3,7,1,9,5,11,3,13,7,15,1,17,9,19,5,21,11,23,3,25,13, ...};

int
mexpk_l (CLINT bas_l, CLINT exp_l, CLINT p_l, CLINT m_l)
{
```

The definitions reserve memory for the exponents plus the leading zero, as well as a pointer clint **aptr_l to the memory still to be allocated, which will take pointers to the powers of bas_l to be precomputed. In acc_l the intermediate results of the exponentiation will be stored.

```
CLINT a_l, a2_l;
clint e_l[CLINTMAXSHORT + 1];
CLINTD acc_l;
clint **aptr_l, *ptr_l;
int noofdigits, s, t, i;
ULONG k;
unsigned int lge, bit, digit, fk, word, pow2k, k_mask;
```

Then comes the usual checking for division by 0 and reduction by 1.

```
if (EQZ_L (m_l))
 {
  return E_CLINT_DBZ;
 }
if (EQONE_L (m_l))
 {
  SETZERO_L (p_l);     /* modulus = 1 ==> residue = 0 */
  return E_CLINT_OK;
 }
```

Base and exponent are copied to the working variables a_l and e_l, and any leading zeros are purged.

```
cpy_l (a_l, bas_l);
cpy_l (e_l, exp_l);
```

Now we process the simple cases $a^0 = 1$ and $0^e = 0$ $(e > 0)$.

```
if (EQZ_L (e_l))
 {
  SETONE_L (p_l);
  return E_CLINT_OK;
 }
if (EQZ_L (a_l))
 {
  SETZERO_L (p_l);
  return E_CLINT_OK;
 }
```

Next, the optimal value for k is determined; the value 2^k is stored in pow2k, and in k_mask the value $2^k - 1$. For this the function ld_l() is used, which returns the number of binary digits of its argument.

```
lge = ld_l (e_l);
k = 8;
while (k > 1 && ((k - 1) * (k << ((k - 1) << 1))/((1 << k ) - k - 1)) >= lge - 1)
  {
    --k;
  }
pow2k = 1U << k;
k_mask = pow2k - 1U;
```

Memory is allocated for the pointers to the powers of a_l to be computed. The base a_l is reduced modulo m_l.

```
if ((aptr_l = (clint **) malloc (sizeof(clint *) * pow2k)) == NULL)
  {
    return E_CLINT_MAL;
  }
mod_l (a_l, m_l, a_l);
aptr_l[1] = a_l;
```

If $k > 1$, then memory is allocated for the powers to be computed. This is not necessary for $k = 1$, since then no powers have to be precomputed. In the following setting of the pointer aptr_l[i] one should note that in the addition of an offset to a pointer p a scaling of the offset by the compiler takes place, so that it counts objects of the pointer type of p.

We have already mentioned that the allocation of working memory can be carried out alternatively in a one-time initialization. The pointers to the CLINT objects would in this case be contained in global variables outside of the function or in static variables within mexpk_l().

```
if (k > 1)
 {
  if ((ptr_l = (clint *) malloc (sizeof(CLINT) * ((pow2k >> 1) - 1)))) == NULL)
   {
    return E_CLINT_MAL;
   }
  aptr_l[2] = a2_l;
  for (aptr_l[3] = ptr_l, i = 5; i < (int)pow2k; i+=2)
   {
    aptr_l[i] = aptr_l[i - 2] + CLINTMAXSHORT;
   }
```

Now comes the precomputation of the powers of the value a stored in a_l. The values $a^3, a^5, a^7, \ldots, a^k - 1$ are computed (a^2 is needed only in an auxiliary role).

```
  msqr_l (a_l, aptr_l[2], m_l);
  for (i = 3; i < (int)pow2k; i += 2)
   {
    mmul_l (aptr_l[2], aptr_l[i - 2], aptr_l[i], m_l);
   }
 }
```

This ends the case distinction for $k > 1$. The exponent is lengthened by the leading zero.

```
*(MSDPTR_L (e_l) + 1) = 0;
```

The determination of the value f (represented by the variable noofdigits).

```
noofdigits = (lge - 1)/k;
fk = noofdigits * k;
```

Word position s_i and bit position d_i of the digit e_i in the variables word and bit.

```
word = fk >> LDBITPERDGT;    /* fk div 16 */
bit = fk & (BITPERDGT-1U);    /* fk mod 16 */
```

Calculation of the digit e_{n-1} with the above-derived formula; e_{n-1} is represented by the variable digit.

```
switch (k)
 {
  case 1:
  case 2:
  case 4:
  case 8:
   digit = ((ULONG)(e_l[word + 1] ) >> bit) & k_mask;
   break;
  default:
   digit = ((ULONG)(e_l[word + 1] | ((ULONG)e_l[word + 2]
                                 << BITPERDGT)) >> bit) & k_mask;
 }
```

First run through step 2 of the algorithm, the case $\text{digit} = e_{n-1} \neq 0$.

```
  if (digit != 0)    /* k-digit > 0 */
   {
    cpy_l (acc_l, aptr_l[oddtab[digit]]);
```

Calculation of p^{2^t}; t is set to the two-part of e_{n-1} via $\text{twotab}[e_{n-1}]$; p is represented by acc_l.

```
    t = twotab[digit];
    for (; t > 0; t--)
     {
      msqr_l (acc_l, acc_l, m_l);
     }
   }
  else    /* k-digit == 0 */
   {
    SETONE_L (acc_l);
   }
```

Loop over noofdigits beginning with $f - 1$.

```
for (--noofdigits, fk -= k; noofdigits >= 0; noofdigits--, fk -= k)
 {
```

> Word position s_i and bit position d_i of the digit e_i in the variables word and bit.

```
word = fk >> LDBITPERDGT;      /* fk div 16 */
bit = fk & (BITPERDGT - 1U);     /* fk mod 16 */
```

> Computation of the digit e_i with the formula derived above; e_i is represented by the variable digit.

```
switch (k)
 {
   case 1:
   case 2:
   case 4:
   case 8:
    digit = ((ULONG)(e_l[word + 1] ) >> bit) & k_mask;
    break;
   default:
    digit = ((ULONG)(e_l[word + 1] | ((ULONG)e_l[word + 2]
                                        << BITPERDGT)) >> bit) & k_mask;
 }
```

> Step 3 of the algorithm, the case digit $= e_i \neq 0$; t is set via the table twotab$[e_i]$ to the two-part of e_i.

```
 if (digit != 0)     /* k-digit > 0 */
  {
   t = twotab[digit];
```

> Calculation of $p^{2^{k-t}} a^u$ in acc_l. Access to a^u with the odd part u of e_i is via aptr_l$[$oddtab$[e_i]]$.

```
   for (s = k - t; s > 0; s--)
    {
     msqr_l (acc_l, acc_l, m_l);
    }
   mmul_l (acc_l, aptr_l[oddtab[digit]], acc_l, m_l);
```

> Calculation of p^{2^t}; p is still represented by acc_l.

```
    for (; t > 0; t--)
      {
        msqr_l (acc_l, acc_l, m_l);
      }
    }
    else     /* k-digit == 0 */
      {
```

> Step 3 of the algorithm, case $e_i = 0$: Calculate p^{2^k}.

```
    for (s = k; s > 0; s--)
      {
        msqr_l (acc_l, acc_l, m_l);
      }
    }
  }
```

> End of the loop; output of acc_l as power residue modulo m_l.

```
cpy_l (p_l, acc_l);
```

> At the end, allocated memory is released.

```
free (aptr_l);
if (ptr_l != NULL)   free (ptr_l);
return E_CLINT_OK;
}
```

The various processes of M-ary exponentiation can be clarified with the help of a numerical example. To this end let us examine the calculation of the power $1234^{667} \bmod 18577$, which will be carried out by the function mexpk_l() in the following steps:

1. **Precomputations**

   The representation of the exponent $e = 667$ can be expressed to the base 2^k with $k = 2$ (cf. the algorithm for M-ary exponentiation on page 89), whereby the exponent e has the representation $e = (10\ 10\ 01\ 10\ 11)_{2^2}$.

   The power $a^3 \bmod 18577$ has the value 17354. Further powers of a do not arise in the precomputation because of the small size of the exponent.

2. **Exponentiation loop**

exponent digit $e_i = 2^t u$	$2^1 \cdot 1$	$2^1 \cdot 1$	$2^0 \cdot 1$	$2^1 \cdot 1$	$2^0 \cdot 3$
$p \leftarrow p^2 \bmod n$	–	14132	13261	17616	13599
$p \leftarrow p^{2^2} \bmod n$	–	–	4239	–	17343
$p \leftarrow pa^u \bmod n$	1234	13662	10789	3054	4445
$p \leftarrow p^2 \bmod n$	18019	7125	–	1262	–

3. **Result**

   $$p = 1234^{667} \bmod 18577 = 4445.$$

As an extension to the general case we shall introduce a special version of exponentiation with a power of two 2^k as exponent. From the above considerations we know that this function can be implemented very easily by means of k-fold exponentiation. The exponent 2^k will be specified by k.

Function: modular exponentiation with exponent a power of 2

Syntax: `int mexp2_l (CLINT a_l, USHORT k, CLINT p_l,`
                       `CLINT m_l);`

Input: a_l (base)
             k (exponent of 2)
             m_l (modulus)

Output: p_l (residue of a_l$^{2^k}$ mod m_l)

Return: E_CLINT_OK if all is ok
               E_CLINT_DBZ if division by 0

```
int
mexp2_l (CLINT a_l, USHORT k, CLINT p_l, CLINT m_l)
{
 CLINT tmp_l;
 if (EQZ_L (m_l))
  {
   return E_CLINT_DBZ;
  }
```

> If k > 0, then a_l is squared k times modulo m_l.

```
if (k > 0)
  {
  cpy_l (tmp_l, a_l);
  while (k-- > 0)
    {
    msqr_l (tmp_l, tmp_l, m_l);
    }
  cpy_l (p_l, tmp_l);
  }
else
```

> Otherwise, if k = 0, we need only to reduce modulo m_l.

```
  {
  mod_l (a_l, m_l, p_l);
  }
return E_CLINT_OK;
}
```

6.3 Addition Chains and Windows

A number of algorithms for exponentiation have been published, some of which are conceived for arbitrary operands and others for special cases. The goal is always to find procedures that employ as few multiplications and divisions as possible. The passage from binary to M-ary exponentiation is an example of how the number of these operations can be reduced.

Binary and M-ary exponentiation are themselves special cases of the construction of *addition chains* (cf. [Knut], Section 4.6.3). We have already taken advantage of the fact that the laws of exponentiation allow the additive decomposition of the exponent of a power: $e = k + l \Rightarrow a^e = a^{k+l} = a^k a^l$. Binary exponentiation decomposes the exponent into a sum

$$e = e_{k-1} \cdot 2^{k-1} + e_{k-2} \cdot 2^{k-2} + \cdots + e_0,$$

from which follows the exponentiation in the form of alternating squarings and multiplications (cf. page 82):

$$a^e \bmod n = \left(\cdots \left(\left(\left(a^{e_{k-1}} \right)^2 \right) a^{e_{k-2}} \right)^2 \right) \cdots \right)^2 a^{e_0} \bmod n.$$

The associated addition chain is obtained by considering the exponents to powers of a that arise as intermediate results in this process:

$$e_{k-1},$$

$$e_{k-1} \cdot 2,$$

$$e_{k-1} \cdot 2 + e_{k-2},$$

$$(e_{k-1} \cdot 2 + e_{k-2}) \cdot 2,$$

$$(e_{k-1} \cdot 2 + e_{k-2}) \cdot 2 + e_{k-3},$$

$$((e_{k-1} \cdot 2 + e_{k-2}) \cdot 2 + e_{k-3}) \cdot 2,$$

$$\vdots$$

$$(\cdots((e_{k-1} \cdot 2 + e_{k-2}) \cdot 2 + e_{k-3}) \cdot 2 + \cdots + e_1) \cdot 2 + e_0.$$

Here terms of the sequence are omitted if $e_j = 0$ for a particular j. For the number 123, for example, based on the binary method the result is the following addition chain with 12 elements: 1, 2, 3, 6, 7, 14, 15, 30, 60, 61, 122, 123.

In general, a sequence of numbers $1 = a_0, a_1, a_2, \ldots, a_r = e$ for which for every $i = 1, \ldots, r$ there exists a pair (j, k) with $j \leq k < i$ such that $a_i = a_j + a_k$ holds is called an *addition chain for e of length r*.

The M-ary method generalizes this principle for the representation of the exponent to other bases. Both methods have the goal of producing addition chains that are as short as possible, in order to minimize the calculational expense for the exponentiation. The addition chain for 123 produced by the 2^3-ary method is 1, 2, 3, 4, 7, 8, 15, 30, 60, 120, 123; with the 2^4-ary method the addition chain 1, 2, 3, 4, 7, 11, 14, 28, 56, 112, 123 is created. These last chains are, as expected, considerably shorter than those obtained by the binary method, which for larger numbers will have a greater effect than in this example. In view of the real savings in time one must, however, note that in the course of initialization for the calculation of $a^e \bmod n$ the M-ary methods construct the powers a^2, a^3, a^5, a^{M-1} also for those exponents that are not needed in the representation of e to the base M or for the construction of the addition chain.

Binary exponentiation represents the worst case of an addition chain: By considering it we obtain a bound on the greatest possible length of an addition chain of $\log_2 e + H(e) - 1$, where $H(e)$ denotes the Hamming weight of e.[1] The length of an addition chain is bounded below by $\log_2 e + \log_2 H(e) - 2.13$, and so a shorter addition chain for e is not to be found (cf. [Scho] or [Knut], Section 4.6.3, Exercises 28, 29). For our example this means that the shortest addition chain for $e = 123$ has length at least 8, and so the results of the M-ary methods cited earlier seem not to be the best possible.

---

[1]   If n possesses a representation $n = (n_{k-1} n_{k-2} \ldots n_0)_2$, then $H(n)$ is defined as $\sum_i n_i$. (See [HeQu], Chapter 8.)

The search for shortest addition chains is a problem for which there is as yet no known polynomial-time procedure. It lies in the complexity class NP of those decision problems that can be solved in polynomial time by nondeterministic methods, that is, those that can be solved by "guessing," where the necessary time for calculation is bounded by a polynomial p that is a function of the size of the input. In contrast to this, the class P contains those problems that can be solved deterministically in polynomial time.[2] It is not surprising that P is a subset of NP, since all polynomial-time deterministic problems can also be solved nondeterministically.

The determination of the shortest addition chain is an NP-*complete problem*, that is, a problem that is at least as difficult to solve as all other problems in the set NP (cf. [Yaco] and [HKW], page 302). The NP-complete problems are therefore of particular interest, since if for even one of them a deterministic polynomial-time procedure could be found, then all other problems in NP could be solved in polynomial time as well. In this case, the classes P and NP would collapse into a single set of problems. Although P $\neq$ NP is conjectured, this problem has remained unsolved, and it represents a central problem of complexity theory .

With this it is clear that all practical procedures for generating addition chains must rest on *heuristics*, that is to say, mathematical rules of thumb such as that for the determination of the exponent k in 2^k-ary exponentiation, of which one knows that it has better time behavior than other methods.

For example, in 1990 Y. Yacobi [Yaco] described a connection between the construction of addition chains and the compression of data according to the Lempel–Ziv procedure; there an exponentiation algorithm based on this compression procedure as well as on the M-ary method is also given.

In the search for the shortest possible addition chains the M-ary exponentiation can be further generalized, which we shall pursue below in greater detail. The *window methods* represent the exponent not as in the M-ary method by digits to a fixed base M, but by digits of varying binary lengths. Thus, for example, long sequences of binary zeros, called *zero windows*, can appear as digits of the exponent. If we recall the M-ary algorithm from page 89, it is clear that for a zero window of length l only the l-fold repetition of squaring is required, and the corresponding step is then

3. Set $p \leftarrow p^{2^l} \mod m = \left(\cdots \left(\left(p^2 \right)^2 \right)^2 \cdots \right)^2$ (l times) $\mod m$.

Digits different from zero will be treated, depending on the process, either as windows of fixed length or as variable windows with a maximal length. As

---

[2] If the input to such a problem is an integer n, then the number of digits of n can serve as a measure of the size of the input. There then exists a polynomial p such that the calculation time is bounded by $p(\log_2 n)$. The difference whether the cost of solving the problem grows with n or with the number of digits of n is decisive.

with the M-ary process, for every nonzero window (in the following called not quite aptly a "1-window") of length t, in addition to the repeated squaring an additional multiplication by a precalculated factor is required, in analogy to the corresponding step of the 2^k-ary procedure:

3'. Set $p \leftarrow p^{2^t} \bmod m$ and then set $p \leftarrow pa^{e_i} \bmod m$.

The number of factors to be precomputed depends on the permitted maximal length of the 1-window. One should note that the 1-windows in the least-significant position always have a 1 and thus are always odd. The factorization of the exponent digit on page 89 into an even and odd factor will thus at first not be needed. On the other hand, in the course of exponentiation the exponent is processed from the most-significant to least-significant place, which means for the implementation that first the *complete* decomposition of the exponent must be carried out and stored before the actual exponentiation can take place.

Yet, if we begin the factorization of the exponent at the most-significant digit and travel from left to right, then every 0- or 1-window can be processed immediately, as soon as it is complete. This means, of course, that we will also obtain 1-windows with an even value, but the exponentiation algorithm is prepared for that.

Both directions of decomposition of the exponent into 1-windows with fixed length l follow essentially the same algorithm, which we formulate below for decomposition from right to left.

Decomposition of an integer e into 0-windows and 1-windows having fixed length l

1. If the least-significant binary digit is equal to 0, then begin a 0-window and go to step 2; otherwise, begin a 1-window and go to step 3.

2. Add the next-higher binary digits in a 0-window as long as no 1 appears. If a 1 appears, then close the 0-window, begin a 1-window, and go to step 3.

3. Collect a further $l - 1$ binary digits into a 1-window. If the next-higher digit is a 0, begin a 0-window and go to step 2; otherwise, begin a 1-window and go to step 3. If in the process all digits of e have been processed, then terminate the algorithm.

The decomposition from left to right begins with the most-significant binary digit and otherwise proceeds analogously. If we suppose that e has no leading binary zeros, then the algorithm cannot reach the end of the representation of e within step 2, and the procedure terminates in step 3 under the same condition given there. The following examples illustrate this process:

- Let $e = 1896837 = (111001111000110000101)_2$, and let $l = 3$. Beginning with the least-significant binary digit, e is decomposed as follows:

$$e = \underline{111}\ \underline{001}\ \underline{111}\ 00\ \underline{011}\ 0000\ \underline{101}.$$

The choice $l = 4$ leads to the following decomposition of e:

$$e = \underline{111}\ 00\ \underline{1111}\ 0\ \underline{0011}\ 000\ \underline{0101}.$$

The 2^k-ary exponentiation considered above yields, for example for $k = 2$, the following decomposition:

$$e = \underline{01}\ \underline{11}\ 00\ \underline{11}\ \underline{11}\ 00\ \underline{01}\ \underline{10}\ 00\ \underline{01}\ \underline{01}.$$

The window decomposition of e for $l = 3$ contains five 1-windows, while that for $l = 4$ has only four, and for each the same number of additional multiplications is required. On the other hand, the 2^2-ary decomposition of e contains eight 1-windows, requires double the number of additional multiplications compared to the case $l = 4$, and is thus significantly less favorable.

- The same procedure, but beginning with the most-significant binary digit, yields for $l = 4$ and $e = 123$ the decomposition

$$e = \underline{1110}\ 0\ \underline{1111}\ 000\ \underline{1100}\ 00\ \underline{101},$$

likewise with four 1-windows, which, as already established above, are not all odd.

Finally, then, exponentiation with a window decomposition of the exponent can be formalized by the following algorithm. Both directions of window decomposition are taken into account.

Algorithm for exponentiation $a^e \bmod m$ with the representation of e in windows of (maximal) length l for odd 1-windows

1. Decompose the exponent e into 0- and 1-windows $(\omega_{k-1} \ldots \omega_0)$ of respective lengths $l_{k-1}, \ldots, l_0$.

2. Calculate and store $a^3 \bmod m$, $a^5 \bmod m$, $a^7 \bmod m, \ldots, a^{2^l - 1} \bmod m$.

3. Set $p \leftarrow a^{\omega_{k-1}} \bmod m$ and $i \leftarrow k - 2$.

4. Set $p \leftarrow p^{l_i} \bmod m$.

5. If $\omega_i \neq 0$, set $p \leftarrow p a^{\omega_i} \bmod m$.

6. Set $i \leftarrow i - 1$; if $i \geq 0$, go to step 4.

7. Output p.

If not all 1-windows are odd, then steps 3 through 6 are replaced by the following, and there is no step 7:

3′. If $\omega_{k-1} = 0$, set $p \leftarrow p^{2^{l_{k-1}}} \mod m = \left(\cdots \left((p^2)^2 \right)^2 \cdots \right)^2$ (l_{k-1} times) $\mod m$. If $\omega_{k-1} \neq 0$, factor $\omega_{k-1} = 2^t u$ with odd u; set $p \leftarrow a^u \mod m$, and then $p \leftarrow p^{2^t} \mod m$. In each case set $i \leftarrow k - 2$.

4′. If $\omega_i = 0$, set $p \leftarrow p^{2^{l_i}} \mod m = \left(\cdots \left((p^2)^2 \right)^2 \cdots \right)^2$ (l_i times) $\mod m$. If $\omega_i \neq 0$, factor $\omega_i = 2^t u$ with odd u; set $p \leftarrow p^{2^{l_i - t}} \mod m$, and then $p \leftarrow pa^u \mod m$; now set $p \leftarrow p^{2^t} \mod m$.

5′. Set $i \leftarrow i - 1$; if $i \geq 0$, go to step 4′.

6′. Output p.

6.4 Montgomery Reduction and Exponentiation

Now we are going to abandon addition chains and turn our attention to another idea, one that is interesting above all from the algebraic point of view. It makes it possible to replace multiplications modulo an odd number n by multiplications modulo a power of 2, that is, 2^k, which requires no explicit division and is therefore more efficient than a reduction modulo an arbitrary number n. This useful method for modular reduction was published in 1985 by P. Montgomery [Mont] and since then has found wide practical application. It is based on the following observation.

Let n and r be relatively prime integers, and let r^{-1} be the multiplicative inverse of r modulo n; and likewise let n^{-1} be the multiplicative inverse of n modulo r; and furthermore, define $n' := -n^{-1} \mod r$ and $m := tn' \mod r$. For integers t we then have

$$\frac{t + mn}{r} \equiv tr^{-1} \mod n. \tag{6.8}$$

Note that on the left side of the congruence we have taken congruences modulo r and a division by r (note that $t + mn \equiv 0 \mod r$, so the division has no remainder), but we have not taken congruences modulo n. By choosing r as a power of 2 in the form 2^s we can reduce a number x modulo r simply by slicing off x at the sth bit (counting from the least-significant bit), and we can carry out the division of x by r by shifting x to the right by s bit positions. The left side of (6.8) thus requires significantly less computational expense than the right side, which is what gives the equation its charm. For the two required operations we can invoke the functions mod2_1() (cf. Section 4.3) and shift_1() (cf. Section 7.1).

This principle of carrying out reduction modulo n is called *Montgomery reduction*. Below, we shall institute Montgomery reduction for the express purpose of speeding up modular exponentiation significantly in comparison to our previous results. Since the procedure requires that n and r be relatively prime, we must take n to be odd. First we have to deal with a couple of considerations.

We can clarify the correctness of the previous congruence with the help of some simple checking. Let us replace m on the left-hand side of (6.8) by the expression $tn' \bmod r$, which is (6.9), and further, replace $tn' \bmod r$ by $tn' - r \lfloor tn'/r \rfloor \in \mathbb{Z}$ to get (6.10), and then in (6.10) for n' the integer expression $(r'r - 1)/n$ for a certain $r' \in \mathbb{Z}$ and obtain (6.11). After reduction modulo n we obtain the result (6.12):

$$\frac{t + mn}{r} \equiv \frac{t + n\left(tn' \bmod r\right)}{r} \tag{6.9}$$

$$\equiv \frac{t + ntn'}{r} - n\left\lfloor \frac{tn'}{r} \right\rfloor \tag{6.10}$$

$$\equiv \frac{t + t\left(rr' - 1\right)}{r} \tag{6.11}$$

$$\equiv tr^{-1} \bmod n. \tag{6.12}$$

To summarize equation (6.8) we record the following: Let $n, t, r \in \mathbb{Z}$ with $\gcd(n, r) = 1, n' := -n^{-1} \bmod r$. For

$$f(t) := t + \left(tn' \bmod r\right) n \tag{6.13}$$

we have

$$f(t) \equiv t \bmod n, \tag{6.14}$$
$$f(t) \equiv 0 \bmod r. \tag{6.15}$$

We shall return to this result later.

To apply Montgomery reduction we shift our calculations modulo n into a complete residue system (cf. Chapter 5)

$$R := R(r, n) := \{ir \bmod n \mid 0 \le i < n\}$$

with a suitable $r := 2^s > 0$ such that $2^{s-1} \le n < 2^s$. Then we define the *Montgomery product* "$\times$" of two numbers a and b in R:

$$a \times b := abr^{-1} \bmod n,$$

with r^{-1} representing the multiplicative inverse of r modulo n. We have

$$a \times b \equiv (ir)(jr)r^{-1} \equiv (ij)r \bmod n \in R,$$

and thus the result of applying $\times$ to members of R is again in R. The Montgomery product is formed by applying Montgomery reduction, where again $n' := -n^{-1} \bmod r$. From n' we derive the representation $1 = \gcd(n, r) = r'r - n'n$, which we calculate in anticipation of Section 10.2 with the help of the extended Euclidean algorithm. From this representation of 1 we immediately obtain

$$1 \equiv r'r \bmod n$$

and

$$1 \equiv -n'n \bmod r,$$

so that $r' = r^{-1} \bmod n$ is the multiplicative inverse of r modulo n, and $n' = -n^{-1} \bmod r$ the negative of the inverse of n modulo r (we are anticipating somewhat; cf. Section 10.2). The calculation of the Montgomery product now takes place according to the following algorithm.

Calculation of the Montgomery product $a \times b$ in $R(r, n)$

1. Set $t \leftarrow ab$.

2. Set $m \leftarrow tn' \bmod r$.

3. Set $u \leftarrow (t + mn)/r$ (the quotient is an integer; see above).

4. If $u \geq n$, output $u - n$, and otherwise u. Based on the above selection of the parameter we have $a, b < n$ as well as $m, n < r$ and finally $u < 2n$; cf. (6.21).

The Montgomery product requires three long-integer multiplications, one in step 1 and two for the reduction in steps 2 and 3. An example with small numbers will clarify the situation: Let $a = 386$, $b = 257$, and $n = 533$. Further, let $r = 2^{10}$. Then $n' = -n^{-1} \bmod r = 707$, $m = 6$, $t + mn = 102400$, and $u = 100$.

A modular multiplication $ab \bmod n$ with odd n can now be carried out by first transforming $a' \leftarrow ar \bmod n$ and $b' \leftarrow br \bmod n$ to R, there forming the Montgomery product $p' \leftarrow a' \times b' = a'b'r^{-1} \bmod n$ and then with $p \leftarrow p' \times 1 = p'r^{-1} = ab \bmod n$ obtaining the desired result. However, we can spare ourselves the reverse transformation effected in the last step by setting $p \leftarrow a' \times b$ at once and thus avoid the transformation of b, so that in the end we have the following algorithm.

Calculation of $p = ab \bmod n$ (n odd) with the Montgomery product

1. Determine $r := 2^s$ with $2^{s-1} \leq n < 2^s$. Calculate $1 = r'r - n'n$ by means of the extended Euclidean algorithm.

2. Set $a' \leftarrow ar \bmod n$.

3. Set $p \leftarrow a' \times b$ and output p.

Again we present an example with small numbers for clarification: Let $a = 123, b = 456, n = 789, r = 2^{10}$. Then $n' = -n^{-1} \bmod r = 963, a' = 501$, and $p = a' \times b = 69 = ab \bmod n$.

Since the precalculation of r' and n' in steps 1 and 2 is very time-consuming and Montgomery reduction in this version also has two long-number multiplications on its balance sheet, there is actually an increased computational expenditure compared with "normal" modular multiplication, so that the computation of *individual* products with Montgomery reduction is not worthwhile.

However, in cases where *many* modular multiplications with a *constant* modulus are required, for which therefore the time-consuming precalculations occur only once, we may expect more favorable results. Particularly suited for the Montgomery product is modular exponentiation, for which we shall suitably modify the M-ary algorithm. To this end let once again $e = (e_{m-1}e_{m-2}\ldots e_0)_B$ and $n = (n_{l-1}n_{l-2}\ldots n_0)_B$ be the representations of the exponent e and the modulus n to the base $B = 2^k$. The following algorithm calculates powers $a^e \bmod n$ in $\mathbb{Z}_n$ with odd n using Montgomery multiplication. The squarings that occur in the exponentiation become Montgomery products $a \times a$, in the computation of which we can use the advantages of squaring.

Exponentiation modulo n (n odd) with the Montgomery product

1. Set $r \leftarrow B^l = 2^{kl}$. Calculate $1 = rr' - nn'$ with the Euclidean algorithm.

2. Set $\bar{a} \leftarrow ar \bmod n$. Calculate and store the powers $\bar{a}^3, \bar{a}^5, \ldots, \bar{a}^{2^k-1}$ using the Montgomery product $\times$ in $R(r, n)$.

3. If $e_{m-1} \neq 0$, factor $e_{m-1} = 2^t u$ with odd u. Set $\bar{p} \leftarrow (\bar{a}^u)^{2^t}$.
   If $e_{m-1} = 0$, set $\bar{p} \leftarrow r \bmod n$.
   In each case set $i \leftarrow m - 2$.

4. If $e_i = 0$, set $\bar{p} \leftarrow \bar{p}^{2^k} = \left(\cdots \left((\bar{p}^2)^2 \right)^2 \cdots \right)^2$ (k-fold squaring $\bar{p}^2 = \bar{p} \times \bar{p}$).
   If $e_i \neq 0$, factor $e_i = 2^t u$ with odd u. Set $\bar{p} \leftarrow \left(\bar{p}^{2^{k-t}} \times \bar{a}^u \right)^{2^t}$.

5. If $i \geq 0$, set $i \leftarrow i - 1$ and go to step 4.

6. Output the Montgomery product $\bar{p} \times 1$.

Further possibilities for improving the algorithm lie less in the exponentiation algorithm than in the implementation of the Montgomery product itself, as demonstrated by S. R. Dussé and B. S. Kaliski in [DuKa]: In calculating the Montgomery product on page 108, in step 2 we can avoid the assignment $m \leftarrow tn' \bmod r$ in the reduction modulo r. Furthermore, we can calculate with $n'_0 := n' \bmod B$ instead of with n' in executing the Montgomery reduction.

We can create a digit $m_i \leftarrow t_i n_0'$ modulo B, multiply it by n, scale by the factor B^i, and add to t. To calculate $ab \bmod n$ with $a, b < n$ the modulus n has the representation $n = (n_{l-1} n_{l-2} \ldots n_0)_B$ as above, and we let $r := B^l$ as well as $rr' - nn' = 1$ and $n_0' := n' \bmod B$.

Calculation of the Montgomery product $a \times b$ à la Dussé and Kaliski

1. Set $t \leftarrow ab$, $n_0' \leftarrow n' \bmod B$, $i \leftarrow 0$.

2. Set $m_i \leftarrow t_i n_0' \bmod B$ (m_i is a one-digit integer).

3. Set $t \leftarrow t + m_i n B^i$.

4. Set $i \leftarrow i + 1$; if $i \leq l - 1$, go to step 2.

5. Set $t \leftarrow t/r$.

6. If $t \geq n$, output $t - n$ and otherwise t.

Dussé and Kaliski state that the basis for their clever simplification is the method of Montgomery reduction to develop t as a multiple of r, but they offer no proof. Before we use this procedure we wish to make more precise why it suffices to calculate $a \times b$. The following is based on a proof of Christoph Burnikel [Zieg]:

In steps 2 and 3 the algorithm calculates a sequence $\left(t^{(i)} \right)_{i=0,\ldots,l}$ by means of the recursion

$$t^{(0)} = ab, \tag{6.16}$$

$$t^{(i+1)} = f\left(\frac{t^{(i)}}{B^i} \right) B^i, \qquad i = 0, \ldots, l - 1, \tag{6.17}$$

where

$$f(t) = t + \left((t \bmod B)\left(-n^{-1} \bmod B \right) \bmod B \right) n$$

is the already familiar function that is induced by the Montgomery equation (cf. (6.13), and there set $r \leftarrow B$ in $f(t)$). The members of the sequence $t^{(i)}$ have the properties

$$t^{(i)} \equiv 0 \bmod B^i, \tag{6.18}$$

$$t^{(i)} \equiv ab \bmod n, \tag{6.19}$$

$$\frac{t^{(l)}}{r} \equiv abr^{-1} \bmod n, \tag{6.20}$$

$$\frac{t^{(l)}}{r} < 2n. \tag{6.21}$$

Properties (6.18) and (6.19) are derived inductively from (6.14), (6.15), (6.16), and (6.17); from (6.18) we obtain $B^l \mid t^{(l)} \Leftrightarrow r \mid t^{(l)}$. From this and from

$t^{(l)} \equiv ab \bmod n$ follows (6.20), and lastly we have (6.21) on account of

$$t^{(l)} = t^{(0)} + n \sum_{i=0}^{l-1} m_i B^i < 2nB^l$$

(note here that $t^{(0)} = ab < n^2 < nB^l$).

The expenditure for the reduction is now determined essentially by multiplication of numbers of order of magnitude the size of the modulus. This variant of Montgomery multiplication can be elegantly implemented in code that forms the core of the multiplication routine mul_l() (cf. page 36).

Function:	Montgomery product
Syntax:	void mulmon_l (CLINT a_l, CLINT b_l, CLINT n_l, USHORT nprime, USHORT logB_r, CLINT p_l);
Input:	a_l, b_l (factors a and b)
	n_l (modulus $n > a, b$)
	nprime ($n' \bmod B$)
	logB_r (logarithm of r to base $B = 2^{16}$; it must hold that $B^{\text{logB}\_\text{r}-1} \le n < B^{\text{logB}\_\text{r}}$)
Output:	p_l (Montgomery product $a \times b = a \cdot b \cdot r^{-1} \bmod n$)

```
void
mulmon_l (CLINT a_l, CLINT b_l, CLINT n_l, USHORT nprime,
          USHORT logB_r, CLINT p_l)
{
 CLINTD t_l;
 clint *tptr_l, *nptr_l, *tiptr_l, *lasttnptr, *lastnptr;
 ULONG carry;
 USHORT mi;
 int i;

 mult (a_l, b_l, t_l);
 lasttnptr = t_l + DIGITS_L (n_l);
 lastnptr = MSDPTR_L (n_l);
```

The earlier use of mult() makes possible the multiplication of a_l and b_l without the possibility of overflow (see page 72); for the Montgomery squaring we simply insert sqr(). The result has sufficient space in t_l. Then t_l is given leading zeros to bring it to double the number of digits of n_l if t_l is smaller than this.

```
for (i = DIGITS_L (t_1) + 1; i <= (DIGITS_L (n_1) << 1); i++)
 {
  t_1[i] = 0;
 }

SETDIGITS_L (t_1, MAX (DIGITS_L (t_1), DIGITS_L (n_1) << 1));
```

> Within the following double loop the partial products $m_i n B^i$ with $m_i := t_i n_0'$ are calculated one after the other and added to t_1. Here again the code is essentially that of our multiplication function.

```
for (tptr_1 = LSDPTR_L (t_1); tptr_1 <= lasttnptr; tptr_1++)
 {
  carry = 0;
  mi = (USHORT)((ULONG)nprime * (ULONG)*tptr_1);

  for (nptr_1 = LSDPTR_L (n_1), tiptr_1 = tptr_1;
    nptr_1 <= lastnptr; nptr_1++, tiptr_1++)
   {
    *tiptr_1 = (USHORT)(carry = (ULONG)mi * (ULONG)*nptr_1 +
      (ULONG)*tiptr_1 + (ULONG)(USHORT)(carry >> BITPERDGT));
   }
```

> In the following inner loop a possible overflow is transported to the most-significant digit of t_1, and t_1 contains an additional digit in case it is needed. This step is essential, since at the start of the main loop t_1 was given a value and not initialized via multiplication by 0 as was the variable p_1.

```
  for ( ;
    ((carry >> BITPERDGT) > 0) && tiptr_1 <= MSDPTR_L (t_1);
    tiptr_1++)
   {
    *tiptr_1 = (USHORT)(carry = (ULONG)*tiptr_1 +
                        (ULONG)(USHORT)(carry >> BITPERDGT));
   }
  if (((carry >> BITPERDGT) > 0))
   {
    *tiptr_1 = (USHORT)(carry >> BITPERDGT);
    INCDIGITS_L (t_1);
   }
 }
```

> Now follows division by B^l, and we shift t_l by logB_r digits to the right, or ignore the logB_r least-significant digits of t_l. Then if applicable the modulus n_l is subtracted from t_l before t_l is returned as result into p_l.

```
tptr_l = t_l + (logB_r);
SETDIGIT_L (tptr_l, DIGITS_L (t_l) - (logB_r));
if (GE_L (tptr_l, n_l))
  {
   sub_l (tptr_l, n_l, p_l);
  }
else
  {
   cpy_l (p_l, tptr_l);
  }
}
```

The *Montgomery squaring* sqrmon_l() differs from this function only marginally: There is no parameter b_l in the function call, and instead of multiplication with mult(a_l, b_l, t_l) we employ the squaring function sqr(a_l, t_l), which likewise ignores a possible overflow. However, in modular squaring in the Montgomery method one must note that after the calculation of $p' \leftarrow a' \times a'$ the reverse transformation $p \leftarrow p' \times 1 = p'r^{-1} = a^2 \bmod n$ must be calculated explicitly (cf. page 108).

Function:	Montgomery square
Syntax:	void sqrmon_l (CLINT a_l, CLINT n_l, USHORT nprime, USHORT logB_r, CLINT p_l);
Input:	a_l (factor a), n_l (modulus $n > a$)
	nprime ($n' \bmod B$)
	logB_r (logarithm of r to base $B = 2^{16}$);
	it must hold that $B^{\text{logB\_r}-1} \leq n < B^{\text{logB\_r}}$
Output:	p_l (Montgomery square $a^2 r^{-1} \bmod n$)

In their article Dussé and Kaliski also present the following variant of the extended Euclidean algorithm, to be dealt with in detail in Section 10.2, for calculating $n'_0 = n' \bmod B$, with which the expenditure for the precalculations can be reduced. The algorithm calculates $-n^{-1} \bmod 2^s$ for an $s > 0$ and for this requires long-number arithmetic.

Algorithm for calculating the inverse $-n^{-1} \bmod 2^s$ **for** $s > 0$, n **odd**

1. Set $x \leftarrow 2$, $y \leftarrow 1$, and $i \leftarrow 2$.

2. If $x < ny \bmod x$, set $y \leftarrow y + x$.

3. Set $x \leftarrow 2x$ and $i \leftarrow i + 1$; if $i \leq s$, go to step 2.

4. Output $x - y$.

With complete induction it can be shown that in step 2 of this algorithm $yn \equiv 1 \bmod x$ always holds, and thus $y \equiv n^{-1} \bmod x$. After x has taken on the value 2^s in step 3, we obtain with $2^s - y \equiv -n^{-1} \bmod 2^s$ the desired result if we choose s such that $2^s = B$. The short function for this can be obtained under the name invmon_l() in the FLINT/C source. It takes only the modulus n as argument and outputs the value $-n^{-1} \bmod B$.

These considerations are borne out in the creation of the functions mexp5m_l() and mexpkm_l(), for which we give here only the interface, together with a computational example.

Function:	modular exponentiation with odd modulus (2^5-ary or 2^k-ary method with Montgomery product)
Syntax:	int mexp5m_l (CLINT bas_l, CLINT exp_l, CLINT p_l, CLINT m_l);
	int mexpkm_l (CLINT bas_l, CLINT exp_l, CLINT p_l, CLINT m_l);
Input:	bas_l (base)
	exp_l (exponent)
	m_l (modulus)
Output:	p_l (power residue)
Return:	E_CLINT_OK if all is ok
	E_CLINT_DBZ if division by 0
	E_CLINT_MAL if malloc() error
	E_CLINT_MOD if even modulus

These functions employ the routines invmon_l(), mulmon_l(), and sqrmon_l() to compute the Montgomery products. Their implementation is based on the functions mexp5_l() and mexpk_l() modified according to the exponentiation algorithm described above.

We would like to reconstruct the processes of Montgomery exponentiation in mexpkm_l() with the same numerical example that we looked at for M-ary exponentiation (cf. page 100). In the following steps we shall calculate the power $1234^{667} \bmod 18577$:

1. **Precomputations**

   The exponent $e = 667$ is represented to the base 2^k with $k = 2$ (cf. the algorithm for Montgomery exponentiation on page 114). The exponent e thereby has the representation

   $$e = (10\ 10\ 01\ 10\ 11)_{2^2}.$$

   The value r for Montgomery reduction is $r = 2^{16} = B = 65536$.
   The value n_0' (cf. page 110) is now calculated as $n_0' = 34703$.
   The transformation of the base a into the residue system $R(r, n)$ (cf. page 107) follows from

   $$\bar{a} = ar \bmod n = 1234 \cdot 65536 \bmod 18577 = 5743.$$

   The power $\bar{a}^3$ in $R(r, n)$ has the value $\bar{a}^3 = 9227$. Because of the small exponent, further powers of $\bar{a}$ do not arise in the precomputation.

2. **Exponentiation loop**

exponent digit $e_i = 2^t u$	$2^1 \cdot 1$	$2^1 \cdot 1$	$2^0 \cdot 1$	$2^1 \cdot 1$	$2^0 \cdot 3$
$\bar{p} \leftarrow \bar{p}^2$	–	16994	3682	14511	11066
$\bar{p} \leftarrow \bar{p}^{2^2}$	–	–	6646	–	12834
$\bar{p} \leftarrow \bar{p} \times \bar{a}^u$	5743	15740	8707	16923	1583
$\bar{p} \leftarrow \bar{p}^2$	9025	11105	–	1628	–

3. **Result**

   The value of the power p after normalization:

   $$p = \bar{p} \times 1 = \bar{p}r^{-1} \bmod n = 1583r^{-1} \bmod n = 4445.$$

Those interested in reconstructing the coding details of the functions mexp5m_1() and mexpkm_1() and the calculational steps of the example related to the function mexpkm_1() are referred to the FLINT/C source code.

At the start of this chapter we developed the function wmexp_1(), which has the advantage for small bases that only multiplications $p \leftarrow pa \bmod m$ of the type CLINT * USHORT mod CLINT occur. In order to profit from the Montgomery procedure in this function, too, we adjust the modular squaring to Montgomery squaring, as in mexpkm_1(), with the use of the fast inverse function invmon_1(), though we leave the multiplication unchanged. We can do this because with the calculational steps for Montgomery squaring and for conventional multiplication modulo n,

$$\left(a^2 r^{-1}\right) b \equiv \left(a^2 b\right) r^{-1} \bmod n,$$

we do not abandon the residue system $R(r,n) = \{\, ir \bmod n \mid 0 \le i < n \,\}$ introduced above. This process yields us both the function wmexpm_l() and the dual function umexpm_l() for USHORT exponents, respectively for odd moduli, which in comparison to the two conventional functions wmexp_l() and umexp_l() again yields a significant speed advantage. For these functions, too, we present here only the interface and a numerical example. The reader is again referred to the FLINT/C source for details.

Function:	modular exponentiation with Montgomery reduction for USHORT-base, respectively USHORT exponents and odd modulus
Syntax:	int wmexpm_l (USHORT bas, CLINT e_l, CLINT p_l, CLINT m_l); int umexpm_l (CLINT bas_l, USHORT e, CLINT p_l, CLINT m_l);
Input:	bas, bas_l (base) e, e_l (exponent) m_l (modulus)
Output:	p_l (residue of bas$^{e\_l}$ mod m_l, resp. bas_l^e mod m_l)
Return:	E_CLINT_OK if all is ok E_CLINT_DBZ if division by 0 E_CLINT_MOD if even modulus

---

The function wmexpm_l() is tailor-made for our primality test in Section 10.5, where we shall profit from our present efforts. The function will be documented with the example used previously of the calculation of $1234^{667} \bmod 18577$.

1. **Precalculations**

   The binary representation of the exponent is $e = (1010011011)_2$.
   The value r for the Montgomery reduction is $r = 2^{16} = B = 65536$.
   The value n_0' (cf. page 110) is calculated as above, yielding $n_0' = 34703$.
   The initial value of $\bar{p}$ is set as $\bar{p} \leftarrow pr \bmod 18577$.

2. **Exponentiation loop**

Exponent bit	1	0	1	0	0	1	1	0	1	1
$\bar{p} \leftarrow \bar{p} \times \bar{p}$ in $R(r,n)$	9805	9025	16994	11105	3682	6646	14511	1628	11066	9350
$\bar{p} \leftarrow \bar{p}a \bmod n$	5743	–	15740	–	–	8707	16923	–	1349	1583

3. **Result**

   The value of the exponent p after normalization:

   $$p = \bar{p} \times 1 = \bar{p}r^{-1} \bmod n = 1583r^{-1} \bmod n = 4445.$$

A detailed analysis of the time behavior of Montgomery reduction with the various optimizations taken into account can be found in [Boss]. There we are promised a ten to twenty percent saving in time over modular exponentiation by using Montgomery multiplication. As can be seen in the overviews in Appendix D of typical calculation times for FLINT/C functions, our implementations bear out this claim fully. To be sure, we have the restriction that the exponentiation functions that use Montgomery reduction can be used only for odd moduli. Nonetheless, for many applications, for example for encryption and decryption, as well as for computing digital signatures according to the RSA procedure (see Chapter 17), the functions mexp5m_l() and mexpkm_l() are the functions of choice.

Altogether, we have at our disposal a number of capable functions for modular exponentiation. To obtain an overview, in Table 6-5 we collect these functions together with their particular properties and domains of application.

Table 6-5. Exponentiation functions in FLINT/C

Function	Domain of Application
mexp5_l()	General 2^5-ary exponentiation, without memory allocation, greater stack requirements.
mexpk_l()	General 2^k-ary exponentiation with optimal k for CLINT numbers, with memory allocation, lower stack requirements.
mexp5m_l()	2^5-ary Montgomery exponentiation for odd moduli, without memory allocation, greater stack requirements.
mexpkm_l()	2^k-ary Montgomery exponentiation for odd moduli, with optimal k for CLINT numbers up to 4096 binary digits, with memory allocation, lower stack requirements.
umexp_l()	Mixed binary exponentiation of a CLINT base with USHORT exponent, lower stack requirements.
umexpm_l()	Mixed binary exponentiation of a CLINT base with USHORT exponent and Montgomery reduction, thus only for odd moduli, lower stack requirements.
wmexp_l()	Mixed binary exponentiation of a USHORT base with CLINT exponent,lower stack requirements.
wmexpm_l()	Mixed binary exponentiation with Montgomery squaring of a USHORT base with CLINT exponent, odd moduli, lower stack requirements.
mexp2_l()	Mixed exponentiation with a power-of-2 exponent, lower stack requirements.

6.5 Cryptographic Application of Exponentiation

We have worked hard in this chapter in our calculation of powers, and it is reasonable to ask at this point what modular exponentiation might have to offer to cryptographic applications. The first example to come to mind is, of course, the RSA procedure, which requires a modular exponentiation for encryption and decryption—assuming suitable keys. However, the author would like to ask his readers for a bit (or perhaps even a byte) of patience, since for the RSA procedure we still must collect a few more items, which we do in the next chapter. We shall return to this extensively in Chapter 17.

For those incapable of waiting, we offer as examples of the application of exponentiation two important algorithms, namely, the procedure suggested in 1976 by Martin E. Hellman and Whitfield Diffie [Diff] for the exchange of cryptographic keys and the encryption procedure of Taher ElGamal as an extension of the Diffie–Hellman procedure.

The Diffie–Hellman procedure represents a cryptographic breakthrough, namely, the first public key, or asymmetric, cryptosystem (see Chapter 17). Two years after its publication, Rivest, Shamir, and Adleman published the RSA procedure (see [Rive]). Variants of the Diffie–Hellman procedure are used today for key distribution in the Internet communications and security protocols IPSec, IPv6, and SSL, which were developed to provide security in the transfer of data packets in the IP protocol layer and the transfer of data at the application level, for example from the realms of electronic commerce. This principle of key distribution thus has a practical significance that would be difficult to overestimate.[3]

With the aid of the Diffie–Hellman protocol two communicators, Ms. A and Mr. B, say, can negotiate in a simple way a secret key that then can be used for the encryption of communications between the two. After A and B have agreed on a large prime number p and a primitive root a modulo p (we shall return to this below), the Diffie–Hellman protocol runs as follows.

Protocol for key exchange à la Diffie–Hellman

1. A chooses an arbitrary value $x_A \leq p - 1$ and sends $y_A := a^{x_A} \bmod p$ as her public key to B.

2. B chooses an arbitrary value $x_B \leq p - 1$ and sends $y_B := a^{x_B} \bmod p$ as his public key to A.

---

[3] IP Security (IPSec), developed by the Internet Engineering Task Force (IETF), is, as an extensive security protocol, a part of the future Internet protocol IPv6. It was created so that it could also be used in the framework of the then current Internet protocol (IPv4). Secure Socket Layer (SSL) is a security protocol developed by Netscape that lies above the TCP protocol, which offers end-to-end security for applications such as HTTP, FTP, and SMTP (for all of this see [Stal], Chapters 13 and 14).

3. A computes the secret key $s_A := y_B^{x_A} \bmod p$.

4. B computes the secret key $s_B := y_A^{x_B} \bmod p$.

Since

$$s_A \equiv y_B^{x_A} \equiv a^{x_B x_A} \equiv y_A^{x_B} \equiv s_B \bmod p,$$

after step 4, A and B are dealing with a common key. The values p and a do not have to be kept secret, nor the values y_A and y_B exchanged in steps 1 and 2. The security of the procedure depends on the difficulty in calculating discrete logarithms in finite fields, and the difficulty of breaking the system is equivalent to that of calculating values x_A or x_B from values y_A or y_B in $\mathbb{Z}_p$.[4] That the calculation of a^{xy} from a^x and a^y in a finite cyclic group (the *Diffie–Hellman problem*) is just as difficult as the calculation of discrete logarithms and thus equivalent to this problem is, in fact, conjectured but has not been proved.

To ensure the security of the procedure under these conditions the modulus p must be chosen sufficiently large (at least 1024 bits, better 2048 or more; see Table 17-1), and one should ensure that $p - 1$ contains a large prime divisor close to $(p - 1)/2$ to exclude particular calculational procedures for discrete logarithms (a constructive procedure for such prime numbers will be presented in Chapter 17 in connection with the generation of *strong* primes, for example for the RSA procedure).

The procedure has the advantage that secret keys can be generated as needed on an ad hoc basis, without the need for secret information to be held for a long time. Furthermore, for the procedure to be used there are no further infrastructure elements necessary for agreeing on the parameters a and b. Nonetheless, this protocol possesses some negative characteristics, the gravest of which is the lack of authentication proofs for the exchanged parameters y_A and y_B. This makes the procedure susceptible to *man-in-the-middle* attacks, whereby attacker X intercepts the messages of A and B with their public keys y_A and y_B and replaces them with falsified messages to A and B containing his own public key y_X.

Then A and B calculate "secret" keys $s_A' := y_X^{x_A} \bmod p$ and $s_B' := y_X^{x_B} \bmod p$, while X on his or her part calculates s_A' from $y_A^{x_X} \equiv a^{x_A x_X} \equiv a^{x_X x_A} \equiv y_X^{x_A} \equiv s_A' \bmod p$ and s_B' analogously. The Diffie–Hellman protocol has now been executed not between A and B, but between X and A as well as between X and B. Now X is in a position to decode messages from A or B and to replace them by falsified messages to A or B. What is fatal is that from a cryptographic point of view the participants A and B are clueless as to what has happened.

To compensate for these defects without giving up the advantages, several variants and extensions have been developed for use in the Internet. They all take into account the necessity that key information be exchanged in such a way that

---

4 For the problem of calculating discrete logarithms see [Schn], Section 11.6, as well as [Odly].

its authenticity can be verified. This can be achieved, for example, by the public keys being digitally signed by the participants and the associated certificate of a certification authority being sent with them (see in this regard page 400, Section 17.3), which is implemented, for example, in the SSL protocol. IPSec and IPv6 use a complexly constructed procedure with the name ISAKMP/Oakley,[5] which overcomes all the drawbacks of the Diffie–Hellman protocol (for details see [Stal], pages 422–423).

To determine a primitive root modulo p, that is, a value a whose powers $a^i \bmod p$ with $i = 0, 1, \ldots, p - 2$ constitute the entire set of elements of the multiplicative group $\mathbb{Z}_p^\times = \{1, \ldots, p - 1\}$ (see in this regard Section 10.2), the following algorithm can be used (see [Knut], Section 3.2.1.2, Theorem C). It is assumed that the prime factorization $p - 1 = P_1^{e_1} \cdots p_k^{e_k}$ of the order of $\mathbb{Z}_p^\times$ is known.

Finding a primitive root modulo p

1. Choose a random integer $a \in [0, p - 1]$ and set $i \leftarrow 1$.

2. Compute $t \leftarrow a^{(p-1)/p_i} \bmod p$.

3. If $t = 1$, go to step 1. Otherwise, set $i \leftarrow i + 1$. If $i \leq k$, go to step 2. If $i > k$, output a and terminate the algorithm.

The algorithm is implemented in the following function.

Function:	ad hoc generation of a primitive root modulo p ($2 < p$ prime)
Syntax:	`int primroot_l (CLINT a_l, unsigned noofprimes,` `                  clint **primes_l);`

Input:	`noofprimes` (number of distinct prime factors in $p - 1$,
	    the order of the group)
	`primes_l` (vector of pointers to `CLINT` objects, beginning with
	    $p - 1$, then follow the prime divisors $p_1, \ldots, p_k$ of the
	    group order $p - 1 = p_1^{e_1} \cdots p_k^{e_k}$, $k = $ `noofprimes`)

Output:	`a_l` (primitive root modulo p_l)
Return:	`E_CLINT_OK` if all is ok -1 if $p - 1$ odd and thus p is not prime

---

[5] ISAKMP: Internet Security Association and Key Management Protocol.

```
int
primroot_l (CLINT a_l, unsigned int noofprimes, clint *primes_l[])
{
 CLINT p_l, t_l, junk_l;
 ULONG i;

 if (ISODD_L (primes_l[0]))
  {
    return -1;
  }
```

primes_l[0] contains $p - 1$, from which we obtain the modulus in p_l.

```
cpy_l (p_l, primes_l[0]);
inc_l (p_l);
SETONE_L (a_l);

do
 {
   inc_l (a_l);
```

As candidates a for the sought-after primitive root only natural numbers greater than or equal to 2 are tested. If a is a square, then a cannot be a primitive root modulo p, since then already $a^{(p-1)/2} \equiv 1 \bmod p$, and the order of a must be less than $\phi(p) = p - 1$. In this case a_l is incremented. We test whether a_l is a square with the function issqr_l() (cf. Section 10.3).

```
 if (issqr_l (a_l, t_l))
  {
    inc_l (a_l);
  }
 i = 1;
```

The calculation of $t \leftarrow a^{(p-1)/p_i} \bmod p$ takes place in two steps. All prime factors p_i are tested in turn; we use Montgomery exponentiation. If a primitive root is found, it is output in a_l.

```
  do
   {
     div_l (primes_l[0], primes_l[i++], t_l, junk_l);
     mexpkm_l (a_l, t_l, t_l, p_l);
   }
```

```
    while ((i <= noofprimes) && !EQONE_L (t_1));
  }
 while (EQONE_L (t_1));

 return E_CLINT_OK;
}
```

As a second example for the application of exponentiation we consider the encryption procedure of ElGamal, which as an extension of the Diffie–Hellman procedure also provides security in the matter of the difficulty of computing discrete logarithms, since breaking the procedure is equivalent to solving the Diffie–Hellman problem (cf. page 119). *Pretty good privacy* (PGP), the workhorse known throughout the world for encrypting and signing e-mail and documents whose development goes back essentially to the work of Phil Zimmermann, uses the ElGamal procedure for key management (see [Stal], Section 12.1).

A participant A selects a public and associated private key as follows.

ElGamal key generation

1. A chooses a large prime number p such that $p - 1$ has a large prime divisor close to $(p - 1)/2$ (cf. page 388) and a primitive root a of the multiplicative group $\mathbb{Z}_p^\times$ as above (cf. page 120).

2. A chooses a random number x with $1 \leq x < p - 1$ and computes $b := a^x \bmod p$ with the aid of Montgomery exponentiation.

3. As public key A uses the triple $\langle p, a, b \rangle_A$, and the associated secret key is $\langle p, a, x \rangle_A$.

Using the public key triple $\langle p, a, b \rangle_A$ a participant B can now encrypt a message $M \in \{1, \ldots, p - 1\}$ and send it to A. The procedure is as follows.

Protocol for encryption à la ElGamal

1. B chooses a random number y with $1 \leq y < p - 1$.

2. B calculates $\alpha := a^y \bmod p$ and $\beta := Mb^y \bmod p = M(a^x)^y \bmod p$.

3. B sends the cryptogram $C := (\alpha, \beta)$ to A.

4. A computes from C the plain text using $M = \beta/\alpha^x$ modulo p.

Since

$$\frac{\beta}{\alpha^x} \equiv \frac{\beta}{(a^x)^y} \equiv M\frac{(a^x)^y}{(a^x)^y} \equiv M \bmod p,$$

the procedure works. The calculation of β/α^x is carried out by means of a multiplication $\beta\alpha^{p-1-x}$ modulo p.

The size of p should be, depending on the application, 1024 bits or longer (see Table 17-1), and for the encryption of different messages M_1 and M_2 unequal random values $y_1 \neq y_2$ should be chosen, since otherwise, from

$$\frac{\beta_1}{\beta_2} = \frac{M_1 b^y}{M_2 b^y} = \frac{M_1}{M_2}$$

it would follow that knowledge of M_1 was equivalent to knowledge of M_2. In view of the practicability of the procedure one should note that the cryptogram C is twice the size of the plain text M, which means that this procedure has a higher transmission cost than others.

The procedure of ElGamal in the form we have presented has an interesting weak point, which is that an attacker can obtain knowledge of the plain text with a small amount of information. We observe that the cyclic group $\mathbb{Z}_p^{\times}$ contains the subgroup $U := \{ a^x \mid x \text{ even} \}$ of order $(p - 1)/2$ (cf. [Fisc], Chapter 1). If now $b = a^x$ or $\alpha = a^y$ lies in U, then this holds, of course, for a^{xy}. If this is the case and the encrypted text β is also in U, then $M = \beta a^{-xy}$ is in U as well. The same holds if a^{xy} and β are both not contained in U. In the other two cases, in which precisely one of a^{xy} and β does not lie in U, then M is also not in U. The following criteria provide information about this situation:

1. $a^{xy} \in U \Leftrightarrow (a^x \in U \text{ or } a^y \in U)$. This, and whether also $\beta \in U$, is tested with

2. For all $u \in \mathbb{Z}_p^{\times}$, $u \in U \Leftrightarrow u^{(p-1)/2} = 1$.

One may ask how bad it might be if an attacker could gain such information about M. From the point of view of cryptography it is a situation difficult to accept, since the message space to be searched is reduced by half with little effort. Whether in practice this is acceptable certainly depends on the application. Surely, it is a valid reason to be generous in choosing the length of a key.

Furthermore, one can take some action against the weakness of the procedure, without, one hopes, introducing new, unknown, weaknesses: The multiplication $M b^y \bmod p$ in step 2 of the algorithm can be replaced with an encryption operation $V \left(H \left(a^{xy} \right), M \right)$ using a suitable symmetric encryption procedure V (such as Triple-DES, IDEA, or Rijndael, which has become the new advanced encryption standard; cf. Chapter 11) and a hash function H (cf. page 398) that so condenses the value a^{xy} that it can be used as a key for V.

So much for our examples of the application of modular exponentiation. In number theory, and therefore in cryptography as well, modular exponentiation is a standard operation, and we shall meet it repeatedly later on, in particular in Chapters 10 and 17. Furthermore, refer to the descriptions and numerous applications in [Schr] as well as in the encyclopedic works [Schn] and [MOV].

CHAPTER 7

Bitwise and
Logical Functions

And sprinkled just a bit
Over each banana split.

> —Tom Lehrer, "In My Home Town"

"Contrariwise," continued Tweedledee, "if it was so, it might be; and if it were so, it would be: but as it isn't, it ain't. That's logic."

> —Lewis Carroll, *Through the Looking-Glass*

IN THIS CHAPTER WE SHALL present functions that carry out bitwise operations on CLINT objects, and we shall also introduce functions for determining the equality and size of CLINT objects, which we have already used quite a bit.

Among the bitwise functions are to be found the shift operations, which shift a CLINT argument in its binary representation by individual bit positions, and certain other functions taking two CLINT arguments that enable the direct manipulation of the binary representation of CLINT objects. How such operations can be applied to arithmetic purposes is most clearly seen in the shift operations described below, but we have also seen, in Section 4.3, how the bitwise AND operation can be used in reduction modulo a power of two.

7.1 Shift Operations

> Necessity devises all manner of shifts.
> —Rabelais

The simplest way to multiply a number a with the representation $a = (a_{n-1}a_{n-2}\ldots a_0)_B$ to the base B by a power B^e is to "shift a to the left by e digits." This works with the binary representation exactly as it does in our familiar decimal system:

$$aB^e = (\hat{a}_{n+e-1}\hat{a}_{n+e-2}\ldots \hat{a}_e\hat{a}_{e-1}\ldots \hat{a}_0)_B \, ,$$

where

$$\hat{a}_{n+e-1} = a_{n-1}, \quad \hat{a}_{n+e-2} = a_{n-2}, \quad \ldots,$$

$$\hat{a}_e = a_0, \qquad \hat{a}_{e-1} = 0, \qquad \ldots, \quad \hat{a}_0 = 0.$$

For $B = 2$ this corresponds to multiplication of a number in binary representation by 2^e, while for $B = 10$ it corresponds to multiplication by a power of ten in the decimal system.

In the analogous procedure for whole-number division by powers of B the digits of a number are "shifted to the right":

$$\left\lfloor \frac{a}{B^e} \right\rfloor = (\hat{a}_{n-1} \ldots \hat{a}_{n-e} \hat{a}_{n-e-1} \hat{a}_{n-e-2} \ldots \hat{a}_0)_B \,,$$

where

$$\hat{a}_{n-1} = \cdots = \hat{a}_{n-e} = 0, \quad \hat{a}_{n-e-1} = a_{n-1}, \quad \hat{a}_{n-e-2} = a_{n-2}, \ldots, \hat{a}_0 = a_e.$$

For $B = 2$ this corresponds to integer division of a number in binary representation by 2^e, and the analogous result holds for other bases.

Since the digits of CLINT objects are represented in memory in binary form, CLINT objects can easily be multiplied by powers of two by shifting left, where the next digit to the right is shifted into each place where a digit has been shifted left, and the binary digits left over on the right are filled with zeros.

In an analogous way CLINT objects can be divided by powers of two by shifting each binary digit to the right into the next lower-valued digit. Digits left free at the end are either filled with zeros or ignored as leading zeros, and at each stage in the process (shifting by one digit) the lowest-valued digit is lost.

The advantage of this process is clear: Multiplication and division of a CLINT object a by a power of two 2^e are simple, and they require at most $e \lceil \log_B a \rceil$ shift operations to shift each USHORT value by one binary digit. Multiplication and division of a by a power B^e uses only $\lceil \log_B a \rceil$ operations for storing USHORT values.

In the following we shall present three functions. The function shl_l() executes a rapid multiplication of a CLINT number by 2, while the function shr_l() divides a CLINT number by 2 and returns the integer quotient.

Lastly, the function shift_l() multiplies or divides a CLINT type a by a power of two 2^e. Which operation is executed is determined by the sign of the exponent e of the power of two that is passed as argument. If the exponent is positive, then the operation is multiplication, while if it negative, then division is carried out. If e has the representation $e = Bk + l, l < B$, then shift_l() carries out the multiplication or division in $(l + 1) \lceil \log_B a \rceil$ operations on USHORT values.

All three functions operate modulo $(N_{\max} + 1)$ on objects of CLINT type. They are implemented as accumulator functions, and thus they change their CLINT operands in that they overwrite the operand with the result of the operation. The functions test for overflow, respectively underflow. However, in shifting, underflow cannot really arise, since in those cases where more positions are to be shifted than there are digits the result is simply zero, almost as it is in real life. The status value E_CLINT_UFL for underflow then merely indicates that there was less to shift than was required, or, in other words, that the power of two by which division was to be carried out was larger than the dividend, and so the quotient is zero. The three functions are implemented in the following manner.

Function:	shift left (multiplication by 2)
Syntax:	int shl_l (CLINT a_l);
Input:	a_l (multiplicand)
Output:	a_l (product)
Return:	E_CLINT_OK if all is ok
	E_CLINT_OFL if overflow

```
int
shl_l (CLINT a_l)
{
 clint *ap_l, *msdptra_l;
 ULONG carry = 0L;
 int error = E_CLINT_OK;

 RMLDZRS_L (a_l);
 if (ld_l (a_l) >= (USHORT)CLINTMAXBIT)
  {
   SETDIGITS_L (a_l, CLINTMAXDIGIT);
   error = E_CLINT_OFL;
  }
 msdptra_l = MSDPTR_L (a_l);
 for (ap_l = LSDPTR_L (a_l); ap_l <= msdptra_l; ap_l++)
  {
   *ap_l = (USHORT)(carry = ((ULONG)*ap_l << 1) | (carry >> BITPERDGT));
  }
 if (carry >> BITPERDGT)
  {
   if (DIGITS_L (a_l) < CLINTMAXDIGIT)
    {
     *ap_l = 1;
     SETDIGITS_L (a_l, DIGITS_L (a_l) + 1);
     error = E_CLINT_OK;
    }
```

```
  else
   {
    error = E_CLINT_OFL;
   }
 }
RMLDZRS_L (a_l);
return error;
}
```

Function:	shift right (integer division by 2)
Syntax:	int shr_l (CLINT a_l);
Input:	a_l (dividend)
Output:	a_l (quotient)
Return:	E_CLINT_OK if all is ok
	E_CLINT_UFL if "underflow"

```
int
shr_l (CLINT a_l)
{
 clint *ap_l;
 USHORT help, carry = 0;

 if (EQZ_L (a_l))
  return E_CLINT_UFL;
 for (ap_l = MSDPTR_L (a_l); ap_l > a_l; ap_l--)
  {
   help = (USHORT)((USHORT)(*ap_l >> 1) | (USHORT)(carry <<
                                    (BITPERDGT - 1)));
   carry = (USHORT)(*ap_l & 1U);
   *ap_l = help;
  }
RMLDZRS_L (a_l);
return E_CLINT_OK;
}
```

```
Function:    left/right shift
             (multiplication and division by powers of two)

Syntax:      int shift_l (CLINT n_l, long int noofbits);

Input:       n_l (operand)
             noofbits (exponent of the power of two)

Output:      n_l (product or quotient, depending on sign of noofbits)

Return:      E_CLINT_OK if all ok
             E_CLINT_UFL if "underflow"
             E_CLINT_OFL if overflow
```

```
int
shift_l (CLINT n_l, long int noofbits)
{
USHORT shorts = (USHORT)((ULONG)(noofbits < 0 ? -noofbits : noofbits) / BITPERDGT);
USHORT bits = (USHORT)((ULONG)(noofbits < 0 ? -noofbits : noofbits) % BITPERDGT);
long int resl;
USHORT i;
int error = E_CLINT_OK;

clint *nptr_l;
clint *msdptrn_l;

RMLDZRS_L (n_l);
resl = (int) ld_l (n_l) + noofbits;
```

If n_l == 0, we need only set the error code correctly, and we are done. The same holds if noofbits == 0.

```
if (*n_l == 0)
 {
  return ((resl < 0) ? E_CLINT_UFL : E_CLINT_OK);
 }
if (noofbits == 0)
 {
  return E_CLINT_OK;
 }
```

Next it is checked whether there is an overflow or underflow to announce. Then a branch is taken depending on the sign of noofbits to shift either to the left or to the right.

```
if ((resl < 0) || (resl > (long) CLINTMAXBIT))
  {
   error = ((resl < 0) ? E_CLINT_UFL : E_CLINT_OFL); /*underflow or overflow*/
  }
msdptrn_l = MSDPTR_L (n_l);
 if (noofbits < 0)
  {
```

If noofbits < 0, then n_l is divided by 2^{noofbits}. The number of digits of n_l to shift is bounded by DIGITS_L (n_l). First the whole digits are shifted, and then the remaining bits with shr_l().

```
   shorts = MIN (DIGITS_L (n_l), shorts);
   msdptrn_l = MSDPTR_L (n_l) - shorts;
   for (nptr_l = LSDPTR_L (n_l); nptr_l <= msdptrn_l; nptr_l++)
    {
     *nptr_l = *(nptr_l + shorts);
    }
   SETDIGITS_L (n_l, DIGITS_L (n_l) - (USHORT)shorts);
   for (i = 0; i < bits; i++)
    {
     shr_l (n_l);
    }
  }
 else
  {
```

If noofbits > 0, then n_l is multiplied by 2^{noofbits}. If the number shorts of digits to be shifted is greater than MAX_B, then the result is zero. Otherwise, first the number of digits of the new value is determined and stored, and then the whole digits are shifted, and the freed-up digits filled with zeros. To avoid an overflow the start position is limited by $\text{n\_l} + \text{MAX}_B$ and stored in nptr_l. As before, the last bits are shifted individually, here with shl_l().

```
  if (shorts < CLINTMAXDIGIT)
   {
    SETDIGITS_L (n_l, MIN (DIGITS_L (n_l) + shorts, CLINTMAXDIGIT));
    nptr_l = n_l + DIGITS_L (n_l);
    msdptrn_l = n_l + shorts;

    while (nptr_l > msdptrn_l)
      {
       *nptr_l = *(nptr_l - shorts);
       --nptr_l;
      }

    while (nptr_l > n_l)
      {
       *nptr_l-- = 0;
      }

    RMLDZRS_L (n_l);

    for (i = 0; i < bits; i++)
      {
       shl_l (n_l);
      }
   }
  else
   {
    SETZERO_L (n_l);
   }
 }
 return error;
}
```

7.2 All or Nothing: Bitwise Relations

The FLINT/C package contains functions that allow the built-in bitwise C operators &, |, and ^ to be used for the type CLINT as well. However, before we program these functions we would like to understand what their implementation will net us.

From a mathematical viewpoint we are looking at relations of the generalized Boolean functions $f : \{0,1\}^k \rightarrow \{0,1\}$ that map a k-tuple $(x_1, \ldots, x_k) \in \{0,1\}^k$ to the value 0 or 1. The effect of a Boolean function is usually presented in the form of a table of values such as that shown in Table 7-1.

Table 7-1. Values of a Boolean function

x_1	x_2	$\cdots$	x_k	$f(x_1, \ldots, x_k)$
0	0	$\ldots$	0	0
1	0	$\ldots$	0	1
0	1	$\ldots$	0	0
$\vdots$	$\vdots$	$\vdots$	$\vdots$	$\vdots$
1	1	$\ldots$	1	1

For the bitwise relations between CLINT types we first regard the variables as bit vectors $(x_1, \ldots, x_n)$, and furthermore, the function values of the Boolean functions will be formed into a sequence. Thus we have functions

$$\overline{f} : \{0, 1\}^n \times \{0, 1\}^n \rightarrow \{0, 1\}^n$$

that map n-bit variables $\overline{x}_1 := \left(x_1^1, x_2^1, \ldots, x_n^1\right)$ and $\overline{x}_2 := \left(x_1^2, x_2^2, \ldots, x_n^2\right)$ by

$$\overline{f}\left(\overline{x}_1, \overline{x}_2\right) := \Big(f_1\left(\overline{x}_1, \overline{x}_2\right), f_2\left(\overline{x}_1, \overline{x}_2\right), \ldots, f_n\left(\overline{x}_1, \overline{x}_2\right)\Big),$$

with $f_i\left(\overline{x}_1, \overline{x}_2\right) := f\left(x_i^1, x_i^2\right)$, again to an n-bit variable $(x_1, \ldots, x_n)$, which is then interpreted as a number of type CLINT.

Decisive for the operation of the function $\overline{f}$ is the definition of the partial functions f_i, each of which is defined in terms of a Boolean function f. For the CLINT functions and_l(), or_l(), and xor_l() the Boolean functions that are implemented are defined as in Tables 7-2 through 7-4.

Table 7-2. Values of the CLINT function and_l()

x_1	x_2	$f(x_1, x_2)$
0	0	0
0	1	0
1	0	0
1	1	1

The implementations of these Boolean functions in the three C functions and_l(), or_l(), and xor_l() do not actually proceed bitwise, but process the digits of CLINT variables by means of the standard C operators &, |, and ^. Each of these functions accepts three arguments of CLINT type, where the first two are the operands and the last the result variable.

Table 7-3. Values of the CLINT *function* or_l()

x_1	x_2	$f(x_1, x_2)$
0	0	0
0	1	1
1	0	1
1	1	1

Table 7-4. Values of the CLINT *function* xor_l()

x_1	x_2	$f(x_1, x_2)$
0	0	0
0	1	1
1	0	1
1	1	0

Function:	operating by bitwise AND
Syntax:	void and_l (CLINT a_l, CLINT b_l, CLINT c_l);
Input:	a_l, b_l (arguments to be operated on)
Output:	c_l (value of the AND operation)

```
void
and_l (CLINT a_l, CLINT b_l, CLINT c_l)
{
CLINT d_l;
clint *r_l, *s_l, *t_l;
clint *lastptr_l;
```

First pointers r_l and s_l are set to the respective digits of the arguments. If the arguments have different numbers of digits, then s_l points to the shorter of the two. The pointer msdptra_l points to the last digit of a_l.

```
if (DIGITS_L (a_l) < DIGITS_L (b_l))
 {
  r_l = LSDPTR_L (b_l);
  s_l = LSDPTR_L (a_l);
  lastptr_l = MSDPTR_L (a_l);
 }
else
 {
  r_l = LSDPTR_L (a_l);
  s_l = LSDPTR_L (b_l);
  lastptr_l = MSDPTR_L (b_l);
 }
```

Now the pointer t_l is set to point to the first digit of the result, and the maximal length of the result is stored in d_l[0].

```
t_l = LSDPTR_L (d_l);
SETDIGITS_L (d_l, DIGITS_L (s_l - 1));
```

The actual operation runs in the following loop over the digits of the shorter argument. The result cannot have a larger number of digits.

```
while (s_l <= lastptr_l)
 {
  *t_l++ = *r_l++ & *s_l++;
 }
```

After the result is copied to c_l, where any leading zeros are expunged, the function is ended.

```
cpy_l (c_l, d_l);
}
```

Function:	operating by bitwise OR
Syntax:	void or_l (CLINT a_l, CLINT b_l, CLINT c_l);
Input:	a_l, b_l (arguments to be operated on)
Output:	c_l (value of the OR operation)

```
void
or_l (CLINT a_l, CLINT b_l, CLINT c_l)
{
 CLINT d_l;
 clint *r_l, *s_l, *t_l;
 clint *msdptrr_l;
 clint *msdptrs_l;
```

> The pointers r_l and s_l are set as above.

```
if (DIGITS_L (a_l) < DIGITS_L (b_l))
  {
   r_l = LSDPTR_L (b_l);
   s_l = LSDPTR_L (a_l);
   msdptrr_l = MSDPTR_L (b_l);
   msdptrs_l = MSDPTR_L (a_l);
  }
else
  {
   r_l = LSDPTR_L (a_l);
   s_l = LSDPTR_L (b_l);
   msdptrr_l = MSDPTR_L (a_l);
   msdptrs_l = MSDPTR_L (b_l);
  }
t_l = LSDPTR_L (d_l);
SETDIGITS_L (d_l, DIGITS_L (r_l - 1));
```

> The actual operation takes place within a loop over the digits of the shorter of the two arguments.

```
while (s_l <= msdptrs_l)
  {
   *t_l++ = *r_l++ | *s_l++;
  }
```

> The remaining digits of the longer argument are taken into the result. After the result is copied to c_l, where any leading zeros are eliminated, the function is terminated.

```
 while (r_l <= msdptrr_l)
  {
   *t_l++ = *r_l++;
  }
 cpy_l (c_l, d_l);
}
```

Function:	operation by bitwise exclusive OR (XOR)
Syntax:	void xor_l (CLINT a_l, CLINT b_l, CLINT c_l);
Input:	a_l, b_l (arguments to be operated on)
Output:	c_l (value of the XOR operation)

```
void
xor_l (CLINT a_l, CLINT b_l, CLINT c_l)
{
 CLINT d_l;
 clint *r_l, *s_l, *t_l;
 clint *msdptrr_l;
 clint *msdptrs_l;
 if (DIGITS_L (a_l) < DIGITS_L (b_l))
  {
   r_l = LSDPTR_L (b_l);
   s_l = LSDPTR_L (a_l);
   msdptrr_l = MSDPTR_L (b_l);
   msdptrs_l = MSDPTR_L (a_l);
  }
 else
  {
   r_l = LSDPTR_L (a_l);
   s_l = LSDPTR_L (b_l);
   msdptrr_l = MSDPTR_L (a_l);
   msdptrs_l = MSDPTR_L (b_l);
  }
 t_l = LSDPTR_L (d_l);
 SETDIGITS_L (d_l, DIGITS_L (r_l - 1));
```

> Now the actual operation takes place. The loop runs over the digits of the shorter of the two arguments.

```
while (s_l <= msdptrs_l)
  {
   *t_l++ = *r_l++ ^ *s_l++;
  }
```

> The remaining digits of the other argument are copied as above.

```
while (r_l <= msdptrr_l)
  {
   *t_l++ = *r_l++;
  }
cpy_l (c_l, d_l);
}
```

The function and_l() can be used to reduce a number a modulo a power of two 2^k by setting a CLINT variable a_l to the value a, a CLINT variable b_l to the value $2^k - 1$, and executing and_l(a_l, b_l, c_l). However, this operation executes faster with the function mod2_l() created for this purpose, which takes into account that the binary representation of $2^k - 1$ consists exclusively of ones (see Section 4.3).

7.3 Direct Access to Individual Binary Digits

Occasionally, it is useful to be able to access individual binary digits of a number in order to read or change them. As an example of this we might mention the initialization of a CLINT object as a power of 2, which can be accomplished easily by setting a single bit.

In the following we shall develop three functions, setbit_l(), testbit_l(), and clearbit_l(), which set an individual bit, test a particular bit, and delete a single bit. The functions setbit_l() and clearbit_l() each return the state of the specified bit before the operation. The bit positions are counted from 0, and thus the specified positions can be understood as logarithms of powers of two: If n_l is equal to 0, then setbit_l(n_l, 0) returns the value 0, and afterwards, n_l has the value $2^0 = 1$; after a call to setbit_l(n_l, 512), n_l has the value 2^{512}.

Function:	test and set a bit in a CLINT object
Syntax:	`int setbit_l (CLINT a_l, unsigned int pos);`
Input:	a_l (CLINT argument)
	pos (bit position counted from 0)
Output:	a_l (result)
Return:	1 if the bit at position pos was already set
	0 if the bit at position pos was not set
	E_CLINT_OFL if overflow

```
int
setbit_l (CLINT a_l, unsigned int pos)
{
 int res = 0;
 unsigned int i;
 USHORT shorts = (USHORT)(pos >> LDBITPERDGT);
 USHORT bitpos = (USHORT)(pos & (BITPERDGT - 1));
 USHORT m = 1U << bitpos;

 if (pos >= CLINTMAXBIT)
  {
   return E_CLINT_OFL;
  }
 if (shorts >= DIGITS_L (a_l))
  {
```

If necessary, a_l is zero filled word by word, and the new length is stored in a_l[0].

```
   for (i = DIGITS_L (a_l) + 1; i <= shorts + 1; i++)
    {
     a_l[i] = 0;
    }
   SETDIGITS_L (a_l, shorts + 1);
  }
```

The digit of a_l that contains the specified bit position is tested by means of the mask prepared in m, and then the bit position is set to 1 via an OR of the relevant digit with m. The function ends by returning the previous status.

```
   if (a_l[shorts + 1] & m)
    {
      res = 1;
    }
  a_l[shorts + 1] |= m;
 return res;
}
```

Function:	test a binary digit of a CLINT object
Syntax:	int testbit_l (CLINT a_l, unsigned int pos);
Input:	a_l (CLINT argument) pos (bit position counted from 0)
Return:	1 if bit at position pos is set 0 otherwise

```
int
testbit_l (CLINT a_l, unsigned int pos)
{
 int res = 0;
 USHORT shorts = (USHORT)(pos >> LDBITPERDGT);
 USHORT bitpos = (USHORT)(pos & (BITPERDGT - 1));
 if (shorts < DIGITS_L (a_l))
  {
   if (a_l[shorts + 1] & (USHORT)(1U << bitpos))
     res = 1;
  }
 return res;
}
```

Function:	test and delete a bit in a CLINT object
Syntax:	int clearbit_l (CLINT a_l, unsigned int pos);
Input:	a_l (CLINT argument) pos (bit position counted from 0)
Output:	a_l (result)
Return:	1 if bit at position pos was set before deletion 0 otherwise

```
int
clearbit_l (CLINT a_l, unsigned int pos)
{
 int res = 0;
 USHORT shorts = (USHORT)(pos >> LDBITPERDGT);
 USHORT bitpos = (USHORT)(pos & (BITPERDGT - 1));
 USHORT m = 1U << bitpos;

 if (shorts < DIGITS_L (a_l))
   {
```

If a_l has enough digits, then the digit of a_l that contains the specified bit position is tested by means of the mask prepared in m, and then the bit position is set to 0 by an AND of the corresponding digit with the complement of m. The previous status of the bit position is returned at the termination of the function.

```
   if (a_l[shorts + 1] & m)
     {
       res = 1;
     }
   a_l[shorts + 1] &= (USHORT)(~m);
   RMLDZRS_L (a_l);
   }
 return res;
}
```

7.4 Comparison Operators

Every program requires the ability to make assertions about the equality or inequality or the size relationship of arithmetic variables, and this holds as well for our dealings with CLINT objects. Here, too, the principle is obeyed that the programmer does not need knowledge of the internal structure of the CLINT type, and the determination of how two CLINT objects are related to each other is left to functions designed for such purposes.

The primary function that accomplishes these tasks is the function cmp_l(). It determines which of the relations a_l < b_l, a_l == b_l, or a_l > b_l holds for two CLINT values a_l and b_l. To this end, first the numbers of digits of the CLINT objects, which have been liberated from any leading zeros, are compared. If the number of digits of the operands is the same, then the process begins with a comparison of the most-significant digits; as soon as a difference is detected, the comparison is terminated.

Function:	comparison of two `CLINT` objects
Syntax:	int cmp_l (CLINT a_l, CLINT b_l);
Input:	a_l, b_l (arguments)
Return:	-1 if (value of a_l) $<$ (value of b_l)
	0 if (value of a_l) $=$ (value of b_l)
	1 if (value of a_l) $>$ (value of b_l)

```
int
cmp_l (CLINT a_l, CLINT b_l)
{
clint *msdptra_l, *msdptrb_l;
int la = DIGITS_L (a_l);
int lb = DIGITS_L (b_l);
```

The first test checks whether both arguments have length, and hence value, 0. Then any leading zeros are eliminated, and a decision is attempted on the basis of the number of digits.

```
if (la == 0 && lb == 0)
  {
   return 0;
  }
while (a_l[la] == 0 && la > 0)
  {
   --la;
  }
while (b_l[lb] == 0 && lb > 0)
  {
   --lb;
  }
if (la == 0 && lb == 0)
  {
   return 0;
  }
if (la > lb)
  {
   return 1;
  }
```

```
if (la < lb)
 {
  return -1;
 }
```

> If the operands have the same number of digits, then the actual values must be compared. For this we begin with a comparison of the most-significant digits and proceed digit by digit until two digits are found that are unequal or until the least-significant digits are reached.

```
msdptra_l = a_l + la;
msdptrb_l = b_l + lb;
while ((*msdptra_l == *msdptrb_l) && (msdptra_l > a_l))
 {
  msdptra_l--;
  msdptrb_l--;
 }
```

> Now we compare the two digits and make our determination, and the corresponding function value is returned.

```
if (msdptra_l == a_l)
 {
  return 0;
 }
if (*msdptra_l > *msdptrb_l)
 {
  return 1;
 }
else
 {
  return -1;
 }
}
```

If we are interested in the equality of two CLINT values, then the application of the function cmp_l() is a bit more than is necessary. In this case there is a simpler variant, which avoids the size comparison.

Function:	comparison of two CLINT objects
Syntax:	int equ_l (CLINT a_l, CLINT b_l);
Input:	a_l, b_l (arguments)
Return:	0 if (value of a_l) $\neq$ (value of b_l)
	1 if (value of a_l) $=$ (value of b_l)

```
int
equ_l (CLINT a_l, CLINT b_l)
{
 clint *msdptra_l, *msdptrb_l;
 int la = DIGITS_L (a_l);
 int lb = DIGITS_L (b_l);
 if (la == 0 && lb == 0)
  {
   return 1;
  }
 while (a_l[la] == 0 && la > 0)
  {
   --la;
  }
 while (b_l[lb] == 0 && lb > 0)
  {
   --lb;
  }
 if (la == 0 && lb == 0)
  {
   return 1;
  }
 if (la != lb)
  {
   return 0;
  }
 msdptra_l = a_l + la;
 msdptrb_l = b_l + lb;
```

```
while ((*msdptra_l == *msdptrb_l) && (msdptra_l > a_l))
 {
  msdptra_l--;
  msdptrb_l--;
 }
return (msdptra_l > a_l ? 0 : 1);
}
```

These two functions in their raw form can easily lead the user into the thickets of error. In particular, the meaning of the function values of cmp_l() must be kept constantly in mind or looked up repeatedly. As a measure against errors a number of macros have been created by means of which comparisons can be formulated in a more mnemonically satisfactory way (see in this regard Appendix C, "Macros with Parameters"). For example, we have the following macros, where we equate the objects a_l and b_l with the values they represent:

GE_L (a_l, b_l)   returns 1 if $a\_l \geq b\_l$, and 0 otherwise;

EQZ_L (a_l)   returns 1 if a_l == 0, and 0 if $a\_l > 0$.

CHAPTER 8

Input, Output, Assignment, Conversion

> The numerals were now being converted automatically from base 2 to base
> 10 ... 881, 883, 887, 907 ... each one confirmed as a prime number.
>
> —Carl Sagan, *Contact*

WE BEGIN THIS CHAPTER WITH assignment, the simplest and also the most important function. To be able to assign to a CLINT object a_l the value of another CLINT object b_l, we require a function that copies the digits of b_l to the reserved storage space for a_l, an event that we shall call *elementwise assignment*. It will not suffice merely to copy the address of the object b_l into the variable a_l, since then both objects would refer to the same location in memory, namely that of b_l, and any change in a_l would be reflected in a change in the object b_l, and conversely. Furthermore, access to the area of memory addressed by a_l could become lost.

We shall return to the problems of elementwise assignment in the second part of this book when we concern ourselves with the implementation of the assignment operator "=" in C++ (see Section 14.3).

The assignment of the value of a CLINT object to another CLINT is effected with the function cpy_l().

Function:	copy a CLINT object as an assignment
Syntax:	void cpy_l (CLINT dest_l, CLINT src_l);
Input:	src_l (assigned value)
Output:	dest_l (destination object)

```
void
cpy_l (CLINT dest_l, CLINT src_l)
{
 clint *lastsrc_l = MSDPTR_L (src_l);
 *dest_l = *src_l;
```

> In the next step leading zeros are found and then ignored. At the same time, the number of digits of the target object is adjusted.

```
while ((*lastsrc_l == 0) && (*dest_l > 0))
  {
   --lastsrc_l;
   --*dest_l;
  }
```

> Now the relevant digits of the source object are copied into the goal object. Then the function is terminated.

```
while (src_l < lastsrc_l)
  {
   *++dest_l = *++src_l;
  }
}
```

The exchange of the values of two CLINT objects can be accomplished with the help of the macro SWAP_L, the FLINT/C variant of the macro SWAP, which manages in an interesting way to accomplish the exchange of two variables using XOR operations without the requirement of intermediate storage in a temporary variable:

```
#define SWAP(a, b) ((a)^=(b), (b)^=(a), (a)^=(b))
#define SWAP_L(a_l, b_l) \
  (xor_l((a_l), (b_l), (a_l)), \
   xor_l((b_l), (a_l), (b_l)), \
   xor_l((a_l), (b_l), (a_l)))
```

Function:	swap the values of two `CLINT` objects
Syntax:	`void fswap_l (CLINT a_l, CLINT b_l);`
Input:	a_l, b_l (values to be exchanged)
Output:	a_l, b_l

The functions in the FLINT/C library for the input and output of numbers in a form readable by human beings are not among the most exciting functions in this library, yet for many applications they are unavoidable. For practical reasons a form was selected to allow for the input and output by means of character strings, as vectors of type char. For this the two essentially complementary functions str2clint_l() and xclint2str_l() were developed: The first transforms a character string with digits into a CLINT object, and the second, conversely, transforms a CLINT object into a character string. The base of the character string's representation is specified, with representations to bases in the range from 2 to 16 allowed.

The conversion to be carried out by the function str2clint_l() of a representation of type CLINT into a representation in the base specified is accomplished by means of a sequence of multiplications and additions to base B (cf. [Knut], Section 4.4). The function registers any overflow that occurs, the use of invalid bases, and the passing of the null pointer and returns the corresponding error code. Any prefixes indicating the number's representation, "0X," "0x," "0B," or "0b," are ignored.

Function:	conversion of a character string into a `CLINT` object
Syntax:	`int str2clint_l (CLINT n_l, char *str, USHORT b);`
Input:	str (pointer to a sequence of char) base (base of the numerical representation of the character string, $2 \leq$ base ≤ 16)
Output:	n_l (target CLINT object)
Return:	E_CLINT_OK if all is ok E_CLINT_BOR if base < 2 or base > 16, or if the number of digits in str is larger than base E_CLINT_OFL if overflow E_CLINT_NPT if in str the null pointer was passed

```
int
str2clint_l (CLINT n_l, char *str, USHORT base)
{
 USHORT n;
 int error = E_CLINT_OK;
 if (str == NULL)
  {
   return E_CLINT_NPT;
  }
 if (2 > base || base > 16)
  {
   return E_CLINT_BOR;     /* error: invalid base */
  }
 SETZERO_L (n_l);
 if (*str == '0')
  {
   if ((tolower_l(*(str+1)) == 'x') ||
     (tolower_l(*(str+1)) == 'b'))     /* ignore any prefix */
    {
     ++str;
     ++str;
    }
  }
 while (isxdigit ((int)*str) || isspace ((int)*str))
  {
   if (!isspace ((int)*str))
    {
     n = (USHORT)tolower_l (*str);
```

> Many implementations of tolower() from non-ANSI-conforming C libraries return undefined results if a character is not uppercase. The FLINT/C function tolower_l() calls tolower() only for uppercase A–Z and otherwise returns the character unchanged.

```
  switch (n)
   {
    case 'a':
    case 'b':
    case 'c':
    case 'd':
    case 'e':
    case 'f':
     n -= (USHORT)('a' -- 10);
     break;
    default:
     n -= (USHORT)'0';
   }
  if (n >= base)
   {
    error = E_CLINT_BOR;
    break;
   }
  if ((error = umul_l (n_l, base, n_l)) != E_CLINT_OK)
   {
    break;
   }
  if ((error = uadd_l (n_l, n, n_l)) != E_CLINT_OK)
   {
    break;
   }
  }
 ++str;
 }

return error;
}
```

The function xclint2str_l(), complementary to str2clint_l(), returns a pointer to an internal buffer of storage class static (cf. [Harb], Section 4.3), which contains the calculated numerical representation and its value until xclint2str_l() is called again or the program is ended.

The function xclint2str_1() carries the required conversion of the CLINT representation into the representation to the specified base by means of a sequence of divisions with remainder to the base B.

Function:	Conversion of a CLINT object into a character string
Syntax:	char * xclint2str_1 (CLINT n_1, USHORT base, int showbase);
Input:	n_1 (CLINT object to be converted)
	base (base of the numerical representation of the character string to be specified);
	showbase (value $\neq 0$: The numerical representation has a "0x" in the case base $= 16$ or "0b" if base $= 2$. Value $= 0$: there is no prefix.)
Return:	pointer to the calculated character string if all ok
	NULL if base < 2 or base > 16

```
static char ntable[16] =
{'0','1','2','3','4','5','6','7','8','9','a','b','c','d','e','f'};

char *
xclint2str_1 (CLINT n_1, USHORT base, int showbase)
{
 CLINTD u_1, r_1;
 int i = 0;
 static char N[CLINTMAXBIT + 3];

 if (2U > base || base > 16U)
  {
   return (char *)NULL;     /* error: invalid base */
  }
 cpy_1 (u_1, n_1);
 do
  {
   (void) udiv_1 (u_1, base, u_1, r_1);
   if (EQZ_L (r_1))
    {
      N[i++] = '0';
    }
   else
```

```
    {
      N[i++] = (char) ntable[*LSDPTR_L (r_l) & 0xff];
    }
  }
while (GTZ_L (u_l));

if (showbase)
  {
    switch (base)
      {
        case 2:
          N[i++] = 'b';
          N[i++] = '0';
          break;
        case 8:
          N[i++] = '0';
          break;
        case 16:
          N[i++] = 'x';
          N[i++] = '0';
          break;
      }
  }

N[i] = '0';

return strrev_l (N);
}
```

For reasons of compatibility with the function clint2str_l() in the first edition of this book, clint2str_l(n_l, base) was defined as a macro that calls the function xclint2str(n_l, base, 0).

Furthermore, macros HEXSTR_L(), DECSTR_L(), OCTSTR_L(), and BINSTR_L() were created, which create, from a passed CLINT object as argument, a character string without prefix with the numerical representation specified by the macro name and thus eliminate the base of the representation as an argument (see Appendix C).

As standard form for the output of CLINT values we have available the macro DISP_L(), which processes a pointer to a character string and a CLINT object as arguments. The character string contains, according to the purpose to which it will be put, information about the following CLINT value to be output, such as "The product of a_l and b_l has the value ... ." The output of the CLINT value is in hexadecimal, that is, to base 16. Additionally, DISP_L() outputs in a new line the number of significant binary digits (that is, without leading zeros) of the indicated CLINT object (cf. Appendix C).

If there are to be conversions between byte vectors and CLINT objects, then the pair of functions byte2clint_l() and clint2byte_l() can be employed (cf. [IEEE], 5.5.1).

It is assumed that the byte vectors embody a numerical representation to base 256 with values increasing from right to left. For the implementation of these functions the reader is referred to the file flint.c. We give here only the function headers.

Function:	conversion of a byte vector into a CLINT object
Syntax:	int byte2clint_l (CLINT n_l, UCHAR *bytestr, int len);
Input:	bytestr (pointer to a sequence of UCHAR)
	len (length of the byte vector)
Output:	n_l (target CLINT object)
Return:	E_CLINT_OK if all ok
	E_CLINT_OFL if overflow
	E_CLINT_NPT if in bytestr the null pointer was passed

Function:	conversion of a CLINT object into a byte vector
Syntax:	UCHAR * clint2byte_l (CLINT n_l, int *len);
Input:	n_l (CLINT object to be converted)
Output:	len (length of the generated byte vector)
Return:	pointer to the calculated byte vector
	NULL, if in len the null pointer was passed

Finally, for the transformation of unsigned values into the CLINT numerical format the two functions u2clint_l() and ul2clint_l() can be used. The function u2clint_l() converts USHORT arguments, and the function ul2clint_l() converts ULONG arguments, into the CLINT numerical format. The function ul2clint_l() will be described in the following as an example.

Function:	conversion of a value of type ULONG into a CLINT object
Syntax:	void ul2clint_l (CLINT num_l, ULONG ul);
Input:	ul (value to be converted)
Output:	num_l (target CLINT object)

```
void
ul2clint_l (CLINT num_l, ULONG ul)
{
 *LSDPTR_L (num_l) = (USHORT)(ul & 0xffff);
 *(LSDPTR_L (num_l) + 1) = (USHORT)((ul >> 16) & 0xffff);
 SETDIGITS_L (num_l, 2);
 RMLDZRS_L (num_l);
}
```

To end this chapter we shall discuss a function that carries out a validity check of a memory object for the CLINT number format. Control functions of this type are called as needed whenever "foreign" values are imported into a system for further processing into a subsystem. Such a subsystem can be, for example, a cryptographic module that before every processing of input data must check whether it is dealing with valid values or arguments. Checking at run time whether the assumptions about the input values of a function have been met is good programming practice, one that helps to avoid undefined situations and that can contribute decisively to the stability of an application. For testing and debugging this usually takes place with *assertions*, with the help of which run-time conditions can be tested. Assertions are inserted as macros and can be decommissioned for the actual running of the program, usually during compilation via #define NDEBUG. In addition to the assert macro of the C standard library (see [Pla1], Chapter 1) there are a number of further implementations of similar mechanisms that take various actions when the test conditions are violated, such as listing recognized exceptional conditions in a log file, with or without program termination in the event of an error. For extensive information in this area the reader is referred to [Magu], Chapters 2 and 3, as well as [Murp], Chapter 4.

The protection of the functions of a program library like the FLINT/C package against being passed values that lie outside of the domain of definition of the respective parameters can occur within the invoked functions themselves or within the calling functions, where in the latter case the responsibility lies with the programmer who employs the library. For performance considerations, in the development of the FLINT/C functions we did not test every passed CLINT argument for a valid address and possible overflow. The thought of carrying out multiply redundant checks of the numerical format in thousands of modular multiplications of an exponentiation moved the author to offload this control task to the programs that use the FLINT/C functions. An exception is the passing of divisors with the value zero, which is checked as a matter of principle and if it occurs is acknowledged with a suitable error notification, even in all the functions for residue class arithmetic. The code of all the functions was particularly carefully tested to make sure that the FLINT/C library generates only valid formats (cf. Chapter 12).

The function vcheck_l() was created for the analysis of CLINT arguments with regard to the validity of their format. It should help to protect the FLINT/C functions from being passed invalid parameters as CLINT values.

Function:	test for a valid CLINT numerical format
Syntax:	int vcheck_l (CLINT n_l);
Input:	n_l (object to be tested)
Return:	E_VCHECK_OK if format ok
	errors and warnings according to Table 8-1

Table 8-1. Diagnostic values of the function vcheck_l()

Return Value	Diagnosis	Explanation
E_VCHECK_OK	Format is ok	Info: The number has a valid representation and a value with the range of definition of a CLINT type.
E_VCHECK_LDZ	leading zeros	Warning: The number has leading zeros, but otherwise a valid definition within the range of definition.
E_VCHECK_MEM	memory error	Error: NULL Pointer was passed.
E_VCHECK_OFL	genuine overflow	Error: The passed number is too large; it cannot be represented as a CLINT object.

```
int
vcheck_l (CLINT n_l)
{
 unsigned int error = E_VCHECK_OK;
```

> Check for the null pointer: the ugliest error of them all.

```
if (n_l == NULL)
 {
  error = E_VCHECK_MEM;
 }
else
 {
```

> Check for overflow: Does the number have too many digits?

```
  if (((unsigned int) DIGITS_L (n_l)) > CLINTMAXDIGIT)
   {
    error = E_VCHECK_OFL;
   }
  else
   {
```

> Check for leading zeros: These we can live with ;-)

```
    if ((DIGITS_L (n_l) > 0) && (n_l[DIGITS_L (n_l)] == 0))
     {
      error = E_VCHECK_LDZ;
     }
   }
 }
 return error;
}
```

The return values of the function are defined as macros in the file flint.h. An explanation of these values is provided in Table 8-1.

The numeric values of the error codes are smaller than zero, so that a simple comparison with zero suffices to distinguish between errors on the one hand and warnings or the valid case on the other.

CHAPTER 9
Dynamic Registers

"What a depressingly stupid machine," said Marvin and trudged away.
—Douglas Adams, *The Restaurant at the End of the Universe*

IN ADDITION TO THE AUTOMATIC, or in exceptional cases global, CLINT objects used up to now, it is sometimes practical to be able to create and purge CLINT variables automatically. To this end we shall create several functions that will enable us to generate, use, clear, and remove a set of CLINT objects, the so-called register bank, as a dynamically allocated data structure, where we take up the sketch presented in [Skal] and work out the details for its use with CLINT objects.

We shall divide the functions into private management functions and public functions; the latter of these will be made available to other external functions for manipulating the registers. However, the FLINT/C functions do not use the registers themselves, so that complete control over the use of the registers can be guaranteed to the user's functions.

The number of registers available should be configurable while the program is running, for which we need a static variable NoofRegs that takes the number of registers, which is predefined in the constant NOOFREGS.

```
static USHORT NoofRegs = NOOFREGS;
```

Now we define the central data structure for managing the register bank:

```
struct clint_registers
{
  int noofregs;
  int created;
  clint **reg_l;     /* pointer to vector of CLINT addresses */
};
```

The structure clint_registers contains the variable noofregs, which specifies the number of registers contained in our register bank, and the variable created, which will indicate whether the set of registers is allocated, as well as the pointer reg_l to a vector that takes the start address of the individual registers:

```
static struct clint_registers registers = {0, 0, 0};
```

Now come the private management functions allocate_reg_l() to set up the register bank and destroy_reg_l() to clear it. After space for the storage of the addresses of the registers to be allocated has been created and a pointer is then set to the variable registers.reg_l, there follows the allocation of memory for each individual register by a call to malloc() from the C standard library. The fact that CLINT registers are memory units allocated by means of malloc() plays an important role in testing the FLINT/C functions. We shall see in Section 13.2 how this makes possible the examination of any memory errors that may occur.

```
static int
allocate_reg_l (void)
{
  USHORT i, j;
```

> First, memory is allocated for the vector of register addresses.

```
  if ((registers.reg_l = (clint **) malloc (sizeof(clint *) * NoofRegs)) == NULL)
    {
      return E_CLINT_MAL;
    }
```

> Now comes the allocation of individual registers. If in the process a call to malloc()
> ends in an error, all previously allocated registers are cleared and the error code
> E_CLINT_MAL is returned.

```
  for (i = 0; i < NoofRegs; i++)
    {
      if ((registers.reg_l[i] = (clint *) malloc (CLINTMAXBYTE)) == NULL)
        {
          for (j = 0; j < i; j++)
            {
              free (registers.reg_l[j]);
            }
          return E_CLINT_MAL;       /* error: malloc */
        }
    }
  return E_CLINT_OK;
}
```

The function destroy_reg_l() is essentially the inverse of the function create_reg_l(): First, the content of the registers is cleared by overwriting them with zeros. Then each individual register is returned by means of free(). Finally, memory pointed to by registers.reg_l is released.

```
static void
destroy_reg_l (void)
{
  unsigned i;
  for (i = 0; i < registers.noofregs; i++)
    {
      memset (registers.reg_l[i], 0, CLINTMAXBYTE);
      free (registers.reg_l[i]);
    }
  free (registers.reg_l);
}
```

Now come the public functions for register management. With the function create_reg_l() we create a set of registers consisting of the number of individual registers determined in NoofRegs. This takes place via a call to the private function allocate_reg_l().

Function:	Allocation of a set of registers of type CLINT
Syntax:	int create_reg_l (void);
Return:	E_CLINT_OK if allocation is ok E_CLINT_MAL if error with malloc()

```
int
create_reg_l (void)
{
  int error = E_CLINT_OK;
  if (registers.created == 0)
    {
      error = allocate_reg_l ();
      registers.noofregs = NoofRegs;
    }
  if (!error)
    {
      ++registers.created;
    }
  return error;
}
```

The structure registers involves the variable registers.created, which is used for counting the number of requested registers to be created. A call to the function free_reg_1() described below results in the set of registers being released only if registers.created has the value 1. Otherwise, registers.created is simply reduced by 1. With the use of this mechanism, called a *semaphore*, we manage to prevent a set of registers allocated by one function being inadvertently released by another function. On the other hand, every function that requests the set of registers by calling create_reg_1() is responsible for releasing it again with free_reg_1(). Moreover, in general, one cannot assume that the registers contain specific values after a function has been called.

The variable NoofRegs, which determines the number of registers created by create_reg_1(), can be changed by the function set_noofregs_1(). This change, however, remains in effect only until the currently allocated set of registers is released and a new set is created with create_reg_1().

Function:	set number of registers
Syntax:	void set_noofregs_l (unsigned int nregs);
Input:	nregs (number of registers in the register bank)

```
void
set_noofregs_l (unsigned int nregs)
{
  NoofRegs = (USHORT)nregs;
}
```

Now that a set of registers can be allocated, one may ask how individual registers can be accessed. For this it is necessary to select the address field reg_l, dynamically allocated by create_reg_1(), of the above-defined structure clint_reg. This will be accomplished with the help of the function get_reg_1(), introduced below, which returns a pointer to an individual register of the set of registers, provided that the specified ordinal number denotes an allocated register.

Function:	output a pointer to a register
Syntax:	clint * get_reg_l (unsigned int reg);
Input:	reg (register number)
Return:	pointer to the desired register reg, if it is allocated NULL if the register is unallocated

```
clint *
get_reg_l (unsigned int reg)
{
  if (!registers.created || (reg >= registers.noofregs))
    {
      return (clint *) NULL;
    }
  return registers.reg_l[reg];
}
```

Since the set of registers can be changed dynamically with respect to its size and location in memory, it is not recommended that addresses of registers once read be stored for further use. It is much to be preferred that one obtain the register addresses afresh for each use. In the file flint.h are to be found several predefined macros of the form

```
#define r0_l get_reg_l(0);
```

with the help of which the registers can be invoked, without additional syntactic effort, by their actual current addresses. With the function purge_reg_l(), introduced below, an individual register of the set can be cleared by overwriting it.

Function:	Clear a CLINT register of the register bank by completely overwriting it with zeros
Syntax:	int purge_reg_l (unsigned int reg);
Input:	reg (register number)
Return:	E_CLINT_OK if deletion is ok E_CLINT_NOR if register is unallocated

```
int
purge_reg_l (unsigned int reg)
{
  if (!registers.created || (reg >= registers.noofregs))
    {
      return E_CLINT_NOR;
    }
  memset (registers.reg_l[reg], 0, CLINTMAXBYTE);
  return E_CLINT_OK;
}
```

Just as an individual register can be cleared with the function purge_reg_l(), with the function purgeall_reg_l() the complete set of registers can be cleared by overwriting.

Function:	clear all CLINT registers by overwriting with zeros
Syntax:	int purgeall_reg_l (void);
Return:	E_CLINT_OK if deletion is ok
	E_CLINT_NOR if registers are not allocated

```
int
purgeall_reg_l (void)
{
  unsigned i;
  if (registers.created)
    {
      for (i = 0; i < registers.noofregs; i++)
        {
          memset (registers.reg_l[i], 0, CLINTMAXBYTE);
        }
      return E_CLINT_OK;
    }
  return E_CLINT_NOR;
}
```

It is good programming style and etiquette to release allocated memory when it is no longer needed. An existing set of registers can be released with the function free_reg_l(). However, as we have explained above, the semaphore

registers.created in the structure registers must have been set to 1 before the
allocated memory is actually released:

```
void
free_reg_l (void)
{
  if (registers.created == 1)
    {
      destroy_reg_l ();
    }
  if (registers.created)
    {
      --registers.created;
    }
}
```

We now present three functions that create, clear, and again free individual
CLINT registers, in analogy to the management of the complete set of registers.

Function:	allocation of a register of type CLINT
Syntax:	clint * create_l (void);
Return:	pointer to allocated registers, if allocation ok NULL if error with malloc()

```
clint *
create_l (void)
{
  return (clint *) malloc (CLINTMAXBYTE);
}
```

It is important to treat the pointer returned by create_l() in such a way that
it does not "become lost," since otherwise, it is impossible to access the created
registers. The sequence

```
clint * do_not_overwrite_l;
clint * lost_l;
/* ... */
do_not_overwrite _l = create_l();
/* ... */
do_not_overwrite _l = lost_l;
```

allocates a register and stores its address in a variable with the suggestive name do_not_overwrite_l. If this variable contains the only reference to the register, then after the last instruction,

```
do_not_overwrite _l = lost_l;
```

the register is lost, which is a typical error in the jungle of pointer management.

A register can, like any other CLINT variable, be cleared with the function purge_l() that follows, whereby the memory reserved for the specified register is overwritten with zeros and thereby cleared.

Function:	clear a CLINT object by completely overwriting with zeros
Syntax:	void purge_l (CLINT n_l);
Input:	n_l (CLINT object)

```
void
purge_l (CLINT n_l)
{
  if (NULL != n_l)
    {
      memset (n_l, 0, CLINTMAXBYTE);
    }
}
```

The following function additionally releases the memory allocated for the specified register after it has been cleared. Afterwards, the register can no longer be accessed.

Function:	clear and release a CLINT register
Syntax:	void free_l (CLINT reg_l);
Input:	reg_l (pointer to a CLINT register)

```
void
free_l (CLINT reg_l)
{
  if (NULL != reg_l)
    {
      memset (reg_l, 0, CLINTMAXBYTE);
      free (n_l);
    }
}
```

Basic Number-Theoretic Functions

I am dying to hear about it, since I always thought
number theory was the Queen of Mathematics—the
purest branch of mathematics—the one branch of
mathematics which has NO applications!

— D. R. Hofstadter, *Gödel, Escher, Bach*

NOW THAT WE ARE FITTED out with a sturdy tool box of arithmetic functions that we developed in the previous chapters, we turn our attention to the implementation of several fundamental algorithms from the realm of number theory. The number-theoretic functions discussed in the following chapters form a collection that on the one hand exemplifies the application of the arithmetic of large numbers and on the other forms a useful foundation for more complex number-theoretic calculations and cryptographic applications. The resources provided here can be extended in a number of directions, so that for almost every type of application the necessary tools can be assembled with the demonstrated methods.

The algorithms on which the following implementations are based are drawn primarily from the publications [Cohe], [HKW], [Knut], [Kran], and [Rose], where as previously, we have placed particular value on efficiency and on as broad a range of application as possible.

The following sections contain the minimum of mathematical theory required to explicate the functions that we present and their possibilities for application. We would like, after all, to have some benefit from all the effort that will be required in dealing with this material. Those readers who are interested in a more thoroughgoing introduction to number theory are referred to the books [Bund] and [Rose]. In [Cohe] in particular the algorithmic aspects of number theory are considered and are treated clearly and concisely. An informative overview of applications of number theory is offered by [Schr], while cryptographic aspects of number theory are treated in [Kobl].

In this chapter we shall be concerned with, among other things, the calculation of the greatest common divisor and the least common multiple of large numbers, the multiplicative properties of residue class rings, the identification of quadratic residues and the calculation of square roots in residue class rings, the Chinese remainder theorem for solving systems of linear congruences, and the identification of prime numbers. We shall supplement the theoretical foundations of these topics with practical tips and explanations, and we shall develop several functions that embody a realization of the algorithms that we describe and make them usable in many practical applications.

10.1 Greatest Common Divisor

> That schoolchildren are taught to use the method of prime factorization rather than the more natural method of the Euclidean algorithm to compute the greatest common divisor of two integers is a disgrace to our system of education.
>
> —W. Heise, P. Quattrocci, *Information and Coding Theory*

Stated in words, the greatest common divisor (gcd) of integers a and b is the positive divisor of a and b that is divisible by all common divisors of a and b. The greatest common divisor is thereby uniquely determined. In mathematical notation the greatest common divisor d of two integers a and b, not both zero, is defined as follows: $d = \gcd(a, b)$ if $d > 0$, $d \mid a$, $d \mid b$, and if for some integer d' we have $d' \mid a$ and $d' \mid b$, then we also have $d' \mid d$.

It is convenient to extend the definition to include

$$\gcd(0, 0) := 0.$$

The greatest common divisor is thus defined for all pairs of integers, and in particular for the range of integers that can be represented by CLINT objects. The following rules hold:

$$
\begin{aligned}
&\text{(i)} && \gcd(a, b) = \gcd(b, a), \\
&\text{(ii)} && \gcd(a, 0) = |a| \ \text{(the absolute value of } a\text{)}, \\
&\text{(iii)} && \gcd(a, b, c) = \gcd(a, \gcd(b, c)), \\
&\text{(iv)} && \gcd(a, b) = \gcd(-a, b),
\end{aligned}
\tag{10.1}
$$

of which, however, only (i)–(iii) are relevant for CLINT objects.

It is obligatory first to consider the classical procedure for calculating the greatest common divisor according to the Greek mathematician Euclid (third century B.C.E.), which Knuth respectfully calls the grandfather of all algorithms (definitely see [Knut], pages 316 ff.). The Euclidean algorithm consists in a sequence of divisions with remainder, beginning with the reduction of $a \bmod b$, then $b \bmod (a \bmod b)$, and so on until the remainder vanishes.

Euclidean algorithm for calculating $\gcd(a, b)$ **for** $a, b \geq 0$

1. If $b = 0$, output a and terminate the algorithm.

2. Set $r \leftarrow a \bmod b$, $a \leftarrow b$, $b \leftarrow r$, and go to step 1.

For natural numbers a_1, a_2 the calculation of the greatest common divisor according to the Euclidean algorithm goes as follows:

$$
\begin{aligned}
a_1 &= a_2 q_1 + a_3, \quad 0 \leq a_3 < a_2, \\
a_2 &= a_3 q_2 + a_4, \quad 0 \leq a_4 < a_3, \\
a_3 &= a_4 q_3 + a_5, \quad 0 \leq a_5 < a_4, \\
&\vdots \\
a_{m-2} &= a_{m-1} q_{m-2} + a_m, \quad 0 \leq a_m < a_{m-1}, \\
a_{m-1} &= a_m q_{m-1}.
\end{aligned}
$$

Result:

$$
\gcd(a_1, a_2) = a_m.
$$

We compute as an example $\gcd(723, 288)$:

$$
\begin{aligned}
723 &= 288 \cdot 2 + 147, \\
288 &= 147 \cdot 1 + 141, \\
147 &= 141 \cdot 1 + 6, \\
141 &= 6 \cdot 23 + 3, \\
6 &= 3 \cdot 2.
\end{aligned}
$$

Result:

$$
\gcd(723, 288) = 3.
$$

This procedure works very well for calculating the greatest common divisor or for letting a computer program do the work. The corresponding program is short, quick, and, due to its brevity, provides few opportunities for error.

A consideration of the following properties of integers and of the greatest common divisor indicates—at least theoretically—possibilities for improvement for programming this procedure:

(i) a and b are even $\Rightarrow \gcd(a, b) = \gcd(a/2, b/2) \cdot 2$.

(ii) a is even and b is odd $\Rightarrow \gcd(a, b) = \gcd(a/2, b)$.

(iii) $\gcd(a, b) = \gcd(a - b, b)$.

(iv) a and b are odd $\Rightarrow a - b$ is even and $|a - b| < \max(a, b)$.

(10.2)

The advantage of the following algorithm based on these properties is that it uses only size comparisons, subtractions, and shifts of CLINT objects, operations that do not require a great deal of computational time and for which we use efficient functions; above all, we need no divisions. The *binary* Euclidean algorithm for calculating the greatest common divisor can be found in almost the identical form in [Knut], Section 4.5.2, Algorithm B, and in [Cohe], Section 1.3, Algorithm 1.3.5.

Binary Euclidean algorithm for calculating $\gcd(a, b)$ **for** $a, b \geq 0$

1. If $a < b$, exchange the values of a and b. If $b = 0$, output a and terminate the algorithm. Otherwise, set $k \leftarrow 0$, and as long as a and b are both even, set $k \leftarrow k + 1, a \leftarrow a/2, b \leftarrow b/2$. (We have exhausted property (i); a and b are now no longer both even.)

2. As long as a is even, set repeatedly $a \leftarrow a/2$ until a is odd. Or else, if b is even, set repeatedly $b \leftarrow b/2$ until b is odd. (We have exhausted property (ii); a and b are now both odd.)

3. Set $t \leftarrow (a - b)/2$. If $t = 0$, output $2^k a$ and terminate the algorithm. (We have used up properties (ii), (iii), and (iv).)

4. As long as t is even, set repeatedly $t \leftarrow t/2$, until t is odd. If $t > 0$, set $a \leftarrow t$; otherwise, set $b \leftarrow -t$; and go to step 3.

This algorithm can be translated step for step into a programmed function, where we take the suggestion from [Cohe] to execute in step 1 an additional division with remainder and set $r \leftarrow a \bmod b, a \leftarrow b$, and $b \leftarrow r$. We thereby equalize any size differences between the operands a and b that could have an adverse effect on the running time.

Function:	greatest common divisor
Syntax:	void gcd_l (CLINT aa_l, CLINT bb_l, CLINT cc_l);
Input:	aa_l, bb_l (operands)
Output:	cc_l (greatest common divisor)

```
void
gcd_l (CLINT aa_l, CLINT bb_l, CLINT cc_l)
{
  CLINT a_l, b_l, r_l, t_l;
  unsigned int k = 0;
  int sign_of_t;
```

Step 1: If the arguments are unequal, the smaller argument is copied to b_l. If b_l is equal to 0, then a_l is output as the greatest common divisor.

```
  if (LT_L (aa_l, bb_l))
    {
      cpy_l (a_l, bb_l);
      cpy_l (b_l, aa_l);
    }
  else
    {
      cpy_l (a_l, aa_l);
      cpy_l (b_l, bb_l);
    }
  if (EQZ_L (b_l))
    {
      cpy_l (cc_l, a_l);
      return;
    }
```

The following division with remainder serves to scale the larger operand a_l. Then the powers of two are removed from a_1 and b_1.

```
  (void) div_l (a_l, b_l, t_l, r_l);
  cpy_l (a_l, b_l);
  cpy_l (b_l, r_l);
  if (EQZ_L (b_l))
    {
      cpy_l (cc_l, a_l);
      return;
    }
```

```
while (ISEVEN_L (a_l) && ISEVEN_L (b_l))
  {
    ++k;
    shr_l (a_l);
    shr_l (b_l);
  }
```

> Step 2.

```
while (ISEVEN_L (a_l))
  {
    shr_l (a_l);
  }
while (ISEVEN_L (b_l))
  {
    shr_l (b_l);
  }
```

> Step 3: Here we have the case that the difference of a_l and b_l can be negative. This situation is caught by a comparison between a_l and b_l. The absolute value of the difference is stored in t_l, and the sign of the difference is stored in the integer variable sign_of_t. If t_l == 0. Then the algorithm is terminated.

```
do
  {
    if (GE_L (a_l, b_l))
      {
        sub_l (a_l, b_l, t_l);
        sign_of_t = 1;
      }
    else
      {
        sub_l (b_l, a_l, t_l);
        sign_of_t = -1;
      }
    if (EQZ_L (t_l))
      {
        cpy_l (cc_l, a_l);       /* cc_l <- a */
        shift_l (cc_l, (long int) k);     /* cc_l <- cc_l*2**k */
        return;
      }
```

Step 4: Depending on the sign of t_1, we have t_1 allocated to a_1 or b_1.

```
      while (ISEVEN_L (t_1))
        {
          shr_l (t_1);
        }
      if (-1 == sign_of_t)
        {
          cpy_l (b_1, t_1);
        }
      else
        {
          cpy_l (a_1, t_1);
        }
    }
  while (1);
}
```

Although the operations used are all linear in the number of digits of the operands, tests show that the simple two-line greatest common divisor on page 168 is hardly slower as a FLINT/C function than this variant. Somewhat surprised at this, we ascribe this situation, for lack of better explanation, to the efficiency of our division routine, as well as to the fact that the latter version of the algorithm requires a somewhat more complex structure.

The calculation of the greatest common divisor for more than two arguments can be carried out with multiple applications of the function gcd_l(), since as we showed above in (10.1)(iii) the general case can be reduced recursively to the case with two arguments:

$$\gcd(n_1, \ldots, n_r) = \gcd(n_1, \gcd(n_2, \ldots, n_r)). \qquad (10.3)$$

With the help of the greatest common divisor it is easy to determine the *least common multiple* (lcm) of two CLINT objects a_1 and b_1. The least common multiple of integers $n_1, \ldots, n_r$, all nonzero, is defined as the smallest element of the set $\{ m \in \mathbb{N}^+ \mid n_i$ divides $m, i = 1, \ldots, r \}$. Since it contains at least the product $\prod_{i=1}^{r} |n_i|$, this set is nonempty. For two arguments $a, b \in \mathbb{Z}$ the least common multiple can be computed as the absolute value of their product divided by the greatest common divisor:

$$\mathrm{lcm}(a, b) \cdot \gcd(a, b) = |ab|. \qquad (10.4)$$

We shall use this relation for the calculation of the least common multiple of a_1 and b_1.

Function:	least common multiple (lcm)
Syntax:	int lcm_l (CLINT a_l, CLINT b_l, CLINT c_l);
Input:	a_l, b_l (operands)
Output:	c_l (lcm)
Return:	E_CLINT_OK if all ok
	E_CLINT_OFL if overflow

```
int
lcm_l (CLINT a_l, CLINT b_l, CLINT c_l)
{
  CLINT g_l, junk_l;
  if (EQZ_L (a_l) || EQZ_L (b_l))
    {
      SETZERO_L (c_l);
      return E_CLINT_OK;
    }
  gcd_l (a_l, b_l, g_l);
  div_l (a_l, g_l, g_l, junk_l);
  return (mul_l (g_l, b_l, c_l));
}
```

It holds for the least common multiple as well that its calculation for more than two arguments can be recursively reduced to the case of two arguments:

$$\mathrm{lcm}\,(n_1, \ldots, n_r) = \mathrm{lcm}\,(n_1, \mathrm{lcm}\,(n_2, \ldots, n_r)) \,. \tag{10.5}$$

Formula (10.4) above does not, however, hold for more than two numbers: The simple fact that $\mathrm{lcm}(2, 2, 2) \cdot \gcd(2, 2, 2) = 4 \neq 2^3$ can serve as a counterexample. There does exist, however, a generalization of this relation between the greatest common divisor and the least common multiple for more than two arguments. Namely, we have

$$\mathrm{lcm}(a, b, c) \cdot \gcd(ab, ac, bc) = |abc| \tag{10.6}$$

and also

$$\gcd(a, b, c) \cdot \mathrm{lcm}(ab, ac, bc) = |abc|. \tag{10.7}$$

The special relationship between the greatest common divisor and the least common multiple is expressed in additional interesting formulas, demonstrating an underlying duality, in the sense that exchanging the roles of greatest common divisor and least common multiple does not affect the validity of the formula, just as in (10.6) and (10.7). We have the *distributive law* for gcd and lcm, namely,

$$\gcd(a, \operatorname{lcm}(b, c)) = \operatorname{lcm}(\gcd(a, b), \gcd(a, c)), \qquad (10.8)$$

$$\operatorname{lcm}(a, \gcd(b, c)) = \gcd(\operatorname{lcm}(a, b), \operatorname{lcm}(a, c)), \qquad (10.9)$$

and to top it all off we have (see [Schr], Section 2.4)

$$\gcd(\operatorname{lcm}(a, b), \operatorname{lcm}(a, c), \operatorname{lcm}(b, c)) = \operatorname{lcm}(\gcd(a, b), \gcd(a, c), \gcd(b, c)).$$
$$(10.10)$$

Aside from the obvious beauty of these formulas on account of their fearful symmetry, they also serve to provide excellent tests for functions that deal with greatest common divisor and least common multiple, where the arithmetic functions used are implicitly tested as well (on the subject of testing, see Chapter 12).

> Don't blame testers for finding your bugs.
> —Steve Maguire

10.2 Multiplicative Inverse in Residue Class Rings

In contrast to the arithmetic of whole numbers, in residue class rings it is possible, under certain assumptions, to calculate with multiplicative inverses. Namely, many elements $\bar{a} \in \mathbb{Z}_n$, not necessarily all, possess a suitable $\bar{x} \in \mathbb{Z}_n$ such that $\bar{a} \cdot \bar{x} = \bar{1}$. This is equivalent to the assertion that the congruence $a \cdot x \equiv 1 \bmod n$ and the statement $a \cdot x \bmod n = 1$ hold. For example, in $\mathbb{Z}_{14}$, $\bar{3}$ and $\bar{5}$ are multiplicative inverses of each other, since $15 \bmod 14 = 1$.

The existence of multiplicative inverses in $\mathbb{Z}_n$ is not obvious. In Chapter 5, on page 69, it was determined only that $(\mathbb{Z}_n, \cdot)$ is a finite commutative semigroup with unit $\bar{1}$. A sufficient condition for an element $\bar{a} \in \mathbb{Z}_n$ to possess a multiplicative inverse can be obtained with the help of the Euclidean algorithm: The second-to-last equation in the Euclidean algorithm procedure on page 169,

$$a_{m-2} = a_{m-1} \cdot q_{m-2} + a_m, \quad 0 \le a_m < a_{m-1},$$

can be transformed into

$$a_m = a_{m-2} - a_{m-1} \cdot q_{m-2}. \qquad (1)$$

If we continue in this fashion, then we obtain in succession

$$a_{m-1} = a_{m-3} - a_{m-2} \cdot q_{m-3}, \qquad (2)$$

$$a_{m-2} = a_{m-4} - a_{m-3} \cdot q_{m-4}, \qquad (3)$$

$$\vdots$$

$$a_3 = a_1 - a_2 \cdot q_1. \qquad (m-2)$$

If in (1) we replace a_{m-1} by the right side of equation (2), then we obtain

$$a_m = a_{m-2} - q_{m-2}\left(a_{m-3} - q_{m-3} \cdot a_{m-2}\right),$$

or

$$a_m = \left(1 + q_{m-3} \cdot q_{m-2}\right) a_{m-2} - q_{m-2} \cdot a_{m-3}.$$

Proceeding thus one obtains in equation $(m - 2)$ an expression for a_m as a linear combination of the starting values a_1 and a_2 with factors composed of the quotients q_i of the Euclidean algorithm.

In this way we obtain a representation of $\gcd(a, b) = u \cdot a + v \cdot b =: g$ as a linear combination of a and b with integer factors u and v, where u modulo a/g and v modulo b/g are uniquely determined. If for an element $\bar{a} \in \mathbb{Z}_n$ we now have $\gcd(a, n) = 1 = u \cdot a + v \cdot n$, then it follows immediately that $1 \equiv u \cdot a \bmod n$, or, equivalently, $\bar{a} \cdot \bar{u} = \bar{1}$. In this case u modulo n is uniquely determined, and $\bar{u}$ is consequently the inverse of $\bar{a}$ in $\mathbb{Z}_n$. We have thus found a condition for the existence of a multiplicative inverse of an element in the residue class ring $\mathbb{Z}_n$, and we have simultaneously obtained a procedure for constructing such an inverse, which shall demonstrate with the following example. From the calculation above of $\gcd(723, 288)$ we obtain by rearrangement

$$3 = 141 - 6 \cdot 23,$$
$$6 = 147 - 141 \cdot 1,$$
$$141 = 288 - 147 \cdot 1,$$
$$147 = 723 - 288 \cdot 2.$$

From this we obtain our representation of the greatest common divisor:

$$3 = 141 - 23 \cdot (147 - 141) = 24 \cdot 141 - 23 \cdot 147$$
$$= 24 \cdot (288 - 147) - 23 \cdot 147 = -47 \cdot 147 + 24 \cdot 288$$
$$= -47 \cdot (723 - 2 \cdot 288) + 24 \cdot 288 = -47 \cdot 723 + 118 \cdot 288.$$

A fast procedure for calculating this representation of the greatest common divisor would consist in storing the quotients q_i (as is done here on the page) so that they would be available for the backward calculation of the desired factors. Because of the high memory requirement, such a procedure would not be practicable. It is necessary to find a compromise between memory requirements and computational time, which is a typical tradeoff in the design and implementation of algorithms. To obtain a realistic procedure we shall further alter the Euclidean algorithm in such a way that the representation of the greatest common divisor as a linear combination can be calculated along with the greatest common divisor itself. For $\bar{a}$ in $\mathbb{Z}_n$ there exists an inverse $\bar{x} \in \mathbb{Z}_n$ if $\gcd(a, n) = 1$. The converse of this statement can also be demonstrated: If $\bar{a}$ in $\mathbb{Z}_n$ has a multiplicative inverse, then $\gcd(a, n) = 1$ (one may find a mathematical proof of this statement in [Nive], the proof to Theorem 2.13). We see, then, that here the issue of having no common factors (that is, being relatively prime) is of great significance: If we consider the subset $\mathbb{Z}_n^\times := \{ \bar{a} \in \mathbb{Z}_n \mid \gcd(a, n) = 1 \}$ of those elements $\bar{a} \in \mathbb{Z}_n$ for which a has no common factor with n other than 1, then with the operation of multiplication one has an abelian group, which we have denoted by $(\mathbb{Z}_n^\times, \cdot)$ already in Chapter 5. The properties of $(\mathbb{Z}_n, \cdot)$ as an abelian semigroup with unit,

- associativity of $(\mathbb{Z}_n, \cdot)$,

- commutativity of $(\mathbb{Z}_n, \cdot)$,

- existence of a unit: For all $\bar{a} \in \mathbb{Z}_n$ one has $\bar{a} \cdot \bar{1} = \bar{a}$,

carry over directly to $(\mathbb{Z}_n^\times, \cdot)$. The existence of multiplicative inverses holds because we have selected precisely those elements that have such inverses, so that we have now only to demonstrate *closure*, namely, that for two elements $\bar{a}$ and $\bar{b}$ in $\mathbb{Z}_n^\times$ the product $\bar{a} \cdot \bar{b}$ is again an element of $\mathbb{Z}_n^\times$. Closure is easily proved: If a and b are relatively prime to n, then the product of a and b cannot have a nontrivial factor in common with n, so that $\bar{a} \cdot \bar{b}$ must belong to the set $\mathbb{Z}_n^\times$. The group $(\mathbb{Z}_n^\times, \cdot)$ is called the *group of residue classes relatively prime to n*.

The number of elements in $\mathbb{Z}_n^\times$, or, equivalently, the number of integers relatively prime to n in the set $\{ 1, 2, \ldots, n - 1 \}$, is given by the Euler phi function $\phi(n)$. For $n = p_1^{e_1} p_2^{e_2} \cdots p_t^{e_t}$ written as a product of distinct primes $p_1, \ldots, p_t$ to positive powers e_i, we have

$$\phi(n) = \prod_{i=1}^{t} p_i^{e_i - 1} (p_i - 1)$$

(see, for example, [Nive], Sections 2.1 and 2.4). This means, for example, that $\mathbb{Z}_p^\times$ has $p - 1$ elements if p is a prime number.[1]

If $\gcd(a, n) = 1$, then according to Euler's generalization of the little theorem of Fermat,[2] $a^{\phi(n)} \equiv 1 \bmod n$, so that the calculation of $a^{\phi(n)-1} \bmod n$ determines the multiplicative inverse of $\bar{a}$. For example, if $n = p \cdot q$ with prime numbers $p \neq q$ and $a \in \mathbb{Z}_n^\times$, then $a^{(p-1)(q-1)} \equiv 1 \bmod n$, and therefore $a^{(p-1)(q-1)-1} \bmod n$ is the inverse of a modulo n. However, this calculation requires, even in the advantageous case that $\phi(n)$ is known, a modular exponentiation whose computational cost is $O\left(\log^3 n\right)$.

We do significantly better, namely with a computational cost of $O\left(\log^2 n\right)$ and without knowing the value of the Euler phi function, by integrating the

---

[1] In this case $\mathbb{Z}_p$ is in fact a *field*, since both $(\mathbb{Z}_p, +)$ and $(\mathbb{Z}_p^\times, \cdot) = (\mathbb{Z}_p \setminus \{0\}, \cdot)$ are abelian groups (see [Nive], Section 2.11). Finite fields have application, for example, to coding theory, and they play an important role in modern cryptography.

[2] The little Fermat theorem states that for a prime number p and for any integer a one has $a^p \equiv a \bmod p$. If p is not a divisor of a, then $a^{p-1} \equiv 1 \bmod p$ (see [Bund], Chapter 2, §3.3). The little theorem of Fermat and its generalization by Euler are among the most important theorems of number theory.

above constructive procedure into the Euclidean algorithm. For this we introduce variables u and v, with the help of which the invariants

$$a_i = u_i \cdot a + v_i \cdot b$$

are maintained in the individual steps of the procedure presented on page 169, in which we have

$$a_{i+1} = a_{i-1} \bmod a_i,$$

and these invariants provide us at the end of the algorithm the desired representation of the greatest common divisor as a linear combination of a and b. Such a procedure is called an *extended Euclidean algorithm*.

The following extension of the Euclidean algorithm is taken from [Cohe], Section 1.3, Algorithm 1.3.6. The variable v in the above invariant condition is employed only implicitly, and only at the end is it calculated as $v := (d - u \cdot a)/b$.

Extended Euclidean algorithm for calculating $\gcd(a, b)$ **and factors** u **and** v **such that** $\gcd(a, b) = u \cdot a + v \cdot b, 0 \leq a, b$

1. Set $u \leftarrow 1, d \leftarrow a$. If $b = 0$, set $v \leftarrow 0$ and terminate the algorithm; otherwise, set $v_1 \leftarrow 0$ and $v_3 \leftarrow b$.

2. Calculate q and t_3 with $d = q \cdot v_3 + t_3$ and $t_3 < v_3$ by a division with remainder, and set $t_1 \leftarrow u - q \cdot v_1, u \leftarrow v_1, d \leftarrow v_3, v_1 \leftarrow t_1$, and $v_3 \leftarrow t_3$.

3. If $v_3 = 0$, set $v \leftarrow (d - u \cdot a)/b$ and terminate the algorithm; otherwise, go to step 2.

The following function xgcd_l() uses the auxiliary functions sadd() and ssub() for the (exceptional) calculation of a signed addition and subtraction. Each of these functions contains a prelude that deals with the sign as an argument to be passed, and then calls the kernel functions add() and sub() (cf. Chapter 5), which execute addition and subtraction, respectively, without consideration of overflow or underflow. Based on the division function div_l() for natural numbers there exists the auxiliary function smod(), which forms the residue $a \bmod b$ with $a, b \in \mathbb{Z}, b > 0$. These auxiliary functions will be needed again later, in connection with the application of the Chinese remainder theorem in the function chinrem_l() (see Section 10.4.3). In a possible extension of the FLINT/C library for processing integers they could be used as models for handling signs.

A hint for using the following function is in order: If the arguments satisfy $a, b \geq N_{\max}/2$, an overflow in the factors u and v, which are returned as the result of xgcd_l(), can occur. In such cases enough space must be reserved for holding u and v, which are then declared by the calling program as type CLINTD or CLINTQ as required (see Chapter 2).

Function:	extended Euclidean algorithm for calculating the representation $\gcd(a, b) = u \cdot a + v \cdot b$ for natural numbers a, b
Syntax:	void xgcd_l (CLINT a_l, CLINT b_l, CLINT g_l, CLINT u_l, int *sign_u, CLINT v_l, int *sign_v);
Input:	a_l, b_l (operands)
Output:	g_l (gcd of a_l and b_l)
	u_l, v_l (factors of a_l and b_l in the representation of g_l)
	*sign_u (sign of u_l)
	*sign_v (sign of v_l).

```
void
xgcd_l (CLINT a_l, CLINT b_l, CLINT d_l, CLINT u_l, int *sign_u, CLINT v_l,
                                                         int *sign_v)
{
  CLINT v1_l, v3_l, t1_l, t3_l, q_l;
  CLINTD tmp_l, tmpu_l, tmpv_l;
  int sign_v1, sign_t1;
```

Step 1: Initialization.

```
  cpy_l (d_l, a_l);
  cpy_l (v3_l, b_l);

  if (EQZ_L (v3_l))
    {
      SETONE_L (u_l);
      SETZERO_L (v_l);
      *sign_u = 1;
      *sign_v = 1;
      return;
    }
SETONE_L (tmpu_l);
*sign_u = 1;
SETZERO_L (v1_l);
sign_v1 = 1;
```

Step 2: Main loop; calculation of the greatest common divisor and of u.

```
while (GTZ_L (v3_l))
  {
    div_l (d_l, v3_l, q_l, t3_l);
    mul_l (v1_l, q_l, q_l);
    sign_t1 = ssub (tmpu_l, *sign_u, q_l, sign_v1, t1_l);

    cpy_l (tmpu_l, v1_l);
    *sign_u = sign_v1;
    cpy_l (d_l, v3_l);
    cpy_l (v1_l, t1_l);
    sign_v1 = sign_t1;
    cpy_l (v3_l, t3_l);
  }
```

Step 3: Calculation of v and the end of the procedure.

```
mult (a_l, tmpu_l, tmp_l);
*sign_v = ssub (d_l, 1, tmp_l, *sign_u, tmp_l);
div_l (tmp_l, b_l, tmpv_l, tmp_l);

cpy_l (u_l, tmpu_l);
cpy_l (v_l, tmpv_l);

return;
}
```

Since dealing with negative numbers within the FLINT/C package requires additional cost, we arrive at the observation that for calculating the inverse of a residue class $\bar{a} \in \mathbb{Z}_n^{\times}$ only the one factor u of the representation $1 = u \cdot a + v \cdot n$ of the greatest common divisor is necessary. A positive representative for u can always be found, and we can thereby spare ourselves the need to deal with negative numbers. The following algorithm is a variant of the previous one that makes use of this observation and eliminates entirely the calculation of v.

Extended Euclidean algorithm for calculating $\gcd(a, n)$ **and the multiplicative inverse of** $a \bmod n, 0 \leq a, 0 < n$

1. Set $u \leftarrow 1, g \leftarrow a, v_1 \leftarrow 0$, and $v_3 \leftarrow n$.

2. Calculate q, t_3 with $g = q \cdot v_3 + t_3$ and $t_3 < v_3$ by division with remainder and set $t_1 \leftarrow u - q \cdot v_1 \bmod n, u \leftarrow v_1, g \leftarrow v_3, v_1 \leftarrow t_1, v_3 \leftarrow t_3$.

3. If $v_3 = 0$, output g as $\gcd(a, n)$ and u as the inverse of $a \bmod n$ and terminate the algorithm; otherwise, return to step 2.

The modular step $t_1 \leftarrow u - q \cdot v_1 \bmod n$ ensures that t_1, v_1, and u do not become negative. At the end we have $u \in \{1, \ldots, n - 1\}$. The coding of the algorithm leads us to the following function.

Function:	calculation of the multiplicative inverse in $\mathbb{Z}_n$
Syntax:	void inv_l (CLINT a_l, CLINT n_l, CLINT g_l, CLINT i_l);
Input:	a_l, n_l (operands)
Output:	g_l (gcd of a_l and n_l)
	i_l (inverse of a_l mod n_l, if defined)

```
void
inv_l (CLINT a_l, CLINT n_l, CLINT g_l, CLINT i_l)
{
  CLINT v1_l, v3_l, t1_l, t3_l, q_l;
```

Test of the operands for 0. If one of the operands is zero, then there does not exist an inverse, but there does exist a greatest common divisor (cf. page 168). The result variable i_l is then undefined, which is indicated by being set to zero.

```
  if (EQZ_L (a_l))
    {
      if (EQZ_L (n_l))
        {
          SETZERO_L (g_l);
          SETZERO_L (i_l);
          return;
        }
      else
        {
          cpy_l (g_l, n_l);
          SETZERO_L (i_l);
          return;
        }
    }
  else
    {
      if (EQZ_L (n_l))
        {
          cpy_l (g_l, a_l);
          SETZERO_L (i_l);
          return;
        }
    }
```

Step 1: Initialization of the variables.

```
cpy_l (g_l, a_l);
cpy_l (v3_l, n_l);
SETZERO_L (v1_l);
SETONE_L (t1_l);
do
  {
```

Step 2: With the test in GTZ_L (t3_l) after the division an unnecessary call to mmul_l() and msub_l() is avoided in the last run through the loop. The assignment to the result variable i_l is not carried out until the end.

```
    div_l (g_l, v3_l, q_l, t3_l);
    if (GTZ_L (t3_l))
      {
        mmul_l (v1_l, q_l, q_l, n_l);
        msub_l (t1_l, q_l, q_l, n_l);
        cpy_l (t1_l, v1_l);
        cpy_l (v1_l, q_l);
        cpy_l (g_l, v3_l);
        cpy_l (v3_l, t3_l);
      }
  }
while (GTZ_L (t3_l));
```

Step 3: As the last requisite assignment we take the greatest common divisor from the variable v3_l, and if the greatest common divisor is equal to 1, we take the inverse to a_l from the variable v1_l.

```
cpy_l (g_l, v3_l);
if (EQONE_L (g_l))
  {
    cpy_l (i_l, v1_l);
  }
else
  {
    SETZERO_L (i_l);
  }
}
```

10.3 Roots and Logarithms

In this section we shall develop functions for calculating the integer part of square roots and logarithms to base 2 of CLINT objects. To this end we first consider the latter of these two functions, since we will need it for the first of them: For a natural number a we are seeking a number e for which $2^e \leq a < 2^{e+1}$. The number $e = \lfloor \log_2 a \rfloor$ is the integer part of the logarithm of a to the base 2 and is easily obtained from the number of relevant bits of a, as determined from the following function ld_1(), reduced by 1. The function ld_1(), which is used in many other functions of the FLINT/C package, disregards leading zeros and counts only the relevant binary digits of a CLINT object.

Function:	number of relevant binary digits of a CLINT object
Syntax:	unsigned int ld_1 (CLINT n_1);
Input:	n_1 (operand)
Return:	number of relevant binary digits of n_1.

```
unsigned int
ld_1 (CLINT n_1)
{
  unsigned int l;
  USHORT test;
```

Step 1: Determine the number of relevant digits to the base B.

```
l = (unsigned int) DIGITS_L (n_1);
while (n_1[l] == 0 && l > 0)
  {
    --l;
  }
if (l == 0)
  {
    return 0;
  }
```

Step 2: Determine the number of relevant bits of the most-significant digit. The macro BASEDIV2 defines the value of a digit that has a 1 in the most-significant bit and otherwise contains 0 (that is, $2^{\text{BITPERDGT}-1}$).

```
test = n_l[1];
l <<= LDBITPERDGT;
while ((test & BASEDIV2) == 0)
  {
    test <<= 1;
    --l;
  }
return l;
}
```

We then calculate the integer part of the square root of a natural number based on the classical method of Newton (also known as the Newton–Raphson method), which is used for determining the zeros of a function by successive approximation: We assume that a function $f(x)$ is twice continuously differentiable on an interval $[a, b]$, that the first derivative $f'(x)$ is positive on $[a, b]$, and that we have

$$\max_{[a,b]} \left| \frac{f(x) \cdot f''(x)}{f'(x)^2} \right| < 1.$$

Then if $x_n \in [a, b]$ is an approximation for a number r with $f(r) = 0$, then $x_{n+1} := x_n - f(x_n)/f'(x_n)$ is a better approximation of r. The sequence defined in this way converges to the zero r of f (cf. [Endl], Section 7.3).

If we set $f(x) := x^2 - c$ with $c > 0$, then $f(x)$ for $x > 0$ satisfies the above conditions for the convergence of the Newton method, and with

$$x_{n+1} := x_n - \frac{f(x_n)}{f'(x_n)} = \frac{1}{2} \left(x_n + \frac{c}{x_n} \right)$$

we obtain a sequence that converges to $\sqrt{c}$. Due to its favorable convergence behavior Newton's method is an efficient procedure for approximating square roots of rational numbers.

Since for our purposes we are interested in only the integer part r of $\sqrt{c}$, for which $r^2 \leq c < (r+1)^2$ holds, where c itself is assumed to be a natural number, we can limit ourselves to computing the integer parts of the elements of the sequence of approximations. We begin with a number $x_1 > \sqrt{c}$ and continue until we obtain a value greater than or equal to its predecessor, at which point the predecessor is the desired value. It is naturally a good idea to begin with a number that is as close to $\sqrt{c}$ as possible. For a CLINT object with value c and $e := \lfloor \log_2 c \rfloor$ we have that $\left\lfloor 2^{(e+2)/2} \right\rfloor$ is always greater than $\sqrt{c}$, and furthermore, we can easily calculate it with the function ld_l(). The algorithm goes as follows.

Algorithm for determining the integer part r of the square root of a natural number $n > 0$

1. Set $x \leftarrow \left\lfloor 2^{(e+2)/2} \right\rfloor$ with $e := \lfloor \log_2 n \rfloor$.

2. Set $y \leftarrow \lfloor (x + n/x)/2 \rfloor$. If $y < x$, set $x \leftarrow y$ and repeat step 2.

3. Output x and terminate the algorithm.

The proof of the correctness of this algorithm is not particularly difficult. The value of x decreases monotonically, and it is an integer and always positive, so that the algorithm certainly terminates. When this occurs, the condition $y = \lfloor (x + n/x)/2 \rfloor \geq x$ holds, and we assume that $x \geq r + 1$. From $x \geq r + 1 > \sqrt{n}$ it follows that $x^2 > n$, or $n - x^2 < 0$.

However,

$$y - x = \left\lfloor \frac{(x + n/x)}{2} \right\rfloor - x = \left\lfloor \frac{(n - x^2)}{2x} \right\rfloor < 0,$$

in contradiction to the condition for terminating the process. Our assertion is therefore false, and we must have $x = r$. The following function, for determining the integer part of the square root, uses integer division with remainder for the operation $y \leftarrow \lfloor (x + c/x)/2 \rfloor$ without putting the validity of the procedure at risk.

Function:	integer part of the square root of a CLINT object
Syntax:	void iroot_l(CLINT n_l, CLINT floor_l);
Input:	n_l (operand > 0)
Output:	floor_l (integer square root of n_l)

```
void
iroot_l (CLINT n_l, CLINT floor_l)
{
  CLINT x_l, y_l, r_l;
  unsigned l;
```

With the function ld_l() and a shift operation l is set to the value $\lfloor (\lfloor \log_2 (n\_l) \rfloor + 2)/2 \rfloor$, and y_l is set to 2^l with the help of setbit_l().

```
l = (ld_l (n_l) + 1) >> 1;
SETZERO_L (y_l);
setbit_l (y_l, l);
do
  {
    cpy_l (x_l, y_l);
```

> Steps 2 and 3. Newton approximation and checking for termination.

```
    div_l (n_l, x_l, y_l, r_l);
    add_l (y_l, x_l, y_l);
    shr_l (y_l);
  }
while (LT_L (y_l, x_l));
cpy_l (floor_l, x_l);
}
```

A generalization of the procedure makes possible the calculation of the integer part of the bth root of n, i.e., $\left\lfloor n^{1/b} \right\rfloor$, for $b > 1$ (see [CrPa], page 3):

Algorithm for calculating the integer part of a bth root

1. Set $x \leftarrow 2^{\lceil \mathrm{ld\_l}(n)/b \rceil}$.

2. Set $y \leftarrow \left\lfloor \left((b-1)x + \left\lfloor n/x^{b-1} \right\rfloor \right) /b \right\rfloor$. If $y < x$, set $x \leftarrow y$ and repeat step 2.

3. Output x as result and terminate the algorithm.

The implementation of the algorithm uses exponentiation modulo N_{max} for the integer power in x^{b-1} in step 2:

Function:	integer part of the bth root of a CLINT object n_l
Syntax:	int
	introot_l(CLINT n_l, USHORT b, CLINT floor_l);
Input:	n_l, b (operands, b > 0)
Output:	floor_l (integer part of the bth root of n_l)

```
int
introot_l (CLINT n_l, USHORT b, CLINT floor_l)
{
  CLINT x_l, y_l, z_l, junk_l, max_l;
  USHORT l;

  if (0 == b)
   {
     return -1;
   }

  if (EQZ_L (n_l))
   {
     SETZERO_L (floor_l);
     return E_CLINT_OK;
   }

  if (EQONE_L (n_l))
   {
     SETONE_L (floor_l);
     return E_CLINT_OK;
   }

  if (1 == b)
   {
     assign_l (floor_l, n_l);
     return E_CLINT_OK;
   }

  if (2 == b)
   {
     iroot_l (n_l, floor_l);
     return E_CLINT_OK;
   }
  /* step 1: set x_l ← 2^⌈ld_l(n_l)/b⌉ */
  setmax_l (max_l);
  l = ld_l (n_l)/b;
  if (l*b != ld_l (n_l)) ++l;

  SETZERO_L (x_l);
  setbit_l (x_l, l);
```

```
/* step 2: loop to approximate the root until y_l ≥ x_l */
while (1)
  {
    umul_l (x_l, (USHORT)(b-1), y_l);
    umexp_l (x_l, (USHORT)(b-1), z_l, max_l);
    div_l (n_l, z_l, z_l, junk_l);
    add_l (y_l, z_l, y_l);
    udiv_l (y_l, b, y_l, junk_l);

    if (LT_L (y_l, x_l))
      {
        assign_l (x_l, y_l);
      }
    else
      {
        break;
      }
  }
  cpy_l (floor_l, x_l);
  return E_CLINT_OK;
}
```

To determine whether a number n is a bth root of another number, it suffices to raise the output value by `introot_l()` to the bth power and compare the result with n. If the values are unequal, then n is clearly not a root. For square roots one must, however, admit that this is not the most efficient method. There are criteria that in many cases can recognize such numbers that are not squares without the explicit calculation of root and square. Such an algorithm is given in [Cohe]. It uses four tables, $q11$, $q63$, $q64$, and $q65$, in which the quadratic residues modulo 11, 63, 64, and 65 are labeled with a "1" and the quadratic nonresidues with a "0":

$$q11[k] \leftarrow 0 \text{ for } k = 0, \ldots, 10, \quad q11[k^2 \bmod 11] \leftarrow 1 \text{ for } k = 0, \ldots, 5,$$
$$q63[k] \leftarrow 0 \text{ for } k = 0, \ldots, 62, \quad q63[k^2 \bmod 63] \leftarrow 1 \text{ for } k = 0, \ldots, 31,$$
$$q64[k] \leftarrow 0 \text{ for } k = 0, \ldots, 63, \quad q64[k^2 \bmod 64] \leftarrow 1 \text{ for } k = 0, \ldots, 31,$$
$$q65[k] \leftarrow 0 \text{ for } k = 0, \ldots, 64, \quad q65[k^2 \bmod 65] \leftarrow 1 \text{ for } k = 0, \ldots, 32.$$

From the representation of the residue class ring as the absolute smallest residue system (cf. page 70) one sees that we obtain all squares in this way.

Algorithm for identifying an integer $n > 0$ as a square. In this case the square root of n is output (from [Cohe], Algorithm 1.7.3)

1. Set $t \leftarrow n \bmod 64$. If $q64[t] = 0$, then n is not a square and we are done. Otherwise, set $r \leftarrow n \bmod (11 \cdot 63 \cdot 65)$.

2. If $q63[r \bmod 63] = 0$, then n is not a square, and we are done.

3. If $q65[r \bmod 65] = 0$, then n is not a square, and we are done.

4. If $q11[r \bmod 11] = 0$, then n is not a square, and we are done.

5. Compute $q \leftarrow \lfloor \sqrt{n} \rfloor$ using the function iroot_l(). If $q^2 \neq n$, then n is not a square and we are done. Otherwise, n is a square, and the square root q is output.

This algorithm appears rather strange due to the particular constants that appear. But this can be explained: A square n has the property for any integer k that if it is a square in the integers, then it is a square modulo k. We have used the contrapositive: If n is not a square modulo k, then it is not a square in the integers. By applying steps 1 through 4 above we are checking whether n is a square modulo 64, 63, 65, or 11. There are 12 squares modulo 64, 16 squares modulo 63, 21 squares modulo 65, and 6 squares modulo 11, so that the probability that we are in the case that a number that is not a square has not been identified by these four steps is

$$\left(1 - \frac{52}{64}\right)\left(1 - \frac{47}{63}\right)\left(1 - \frac{44}{65}\right)\left(1 - \frac{5}{11}\right) = \frac{12}{64} \cdot \frac{16}{63} \cdot \frac{21}{65} \cdot \frac{6}{11} = \frac{6}{715}.$$

It is only for these relatively rare cases that the test in step 5 is carried out. If this test is positive, then n is revealed to be a square, and the square root of n is determined. The order of the tests in steps 1 through 4 is determined by the individual probabilities. We have anticipated the following function in Section 6.5 to exclude squares as candidates for primitive roots modulo p.

Function:	determining whether a CLINT number n_l is a square
Syntax:	unsigned int issqr_l(CLINT n_l, CLINT r_l);
Input:	n_l (operand)
Output:	r_l (square root of n_l, or 0 if n_l is not a square)
Return:	1 if n_l is a square
	0 otherwise

```
static const UCHAR q11[11]=
  {1, 1, 0, 1, 1, 1, 0, 0, 0, 1, 0};
static const UCHAR q63[63]=
  {1, 1, 0, 0, 1, 0, 0, 1, 0, 1, 0, 0, 0, 0, 0, 0, 1, 0, 1, 0, 0, 0, 1,
   0, 0, 1, 0, 0, 1, 0, 0, 0, 0, 0, 0, 0, 1, 1, 0, 0, 0, 0, 0, 1, 0, 0,
   1, 0, 0, 1, 0, 0, 0, 0, 0, 0, 0, 1, 0, 0, 0, 0};
```

```
static const UCHAR q64[64]=
  {1, 1, 0, 0, 1, 0, 0, 0, 0, 1, 0, 0, 0, 0, 0, 0, 1, 1, 0, 0, 0, 0, 0, 0,
    0, 0, 1, 0, 0, 0, 0, 0, 0, 0, 1, 0, 0, 1, 0, 0, 0, 0, 1, 0, 0, 0, 0, 0,
    0, 0, 0, 1, 0, 0, 0, 0, 0, 0, 0, 1, 0, 0, 0, 0, 0, 0};
static const UCHAR q65[65]=
  {1, 1, 0, 0, 1, 0, 0, 0, 0, 1, 1, 0, 0, 0, 1, 0, 1, 0, 0, 0, 0, 0, 0, 0,
    0, 0, 1, 1, 0, 0, 1, 1, 0, 0, 0, 0, 1, 1, 0, 0, 1, 1, 0, 0, 0, 0, 0, 0,
    0, 0, 0, 1, 0, 1, 0, 0, 0, 1, 1, 0, 0, 0, 0, 1, 0, 0, 1};
unsigned int
issqr_l (CLINT n_l, CLINT r_l)
{
  CLINT q_l;
  USHORT r;

  if (EQZ_L (n_l))
    {
      SETZERO_L (r_l);
      return 1;
    }
```

The case q64[n_l mod 64]

```
  if (1 == q64[*LSDPTR_L (n_l) & 63])
    {
      r = umod_l (n_l, 45045);      /* n_l mod (11·63·65) */
      if ((1 == q63[r % 63]) && (1 == q65[r % 65]) && (1 == q11[r % 11]))
```

Note that evaluation of the previous expression takes place from left to right; cf. [Harb], Section 7.7

```
        {
          iroot_l (n_l, r_l);
          sqr_l (r_l, q_l);
          if (equ_l (n_l, q_l))
            {
              return 1;
            }
        }
    }
  SETZERO_L (r_l);
  return 0;
}
```

10.4 Square Roots in Residue Class Rings

Now that we have calculated square roots of whole numbers, or their integer parts, we turn our attention once again to residue classes, where we shall do the same thing, that is, calculate square roots. Under certain assumptions there exist square roots in residue class rings, though in general they are not uniquely determined (that is, an element may have more than one square root). Put algebraically, the question is to determine whether for an element $\bar{a} \in \mathbb{Z}_m$ there exist roots $\bar{b}$ for which $\bar{b}^2 = \bar{a}$. In number-theoretic notation (see Chapter 5) this would appear in congruence notation, and we would ask whether the quadratic congruence $x^2 \equiv a \bmod m$ has any solutions, and if it does, what they are.

If $\gcd(a, m) = 1$ and there exists a solution b with $b^2 \equiv a \bmod m$, then a is called a *quadratic residue modulo m*. If there is no solution to the congruence, then a is called a *quadratic nonresidue modulo m*. If b is a solution to the congruence, then so is $b + m$, and therefore we can restrict our attention to those residues that differ modulo m.

Let us clarify the situation with the help of an example: 2 is a quadratic residue modulo 7, since $3^2 \equiv 9 \equiv 2 \pmod 7$, while 3 is a quadratic nonresidue modulo 5.

In the case that m is a prime number, then the determination of square roots modulo m is easy, and in the next chapter we shall present the functions required for this purpose. However, the calculation of square roots modulo a composite number depends on whether the prime factorization of m is known. If it is not, then the determination of square roots for large m is a mathematically difficult problem in the complexity class NP (see page 103), and it is this level of complexity that ensures the security of modern cryptographic systems.[3] We shall return to more elucidative examples in Section 10.4.4

The determination of whether a number has the property of being a quadratic residue and the calculation of square roots are two different computational problems each with its own particular algorithm, and in the following sections we will provide explanations and implementations. We first consider procedures for determining whether a number is a quadratic residue modulo a given number. Then we shall calculate square roots modulo prime numbers, and in a later section we shall give approaches to calculating square roots of composite numbers.

---

[3] The analogy between mathematical and cryptographic complexity should be approached with caution: In [Rein] we are informed that the question of whether P $\neq$ NP has little relevance in cryptographic practice. A *polynomial* algorithm for factorization with running time $O\left(n^{20}\right)$ would still be insuperable for even relatively small values of n, while an *exponential* algorithm with running time $O\left(e^{n^{0.1}}\right)$ would conquer even relatively large moduli. The security of cryptographic procedures in practice is really not dependent on whether P and NP are the same, despite the fact that one often sees precisely this formulation.

10.4.1 The Jacobi Symbol

We plunge right into this section with a definition: Let $p \neq 2$ be a prime number and a an integer. The *Legendre symbol* $\left(\frac{a}{p}\right)$ (say "a over p") is defined to be 1 if a is a quadratic residue modulo p and to be -1 if a is a quadratic nonresidue modulo p. If p is a divisor of a, then $\left(\frac{a}{p}\right) := 0$. As a definition the Legendre symbol does not seem to help us much, since in order to know its value we have to know whether a is a quadratic residue modulo p. However, the Legendre symbol has properties that will allow us to do calculations with it and above all to determine its value. Without going too far afield we cannot go into the theoretical background. For that the reader is referred to, for example, [Bund], Section 3.2. Nonetheless, we would like to cite some of these properties to give the reader an idea of the basis for calculation with the Legendre symbol:

(i)   The number of solutions of the congruence $x^2 \equiv a \pmod{p}$ is $1 + \left(\frac{a}{p}\right)$.

(ii) There are as many quadratic residues as nonresidues modulo p, namely $(p-1)/2$.

(iii) $a \equiv b \pmod{p} \Rightarrow \left(\frac{a}{p}\right) = \left(\frac{b}{p}\right)$.

(iv) The Legendre symbol is multiplicative: $\left(\frac{ab}{p}\right) = \left(\frac{a}{p}\right)\left(\frac{b}{p}\right)$.

(v) $\displaystyle\sum_{i=1}^{p-1} \left(\frac{i}{p}\right) = 0$.

(vi) $a^{(p-1)/2} \equiv \left(\frac{a}{p}\right) \pmod{p}$ (Euler criterion).

(vii) For an odd prime q, $q \neq p$, we have $\left(\frac{p}{q}\right) = (-1)^{(p-1)(q-1)/4} \left(\frac{q}{p}\right)$ (law of quadratic reciprocity of Gauss).

(viii) $\left(\frac{-1}{p}\right) = (-1)^{(p-1)/2}$, $\left(\frac{2}{p}\right) = (-1)^{(p^2-1)/8}$, $\left(\frac{1}{p}\right) = 1$.

The proofs of these properties of the Legendre symbol can be found in the standard literature on number theory, for example [Bund] or [Rose].

Two ideas for calculating the Legendre symbol come at once to mind: We can use the Euler criterion (vi) and compute $a^{(p-1)/2} \pmod{p}$. This requires a modular exponentiation (an operation of complexity $O\left(\log^3 p\right)$). Using the reciprocity law, however, we can employ the following recursive procedure, which is based on properties (iii), (iv), (vii), and (viii).

Recursive algorithm for calculating the Legendre symbol $\left(\frac{a}{p}\right)$ of an integer a and an odd prime p

1. If $a = 1$, then $\left(\frac{a}{p}\right) = 1$ (property (viii)).

2. If a is even, then $\left(\frac{a}{p}\right) = (-1)^{(p^2-1)/8} \left(\frac{a/2}{p}\right)$ (properties (iv), (viii)).

3. If $a \neq 1$ and $a = q_1 \cdots q_k$ is the product of odd primes $q_1, \ldots, q_k$, then

$$\left(\frac{a}{p}\right) = \prod_{i=1}^{k} \left(\frac{q_i}{p}\right).$$

For each i we compute

$$\left(\frac{q_i}{p}\right) = (-1)^{(p-1)(q_i-1)/4} \left(\frac{p \bmod q_i}{q_i}\right)$$

by means of steps 1 through 3 (properties (iii), (iv), and (vii)).

Before we examine the programming techniques required for computing the Legendre symbol we consider a generalization that can be carried out without the prime decomposition, such as would be required by the direct application of the reciprocity law in the version above (vii), which for large numbers takes an enormous amount of time (for the factoring problem see page 203). At that point we will be able to fall back on a nonrecursive procedure: For an integer a and an integer $b = p_1 p_2 \cdots p_k$ with not necessarily distinct prime factors p_i the Jacobi symbol (or Jacobi–Kronecker, Kronecker–Jacobi, or Kronecker symbol) $\left(\frac{a}{b}\right)$ is defined as the product of the Legendre symbols $\left(\frac{a}{p_i}\right)$:

$$\left(\frac{a}{b}\right) := \prod_{i=1}^{k} \left(\frac{a}{p_i}\right),$$

where

$$\left(\frac{a}{2}\right) := \begin{cases} 0 & \text{if } a \text{ is even,} \\ (-1)^{(a^2-1)/8} & \text{if } a \text{ is odd.} \end{cases}$$

For the sake of completeness we set $\left(\frac{a}{1}\right) := 1$ for $a \in \mathbb{Z}$, $\left(\frac{a}{0}\right) := 1$ if $a = \pm 1$, and $\left(\frac{a}{0}\right) := 0$ otherwise.

If b is itself an odd prime (that is, $k = 1$), then the values of the Jacobi and Legendre symbols are the same. In this case the Jacobi (Legendre) symbol specifies whether a is a quadratic residue modulo b, that is, whether there is a number c with $c^2 \equiv a \bmod b$, in which case $\left(\frac{a}{b}\right) = 1$. Otherwise, $\left(\frac{a}{b}\right) = -1$ (or $\left(\frac{a}{b}\right) = 0$ if $a \equiv 0 \bmod b$). If b is not a prime (that is, $k > 1$), then we have that a is a quadratic residue modulo b if and only if $\gcd(a, b) = 1$ and a is a quadratic residue modulo all primes that divide b, that is, if all Legendre symbols $\left(\frac{a}{p_i}\right)$, $i = 1, \ldots, k$, have the value 1. This is clearly not equivalent to the Jacobi symbol $\left(\frac{a}{b}\right)$ having the value 1: Since $x^2 \equiv 2 \bmod 3$ has no solution, we have $\left(\frac{2}{3}\right) = -1$. However, by definition, $\left(\frac{2}{9}\right) = \left(\frac{2}{3}\right)\left(\frac{2}{3}\right) = 1$, although for $x^2 \equiv 2 \bmod 9$ there is likewise no solution. On the other hand, if $\left(\frac{a}{b}\right) = -1$, then a is in every case a quadratic nonresidue modulo b. The relation $\left(\frac{a}{b}\right) = 0$ is equivalent to $\gcd(a, b) \neq 1$.

From the properties of the Legendre symbol we can conclude the following about the Jacobi symbol:

(i) $\left(\frac{ab}{c}\right) = \left(\frac{a}{c}\right)\left(\frac{b}{c}\right)$, and if $b \cdot c \neq 0$, then $\left(\frac{a}{bc}\right) = \left(\frac{a}{b}\right)\left(\frac{a}{c}\right)$.

(ii) $a \equiv c \bmod b \Rightarrow \left(\frac{a}{b}\right) = \left(\frac{c}{b}\right)$.

(iii) For odd $b > 0$ we have $\left(\frac{-1}{b}\right) = (-1)^{(b-1)/2}$, $\left(\frac{2}{b}\right) = (-1)^{\left(b^2-1\right)/8}$, and $\left(\frac{1}{b}\right) = 1$ (see (viii) above).

(iv) For odd a and b with $b > 0$ we have the reciprocity law (see (viii) above)
$$\left(\frac{a}{b}\right) = (-1)^{(a-1)(b-1)/4}\left(\frac{b}{|a|}\right).$$

From these properties (see the above references for the proofs) of the Jacobi symbol we have the following algorithm of Kronecker, taken from [Cohe], Section 1.4, that calculates the Jacobi symbol (or, depending on the conditions, the Legendre symbol) of two integers in a nonrecursive way. The algorithm deals with a possible sign of b, and for this we set $\left(\frac{a}{-1}\right) := 1$ for $a \geq 0$ and $\left(\frac{a}{-1}\right) := -1$ for $a < 0$.

Algorithm for calculating the Jacobi symbol $\left(\frac{a}{b}\right)$ of integers a and b

1. If $b = 0$, output 1 if the absolute value $|a|$ of a is equal to 1; otherwise, output 0 and terminate the algorithm.

2. If a and b are both even, output 0 and terminate the algorithm. Otherwise, set $v \leftarrow 0$, and as long as b is even, set $v \leftarrow v + 1$ and $b \leftarrow b/2$. If now v is even, set $k \leftarrow 1$; otherwise, set $k \leftarrow (-1)^{\left(a^2-1\right)/8}$. If $b < 0$, then set $b \leftarrow -b$. If $a < 0$, set $k \leftarrow -k$ (cf. (iii)).

3. If $a = 0$, output 0 if $b > 1$, otherwise k, and terminate the algorithm. Otherwise, set $v \leftarrow 0$, and as long as a is even, set $v \leftarrow v + 1$ and $a \leftarrow a/2$. If now v is odd, set $k \leftarrow (-1)^{\left(b^2-1\right)/8} \cdot k$ (cf. (iii)).

4. Set $k \leftarrow (-1)^{(a-1)(b-1)/4} \cdot k$, $r \leftarrow |a|$, $a \leftarrow b \bmod r$, $b \leftarrow r$, and go to step 3 (cf. (ii) and (iv)).

The run time of this procedure is $O\left(\log^2 N\right)$, where $N \geq a, b$ represents an upper bound for a and b. This is a significant improvement over what we achieved with the Euler criterion. The following tips for the implementation of the algorithm are given in Section 1.4 of [Cohe].

- The values $(-1)^{(a^2-1)/8}$ and $(-1)^{(b^2-1)/8}$ in steps 2 and 3 are best computed with the aid of a prepared table.

- The value $(-1)^{(a-1)(b-1)/4} \cdot k$ in step 4 can be efficiently determined with the C expression if(a&b&2) k = -k, where & is bitwise AND.

In both cases the explicit computation of a power can be avoided, which of course has a positive effect on the total run time.

We would like to clarify the first tip with the help of the following considerations: If k in step 2 is set to the value $(-1)^{(a^2-1)/8}$, then a is odd. The same holds for b in step 3. For odd a we have

$$2 \mid (a - 1) \quad \text{and} \quad 4 \mid (a + 1)$$

or

$$4 \mid (a - 1) \quad \text{and} \quad 2 \mid (a + 1),$$

so that 8 is a divisor of $(a - 1)(a + 1) = a^2 - 1$. Thus $(-1)^{(a^2-1)/8}$ is an integer. Furthermore, we have $(-1)^{(a^2-1)/8} = (-1)^{((a\,\text{mod}\,8)^2-1)/8}$ (this can be seen by placing the representation $a = k \cdot 8 + r$ in the exponent). The exponent must therefore be determined only for the four values $a \bmod 8 = \pm 1$ and ± 3, for which the results are $1, -1, -1$, and 1. These are placed in a vector $\{0, 1, 0, -1, 0, -1, 0, 1\}$, so that by knowing $a \bmod 8$ one can access the value of $(-1)^{((a\,\text{mod}\,8)^2-1)/8}$. Observing that $a \bmod 8$ can be represented by the expression a & 7, where again & is binary AND, then the calculation of the power is reduced to a few fast CPU operations. For an understanding of the second tip we note that $(a \,\&\, b \,\&\, 2) \neq 0$ if and only if $(a - 1)/2$ and $(b - 1)/2$, and hence $(a - 1)(b - 1)/4$, are odd.

Finally, we use the auxiliary function twofact_l(), which we briefly introduce here, for determining v and b in step 2, for the case that b is even, as well as in the analogous case for the values v and a in step 3. The function twofact_l() decomposes a CLINT value into a product consisting of a power of two and an odd factor.

Function:	decompose a CLINT object $a = 2^k u$ with odd u
Syntax:	int twofact_l (CLINT a_l, CLINT b_l);
Input:	a_l (operand)
Output:	b_l (odd part of a_l)
Return:	k (logarithm to base 2 of the two-part of a_l)

```
int
twofact_l (CLINT a_l, CLINT b_l)
{
  int k = 0;
  if (EQZ_L (a_l))
    {
      SETZERO_L (b_l);
      return 0;
    }
  cpy_l (b_l, a_l);
  while (ISEVEN_L (b_l))
    {
      shr_l (b_l);
      ++k;
    }
  return k;
}
```

Thus equipped we can now create an efficient function `jacobi_l()` for calculating the Jacobi symbol.

Function:	calculate the Jacobi symbol of two CLINT objects
Syntax:	int jacobi_l (CLINT aa_l, CLINT bb_l);
Input:	aa_l, bb_l (operands)
Return:	± 1 (value of the Jacobi symbol of aa_l over bb_l)

```
static int tab2[] = 0, 1, 0, -1, 0, -1, 0, 1;

int
jacobi_l (CLINT aa_l, CLINT bb_l)
{
  CLINT a_l, b_l, tmp_l;
  long int k, v;
```

Step 1: The case bb_l = 0.

```
  if (EQZ_L (bb_l))
    {
      if (equ_l (aa_l, one_l))
        {
```

```
        return 1;
      }
    else
      {
        return 0;
      }
  }
```

Step 2: Remove the even part of bb_l.

```
if (ISEVEN_L (aa_l) && ISEVEN_L (bb_l))
  {
    return 0;
  }
cpy_l (a_l, aa_l);
cpy_l (b_l, bb_l);
v = twofact_l (b_l, b_l);
if ((v & 1) == 0)     /* v even? */
  {
    k = 1;
  }
else
  {
    k = tab2[*LSDPTR_L (a_l) & 7];   /* *LSDPTR_L (a_l) & 7 == a_l % 8 */
  }
```

Step 3: If a_l = 0, then we are done. Otherwise, the even part of a_l is removed.

```
while (GTZ_L (a_l))
  {
    v = twofact_l (a_l, a_l);
    if ((v & 1) != 0)
      {
        k = tab2[*LSDPTR_L (b_l) & 7];
      }
```

Step 4: Application of the quadratic reciprocity law.

```
    if (*LSDPTR_L (a_l) & *LSDPTR_L (b_l) & 2)
      {
        k = -k;
      }
```

```
        cpy_l (tmp_l, a_l);
        mod_l (b_l, tmp_l, a_l);
        cpy_l (b_l, tmp_l);
      }
    if (GT_L (b_l, one_l))
      {
        k = 0;
      }
    return (int) k;
}
```

10.4.2 Square Roots Modulo p^k

We now have an idea of the property possessed by an integer of being or not being a quadratic residue modulo another integer, and we also have at our disposal an efficient program to determine which case holds. But even if we know whether an integer a is a quadratic residue modulo an integer n, we still cannot compute the square root of a, especially not in the case where n is large. Since we are modest, we will first attempt this feat for those n that are prime. Our task, then, is to solve the quadratic congruence

$$x^2 \equiv a \bmod p, \tag{10.11}$$

where we assume that p is an odd prime and a is a quadratic residue modulo p, which guarantees that the congruence has a solution. We shall distinguish the two cases $p \equiv 3 \bmod 4$ and $p \equiv 1 \bmod 4$. In the former, simpler, case, $x := a^{(p+1)/4} \bmod p$ solves the congruence, since

$$x^2 \equiv a^{(p+1)/2} \equiv a \cdot a^{(p-1)/2} \equiv a \bmod p, \tag{10.12}$$

where for $a^{(p-1)/2} \equiv \left(\frac{a}{p}\right) \equiv 1 \bmod p$ we have used property (vi) of the Legendre symbol, the Euler criterion, cited above.

The following considerations, taken from [Heid], lead to a general procedure for solving quadratic congruences, and in particular for solving congruences of the second case, $p \equiv 1 \bmod 4$: We write $p - 1 = 2^k q$, with $k \geq 1$ and q odd, and we look for an arbitrary quadratic nonresidue $n \bmod p$ by choosing a random number n with $1 \leq n < p$ and calculating the Legendre symbol $\left(\frac{n}{p}\right)$. This has value -1 with probability $\frac{1}{2}$, so that we should find such an n relatively quickly.

We set

$$x_0 \equiv a^{(q+1)/2} \bmod p,$$
$$y_0 \equiv n^q \bmod p,$$
$$z_0 \equiv a^q \bmod p, \tag{10.13}$$
$$r_0 := k.$$

Since by Fermat's little theorem we have $a^{(p-1)/2} \equiv x^{2(p-1)/2} \equiv x^{p-1} \equiv 1 \bmod p$ for a and for a solution x of (10.11), and since additionally, for quadratic nonresidues n we have $n^{(p-1)/2} \equiv -1 \bmod p$ (cf. (vi), page 221), we have

$$a z_0 \equiv x_0^2 \bmod p,$$
$$y_0^{2^{r_0-1}} \equiv -1 \bmod p, \tag{10.14}$$
$$z_0^{2^{r_0-1}} \equiv 1 \bmod p.$$

If $z_0 \equiv 1 \bmod p$, then x_0 is already a solution of the congruence (10.11). Otherwise, we recursively define numbers x_i, y_i, z_i, r_i such that

$$a z_i \equiv x_i^2 \bmod p,$$
$$y_i^{2^{r_i-1}} \equiv -1 \bmod p, \tag{10.15}$$
$$z_i^{2^{r_i-1}} \equiv 1 \bmod p,$$

and $r_i > r_{i-1}$. After at most k steps we must have $z_i \equiv 1 \bmod p$ and that x_i is a solution to (10.11). To this end we choose m_0 as the smallest natural number such that $z_0^{2^{m_0}} \equiv 1 \bmod p$, whereby $m_0 \leq r_0 - 1$. We set

$$x_{i+1} \equiv x_i y_i^{2^{r_i-m_i-1}} \bmod p,$$
$$y_{i+1} \equiv y_i^{2^{r_i-m_i}} \bmod p, \tag{10.16}$$
$$z_{i+1} \equiv z_i y_i^{2^{r_i-m_i}} \bmod p,$$

with $r_{i+1} := m_i := \min\left\{ m \geq 1 \mid z_i^{2^m} \equiv 1 \bmod p \right\}$. Then

$$x_{i+1}^2 \equiv x_i^2 y_i^{2^{r_i-m_i}} \equiv a z_i y_i^{2^{r_i-m_i}} \equiv a z_{i+1} \bmod p,$$
$$y_{i+1}^{2^{r_{i+1}-1}} \equiv y_{i+1}^{2^{m_i-1}} \equiv \left(y_i^{2^{r_i-m_i}} \right)^{2^{m_i-1}} \equiv y_i^{2^{r_i-1}} \equiv -1 \bmod p, \tag{10.17}$$
$$z_{i+1}^{2^{r_{i+1}-1}} \equiv z_{i+1}^{2^{m_i-1}} \equiv \left(z_i y_i^{2^{r_i-m_i}} \right)^{2^{m_i-1}} \equiv -z_i^{2^{m_i-1}} \equiv 1 \bmod p,$$

since $\left(z_i^{2^{m_i-1}} \right)^2 \equiv z_i^{2^{m_i}} \equiv 1 \bmod p$, and therefore by the minimality of m_i only $z_i^{2^{m_i-1}} \equiv -1 \bmod p$ is possible.

We have thus proved a solution procedure for quadratic congruence, on which the following algorithm of D. Shanks is based (presented here as in [Cohe], Algorithm 1.5.1).

Algorithm for calculating square roots of an integer a modulo an odd prime p

1. Write $p - 1 = 2^k q$, q odd. Choose random numbers n until $\left(\frac{n}{p}\right) = -1$.

2. Set $x \leftarrow a^{(q-1)/2} \bmod p$, $y \leftarrow n^q \bmod p$, $z \leftarrow a \cdot x^2 \bmod p$, $x \leftarrow a \cdot x \bmod p$, and $r \leftarrow k$.

3. If $z \equiv 1 \bmod p$, output x and terminate the algorithm. Otherwise, find the smallest m for which $z^{2^m} \equiv 1 \bmod p$. If $m = r$, then output the information that a is not a quadratic residue p and terminate the algorithm.

4. Set $t \leftarrow y^{2^{r-m-1}} \bmod p$, $y \leftarrow t^2 \bmod p$, $r \leftarrow m \bmod p$, $x \leftarrow x \cdot t \bmod p$, $z \leftarrow z \cdot y \bmod p$, and go to step 3.

It is clear that if x is a solution of the quadratic congruence, then so is $-x \bmod p$, since $(-x)^2 \equiv x^2 \bmod p$.

Out of practical considerations in the following implementation of the search for a quadratic nonresidue modulo p we shall begin with 2 and run through all the natural numbers testing the Legendre symbol in the hope of finding a nonresidue in polynomial time. In fact, this hope would be a certainty if we knew that the still unproved extended Riemann hypothesis were true (see, for example, [Bund], Section 7.3, Theorem 12, or [Kobl], Section 5.1, or [Kran], Section 2.10). To the extent that we doubt the truth of the extended Riemann hypothesis the algorithm of Shanks is probabilistic.

For the practical application in constructing the following function `proot_l()` we ignore these considerations and simply expect that the calculational time is polynomial. For further details see [Cohe], pages 33 f.

Function:	compute the square root of a modulo p
Syntax:	`int proot_l (CLINT a_l, CLINT p_l, CLINT x_l);`
Input:	`a_l, p_l` (operands, `p_l` > 2 a prime)
Output:	`x_l` (square root of `a_l` modulo `p_l`)
Return:	0 if `a_l` is a quadratic residue modulo `p_l`
	-1 otherwise

```
int
proot_l (CLINT a_l, CLINT p_l, CLINT x_l)
{
  CLINT b_l, q_l, t_l, y_l, z_l;
  int r, m;
  if (EQZ_L (p_l) || ISEVEN_L (p_l))
    {
      return -1;
    }
```

If a_l == 0, the result is 0.

```
  if (EQZ_L (a_l))
    {
      SETZERO_L (x_l);
      return 0;
    }
```

Step 1: Find a quadratic nonresidue.

```
  cpy_l (q_l, p_l);
  dec_l (q_l);
  r = twofact_l (q_l, q_l);
  cpy_l (z_l, two_l);
  while (jacobi_l (z_l, p_l) == 1)
    {
      inc_l (z_l);
    }
  mexp_l (z_l, q_l, z_l, p_l);
```

Step 2: Initialization of the recursion.

```
  cpy_l (y_l, z_l);
  dec_l (q_l);
  shr_l (q_l);
  mexp_l (a_l, q_l, x_l, p_l);
  msqr_l (x_l, b_l, p_l);
  mmul_l (b_l, a_l, b_l, p_l);
  mmul_l (x_l, a_l, x_l, p_l);
```

Step 3: End of the procedure; otherwise, find the smallest m such that
$z^{2^m} \equiv 1 \mod p$.

```
mod_l (b_l, p_l, q_l);
while (!equ_l (q_l, one_l))
  {
    m = 0;
    do
      {
        ++m;
        msqr_l (q_l, q_l, p_l);
      }
    while (!equ_l (q_l, one_l));

    if (m == r)
      {
        return -1;
      }
```

Step 4: Recursion step for x, y, z, and r.

```
    mexp2_l (y_l, (ULONG)(r - m - 1), t_l, p_l);
    msqr_l (t_l, y_l, p_l);
    mmul_l (x_l, t_l, x_l, p_l);
    mmul_l (b_l, y_l, b_l, p_l);
    cpy_l (q_l, b_l);
    r = m;
  }
  return 0;
}
```

The calculation of roots modulo prime powers p^k can now be accomplished on the basis of our results modulo p. To this end we first consider the congruence

$$x^2 \equiv a \mod p^2 \tag{10.18}$$

based on the following approach: Given a solution x_1 of the above congruence $x^2 \equiv a \mod p$ we set $x := x_1 + p \cdot x_2$, from which follows

$$x^2 - a \equiv x_1^2 - a + 2px_1x_2 + p^2x_2^2 \equiv p\left(\frac{x_1^2 - a}{p} + 2x_1x_2\right) \mod p^2.$$

From this we deduce that for solving (10.18) we will be helped by a solution x_2 of the *linear* congruence

$$x \cdot 2x_1 + \frac{x_1^2 - a}{p} \equiv 0 \bmod p.$$

Proceeding recursively one obtains in a number of steps a solution of the congruence $x^2 \equiv a \bmod p^k$ for any $k \in \mathbb{N}$.

10.4.3 Square Roots Modulo n

The ability to calculate square roots modulo a prime power is a step in the right direction for what we really want, namely, the solution of the more general problem $x^2 \equiv a \bmod n$ for a composite number n. However, we should say at once that the solution of such a quadratic congruence is in general a difficult problem. In principle, it is solvable, but it requires a great deal of computation, which grows exponentially with the size of n: The solution of the congruence is as difficult (in the sense of complexity theory) as factorization of the number n. Both problems lie in the complexity class NP (cf. page 103). The calculation of square roots modulo composite numbers is therefore related to a problem for whose solution there has still not been discovered a polynomial-time algorithm. Therefore, for large n we cannot expect to find a fast solution to this general case.

Nonetheless, it is possible to piece together solutions of quadratic congruences $y^2 \equiv a \bmod r$ and $z^2 \equiv a \bmod s$ with relatively prime numbers r and s to obtain a solution of the congruence $x^2 \equiv a \bmod rs$. Here we will be assisted by the *Chinese remainder theorem*:

> *Given congruences $x \equiv a_i \bmod m_i$ with natural numbers $m_1, \ldots, m_r$*
> *that are pairwise relatively prime (that is, $\gcd(m_i, m_j) = 1$ for $i \neq j$)*
> *and integers $a_1, \ldots, a_r$, there exists a common solution to the set of*
> *congruences, and furthermore, such a solution is unique modulo the*
> *product $m_1 \cdot m_2 \cdots m_r$.*

We would like to spend a bit of time in consideration of the proof of this theorem, for it contains hidden within itself in a remarkable way the promised solution: We set $m := m_1 \cdot m_2 \cdots m_r$ and $m_j' := m/m_j$. Then m_j' is an integer and $\gcd(m_j', m_j) = 1$. From Section 10.2 we know that that there exist integers u_j and v_j with $1 = m_j' u_j + m_j v_j$, that is, $m_j' u_j \equiv 1 \bmod m_j$, for $j = 1, \ldots, r$ and how to calculate them.

We then form the sum

$$x_0 := \sum_{j=1}^{r} m_j' u_j a_j,$$

and since $m'_j u_j \equiv 0 \bmod m_i$ for $i \neq j$, we obtain

$$x_0 \equiv \sum_{j=1}^{r} m'_j u_j a_j \equiv m'_i u_i a_i \equiv a_i \bmod m_i, \tag{10.19}$$

and in this way have constructed a solution to the problem. For two solutions $x_0 \equiv a_i \bmod m_i$ and $x_1 \equiv a_i \bmod m_i$ we have $x_0 \equiv x_1 \bmod m_i$. This is equivalent to the difference $x_0 - x_1$ being simultaneously divisible by all m_i, that is, by the least common multiple of the m_i. Due to the pairwise relative primality of the m_i we have that the least common multiple is, in fact, the product of the m_i, so that finally, we have that $x_0 \equiv x_1 \bmod m$ holds.

We now apply the Chinese remainder theorem to obtain a solution of $x^2 \equiv a \bmod rs$ with $\gcd(r, s) = 1$, where r and s are distinct odd primes and neither r nor s is a divisor of a, on the assumption that we have already obtained roots of $y^2 \equiv a \bmod r$ and $z^2 \equiv a \bmod s$. We now construct as above a common solution to the congruences

$$x \equiv y \bmod r,$$
$$x \equiv z \bmod s,$$

by

$$x_0 := (zur + yvs) \bmod rs,$$

where $1 = ur + vs$ is the representation of the greatest common divisor of r and s. We thus have $x_0^2 \equiv a \bmod r$ and $x_0^2 \equiv a \bmod s$, and since $\gcd(r, s) = 1$, we also have $x_0^2 \equiv a \bmod rs$, and so we have found a solution of the above quadratic congruence. Since as shown above every quadratic congruence modulo r and modulo s possesses two solutions, namely $\pm y$ and $\pm z$, the congruence modulo rs has four solutions, obtained by substituting in $\pm y$ and $\pm z$ above:

$$x_0 := zur + yvs \bmod rs, \tag{10.20}$$
$$x_1 := -zur - yvs \bmod rs = -x_0 \bmod rs, \tag{10.21}$$
$$x_2 := -zur + yvs \bmod rs, \tag{10.22}$$
$$x_3 := zur - yvs \bmod rs = -x_2 \bmod rs. \tag{10.23}$$

We have thus found in principle a way to reduce the solution of quadratic congruences $x^2 \equiv a \bmod n$ with n odd to the case $x^2 \equiv a \bmod p$ for primes p. For this we determine the prime factorization $n = p_1^{k_1} \cdots p_t^{k_t}$ and then calculate the roots modulo the p_i, which by the recursion in Section 10.4.2 can be used to obtain solutions of the congruences $x_2 \equiv a \bmod p_i^{k_i}$. As the crowning glory of all this we then assemble these solutions with the help of the Chinese remainder theorem into a solution of $x^2 \equiv a \bmod n$. The function that we give takes this path to solving a congruence $x^2 \equiv a \bmod n$. However, it assumes the restricted hypothesis that $n = p \cdot q$ is the product of two odd primes p and q, and first calculates solutions x_1 and x_2 of the congruences

$$x^2 \equiv a \bmod p,$$
$$x^2 \equiv a \bmod q.$$

From x_1 and x_2 we assemble according to the method just discussed the solutions to the congruence

$$x^2 \equiv a \bmod pq,$$

and the output is the smallest square root of a modulo pq.

Function: calculate the square root of a modulo $p \cdot q$
                for odd primes p, q

Syntax: `int root_l (CLINT a_l, CLINT p_l, CLINT q_l, CLINT x_l);`

Input: `a_l, p_l, q_l` (operands, primes `p_l, q_l` > 2)

Output: `x_l` (square root of `a_l` modulo `p_l * q_l`)

Return: 0 if `a_l` is a quadratic residue modulo `p_l * q_l`
                −1 otherwise

```
int
root_l (CLINT a_l, CLINT p_l, CLINT q_l, CLINT x_l)
 {
  CLINT x0_l, x1_l, x2_l, x3_l, xp_l, xq_l, n_l;
  CLINTD u_l, v_l;
  clint *xptr_l;
  int sign_u, sign_v;
```

Calculate the roots modulo `p_l` and `q_l` with the function `proot_l()`. If `a_l == 0`, the result is 0.

```
  if (0 != proot_l (a_l, p_l, xp_l) || 0 != proot_l (a_l, q_l, xq_l))
    {
      return -1;
    }
  if (EQZ_L (a_l))
    {
      SETZERO_L (x_l);
      return 0;
    }
```

For the application of the Chinese remainder theorem we must take into account the signs of the factors u_l and v_l, represented by the auxiliary variables sign_u and sign_v, which assume the values calculated by the function xgcd_l(). The result of this step is the root x_0.

```
mul_l (p_l, q_l, n_l);
xgcd_l (p_l, q_l, x0_l, u_l, &sign_u, v_l, &sign_v);
mul_l (u_l, p_l, u_l);
mul_l (u_l, xq_l, u_l);
mul_l (v_l, q_l, v_l);
mul_l (v_l, xp_l, v_l);

sign_u = sadd (u_l, sign_u, v_l, sign_v, x0_l);

smod (x0_l, sign_u, n_l, x0_l);
```

Now we calculate the roots x_1, x_2, and x_3.

```
sub_l (n_l, x0_l, x1_l);
msub_l (u_l, v_l, x2_l, n_l);
sub_l (n_l, x2_l, x3_l);
```

The smallest root is returned as result.

```
xptr_l = MIN_L (x0_l, x1_l);
xptr_l = MIN_L (xptr_l, x2_l);
xptr_l = MIN_L (xptr_l, x3_l);
cpy_l (x_l, xptr_l);

return 0;
}
```

From this we can now easily deduce an implementation of the Chinese remainder theorem by taking the code sequence from the above function and extending it by the number of congruences that are to be simultaneously solved. Such a procedure is described in the following algorithm, due to Garner (see [MOV], page 612), which has an advantage with respect to the application of the Chinese remainder theorem in the above form in that reduction must take place only modulo the m_i, and not modulo $m = m_1 m_2 \cdots m_r$. This results in a significant savings in computing time.

Algorithm 1 for a simultaneous solution of a system of linear congruences
$x \equiv a_i \bmod m_i, 1 \le i \le r,$ **with** $\gcd(m_i, m_j) = 1$ **for** $i \ne j$

1. Set $u \leftarrow a_1, x \leftarrow u,$ and $i \leftarrow 2$.

2. Set $C_i \leftarrow 1, j \leftarrow 1$.

3. Set $u \leftarrow m_j^{-1} \bmod m_i$ (computed by means of the extended Euclidean algorithm; see page 181) and $C_i \leftarrow uC_i \bmod m_i$.

4. Set $j \leftarrow j + 1$; if $j \le i - 1$, go to step 3.

5. Set $u \leftarrow (a_i - x) C_i \bmod m_i$, and $x \leftarrow x + u \prod_{j=1}^{i-1} m_j$.

6. Set $i \leftarrow i + 1$; if $i \le r$, go to step 2. Otherwise, output x.

It is not obvious that the algorithm does what it is supposed to, but this can be shown by an inductive argument. To this end let $r = 2$. In step 5 we then have

$$x = a_1 + ((a_2 - a_1) u \bmod m_2) m_1.$$

It is seen at once that $x \equiv a_1 \bmod m_1$. However, we also have

$$x \equiv a_1 + (a_2 - a_1)m_1 \left(m_1^{-1} \bmod m_2\right) \equiv a_2 \bmod m_2.$$

To finish the induction by passing from r to $r + 1$ we assume that the algorithm returns the desired result x_r for some $r \ge 2$, and we append a further congruence $x \equiv a_{r+1} \bmod m_{r+1}$. Then by step 5 we have

$$x \equiv x_r + \left(\left((a_{r+1} - x) \prod_{j=1}^{r} m_j^{-1} \right) \bmod m_{r+1} \right) \cdot \prod_{j=1}^{r} m_j.$$

Here we have $x \equiv x_r \equiv a_i \bmod m_i$ for $i = 1, \ldots, r$ according to our assumption. But we also have

$$x \equiv x_r + \left((a_{r+1} - x) \prod_{j=1}^{r} m_j \cdot \prod_{j=1}^{r} m_j^{-1} \right) \equiv a_{r+1} \bmod m_{r+1},$$

which completes the proof.

For the application of the Chinese remainder theorem in programs one function would be particularly useful, one that is not dependent on a predetermined number of congruences, but rather allows the number of congruences to be specified at run time. This method is supported by an adaptation of the above construction procedure, which does not, alas, have the advantage that reduction need take place only modulo m_i, but it does make it possible to process the parameters a_i and m_i of a system of congruences with $i = 1, \ldots, r$ with variable r with a constant memory expenditure. Such a solution is contained in the following algorithm from [Cohe], Section 1.3.3.

Algorithm 2 for calculating a simultaneous solution of a system of linear congruences $x \equiv a_i \bmod m_i, 1 \leq i \leq r,$ **with** $\gcd(m_i, m_j) = 1$ **for** $i \neq j$

1. Set $i \leftarrow 1, m \leftarrow m_1,$ and $x \leftarrow a_1.$

2. If $i = r,$ output x and terminate the algorithm. Otherwise, increase $i \leftarrow i+1$ and calculate u and v with $1 = um + vm_i$ using the extended Euclidean algorithm (cf. page 179).

3. Set $x \leftarrow uma_i + vm_ix, m \leftarrow mm_i, x \leftarrow x \bmod m$ and go to step 2.

The algorithm immediately becomes understandable if we carry out the computational steps for three equations $x = a_i \bmod m_i, i = 1, 2, 3$: For $i = 2$ we have in step 2

$$1 = u_1 m_1 + v_1 m_2$$

and in step 3

$$x_1 = u_1 m_1 a_2 + v_1 m_2 a_1 \bmod m_1 m_2.$$

In the next pass through the loop with $i = 3$ the parameters a_3 and m_3 are processed. In step 2 we then have

$$1 = u_2 m + v_2 m_3 = u_2 m_1 m_2 + v_2 m_3$$

and in step 3

$$x_2 = u_2 m a_3 + v_2 m_3 x_1 \bmod mm_1$$

$$= u_2 m_1 m_2 a_3 + v_2 m_3 u_1 m_1 a_2 + v_2 m_3 v_1 m_2 a_1 \bmod m_1 m_2 m_3.$$

The summands $u_2 m_1 m_2 a_3$ and $v_2 m_3 u_1 m_1 a_2$ disappear in forming the residue x_2 modulo m_1; furthermore, $v_2 m_3 \equiv v_1 m_2 \equiv 1 \bmod m_1$ by construction, and thus $x_2 \equiv a_1 \bmod m_1$ solves the first congruence. Analogous considerations lead us to see that x_2 also solves the remaining congruences.

We shall implement this inductive variant of the construction principle according to the Chinese remainder theorem in the following function chinrem_l(), whose interface enables the passing of coefficients of a variable number of congruences. For this a vector with an even number of pointers to CLINT objects is passed, which in the order $a_1, m_1, a_2, m_2, a_3, m_3, \ldots$ are processed as coefficients of congruences $x \equiv a_i \bmod m_i$. Since the number of digits of the solution of a congruence system $x \equiv a_i \bmod m_i$ is of order $\sum_i \log(m_i)$, the procedure is subject to overflow in its dependence on the number of congruences and the size of the parameters. Therefore, such errors will be noted and indicated in the return value of the function.

Function:	solution of linear congruences with the Chinese remainder theorem
Syntax:	int chinrem_l (int noofeq, clint **coeff_l, CLINT x_l);
Input:	noofeq (number of congruences) coeff_l (vector of pointers to CLINT coefficients a_i, m_i of congruences $x \equiv a_i \bmod m_i, i = 1, \ldots, $ noofeq)
Output:	x_l (solution of the system of congruences)
Return:	E_CLINT_OK if all is ok E_CLINT_OFL if overflow 1 if noofeq is 0 2 if mi are not pairwise relatively prime

```
int
chinrem_l (unsigned int noofeq, clint** coeff_l, CLINT x_l)
{
  clint *ai_l, *mi_l;
  CLINT g_l, u_l, v_l, m_l;
  unsigned int i;
  int sign_u, sign_v, sign_x, err, error = E_CLINT_OK;
  if (0 == noofeq)
    {
      return 1;
    }
```

Initialization: The coefficients of the first congruence are taken up.

```
cpy_l (x_l, *(coeff_l++));
cpy_l (m_l, *(coeff_l++));
```

If there are additional congruences, that is, if no_of_eq > 1, the parameters of the remaining congruences are processed. If one of the mi_l is not relatively prime to the previous moduli occurring in the product m_l, then the function is terminated and 2 is returned as error code.

```
for (i = 1; i < noofeq; i++)
  {
    ai_l = *(coeff_l++);
    mi_l = *(coeff_l++);
    xgcd_l (m_l, mi_l, g_l, u_l, &sign_u, v_l, &sign_v);
    if (!EQONE_L (g_l))
      {
        return 2;
      }
```

In the following an overflow error is recorded. At the end of the function the status is indicated in the return of the error code stored in error.

```
    err = mul_l (u_l, m_l, u_l);
    if (E_CLINT_OK == error)
      {
        error = err;
      }
    err = mul_l (u_l, ai_l, u_l);
    if (E_CLINT_OK == error)
      {
        error = err;
      }
    err = mul_l (v_l, mi_l, v_l);
    if (E_CLINT_OK == error)
      {
        error = err;
      }
    err = mul_l (v_l, x_l, v_l);
    if (E_CLINT_OK == error)
      {
        error = err;
      }
```

The auxiliary functions sadd() and smod() take care of the signs sign_u and sign_v (respectively sign_x) of the variables u_l and v_l (respectively 4).

```
    sign_x = sadd (u_1, sign_u, v_1, sign_v, x_1);
    err = mul_1 (m_1, mi_1, m_1);
    if (E_CLINT_OK == error)
    {
        error = err;
    }
    smod (x_1, sign_x, m_1, x_1);
  }
  return error;
}
```

10.4.4 Cryptography with Quadratic Residues

We come now to the promised examples for the cryptographic application of
quadratic residues and their roots. To this end we consider first the encryption
procedure of Rabin and then the identification schema of Fiat and Shamir.[4]

The encryption procedure published in 1979 by Michael Rabin (see [Rabi])
depends on the difficulty of calculating square roots in $\mathbb{Z}_{pq}$. Its most important
property is the *provable* equivalence of this calculation to the factorization
problem (see also [Kran], Section 5.6). Since for encryption the procedure
requires only a squaring modulo n, it is simple to implement, as the following
demonstrates.

Rabin key generation

1. Ms. A generates two large primes $p \approx q$ and computes $n = p \cdot q$.

2. Ms. A publishes n as a public key and uses the pair $\langle p, q \rangle$ as private key.

With the public key n_A a correspondent Mr. B can encode a message $M \in \mathbb{Z}_n$
in the following way and send it to Ms. A.

Rabin encryption

1. Mr. B computes $C := M^2 \bmod n_A$ with the function msqr_1() on page 77
   and sends the encrypted text C to A.

2. To decode the message, A computes from C the four square roots M_i
   modulo n_A, $i = 1, \ldots, 4$, with the aid of the function root_1() (cf. page
   205), which here is modified so that not only the smallest but all four square
   roots are output.[5] One of these roots is the plain text M.

---

[4] For the fundamental concepts of asymmetric cryptography, see Chapter 17.
[5] We may assume that gcd $(M, n_A) = 1$ and that therefore there really exist four distinct roots
   of C. Otherwise, the sender B could factor the modulus n_A of the receiver A by calculating
   gcd (M, n_A). This, of course, is not the way a public key system should operate.

Ms. A now has the problem of deciding which of the four roots M_i represents the original plain text M. If prior to encoding the message B adds some redundant material, say a repetition of the last r bits, and informs A of this, then A will have no trouble in choosing the right text, since the probability that one of the other texts will have the same identifier is very slight.

Furthermore, redundancy prevents the following attack strategy against the Rabin procedure: If an attacker X chooses at random a number $R \in \mathbb{Z}_{n_A}^{\times}$ and is able to obtain from A one of the roots R_i of $X := R^2 \bmod n_A$ (no matter how he or she may motivate A to cooperate), then $R_i \not\equiv \pm R \bmod n_A$ will hold with probability $\frac{1}{2}$.

From $n_A = p \cdot q \mid \left(R_i^2 - R^2 \right) = \left(R_i - R \right) \left(R_i + R \right) \neq 0$, however, one would have $1 \neq \gcd \left(R - R_i, n_A \right) \in \{\, p, q \,\}$, and X would have broken the code with the factorization of n_A (cf. [Bres], Section 5.2). On the other hand, if the plain text is provided with redundancy, then A can always recognize which root represents a valid plain text. Then A would at most reveal R (on the assumption that R had the right format), which for Mr. or Ms. X, however, would be useless.

The avoidance of deliberate or accidental access to the roots of a pretended cipher text is a necessary condition for the use of the procedure in the real world.

The following example of the cryptographic application of quadratic residues deals with an identification schema published in 1986 by Amos Fiat and Adi Shamir. The procedure, conceived especially for use in connection with smart cards, uses the following aid: Let I be a sequence of characters with information for identifying an individual A, let m be the product of two large primes p and q, and let $f(Z, n) \to \mathbb{Z}_m$ be a random function that maps arbitrary finite sequences of characters Z and natural numbers n in some unpredictable fashion to elements of the residue class ring $\mathbb{Z}_m$. The prime factors p and q of the modulus m are known to a central authority, but are otherwise kept secret. For the identity represented by I and a yet to be determined $k \in \mathbb{N}$ the central authority has now the task of producing key components as follows.

Algorithm for key generation in the Fiat–Shamir procedure

1. Compute numbers $v_i = f(I, i) \in \mathbb{Z}_m$ for some $i \geq k \in \mathbb{N}$.

2. Choose k different quadratic residues $v_{i_1}, \ldots, v_{i_k}$ from among the v_i and compute the smallest square roots $s_{i_1}, \ldots, s_{i_k}$ of $v_{i_1}^{-1}, \ldots, v_{i_k}^{-1}$ in $\mathbb{Z}_m$.

3. Store the values I and $s_{i_1}, \ldots, s_{i_k}$ securely against unauthorized access (such as in a smart card).

For generating keys s_{i_j} we can use our functions jacobi_1() and root_1(); the function f can be constructed from one of the *hash functions* from Chapter 17, such as RIPEMD-160. As Adi Shamir once said at a conference, "Any crazy function will do."

With the help of the information stored by the central authority on the smart card Ms. A can now authenticate herself to a communication partner Mr. B.

Protocol for authentication à la Fiat–Shamir

1. A sends I and the numbers i_j, $j = 1, \ldots, k$, to B.

2. B generates $v_{i_j} = f(I, i_j) \in \mathbb{Z}_m$ for $j = 1, \ldots, k$. The following steps 3–6 are repeated for $\tau = 1, \ldots, t$ (for a value $t \in \mathbb{N}$ yet to be determined):

3. A chooses a random number $r_\tau \in \mathbb{Z}_m$ and sends $x_\tau = r_\tau^2$ to B.

4. B sends a binary vector $(e_{\tau_1}, \ldots, e_{\tau_k})$ to A.

5. A sends numbers $y_\tau := r_\tau \prod_{e_{\tau_i} = 1} s_i \in \mathbb{Z}_m$ to B.

6. B verifies that $x_\tau = y_\tau^2 \prod_{e_{\tau_i} = 1} v_i$.

If A truly possesses the values $s_{i_1}, \ldots, s_{i_k}$, then in step 6

$$y_\tau^2 \prod_{e_{\tau_i}=1} v_i = r_\tau^2 \prod_{e_{\tau_i}=1} s_i^2 \cdot \prod_{e_{\tau_i}=1} v_i = r_\tau^2 \prod_{e_{\tau_i}=1} v_i^{-1} v_i = r_\tau^2$$

holds (all calculations are in $\mathbb{Z}_m$), and A thereby has proved her identity to B. An attacker who wishes to assume the identity of A can with probability 2^{-kt} *guess* the vectors $(e_{\tau_1}, \ldots, e_{\tau_k})$ that B will send in step 4, and as a precaution in step 3 send the values $x_\tau = r_\tau^2 \prod_{e_{\tau_i}=1} v_i$ to B; for $k = t = 1$, for example, this would give the attacker an average hit number of $\frac{1}{2}$. Thus the values of k and t should be chosen such that an attacker has no realistic probability of success and such that furthermore—depending on the application—suitable values result for

- the size of the secret key;

- the set of data to be exchanged between A and B;

- the required computer time, measured as the number of multiplications.

Such parameters are given in [Fiat] for various values of k and t with $kt = 72$.

All in all, the security of the procedure depends on the secure storage of the values s_{i_j}, on the choice of k and t, and on the factorization problem: Anyone who can factor the modulus m into the factors p and q can compute the secret key components s_{i_j}, and the procedure has been broken. It is a matter, then, of choosing the modulus in such a way that it is not easily factorable. In this regard the reader is again referred to Chapter 17, where we discuss the generation of RSA moduli, subject to the same requirements.

A further security property of the procedure of Fiat and Shamir is that A can repeat the process of authentication as often as she wishes without thereby giving away any information about the secret key values. Algorithms with such properties are called *zero knowledge processes* (see, for example, [Schn], Section 32.11).

10.5 A Primality Test

Primes is in P

— M. Agrawa, N. Kaval, N. Saxena, 2002

Not to stretch out the suspense, the largest known Mersenne prime, M_{11213}, and, I believe, the largest prime known at present, has 3375 digits and is therefore just about T-281$\frac{1}{4}$.[6]

— Isaac Asimov, *Adding a Dimension*, 1964

Forty-First Known Mersenne Prime Found!!

— http://www.mersenne.org/prime.htm (May 2004)

The study of prime numbers and their properties is one of the oldest branches of number theory and one of fundamental significance for cryptography. From the seemingly harmless definition of a prime number as a natural number greater than 1 that has no divisors other than itself and 1 there arises a host of questions and problems with which mathematicians have been grappling for centuries and many of which remain unanswered and unsolved to this day. Examples of such questions are, "Are there infinitely many primes?" "How are the primes distributed among the natural numbers?" "How can one tell whether a number is prime?" "How can one identify a natural number that is not prime, that is, a number that is composite?" "How does one find all the prime factors of a composite number?"

That there are infinitely many primes was proven already by Euclid about 2300 years ago (see, for example, [Bund], page 5, and especially the amusing proof variant and the serious proof variant on pages 39 and 40). Another important fact, which up to now we have tacitly assumed, will be mentioned here explicitly: The fundamental theorem of arithmetic states that every natural number greater than 1 has a unique decomposition as a product of finitely many prime numbers, where the uniqueness is up to the order of the factors. Thus prime numbers are truly the building blocks of the natural numbers.

As long as we stick close to home in the natural numbers and do not stray among numbers that are too big for us to deal with easily we can approach a number of questions empirically and carry out concrete calculations. Take note, however, that the degree to which results are achievable depends in large measure on the efficiency of the algorithms used and the capacities of available computers.

---

[6]   T is for *trillion*, whereby Asimov denotes the order of magnitude 10^{12}. Thus T-281$\frac{1}{4}$ stands for $10^{12 \cdot 281.25} = 10^{3375} \approx 2^{11211.5}$.

A list of the largest numbers identified as prime, published on the Internet, demonstrates the impressive size of the most recent discoveries (see Table 10-1 and `http://www.mersenne.org`).

Table 10-1. The ten largest known primes (as of December 2004)

Prime	Digits	Discoverer	Year
$2^{24\,036\,583} - 1$	7 235 733	Findley	2004
$2^{20\,996\,011} - 1$	6 320 430	Shafer	2003
$2^{13\,466\,917} - 1$	4 053 946	Cameron, Kurowski	2001
$2^{6\,972\,593} - 1$	2 098 960	Hajratwala, Woltman, Kurowski	1999
$5\,539 \cdot 2^{5\,054\,502} + 1$	1 521 561	Sundquist	2003
$2^{3\,021\,377} - 1$	909 526	Clarkson, Woltman, Kurowski	1998
$2^{2\,976\,221} - 1$	895 932	Spence, Woltman	1997
$1\,372\,930^{131\,072} + 1$	804 474	Heuer	2003
$1\,361\,244^{131\,072} + 1$	803 988	Heuer	2004
$1\,176\,694^{131\,072} + 1$	795 695	Heuer	2003

The largest known prime numbers are of the form $2^p - 1$. Primes that can be represented in this way are called *Mersenne* primes, named for Marin Mersenne (1588–1648), who discovered this particular structure of prime numbers in his search for perfect numbers. (A natural number is said to be *perfect* if it equals the sum of its proper divisors. Thus, for example, 496 is a perfect number, since $496 = 1 + 2 + 4 + 8 + 16 + 31 + 62 + 124 + 248$.)

For every divisor t of p we have that $2^t - 1$ is a divisor of $2^p - 1$, since if $p = ab$, then

$$2^p - 1 = (2^a - 1)\left(2^{a(b-1)} + 2^{a(b-2)} + \cdots + 1\right).$$

Therefore, we see that $2^p - 1$ can be prime only if p is prime. Mersenne himself announced in 1644, without being in possession of a complete proof, that for $p \leq 257$ the only primes of the form $2^p - 1$ were those for the primes $p \in \{\,2, 3, 5, 7, 13, 17, 19, 31, 67, 127, 257\,\}$. With the exception of $p = 67$ and $p = 257$, for which $2^p - 1$ is not prime, Mersenne's conjecture has been verified, and analogous results for many additional exponents have been established as well (see [Knut], Section 4.5.4, and [Bund], Section 3.2.12).

On the basis of the discoveries thus far of Mersenne primes one may conjecture that there exist Mersenne primes for infinitely many prime numbers p. However, there is as yet no proof of this conjecture (see [Rose], Section 1.2). An interesting overview of additional unsolved problems in the realm of prime numbers can be found in [Rose], Chapter 12.

Because of their importance in cryptographic public key algorithms prime numbers and their properties have come increasingly to public attention, and it is a pleasure to see how algorithmic number theory in regard to this and other topics has become popular as never before. The problems of identifying a number as prime and the decomposition of a number into its prime factors are the problems that have attracted the greatest interest. The cryptographic invulnerability of many public key algorithms (foremost among them the famous RSA procedure) is based on the fact that factorization is a difficult problem (in the sense of complexity theory), which at least at present is unsolvable in polynomial time.[7]

Until recently, the same held true, in a weakened form, for the identification of a number as prime if one were looking for a definitive proof that a number is prime. On the other hand, there are tests that determine, up to a small degree of uncertainty, whether a number is prime; furthermore, if the test determines that the number is composite, then that determination is definitive. Such probabilistic tests are, in compensation for the element of doubt, executable in polynomial time, and the probability of a "false positive" can be brought below any given positive bound, as we shall see, by repeating the test a sufficient number of times.

A venerable, but nonetheless still useful, method of determining all primes up to a given natural number N was developed by the Greek philosopher and astronomer Eratosthenes (276–195 B.C.E.; see also [Saga]), and in his honor it is known as the *sieve of Eratosthenes*. Beginning with a list of all natural numbers greater than 1 and less than or equal to N, we take the first prime number, namely 2, and strike from the list all multiples of 2 greater than 2 itself. The first remaining number above the prime number just used (2 in this case) is then identified as a prime p, whose multiples $p(p + 2i)$, $i = 0, 1, \ldots$, are likewise struck from the list. This process is continued until a prime number greater than $\sqrt{N}$ is found, at which point the procedure is terminated. The numbers in the list that have not been struck are the primes less than or equal to N. They have been "caught" in the sieve.

We would like to elucidate briefly why it is that the sieve of Eratosthenes works as advertised: First, an induction argument makes it immediately plain that the next unstruck number above a prime is itself prime, since otherwise, the number would have a smaller prime divisor and thus would already have been struck from the list as a multiple of this prime factor. Since only composite numbers are struck, no prime numbers can be lost in the process.

Furthermore, it suffices to strike out only multiples of primes p for which $p \leq \sqrt{N}$, since if T is the smallest proper divisor of N, then $T \leq \sqrt{N}$. Thus if a composite number $n \leq N$ were to remain unstruck, then this number would have a smallest prime divisor $p \leq \sqrt{n} \leq \sqrt{N}$, and n would have been struck as a

---

[7] For a discussion of the complexity-theoretic aspects of cryptography one might have a look at [HKW], Chapter 6, or [Schn], Sections 19.3 and 20.8, and the many further references therein. One should also read the footnote in the present book on page 191.

multiple of p, in contradiction to our assumption. Now we would like to consider how this sieve might be implemented, and as preparation we shall develop a programmable algorithm, for which we take the following viewpoint: Since except for 2 there are no even prime numbers, we shall consider only odd numbers as candidates for primality. Instead of making a list of odd numbers, we form the list $f_i, 1 \leq i \leq \lfloor (N-1)/2 \rfloor$, which represents the primality property of the numbers $2i + 1$. Further, we use a variable p that will contain the current value $2i + 1$ of our (imagined) list of odd numbers, as well as a variable s for which the relation $2s + 1 = p^2 = (2i + 1)^2$, that is, $s = 2i^2 + 2i$, always holds. We may now formulate the following algorithm (cf. [Knut], Section 4.5.4, Exercise 8).

Sieve of Eratosthenes, algorithm for calculating all prime numbers less than or equal to a natural number N

1. Set $L \leftarrow \lfloor (N-1)/2 \rfloor$ and $B \leftarrow \lceil \sqrt{N}/2 \rceil$. Set $f_i \leftarrow 1$ for $1 \leq i \leq L$. Set $i \leftarrow 1, p \leftarrow 3$, and $s \leftarrow 4$.

2. If $f_i = 0$, go to step 4. Otherwise, output p as a prime and set $k \leftarrow s$.

3. If $k \leq L$, set $f_k \leftarrow 0, k \leftarrow k + p$, and repeat step 3.

4. If $i \leq B$, then set $i \leftarrow i + 1, s \leftarrow s + 2p, p \leftarrow p + 2$, and go to step 2. Otherwise, terminate the algorithm.

The algorithm leads us to the following program, which as result returns a pointer to a list of ULONG values that contains, in ascending order, all primes below the input value. The first number in the list is the number of prime numbers found.

Function:	prime number generator (sieve of Eratosthenes)
Syntax:	ULONG * genprimes (ULONG N;)
Input:	N (upper bound for the prime search)
Return:	a pointer to vector of ULONG values with primes less than or equal to N. (At position 0 the vector contains the number of primes found.)
	NULL, if an error with malloc().

```
ULONG *
genprimes (ULONG N)
{
  ULONG i, k, p, s, B, L, count;
  char *f;
  ULONG *primes;
```

Step 1: Initialization of the variables. The auxiliary function `ul_iroot()` computes the integer part of the square root of a `ULONG` variable. For this it uses the procedure elucidated in Section 10.3. Then comes the allocation of the vector f for marking the composite numbers.

```
B = (1 + ul_iroot (N)) >> 1;
L = N >> 1;
if (((N & 1) == 0) && (N > 0))
  {
     --L;
  }

if ((f = (char *) malloc ((size_t) L+1)) == NULL)
  {
     return (ULONG *) NULL;
  }

for (i = 1;  i <= L;  i++)
  {
     f[i] = 1;
  }
p = 3;
s = 4;
```

Steps 2, 3, and 4 constitute the actual sieve. The variable i represents the numerical value $2i + 1$.

```
for (i = 1;  i <= B;  i++)
  {
    if (f[i])
      {
        for (k = s;  k <= L;  k += p)
          {
             f[k] = 0;
          }
      }
  s += p + p + 2;
  p += 2;
}
```

Now the number of primes found is reported, and a field of ULONG variables of commensurate size is allocated.

```
for (count = i = 1; i <= L; i++)
  {
    count += f[i];
  }
if ((primes = (ULONG*)malloc ((size_t)(count+1) * sizeof (ULONG))) == NULL)
  {
    return (ULONG*)NULL;
  }
```

The field f[ ] is evaluated, and all the numbers $2i + 1$ marked as primes are stored in the field primes. If $N \geq 2$, then the number 2 is counted as well.

```
for (count = i = 1; i <= L; i++)
  {
    if (f[i])
      {
        primes[++count] = (i << 1) + 1;
      }
  }
if (N < 2)
  {
    primes[0] = 0;
  }
else
  {
    primes[0] = count;
    primes[1] = 2;
  }
  free (f);
  return primes;
}
```

To determine whether a number n is composite it is sufficient, according to what we have said above, to institute a division test that divides n by all prime numbers less than or equal to $\sqrt{n}$. If one fails to find a divisor, then n is itself prime; the prime test divisors are given to us by the sieve of Eratosthenes. However, this method is not practicable, since the number of primes that have to be tested becomes rapidly too large. In particular, we have the *prime number theorem*, formulated as a conjecture by A. M. Legendre, that the number $\pi\,(x)$ of primes p, $2 \leq p \leq x$, approaches $x/\ln x$ asymptotically as x goes to infinity (see, for example, [Rose], Chapter 12).[8] A few values of the number of primes less than a given x will help to make clear the size of numbers we are dealing with. Table 10-2 gives the values of both $\pi\,(x)$, the actual number of primes less than or equal to x, and the asymptotic approximation $x/\ln x$. The question mark in the last cell indicates a number to be filled in by the reader. ;-)

Table 10-2. The number of primes up to various limits x

x	10^2	10^4	10^8	10^{16}	10^{18}	10^{100}
$x/\ln x$	22	1,086	5,428,681	271,434,051,189,532	24,127,471,216,847,323	4×10^{97}
$\pi\,(x)$	25	1,229	5,761,455	279,238,341,033,925	24,739,954,287,740,860	?

The number of necessary calculations for the division test of x grows almost with the number of digits of x in the exponent. Therefore, the division test alone is not a practicable method for determining the primality of large numbers. We shall see, in fact, that the division test is an important aid in connection with other tests, but in principle we would be content to have a test that gave information about the primality of a number without revealing anything about its factorization. An improvement in the situation is offered by the little theorem of Fermat, which tells us that for a prime p and all numbers a that are not multiples of p the congruence $a^{p-1} \equiv 1 \bmod p$ holds (see page 177).

From this fact we can derive a primality test, called the Fermat test: If for some number a we have $\gcd(a, n) \neq 1$ or $\gcd(a, n) = 1$ and $1 \not\equiv a^{n-1} \bmod n$, then n is composite. An exponentiation $a^{n-1} \equiv 1 \bmod n$ requires $O\left(\log^3 n\right)$ CPU operations, and experience indicates that in only a few tries a composite number will reveal its lack of primality. However, there are exceptions, and these limit the utility of the Fermat test. Therefore, we shall have to have a closer look at them.

We must face the fact that the converse of Fermat's little theorem does not hold: Not every number n with $\gcd(a, n) = 1$ and $a^{n-1} \equiv 1 \bmod n$ for $1 \leq a \leq n - 1$ is prime. There exist composite numbers n that pass the Fermat test as long as a and n are relatively prime. Such numbers are called Carmichael numbers, named for their discoverer, Robert Daniel Carmichael (1879–1967). The smallest of these curious objects are

$$561 = 3 \cdot 11 \cdot 17, \quad 1105 = 5 \cdot 13 \cdot 17, \quad 1729 = 7 \cdot 13 \cdot 19.$$

All Carmichael numbers have in common the property that each of them possesses at least three different prime factors (see [Kobl], Chapter 5). It was only

---

[8] The prime number theorem was proved independently in 1896 by Jacques Hadamard and Charles-Jacques de la Vallée Poussin (see [Bund], Section 7.3).

in the early 1990s that it was proven that there are infinitely many Carmichael numbers (see [Bund], Section 2.3).

The relative frequency of numbers less than n that are relatively prime to n is

$$1 - \frac{\phi(n)}{n-1} \tag{10.24}$$

(for the Euler ϕ function see page 177), so that the proportion of numbers that are not relatively prime to n is close to 0 for large n. Therefore, in most cases one must run through the Fermat test very often to determine that a Carmichael number is composite. Letting a run through the range $2 \leq a \leq n - 1$, eventually, one encounters the smallest prime divisor of n, and it is only when a assumes this value that n is exposed as composite.

In addition to the Carmichael numbers there are further odd composite numbers n for which there exist natural numbers a with $\gcd(a, n) = 1$ and $a^{n-1} \equiv 1 \bmod n$. Such numbers are known as *pseudoprimes to the base a*. To be sure, one can make the observation that there are only a few pseudoprimes to the bases 2 and 3, or that, for example, up to 25×10^9 there are only 1770 integers that are simultaneously pseudoprimes to the bases 2, 3, 5, and 7 (see [Rose], Section 3.4), yet the sad fact remains that there is no general estimate of the number of solutions of the Fermat congruence for composite numbers. Thus the problem with the Fermat test is that the uncertainty as to whether the method of random tests will reveal a composite number as such cannot be correlated with the number of tests.

However, such a connection is offered on the basis of the Euler criterion (see Section 10.4.1): For an odd prime p and for all integers a that are not multiples of p, we have

$$a^{(p-1)/2} \equiv \left(\frac{a}{p}\right) \bmod p, \tag{10.25}$$

where $\left(\frac{a}{p}\right) \equiv \pm 1 \bmod p$ denotes the Legendre–Jacobi symbol. In analogy to Fermat's little theorem we obtain an exclusionary criterion by taking the contrapositive of the following statement:

> If for a natural number n there exists an integer a with $\gcd(a, n) = 1$ and $a^{(n-1)/2} \equiv \left(\frac{a}{n}\right) \bmod n$, then n cannot be a prime number.

The required computational expenditure for establishing this criterion is the same as that for the Fermat test, namely $O\left(\log^3 n\right)$.

As with the Fermat test, where there is the problem of pseudoprimes, there exist integers n that for certain a satisfy the Euler criterion although they are composite. Such n are called *Euler pseudoprimes* to the base a. An example is

$n = 91 = 7 \cdot 13$ to the bases 9 and 10, for which we have $9^{45} \equiv \left(\frac{9}{91}\right) \equiv 1 \bmod 91$ and $10^{45} \equiv \left(\frac{10}{91}\right) \equiv -1 \bmod 91$.[9]

An Euler pseudoprime to a base a is always a pseudoprime to the base a (see page 221), since by squaring $a^{(n-1)/2} \equiv \left(\frac{a}{n}\right) \bmod n$ it follows that $a^{n-1} \equiv 1 \bmod n$.

There is, however, no counterpart to the Carmichael numbers for the Euler criterion, and based on the following observations of R. Solovay and V. Strassen we can see that the risk of a false test result for Euler pseudoprimes is favorably bounded from above.

(i) For a composite number n the number of integers a relatively prime to n for which $a^{(n-1)/2} \equiv \left(\frac{a}{n}\right) \bmod n$ is at most $\frac{1}{2}\phi(n)$ (see [Kobl], Section 2.2, Exercise 21). From this we have the following proposition.

(ii) The probability that for a composite number n and k randomly selected numbers $a_1, \ldots, a_k$ relatively prime to n one has $a_r^{(n-1)/2} \equiv \left(\frac{a_r}{n}\right) \bmod n$, for $1 \le r \le k$, is at most 2^{-k}.

These results make it possible to implement the Euler criterion as a probabilistic primality test, where "probabilistic" means that if the test returns that result "n is not prime," then this result is definitive, but it is only with a certain probability of error that we may infer that n is in fact prime.

Algorithm: Probabilistic primality test à la Solvay–Strassen for testing a natural number n for compositeness

1. Choose a random number $a \le n - 1$ with $\gcd(a, n) = 1$.

2. If has $a^{(n-1)/2} \equiv \left(\frac{a}{n}\right) \bmod n$, then output "$n$ is a probable prime." Otherwise, output "n is composite."

This test requires computation time $O\left(\log^3 n\right)$ for the calculation of the exponent and the Jacobi symbol. By repeated application of this test we can reduce the probability of error in step (ii). For example, for $k = 60$ we obtain a vanishingly small probability of error less than $2^{-60} \approx 10^{-18}$, and D. Knuth has indicated that this value is less than that of a transient hardware error, caused, for example, by an alpha particle that has found its way into the CPU or memory of a computer and thereby switched the value of a bit.

We might be satisfied with this test, since we have control over the probability of error and we have efficient algorithms for all the required computations. However, there are results that lead to a more efficient algorithm. For this we

---

[9] We have $9^3 \equiv 10^6 \equiv 1 \bmod 91$, since 3 is the order of 9 and 6 is the order of 10 in $\mathbb{Z}_{91}$. Therefore, $9^{45} \equiv 9^{3 \cdot 15} \equiv 1 \bmod 91$ and $10^{45} \equiv 10^{6 \cdot 7 + 3} \equiv 10^3 \equiv -1 \bmod 91$.

would like to introduce a few considerations that will improve our understanding of the most widely used probabilistic primality tests

Let us make the hypothesis that n is prime. Then by Fermat's little theorem we have $a^{n-1} \equiv 1 \bmod n$ for integers a that are not multiples of n. The square root of $a^{n-1} \bmod n$ can assume only the value 1 or -1, since these are the only solutions of the congruence $x^2 \equiv 1 \bmod n$ (see Section 10.4.1). If we also compute from $a^{n-1} \bmod n$ the successive square roots

$$a^{(n-1)/2} \bmod n, \quad a^{(n-1)/4} \bmod n, \quad \ldots, \quad a^{(n-1)/2^t} \bmod n,$$

one after another until $(n-1)/2^t$ is odd, and if in the process we arrive at a residue not equal to 1, then this residue must have the value -1, for otherwise, n cannot be prime, which we have hypothesized. For the case that the first square root different from 1 has the value -1, we stick by our hypothesis that n is prime. If n is nevertheless composite, then we shall call n on the basis of this special property a *strong pseudoprime to the base* a. Strong pseudoprimes to a base a are always Euler pseudoprimes to the base a (see [Kobl], Chapter 5).

We assemble all of this into the following probabilistic primality test, though for the sake of efficiency we shall first compute the power $b = a^{(n-1)/2^t} \bmod n$ with odd $(n-1)/2^t$, and if this is not equal to 1, we continue to square b until we obtain a value of ± 1 or have reached $a^{(n-1)/2} \bmod n$. In the last case we must have either $b = -1$ or that n is composite. The idea of shortening the algorithm so that the last square does not have to be calculated has been taken from [Cohe], Section 8.2.

Probabilistic primality test à la Miller–Rabin for odd integers $n > 1$

1. Determine q and t with $n - 1 = 2^t q$, with q odd.

2. Choose a random integer a, $1 < a < n$. Set $e \leftarrow 0$, $b \leftarrow a^q \bmod n$. If $b = 1$, output "n is probably prime" and terminate the algorithm.

3. As long as we have $b \not\equiv \pm 1 \bmod n$ and $e < t - 1$, set $b \leftarrow b^2 \bmod n$ and $e \leftarrow e + 1$. If now $b \neq n - 1$, then output "n is composite." Otherwise, output "n is probably prime."

With a running time of $O\left(\log^3 n\right)$ for the exponentiations, the Miller–Rabin test (MR test for short) has complexity the same order of magnitude as the Solovay–Strassen test.

The existence of strong pseudoprimes means that the Miller–Rabin primality test offers us certainty only about the compositeness of numbers. The number 91, which we trotted out above as an example of an Euler pseudoprime (to base 9) is also—again to base 9—a strong pseudoprime. Further examples of strong pseudoprimes are

$$2152302898747 = 6763 \cdot 10627 \cdot 29947$$

and

$$3474749660383 = 1303 \cdot 16927 \cdot 157543.$$

These two numbers are the only pseudoprimes below 10^{13} to the prime bases $2, 3, 5, 7$, and 11 (see [Rose], Section 3.4).

Fortunately, the number of bases of strong pseudoprimes is again diminished by these numbers themselves. M. Rabin has proved that for a composite number n there are fewer than $n/4$ bases a, $2 \leq a \leq n-1$, to which n is a strong pseudoprime (see [Knut], Section 4.5.4, Exercise 22, and [Kobl], Chapter 5). From this we obtain with k-fold repetition of the test with k randomly chosen bases $a_1, \ldots, a_k$ a probability smaller than 4^{-k} that a strong pseudoprime has been falsely accepted as a prime. Therefore, for the same amount of work, the Miller–Rabin test is superior to the Solovay–Strassen test, which with k repetitions has probability of error bounded by 2^{-k}.

In practice, the Miller–Rabin test does much better than advertised, since the actual probability of error is in most cases much smaller than that guaranteed by the theorem of Rabin (see [MOV], Section 4.4, and [Schn], Section 11.5).

Before we get down to implementing the Miller–Rabin test, we look at two approaches to improving efficiency.

By beginning the Miller–Rabin test with a division sieve that divides the prime candidates by small primes, we obtain an advantage: If a factor is found in the process, then the candidate can be eliminated from consideration without the expense of a Miller–Rabin test. The question at once presents itself as to how many prime numbers would be optimal to divide by before undertaking the MR test. We give a recommendation due to A. K. Lenstra: The greatest efficiency is achieved if one divides by the 303 prime numbers less than 2000 (see [Schn], Section 11.5). The reason for this arises from the observation that the relative frequency of odd numbers without prime divisors less than the bound n is about $1.12/\ln n$. Dividing by prime numbers under 2000 eliminates about 85 percent of all composite numbers without using the MR test, which is then used only on the remaining candidates.

Each division by a small divisor requires computation time of order only $O(\ln n)$. We make use of an efficient division routine especially for small divisors and use it in instituting the division sieve.

The division sieve is implemented in the following function `sieve_1()`. It, in turn, uses the primes less than 65536 stored in the field `smallprimes[NOOFSMALLPRIMES]`. The primes are stored as differences, where for each prime only a byte of storage is required. The diminished access to these primes is not a serious problem, since we are using them in their natural order. The case that the candidate itself is a small prime and is contained in the prime number table must be specially indicated.

Finally, we profit from the exponentiation function for small bases (see Chapter 6) by applying the MR test with small primes $2, 3, 5, 7, 11, \ldots < B$

instead of randomly selected bases. According to experience this in no way impairs the results of the test.

We now introduce the division sieve. The function uses the division routine for short divisors that we developed for the function div_l().

Function:	division sieve
Syntax:	USHORT sieve_l (CLINT a_l, unsigned no_of_smallprimes);
Input:	a_l (candidate for primality search)
	no_of_smallprimes (number of primes to serve as divisors, without 2)
Return:	prime factor, if one is found
	1, if the candidate itself is prime
	0, if no factor is found

```
USHORT
sieve_l (CLINT a_l, unsigned int no_of_smallprimes)
{
  clint *aptr_l;
  USHORT bv, rv, qv;
  ULONG rhat;
  unsigned int i = 1;
```

For the sake of completeness we first test whether a_1 is a multiple of 2. If, in fact, a_1 has the value 2, then 1 is returned, while if a_1 is greater than 2 and is even, then 2 is returned as a factor.

```
if (ISEVEN_L (a_l))
  {
    if (equ_l (a_l, two_l))
      {
        return 1;
      }
    else
      {
        return 2;
      }
  }
bv = 2;
do
  {
```

> The prime numbers are computed by successive addition of the numbers stored
> in smallprimes[] and stored in bv. The first prime that serves as a divisor is 3. We
> use the code of the fast routine for division by a USHORT (see Section 4.3).

```
    rv = 0;
    bv += smallprimes[i];
    for (aptr_l = MSDPTR_L (a_l); aptr_l >= LSDPTR_L (a_l); aptr_l--)
      {
        qv = (USHORT)((rhat = (((((ULONG)rv) << BITPERDGT) + (ULONG)*aptr_l)) / bv);
        rv = (USHORT)(rhat - (ULONG)bv * (ULONG)qv);
      }
  }
while (rv != 0 && ++i <= no_of_smallprimes);
```

> If an actual divisor was found (rv == 0 and bv $\neq$ a_l; otherwise, a_l itself is
> prime!), this is returned. If a_l is itself a small prime, then 1 is returned. Otherwise,
> 0 is returned.

```
  if (0 == rv)
    }
      if (DIGITS_L (a_l) == 1 && *LSDPTR_L (a_l) == bv)
        }
          bv = 1;
        }
      /* else: result in bv is a prime factor of a_l */
    }
  else /* no factor of a_l was found */
    }
      bv = 0;
    }
  return bv;
}
```

The function sieve_l() can be used for splitting off prime factors under
65536 from CLINT objects. To enable this, the macro SFACTOR_L(n_l) is defined
in flint.h, which uses the call sieve_l(n_l, NOOFSMALLPRIMES) to test divide
n_l by the primes stored in smallprimes[]; SFACTOR_L() returns the same value
as sieve_l(). By repeated calls to SFACTOR_L() with subsequent division by the
factors found, integers below 2^{32}, that is, integers that can be represented by the
standard integer types, can be completely factored. If no factor is found, then we
are dealing with a prime number.

The full-blown test function `prime_l()` integrates the division sieve and the Miller–Rabin test. To retain maximum flexibility the function is constituted in such a way that the number of divisions in the pretest and the number of passes through the Miller–Rabin test can be passed as parameters. To simplify the situation in applications, the macro `ISPRIME_L(CLINT n_l)` can be used, which in turn calls the function `prime_l()` with preset parameters.

There is differing advice in the literature in relation to the open question of how many repetitions of the Miller–Rabin test should be made in order to ensure reliable results. For example, [Gord] and [Schn] recommend five repetitions for cryptographic purposes, while the algorithm in [Cohe] prescribes 25 passes. In [Knut], the recommendation is that in 25 passes through the test, the number of errors for a set of a billion candidates accepted as prime numbers is under 10^{-6}, although the value 25 is not explicitly endorsed, and he asks the philosophical question, "Do we really need to have a rigorous proof of primality?"[10]

For the application area of digital signatures, there is the opinion that error probabilities less than $2^{-80} \approx 10^{-24}$ in the generation of prime numbers is acceptable (in Europe, the bound $2^{-60} \approx 10^{-18}$ is also under discussion), so that errors are almost entirely excluded even when large numbers of keys are generated. In [RegT] it is suggested that in 2010, the threshold value should be lowered to 2^{-100}. Applied to the estimate of the probability of error by Rabin, this would mean that 40, respectively 30, rounds of Miller–Rabin tests would be run, with longer calculation times as the size of the numbers being tested grows. In fact, however, there exist very much sharper estimates that depend not only on the number of passes, but also on the length of the prime number candidate (see [DaLP] and [Burt]). In [DaLP], the following inequalities are proved, where $p_{l,k}$ denotes the probability that a randomly selected odd number with l binary digits that is declared prime after k passes through the Miller–Rabin test is actually composite:

$$p_{l,1} < l^2 4^{2-\sqrt{l}} \quad \text{for } l \geq 2; \tag{10.26}$$

$$p_{l,k} < l^{3/2} 2^k k^{-1/2} 4^{2-\sqrt{kl}} \quad \text{for } k = 2,\ l \geq 88 \text{ or } 3 \leq k \leq l/9,\ l \geq 21; \tag{10.27}$$

$$p_{l,k} < \frac{7}{20} l \cdot 2^{-5k} + \frac{1}{7} l^{15/4} 2^{l/2-2k} + 12 \cdot l \cdot 2^{-l/4-3k} \tag{10.28}$$
$$\text{for } l/9 \leq k \leq l/4,\ l \geq 21;$$

$$p_{l,k} < \frac{1}{7} l^{15/4} 2^{-l/2-2k} \quad \text{for } k \geq l/4,\ l \geq 21. \tag{10.29}$$

---

[10] In [BCGP] it is mentioned that Knuth's assertion holds only because the probability of error for most composite numbers is significantly less than one-fourth; otherwise, the error bound given by Knuth would lie significantly above the given number.

From these inequalities we can calculate what probabilities we can get below with how many passes of the Miller–Rabin test for a given number of digits, or how many passes are necessary to get below given probabilities of error. The results are far below those of Rabin, according to whom k repetitions are necessary to reach a probability of error beneath 4^{-k}. Table 10-3 shows values of k necessary to reach probabilities below 2^{-80} and 2^{-100} as a function of the number l of binary digits of the numbers being tested.

Table 10-3. The number **k** *of passes through the Miller–Rabin test to achieve probabilities of error less than* 2^{-80} *and* 2^{-100} *as a function of the number* **l** *of binary digits (after [DaLP]).*

Probability $< 2^{-80}$		Probability $< 2^{-100}$	
l	k	l	k
49	37	49	47
73	32	73	42
105	25	105	35
137	19	132	29
197	15	198	23
220 to 234	13	223	20
235 to 251	12	242	18
252 to 272	11	253	17
273 to 299	10	265	16
300 to 331	9	335	12
332 to 374	8	480 to 542	8
375 to 432	7	543 to 626	7
433 to 513	6	627 to 746	6
514 to 637	5	747 to 926	5
638 to 846	4	927 to 1232	4
847 to 1274	3	1233 to 1853	3
1275 to 2860	2	1854 to 4095	2
≥ 2861	1	≥ 4096	1

The effect of using the division sieve before the Miller–Rabin test is not considered in inequalities (10.26) through (10.29). Since the sieve greatly reduces the relative frequency of composite candidates, one may expect that the probabilities of error for a given choice of l and k would be further reduced.

For a discussion of the subtle problems of conditional probabilities in relation to the probability of error in the generation of randomly selected prime numbers, see [BCGP] and [MOV], Section 4.4.

In the following function prime_l, the values from Table 10-3 will be considered. We use the exponentiation function wmexpm_l(), which combines Montgomery reduction with the advantages that accrue from exponentiation of small bases (see Chapter 6).

Function:	probabilistic primality test à la Miller–Rabin with division sieve
Syntax:	int prime_l (CLINT n_l, unsigned int no_of_smallprimes, unsigned int iterations);
Input:	n_l (candidate for primality) no_of_smallprimes (number of primes for the division sieve) iterations (number of Miller–Rabin test iterations; if iterations == 0, this is determined from Table 10-3)
Return:	1 if the candidate is "probably" prime 0 if the candidate is composite or equal to 1

```
int
prime_l (CLINT n_l, unsigned int no_of_smallprimes, unsigned int iterations)
{
  CLINT d_l, x_l, q_l;
  USHORT i, j, k, p;
  int isprime = 1;

  if (EQONE_L (n_l))
    {
      return 0;
    }
```

Now the division test is executed. If a factor is found, then the function is terminated with 0 returned. If 1 is returned by sieve_l(), indicating that n_l is itself prime, then the function is terminated with return value 1. Otherwise, the Miller–Rabin test is carried out.

```
k = sieve_1 (n_1, no_of_smallprimes);
if (1 == k)
  {
    return 1;
  }
if (1 < k)
  {
    return 0;
  }
else
  {
    if (0 == iterations)
```

If iterations == 0 is passed as parameter, then based on the number of digits of n_1, the optimized number of iterations for coming in under the bound of 2^{-80} is determined.

```
      {
        k = ld_1 (n_1);
        if (k < 73) iterations = 37;
        else if (k < 105) iterations = 32;
        else if (k < 137) iterations = 25;
        else if (k < 197) iterations = 19;
        else if (k < 220) iterations = 15;
        else if (k < 235) iterations = 13;
        else if (k < 253) iterations = 12;
        else if (k < 275) iterations = 11;
        else if (k < 300) iterations = 10;
        else if (k < 332) iterations = 9;
        else if (k < 375) iterations = 8;
        else if (k < 433) iterations = 7;
        else if (k < 514) iterations = 6;
        else if (k < 638) iterations = 5;
        else if (k < 847) iterations = 4;
        else if (k < 1275) iterations = 3;
        else if (k < 2861) iterations = 2;
        else iterations = 1;
      }
```

Step 1. The decomposition of $n - 1$ as $n - 1 = 2^k q$ with odd q is carried out by the function twofact_l(). The value $n - 1$ is retained in d_l.

```
cpy_l (d_l, n_l);
dec_l (d_l);
k = (USHORT)twofact_l (d_l, q_l);
p = 0;
i = 0;
isprime = 1;
do
    {
```

Step 2. The bases p are formed from the differences stored in the field smallprimes[]. For the exponentiation we use the Montgomery function wmexpm_l, since the base is always of type USHORT and, after the pretest with the division sieve of the prime candidate n_l, always odd. If afterwards the power in x_l is equal to 1, then the next test iteration begins.

```
p += smallprimes[i++];
wmexpm_l (p, q_l, x_l, n_l);
if (!EQONE_L (x_l))
    {
        j = 0;
```

Step 3. Squaring, as long as x_l is different from ± 1 and $k - 1$ iterations have not yet been executed.

```
while (!EQONE_L (x_l) && !equ_l (x_l, d_l) && ++j < k)
    {
        msqr_l (x_l, x_l, n_l);
        }
    if (!equ_l (x_l, d_l))
        {
            isprime = 0;
        }
    }
}
```

> Loop over the number iterations of test iterations.

```
        while ((--iterations > 0) && isprime);
        return isprime;
    }
}
```

For the cases in which definitive test results are required, the APRCL test, published in 1981 by its developers L. Adleman, C. Pomerance, R. Rumely, H. Cohen, and A. K. Lenstra, shows the direction of development of such tests. H. Riesel praised this test as a breakthrough, proving that fast, generally applicable, definitive primality tests were possible (see [Ries], page 131). The test determines the primality property of an integer n in time of order $O\left((\ln n)^{C \ln \ln \ln n}\right)$ for a suitable constant C. Since the exponent $\ln \ln \ln n$ behaves like a constant for all practical purposes, it can be considered a polynomial-time procedure, and integers with several hundreds of decimal digits can have their primality or lack thereof determined definitively in times that are otherwise achieved only by probabilistic tests.[11] The algorithm, which uses analogues of Fermat's little theorem for higher algebraic structures, is theoretically complicated and difficult to implement. For further information see [Cohe], Chapter 9, or the original article cited therein, as well as the extensive explication in [Ries].

One might also ask whether one would obtain a definitive proof of primality by testing sufficiently many bases with the Miller–Rabin test. In fact, G. Miller has proved, on the assumption of the extended Riemann hypothesis (see page 200) that an odd natural number n is prime if and only if for all bases a, $1 \leq a \leq C \cdot \ln^2 n$, the Miller–Rabin test indicates the primality of n (the constant C is specified in [Kobl], Section 5.2, as 2). Used in this way the Miller–Rabin test is a deterministic polynomial-time primality test that uses about 10^6 iterations, for primes of about 1024 binary digits, to produce a definitive answer. If we suppose 10^{-3} seconds for each iteration (this is the order of magnitude for the time required for an exponentiation on a fast PC; cf. Appendix D), then a definitive test would take about an hour. Considering that there is an unproven hypothesis to be reckoned with, this theoretical result will satisfy neither the mathematical purists nor the computational pragmatists interested in fast procedures.

A surprising mathematical breakthrough occurred in 2002, when Maninda Agrawal, Neeraj Kayal, and Nitin Saxena, of the Indian Institute of Technology, in Kanpur, published an algorithm that provided a definitive proof of primality in polynomial time, thereby proving that the problem of recognizing a number

---

[11] Cohen suggests in this connection that the practicably implementable variant of the APRCL algorithm is again probabilistic, but that nonetheless a less practical, but deterministic, version exists (see [Cohe], Chapter 9).

to be prime belongs in the computational complexity class P. The algorithm was declared "brilliant and beautiful" by Carl Pomerance. The proof is elegant and surprisingly without any deep complexity, in contrast to what had been supposed, since a solution to the problem had been sought for centuries. Above all, we note that the proof does not rely on any unproven conjectures (see [AgKS]).

AKS algorithm for determining whether an integer n is prime

1. If n is a power of a natural number, go to step 8.

2. Set $r \leftarrow 2$.

3. If $\gcd(r, n) \neq 1$, go to step 8.

4. If r is not prime, go to step 5. Otherwise, let q be the largest prime factor of $r - 1$. If $q \geq \sqrt[4]{r} \log n$ and $n^{(r-1)/q} \neq r$, go to step 6.

5. Set $r \leftarrow r + 1$ and go to step 3.

6. If for some a in the set $\{1, \ldots, \lfloor 2\sqrt{r} \log n \rfloor\}$ it is the case that $(X - a)^n \not\equiv X^n - a \pmod{X^r - 1, n}$, go to step 8.[12]

7. Output "n is prime."

8. Output "n is composite."

To exclude powers of natural numbers in step 1 of the AKS test it suffices to test whether $\left\lfloor n^{1/b} \right\rfloor^b \neq b$ for $2 \leq b < \log n$. The integer part of the root $\left\lfloor n^{1/b} \right\rfloor$ is calculated with the algorithm previously presented in this chapter.

The AKS algorithm is based on a variant of Fermat's little theorem together with the binomial theorem, according to which for $1 < n \in \mathbb{N}$ and $a \in \mathbb{Z}_n^\times$, the integer n is prime precisely when in the polynomial ring $\mathbb{Z}_n[X]$ (see [AgKS], page 2), one has

$$(X + a)^n = (X^n + a). \tag{10.30}$$

A test based on this fact for an element a of $\mathbb{Z}_n[X]$ would then be able to determine definitively whether an integer n is prime. However, there would be considerable computation to determine the n coefficients of the polynomial $(X + a)^n$, even more than in applying the sieve of Eratosthenes. Following the idea of Agrawal, Kayal, and Saxena, it turns out that both sides of equation (10.30) can be reduced modulo $(X^r - 1)$ for a suitable value of r. If for *sufficiently* many values of a one has the equality

$$(X + a)^n = (X^n + a) \tag{10.31}$$

---

[12] According to the notation of Agrawal, Kayal and Saxena, $p(x) \equiv q(x) \pmod{x^r - 1, n}$ if $p(x)$ and $q(x)$ have the same remainders on division by both $x^r - 1$ and n.

in the ring $\mathbb{Z}_n[x]/(X^r - 1)$, then n is prime. Conversely, for a composite number n, there exist values of a and r such that $(X + a)^n \neq (X^n + a)$ in $\mathbb{Z}_n[x]/(X^r - 1)$. What is decisive here is that such values of a and r can be found in polynomial time if n is not prime, while if n is prime, it can be determined in polynomial time that such values do not exist. The size of the polynomial coefficients are bounded by r, and thus the calculation is faster, the smaller r is. If r is of order $\log n$, the polynomial residue can be computed in polynomial time.

Agrawal, Kayal, and Saxena showed that suitable values of r can be found of size $O\left(\log^5 n\right)$ and that the AKS test must be run only for values $1 \leq a \leq 2\sqrt{r}\log n$. The running time of the AKS test is therefore polynomial in $\log_2 n$, given by $O\left(\log^{7.5+\varepsilon} n\right)$.[13] The problem is solved.

There remains the fascinating question what practical relevance the AKS test has from the point of view of cryptography: The expected calculation time determines whether it is of any practical use.

Crandall gives the values in Table 10-4 for small values of n from a small experimental C implementation on a "decent workstation."

Table 10-4. Approximate calculation times for the AKS test, after [CrPa]

n	Approximate Time
70 001	3 seconds
700 001	15 seconds
2 147 483 647	200 seconds
1 125 899 906 842 679	4000 seconds (ca. 1 hour)
618 970 019 642 690 137 449 562 111	100 000 seconds (ca. 1 day)

The times in the table correspond to about $10^{-6} \log^6 n$ seconds. An implementation by F. Bornemann based on the Pari-GP library requires nine seconds on a 1.7-GHz PC for proving the primality of $628\,363\,443\,011$ (see http://www-m3.ma.tum.de/m3/ftp/Bornemann/PARI/aks2.txt). The running time for a 512-bit prime number would then take several days. We thus obtain a definitive result, whose certainty we can approach only asymptotically using probabilistic primality tests. Since we can make the remaining probability of error, say by using the Miller–Rabin test, arbitrarily small, the disadvantage of not having that last bit of certainty is not very large in practice.

---

[13] Improvements in these numbers have been considered on the basis of suggestions by H. Lenstra and D. Bernstein (see [Bern]). If we consider a conjecture about the density of Sophie Germain primes (prime numbers n for which $2n + 1$ is also prime) by Hardy and Littlewood (1922), we would have a run time for the AKS test of $O\left(\log^{6+\varepsilon} n\right)$. Hardy and Littlewood conjectured that the cardinality of the set $\{\, p \leq x \mid p \text{ and } 2p + 1 \text{ are prime}\,\}$ is asymptotic to $2C_2/\ln^2 x$, with $C_2 = 0.6601618158\ldots$, the so-called twin-primes constant. This conjecture has been verified up to $x = 10\,000\,000\,000$, and therefore, the more favorable run-time estimate for the AKS test holds at least for numbers with up to 100 000 digits (see [Born]).

In sum, we should recognize that the AKS test represents a sensational result from the point of view of complexity theory, but that the Miller–Rabin test will continue to be the test of choice for cryptographic applications due to its enormous advantage in speed, even if Henri Cohen seems to be answering the above-quoted question of Knuth when he categorically asserts ([Cohe], Section 8.2), "Primality testing, however, requires rigorous mathematical proofs."

Rijndael: A Successor to the Data Encryption Standard

> I don't know if we have any real chance. He can multiply and all we can do is add. He represents progress and I just drag my feet.
>
> —Sten Nadolny (translated by Breon Mitchell), *God of Impertinence*

THE AMERICAN NATIONAL INSTITUTE OF Standards and Technology (NIST) launched a competition in 1997 under the aegis of an *Advanced Encryption Standard* (AES) with the goal of creating a new national standard (federal information processing standard, or FIPS) for encryption with a symmetric algorithm. Although we have concentrated our attention in this book on asymmetric cryptography, this development is important enough that we should give it some attention, if only cursorily. Through the new standard FIPS 197 [F197], an encryption algorithm will be established that satisfies all of today's security requirements and that in all of its design and implementation aspects will be freely available without cost throughout the world. Finally, it replaces the dated *data encryption standard* (DES), which, however, as *triple DES* remains available for use in government agencies. However, the AES represents the cryptographic basis of the American administration for the protection of sensitive data.

The AES competition received a great deal of attention abroad as well as in the USA, not only because whatever happens in the United States in the area of cryptography produces great effects worldwide, but because international participation was specifically encouraged in the development of the new block encryption procedure.

From an original field of fifteen candidates who entered the contest in 1998, by 1999 ten had been eliminated, a process with involvement of an international group of experts. There then remained in competition the algorithms MARS, of IBM; RC6, of RSA Laboratories; Rijndael, of Joan Daemen and Vincent Rijmen; Serpent, of Ross Anderson, Eli Biham, and Lars Knudson; and Twofish, of Bruce Schneier et al. Finally, in October 2000 the winner of the selection process was announced. The algorithm with the name "Rijndael," by Joan Daemen and

Vincent Rijmen, of Belgium, was named as the future advanced encryption standard (cf. [NIST]).[1] Rijndael is a successor of the block cipher "Square," published earlier by the same authors (cf. [Squa]), which, however, had proved to be not as powerful. Rijndael was especially strengthened to attack the weaknesses of Square. The AES report of NIST gives the following basis for its decision.

1. **Security**

   All candidates fulfill the requirements of the AES with respect to security against all known attacks. In comparison to the other candidates, the implementations of Serpent and Rijndael can at the least cost be protected against attacks that are based on measurements of the time behavior of the hardware (so-called timing attacks) or changes in electrical current use (so-called power or differential power analysis attacks).[2] The degradation in performance associated with such protective measures is least for Rijndael, Serpent, and Twofish, with a greater advantage to Rijndael.

2. **Speed**

   Rijndael is among the candidates that permit the most rapid implementation, and it is distinguished by equally good performance across all platforms considered, such as 32-bit processors, 8-bit microcontrollers, smart cards, and implementations in hardware (see below). Of all the candidates Rijndael allows the most rapid calculation of round keys.

3. **Memory requirement**

   Rijndael makes use of very limited resources of RAM and ROM memory and is thus an excellent candidate for use in restricted-resource environments. In particular, the algorithm offers the possibility to calculate round keys separately "on the fly" for each round. These properties have great significance for applications on microcontrollers such as used in smart cards. Due to the structure of the algorithm, the requirements on ROM storage are least when only one direction, that is, either encryption or decryption, is realized, and they increase when both functions are needed. Nonetheless, with respect to resource requirements Rijndael is not beaten by any of the other four contestants.

4. **Implementation in hardware**

---

[1] The name "Rijndael" is a portmanteau word derived from the names of the authors. Sources tell me that the correct pronunciation is somewhere between "rain doll" and "Rhine dahl." Perhaps NIST should include in the standard a pronunciation key in the international phonetic alphabet.

[2] Power analysis attacks (simple PA/differential PA) are based on correlations between individual bits or groups of bits of a secret cryptographic key and the average consumption of electricity for the execution of individual instructions or code sequences depending on the key (see, for example, [KoJJ], [CJRR], [GoPa]).

Rijndael and Serpent are the candidates with the best performance in hardware implementations, with a slight advantage going to Rijndael due to its better performance in output and cipher feedback modes.

The report offers further criteria that contributed to the decision in favor of Rijndael, which are collected into a closing summary (see [NIST], Section 7):

> There are many unknowns regarding future computing platforms and the wide range of environments in which the AES will be implemented. However, when considered together, Rijndael's combination of security, performance, efficiency, implementability, and flexibility make it an appropriate selection for the AES for use in the technology of today and in the future.

Given the openness of the selection process and the politically interesting fact that with Rijndael an algorithm of European vintage was selected, one might expect future speculation about secret properties, hidden trap doors, and deliberately built-in weaknesses to be silenced, which never quite succeeded with DES.

Before we get involved with the functionality of Rijndael, we would like as preparation to go on a brief excursion into the arithmetic of polynomials over finite fields, which leans heavily on the presentation in [DaRi], Section 2.

11.1 Arithmetic with Polynomials

We start by looking at arithmetic in the field $\mathbb{F}_{2^n}$, the finite field with 2^n elements, where an element of $\mathbb{F}_{2^n}$ is represented as a polynomial $f(x) = a_{n-1}x^{n-1} + a_{n-2}x^{n-2} + \cdots + a_1 x + a_0$ with coefficients a_i in $\mathbb{F}_2$ (which is isomorphic to $\mathbb{Z}_2$). Equivalently, an element of $\mathbb{F}_{2^n}$ can be represented simply as an n-tuple of polynomial coefficients, each representation offering its own advantages. The polynomial representation is well suited for manual calculation, while the representation as a tuple of coefficients corresponds well to a computer's binary representation of numbers. To demonstrate this, we notate $\mathbb{F}_{2^3}$ as a sequence of eight polynomials and again as eight 3-tuples with their associated numerical values (see Table 11-1).

Addition of polynomials proceeds by adding the coefficients in $\mathbb{F}_2$: If $f(x) := x^2 + x$ and $g(x) := x^2 + x + 1$, then $f(x) + g(x) = 2x^2 + 2x + 1 = 1$, since $1 + 1 = 0$ in $\mathbb{F}_2$. We can carry out addition of 3-tuples in $\mathbb{F}_{2^3}$ column by column. We see, then, for example, that the sum of $(1\ 1\ 0)$ and $(1\ 1\ 1)$ is $(0\ 0\ 1)$:

$$
\begin{array}{ccc}
 & 1 \quad 1 \quad 0 \\
\oplus & \underline{1 \quad 1 \quad 1} \\
 & 0 \quad 0 \quad 1
\end{array}
$$

Table 11-1. Elements of $\mathbb{F}_{2^3}$

Polynomials in $\mathbb{F}_{2^3}$	3-Tuples in $\mathbb{F}_{2^3}$			Numerical Value
0	0	0	0	'00'
1	0	0	1	'01'
x	0	1	0	'02'
$x+1$	0	1	1	'03'
x^2	1	0	0	'04'
x^2+1	1	0	1	'05'
x^2+x	1	1	0	'06'
x^2+x+1	1	1	1	'07'

The addition of digits takes place in $\mathbb{Z}_2$ and is not to be confused with binary addition, which can involve a carry. This process is reminiscent of our XOR function in Section 7.2, which executes the same operation in $\mathbb{Z}_n$ for large n.

Multiplication in $\mathbb{F}_{2^3}$ is accomplished by multiplying each term of the first polynomial by each term of the second and then summing the partial products. The sum is then reduced by an irreducible polynomial of degree 3 (in our example modulo $m(x) := x^3 + x + 1$):[3]

$$
\begin{aligned}
f(x) \cdot g(x) &= \left(x^2+x\right) \cdot \left(x^2+x+1\right) \bmod \left(x^3+x+1\right) \\
&= x^4 + 2x^3 + 2x^2 + x \bmod \left(x^3+x+1\right) \\
&= x^4 + x \bmod \left(x^3+x+1\right) \\
&= x^2.
\end{aligned}
$$

This corresponds to the product of 3-tuples $(1\ 1\ 0) \bullet (1\ 1\ 1) = (1\ 0\ 0)$, or, expressed numerically, '06' $\bullet$ '07' = '04'.

The abelian group laws hold in $\mathbb{F}_{2^3}$ with respect to addition and in $\mathbb{F}_{2^3} \setminus \{0\}$ with respect to multiplication (cf. Chapter 5). The distributive law holds as well.

The structure and arithmetic of $\mathbb{F}_{2^3}$ can be carried over directly to the field $\mathbb{F}_{2^8}$, which is the field that is actually of interest in studying Rijndael. Addition and multiplication are carried out as in our above example, the only differences being that $\mathbb{F}_{2^8}$ has 256 elements and that an irreducible polynomial of degree 8 will be used for reduction. For Rijndael this polynomial is $m(x) := x^8 + x^4 + x^3 + x + 1$, which in tuple representation is $(1\ 0\ 0\ 0\ 1\ 1\ 0\ 1\ 1)$, corresponding to the hexadecimal number '011B'.

Multiplication of a polynomial

$$
f(x) = a_7 x^7 + a_6 x^6 + a_5 x^5 + a_4 x^4 + a_3 x^3 + a_2 x^2 + a_1 x + a_0
$$

---

[3]　A polynomial is said to be *irreducible* if it divisible (without remainder) only by itself and 1.

by x (corresponding to a multiplication $\bullet$ '02') is particularly simple:

$$f(x) \cdot x = a_7 x^8 + a_6 x^7 + a_5 x^6 + a_4 x^5 + a_3 x^4 + a_2 x^3 + a_1 x^2 + a_0 x \bmod m(x),$$

where the reduction modulo $m(x)$ is required only in the case $a_7 \neq 0$, and then it can be carried out by subtracting $m(x)$, that is, by a simple XOR of the coefficients.

For programming one therefore regards the coefficients of a polynomial as binary digits of integers and executes a multiplication by x by a left shift of one bit, followed by, if $a_7 = 1$, a reduction by an XOR operation with the eight least-significant digits '1B' of the number '011B' corresponding to $m(x)$ (whereby a_7 is simply "forgotten"). The operation $a \bullet$ '02' for a polynomial f, or its numerical value a, is denoted by Daemen and Rijmen by b = xtime(a). Multiplication by powers of x can be executed by successive applications of xtime().

For example, multiplication of $f(x)$ by $x + 1$ (or '03') is carried out by shifting the binary digits of the numerical value a of f one place to the left and XOR-ing the result with a. Reduction modulo $m(x)$ proceeds exactly as with xtime. Two lines of C code demonstrate the procedure:

```
f ^= f << 1;      /* multiplication of f by (x + 1) */
if (f & 0x100) f ^= 0x11B;   /* reduction modulo m(x) */
```

Multiplication of two polynomials f and h in $\mathbb{F}_{2^8} \setminus \{0\}$ can be speeded up by using logarithms: Let $g(x)$ be a generating polynomial[4] of $\mathbb{F}_{2^8} \setminus \{0\}$. Then there exist m and n such that $f \equiv g^m$ and $h \equiv g^n$. Thus $f \cdot h \equiv g^{m+n} \bmod m(x)$.

From a programming point of view this can be transposed with the help of two tables, into one of which we place the 255 powers of the generator polynomial $g(x) := x + 1$ and into the other the logarithms to the base $g(x)$ (see Tables 11-2 and 11-3). The product $f \cdot h$ is now determined by three accesses to these tables: From the logarithm table are taken values m and n for which $g^m = f$ and $g^n = h$. From the table of powers the value $g^{((n+m) \bmod 255)}$ is taken (note that $g^{\mathrm{ord}(g)} = 1$). Table 11-2 contains the powers of g twice in succession, and so one can avoid having to reduce the exponent of g in $f \cdot h = g^{n+m}$.

With the help of this mechanism we can also carry out polynomial division in $\mathbb{F}_{2^8}$. Thus for $f, g \in \mathbb{F}_{2^8} \setminus \{0\}$,

$$\frac{f}{h} = fh^{-1} = g^m (g^n)^{-1} = g^{m-n} = g^{(m-n) \bmod 255}.$$

This procedure for polynomial multiplication in $\mathbb{F}_{2^8}$ is illustrated in the function polymul():

---

[4] g generates $\mathbb{F}_{2^8} \setminus \{0\}$ if g has order 255. That is, the powers of g run through all the elements of $\mathbb{F}_{2^8} \setminus \{0\}$.

Table 11-2. Powers of $g(x) = x + 1$, ascending left to right

01	03	05	0F	11	33	55	FF	1A	2E	72	96	A1	F8	13	35
5F	E1	38	48	D8	73	95	A4	F7	02	06	0A	1E	22	66	AA
E5	34	5C	E4	37	59	EB	26	6A	BE	D9	70	90	AB	E6	31
53	F5	04	0C	14	3C	44	CC	4F	D1	68	B8	D3	6E	B2	CD
4C	D4	67	A9	E0	3B	4D	D7	62	A6	F1	08	18	28	78	88
83	9E	B9	D0	6B	BD	DC	7F	81	98	B3	CE	49	DB	76	9A
B5	C4	57	F9	10	30	50	F0	0B	1D	27	69	BB	D6	61	A3
FE	19	2B	7D	87	92	AD	EC	2F	71	93	AE	E9	20	60	A0
FB	16	3A	4E	D2	6D	B7	C2	5D	E7	32	56	FA	15	3F	41
C3	5E	E2	3D	47	C9	40	C0	5B	ED	2C	74	9C	BF	DA	75
9F	BA	D5	64	AC	EF	2A	7E	82	9D	BC	DF	7A	8E	89	80
9B	B6	C1	58	E8	23	65	AF	EA	25	6F	B1	C8	43	C5	54
FC	1F	21	63	A5	F4	07	09	1B	2D	77	99	B0	CB	46	CA
45	CF	4A	DE	79	8B	86	91	A8	E3	3E	42	C6	51	F3	0E
12	36	5A	EE	29	7B	8D	8C	8F	8A	85	94	A7	F2	0D	17
39	4B	DD	7C	84	97	A2	FD	1C	24	6C	B4	C7	52	F6	01
03	05	0F	11	33	55	FF	1A	2E	72	...	...	...	F6		

Function:	multiplication of polynomials in $\mathbb{F}_{2^8}$
Syntax:	UCHAR polymul (unsigned int f, unsigned int h);
Input:	unsigned int f (summand), unsigned int h (summand)
Return:	the product f · h

```
UCHAR
polymul (unsigned int f, unsigned int h)
{
  if ((f != 0) && (h != 0))
    {
```

Note that for the following access to the table of powers of g, the reduction of the exponent m + n = LogTable[f] + LogTable[h] is unnecessary.

```
      return (AntiLogTable[LogTable[f] + LogTable[h]]);
   }
 else
   {
      return 0;
   }
}
```

Table 11-3. Logarithms to base $g(x) = x + 1$ (e.g., $\log_{g(x)} 2 = 25 = 19$ in hexadecimal, $\log_{g(x)} 255 = 7$).

	00	19	01	32	02	1A	C6	4B	C7	1B	68	33	EE	DF	03
64	04	E0	0E	34	8D	81	EF	4C	71	08	C8	F8	69	1C	C1
7D	C2	1D	B5	F9	B9	27	6A	4D	E4	A6	72	9A	C9	09	78
65	2F	8A	05	21	0F	E1	24	12	F0	82	45	35	93	DA	8E
96	8F	DB	BD	36	D0	CE	94	13	5C	D2	F1	40	46	83	38
66	DD	FD	30	BF	06	8B	62	B3	25	E2	98	22	88	91	10
7E	6E	48	C3	A3	B6	1E	42	3A	6B	28	54	FA	85	3D	BA
2B	79	0A	15	9B	9F	5E	CA	4E	D4	AC	E5	F3	73	A7	57
AF	58	A8	50	F4	EA	D6	74	4F	AE	E9	D5	E7	E6	AD	E8
2C	D7	75	7A	EB	16	0B	F5	59	CB	5F	B0	9C	A9	51	A0
7F	0C	F6	6F	17	C4	49	EC	D8	43	1F	2D	A4	76	7B	B7
CC	BB	3E	5A	FB	60	B1	86	3B	52	A1	6C	AA	55	29	9D
97	B2	87	90	61	BE	DC	FC	BC	95	CF	CD	37	3F	5B	D1
53	39	84	3C	41	A2	6D	47	14	2A	9E	5D	56	F2	D3	AB
44	11	92	D9	23	20	2E	89	B4	7C	B8	26	77	99	E3	A5
67	4A	ED	DE	C5	31	FE	18	0D	63	8C	80	C0	F7	70	07

We now ratchet the complexity level up one notch and consider arithmetic with polynomials of the form $f(x) = f_3 x^3 + f_2 x^2 + f_1 x + f_0$ with coefficients f_i in $\mathbb{F}_{2^8}$, that is, coefficients that are themselves polynomials. The coefficients of such polynomials can be represented as fields of four bytes each. Now things begin to get interesting: While addition of such polynomials $f(x)$ and $g(x)$ again takes place by means of a bitwise XOR of the coefficients, the product $h(x) = f(x)g(x)$ is calculated to be

$$h(x) = h_6 x^6 + h_5 x^5 + h_4 x^4 + h_3 x^3 + h_2 x^2 + h_1 x + h_0,$$

with coefficients $h_k := \sum_{i+j=0}^{k} f_i \bullet g_j$, where the summation sign indicates addition $\oplus$ in $\mathbb{F}_{2^8}$.

After reduction of $h(x)$ by a polynomial of degree 4, one again obtains a polynomial of degree 3 over $\mathbb{F}_{2^8}$.

For this Rijndael uses the polynomial $M(x) := x^4 + 1$. Usefully, $x^j \bmod M(x) = x^{j \bmod 4}$, so that $h(x) \bmod M(x)$ can be easily computed as

$$d(x) := f(x) \otimes g(x) := h(x) \bmod M(x) = d_3 x^3 + d_2 x^2 + d_1 x + d_0,$$

with

$$d_0 = a_0 \bullet b_0 \oplus a_3 \bullet b_1 \oplus a_2 \bullet b_2 \oplus a_1 \bullet b_3,$$
$$d_1 = a_1 \bullet b_0 \oplus a_0 \bullet b_1 \oplus a_3 \bullet b_2 \oplus a_2 \bullet b_3,$$
$$d_2 = a_2 \bullet b_0 \oplus a_1 \bullet b_1 \oplus a_0 \bullet b_2 \oplus a_3 \bullet b_3,$$
$$d_3 = a_3 \bullet b_0 \oplus a_2 \bullet b_1 \oplus a_1 \bullet b_2 \oplus a_0 \bullet b_3.$$

From this one concludes that the coefficients d_i can be computed by matrix multiplication over $\mathbb{F}_{2^8}$:

$$\begin{bmatrix} d_0 \\ d_1 \\ d_2 \\ d_3 \end{bmatrix} = \begin{bmatrix} a_0 & a_3 & a_2 & a_1 \\ a_1 & a_0 & a_3 & a_2 \\ a_2 & a_1 & a_0 & a_3 \\ a_3 & a_2 & a_1 & a_0 \end{bmatrix} \cdot \begin{bmatrix} b_0 \\ b_1 \\ b_2 \\ b_3 \end{bmatrix}. \tag{11.1}$$

It is precisely this operation with the constant, invertible modulo $M(x)$, polynomial $a(x) := a_3 x^3 + a_2 x^2 + a_1 x + a_0$ over $\mathbb{F}_{2^8}$, with coefficients $a_0(x) = x$, $a_1(x) = 1$, $a_2(x) = 1$, and $a_3(x) = x + 1$, that is executed in the so-called *MixColumns* transformation, which constitutes a principal component of the round transformations of Rijndael.

11.2 The Rijndael Algorithm

Rijndael is a symmetric block encryption algorithm with variable block and key lengths. It can process blocks of 128, 192, and 256 bits and keys of the same lengths, where all combinations of block and key lengths are possible. The accepted key lengths correspond to the guidelines for AES, though the "official" block length is only 128 bits. Each block of plain text is encrypted several times with a repeating sequence of various functions, in so-called *rounds*. The number of rounds is dependent on the block and key lengths (see Table 11-4).

Rijndael is not a Feistel algorithm, whose essential characteristic is that blocks are divided into left and right halves, the round transformations applied to one half, and the result XOR-ed with the other half, after which the two halves are exchanged. DES is the best-known block algorithm built along these lines. Rijndael, on the other hand, is built up of separate layers, which successively apply various effects to an entire block. For the encryption of a block the following transformations are sequentially applied:

1. The first round key is XOR-ed with the block.

2. $L_r - 1$ regular rounds are executed.

3. A terminal round is executed, in which the MixColumns transformation of the regular rounds is omitted.

Table 11-4. Number of Rijndael rounds as a function of block and key length

	Block Length (Bits)		
Key Length (Bits)	128	192	256
128	10	12	14
192	12	12	14
256	14	14	14

Each regular round of step 2 consists of four individual steps, which we shall now examine:

1. **Substitution:** Each byte of a block is replaced by application of an S-box.

2. **Permutation:** The bytes of the block are permuted in a *ShiftRows* transformation.

3. **Diffusion:** The *MixColumns* transformation is executed.

4. **Round key addition:** The current round key is XOR-ed with the block.

The layering of transformations within a round is shown schematically in Figure 11-1.

Each layer exercises a particular effect within a round and thus on each block of plain text:

1. **Influence of the key**

   XOR-ing with the round key before the first round and as the last step within each round has an effect on every bit of the round result. In the course of encryption of a block there is no step whose result is not dependent in every bit on the key.

2. **Nonlinear layer**

   The substitution effected via the S-box is a nonlinear operation. The construction of the S-box provides almost ideal protection against differential and linear cryptanalysis (see [BiSh] and [NIST]).

3. **Linear layer**

   The ShiftRows and MixColumns transformations ensure an optimal mixing up of the bits of a block.

In the following description of the internal Rijndael functions L_b will denote the block length in 4-byte words, L_k the length of the user key in 4-byte words (that is, $L_b, L_k \in \{4, 6, 8\}$), and L_r the number of rounds as indicated in Table 11-4.

Plain text and encrypted text are input, respectively output, as fields of bytes. A block of plain text, passed as a field $m_0, \ldots, m_{4L_b-1}$, will be regarded in the following as a two-dimensional structure $\mathfrak{B}$ as depicted in Table 11-5,

Table 11-5. Representation of message blocks

$b_{0,0}$	$b_{0,1}$	$b_{0,2}$	$b_{0,3}$	$b_{0,4}$	$\ldots$	b_{0,L_b-1}
$b_{1,0}$	$b_{1,1}$	$b_1,2$	$b_{1,3}$	$b_{1,4}$	$\ldots$	b_{1,L_b-1}
$b_{2,0}$	$b_{2,1}$	$b_{2,2}$	$b_{2,3}$	$b_{2,4}$	$\ldots$	b_{2,L_b-1}
$b_{3,0}$	$b_{3,1}$	$b_{3,2}$	$b_{3,3}$	$b_{3,4}$	$\ldots$	b_{3,L_b-1}

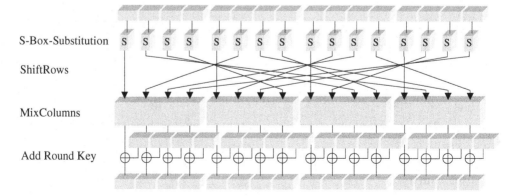

Figure 11-1. Layering of transformations in the Rijndael rounds

where the bytes of plain text are sorted according to the following ordering:

$$m_0 \to b_{0,0}, \quad m_1 \to b_{1,0}, \quad m_2 \to b_{2,0}, \quad m_3 \to b_{3,0},$$
$$m_4 \to b_{0,1}, \quad m_5 \to b_{1,1}, \qquad \ldots \qquad m_n \to b_{i,j}, \quad \ldots$$

with $i = n \bmod 4$ and $j = \lfloor n/4 \rfloor$.

Access to $\mathfrak{B}$ within the Rijndael functions takes place in different ways according to the operation. The S-box transformation operates bytewise, ShiftRows operates on rows $(b_{i,0}, b_{i,1}, b_{i,2}, \ldots, b_{i,L_b-1})$ of $\mathfrak{B}$, and the functions AddRoundKey and MixColumns operate on 4-byte words and access the values of $\mathfrak{B}$ by columns $(b_{0,j}, b_{1,j}, b_{2,j}, b_{3,j})$.

11.3 Calculating the Round Key

Encryption and decryption each require the generation of L_r round keys, called collectively the *key schedule*. This occurs through expansion of the secret user key by attaching recursively derived 4-byte words $k_i = (k_{0,i}, k_{1,i}, k_{2,i}, k_{3,i})$ to the user key.

The first L_k words $k_0, \ldots, k_{L_k-1}$ of the key schedule are formed from the secret user key itself. For $L_k \in \{4, 6\}$ the next 4-byte word k_i is determined by XOR-ing the preceding word k_{i-1} with k_{i-L_k}. If $i \equiv 0 \bmod L_k$, then a function $F_{L_k}(k, i)$ is applied before the XOR operation, which is composed of a cyclic left shift (left rotation) $r(k)$ of k bytes, a substitution $S(r(k))$ from the Rijndael S-box (we shall return to this later), and an XOR with a constant $c(\lfloor i/L_k \rfloor)$, so that altogether the function F is given by $F_{L_k}(k, i) := S(r(k)) \oplus c(\lfloor i/L_k \rfloor)$.

The constants $c(j)$ are defined by $c(j) := (\mathrm{rc}(j), 0, 0, 0)$, where $\mathrm{rc}(j)$ are recursively determined elements from $\mathbb{F}_{2^8}$: $\mathrm{rc}(1) := 1$, $\mathrm{rc}(j) := \mathrm{rc}(j-1) \cdot x = x^{j-1}$. Expressed in numerical values, this is equivalent to $\mathrm{rc}(1) := \text{`01'}$, $\mathrm{rc}(j) := \mathrm{rc}(j-1) \bullet \text{`02'}$. From the standpoint of programming, $\mathrm{rc}(j)$ is computed by a $(j-1)$-fold execution of the function xtime described above, beginning with the argument 1, or more rapidly by access to a table (Tables 11-6 and 11-7).

Table 11-6. $\mathrm{rc}(j)$ constants (hexadecimal)

'01'	'02'	'04'	'08'	'10'	'20'	'40'	'80'	'1B'	'36'
'6C'	'D8'	'AB'	'4D'	'9A'	'2F'	'5E'	'BC'	'63'	'C6'
'97'	'35'	'6A'	'D4'	'B3'	'7D'	'FA'	'EF'	'C5'	'91'

For keys of length 256 bits (that is, $L_k = 8$) an additional S-box operation is inserted: If $i \equiv 4 \bmod L_k$, then before the XOR operation k_{i-1} is replaced by $S(k_{i-1})$.

Table 11-7. $\text{rc}(j)$ *constants (binary)*

00000001	00000010	00000100	00001000	00010000
00100000	01000000	10000000	00011011	00110110
01101100	11011000	10101011	01001101	10011010
00101111	01011110	10111100	01100011	11000110
10010111	00110101	01101010	11010100	10110011
01111101	11111010	11101111	11000101	10010001

Thus a key schedule is built up of $L_b \cdot (L_r + 1)$ 4-byte words, including the secret user key. At each round $i = 0, \ldots, L_r - 1$ the next L_b 4-byte words $k_{L_b \cdot i}$ through $kL_{b \cdot (i+1)}$ are taken as round keys from the key schedule. The round keys are conceptualized, in analogy to the structuring of the message blocks, as a two-dimensional structure of the form depicted in Table 11-8.

Table 11-8. Representation of the round keys

$k_{0,0}$	$k_{0,1}$	$k_{0,2}$	$k_{0,3}$	$k_{0,4}$	$\ldots$	k_{0,L_b-1}
$k_{1,0}$	$k_{1,1}$	$k_{1,2}$	$k_{1,3}$	$k_{1,4}$	$\ldots$	k_{1,L_b-1}
$k_{2,0}$	$k_{2,1}$	$k_{2,2}$	$k_{2,3}$	$k_{2,4}$	$\ldots$	k_{2,L_b-1}
$k_{3,0}$	$k_{3,1}$	$k_{3,2}$	$k_{3,3}$	$k_{3,4}$	$\ldots$	k_{3,L_b-1}

For key lengths of 128 bits key generation can be understood from an examination of Figure 11-2.

Secret Key of User

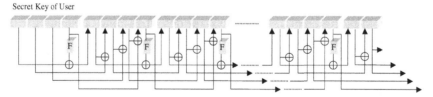

Figure 11-2. Diagram for round keys for $L_k = 4$

There are no *weak* keys known, those whose use would weaken the procedure.

11.4 The S-Box

The substitution box, or S-box, of the Rijndael algorithm specifies how in each round each byte of a block is to be replaced by another value.

The S-box has the task of minimizing the susceptibility of the algorithm to methods of linear and differential cryptanalysis and to algebraic attacks. To accomplish this, the S-box operation should possess a high algebraic complexity in $\mathbb{F}_{2^8}$ and thus create a good extension to the ShiftRows and MixColumns operations. Not having such a function would support attacks within $\mathbb{F}_{2^8}$ and thereby decisively weaken the procedure.

In addition to the requirement of complexity, the S-box function must of course be invertible; it must have no fixed points $S(a) = a$ or complementary fixed points $S(a) = \bar{a}$; and it must also execute rapidly and be easy to implement.

All these desiderata were achieved through a combination of multiplicative inversion in $\mathbb{F}_{2^8}$ and the previously mentioned affine mapping from $\mathbb{F}_{2^8}$ to itself. The S-box consists of a list of 256 bytes, which are constructed by first thinking of each nonzero byte as a representative of $\mathbb{F}_{2^8}$ and replacing it with its multiplicative inverse (zero remains unchanged). Then an affine transformation over $\mathbb{F}_2$ is calculated as a matrix multiplication and addition of $(1\ 1\ 0\ 0\ 0\ 1\ 1\ 0)$:

$$\begin{bmatrix} y_0 \\ y_1 \\ y_2 \\ y_3 \\ y_4 \\ y_5 \\ y_6 \\ y_7 \end{bmatrix} = \begin{bmatrix} 1 & 0 & 0 & 0 & 1 & 1 & 1 & 1 \\ 1 & 1 & 0 & 0 & 0 & 1 & 1 & 1 \\ 1 & 1 & 1 & 0 & 0 & 0 & 1 & 1 \\ 1 & 1 & 1 & 1 & 0 & 0 & 0 & 1 \\ 1 & 1 & 1 & 1 & 1 & 0 & 0 & 0 \\ 0 & 1 & 1 & 1 & 1 & 1 & 0 & 0 \\ 0 & 0 & 1 & 1 & 1 & 1 & 1 & 0 \\ 0 & 0 & 0 & 1 & 1 & 1 & 1 & 1 \end{bmatrix} \cdot \begin{bmatrix} x_0 \\ x_1 \\ x_2 \\ x_3 \\ x_4 \\ x_5 \\ x_6 \\ x_7 \end{bmatrix} + \begin{bmatrix} 1 \\ 1 \\ 0 \\ 0 \\ 0 \\ 1 \\ 1 \\ 0 \end{bmatrix}. \tag{11.2}$$

In this representation x_0 and y_0 denote the least-significant, and x_7 and y_7 the most-significant, bits of a byte, where the 8-tuple $(1\ 1\ 0\ 0\ 0\ 1\ 1\ 0)$ corresponds to the hexadecimal value '63'.

Through this construction, all of the requisite design criteria were satisfied. The substitution is thereby an ideal strengthening of the algorithm. Successive application of the construction plan to the values 0 to 255 leads to Table 11-9 (in hexadecimal form; read horizontally from left to right).

For decryption the S-box must be used backwards: The affine inverse transformation is used, followed by multiplicative inversion in $\mathbb{F}_{2^8}$. The inverted S-box appears in Table 11-10.

11.5 The ShiftRows Transformation

The next step in the cycle of a round consists in the permutation of a block at the byte level. To this end the bytes are exchanged within the individual lines $(b_{i,0}, b_{i,1}, b_{i,2}, \ldots, b_{i,L_b-1})$ of a block according to the schemata depicted in Tables 11-11 through 11-13.

Table 11-9. The values of the S-box

63	7C	77	7B	F2	6B	6F	C5	30	01	67	2B	FE	D7	AB	76
CA	82	C9	7D	FA	59	47	F0	AD	D4	A2	AF	9C	A4	72	C0
B7	FD	93	26	36	3F	F7	CC	34	A5	E5	F1	71	D8	31	15
04	C7	23	C3	18	96	05	9A	07	12	80	E2	EB	27	B2	75
09	83	2C	1A	1B	6E	5A	A0	52	3B	D6	B3	29	E3	2F	84
53	D1	00	ED	20	FC	B1	5B	6A	CB	BE	39	4A	4C	58	CF
D0	EF	AA	FB	43	4D	33	85	45	F9	02	7F	50	3C	9F	A8
51	A3	40	8F	92	9D	38	F5	BC	B6	DA	21	10	FF	F3	D2
CD	0C	13	EC	5F	97	44	17	C4	A7	7E	3D	64	5D	19	73
60	81	4F	DC	22	2A	90	88	46	EE	B8	14	DE	5E	0B	DB
E0	32	3A	0A	49	06	24	5C	C2	D3	AC	62	91	95	E4	79
E7	C8	37	6D	8D	D5	4E	A9	6C	56	F4	EA	65	7A	AE	08
BA	78	25	2E	1C	A6	B4	C6	E8	DD	74	1F	4B	BD	8B	8A
70	3E	B5	66	48	03	F6	0E	61	35	57	B9	86	C1	1D	9E
E1	F8	98	11	69	D9	8E	94	9B	1E	87	E9	CE	55	28	DF
8C	A1	89	0D	BF	E6	42	68	41	99	2D	0F	B0	54	BB	16

In each first row (row index $i = 0$) no exchange takes place. In lines $i = 1, 2, 3$ the bytes are rotated left by $c_{L_b,i}$ positions, from position j to position $j - c_{L_b,i} \bmod L_b$, where $c_{L_b,i}$ is taken from Table 11-14.

For inverting this step, positions j in rows $i = 1, 2, 3$ are shifted to positions $j + c_{L_b,i} \bmod L_b$.

11.6 The MixColumns Transformation

After the rowwise permutation in the last step, in this step each column $(b_{i,j})$, $i = 0, \ldots, 3, j = 0, \ldots, L_b$ of a block is taken to be a polynomial over $\mathbb{F}_{2^8}$ and multiplied by the constant polynomial $a(x) := a_3 x^3 + a_2 x^2 + a_1 x + a_0$, with coefficients $a_0(x) = x$, $a_1(x) = 1$, $a_2(x) = 1$, $a_3(x) = x + 1$, and reduced modulo $M(x) := x^4 + 1$. Each byte of a column thus interacts with every other byte of the column. The rowwise operating ShiftRows transformation has the effect that in each round, other bytes are mixed with one another, resulting in strong diffusion.

Table 11-10. The values of the inverted S-box

52	09	6A	D5	30	36	A5	38	BF	40	A3	9E	81	F3	D7	FB
7C	E3	39	82	9B	2F	FF	87	34	8E	43	44	C4	DE	E9	CB
54	7B	94	32	A6	C2	23	3D	EE	4C	95	0B	42	FA	C3	4E
08	2E	A1	66	28	D9	24	B2	76	5B	A2	49	6D	8B	D1	25
72	F8	F6	64	86	68	98	16	D4	A4	5C	CC	5D	65	B6	92
6C	70	48	50	FD	ED	B9	DA	5E	15	46	57	A7	8D	9D	84
90	D8	AB	00	8C	BC	D3	0A	F7	E4	58	05	B8	B3	45	06
D0	2C	1E	8F	CA	3F	0F	02	C1	AF	BD	03	01	13	8A	6B
3A	91	11	41	4F	67	DC	EA	97	F2	CF	CE	F0	B4	E6	73
96	AC	74	22	E7	AD	35	85	E2	F9	37	E8	1C	75	DF	6E
47	F1	1A	71	1D	29	C5	89	6F	B7	62	0E	AA	18	BE	1B
FC	56	3E	4B	C6	D2	79	20	9A	DB	C0	FE	78	CD	5A	F4
1F	DD	A8	33	88	07	C7	31	B1	12	10	59	27	80	EC	5F
60	51	7F	A9	19	B5	4A	0D	2D	E5	7A	9F	93	C9	9C	EF
A0	E0	3B	4D	AE	2A	F5	B0	C8	EB	BB	3C	83	53	99	61
17	2B	04	7E	BA	77	D6	26	E1	69	14	63	55	21	0C	7D

Table 11-11. ShiftRows for blocks of length 128 bits ($L_b = 4$)

Before ShiftRows				After ShiftRows			
0	4	8	12	0	4	8	12
1	5	9	13	5	9	13	1
2	6	10	14	10	14	2	6
3	7	11	15	15	3	7	11

We have already seen (see page 244) how this step can be reduced to a matrix multiplication

$$\begin{bmatrix} b_{0,j} \\ b_{1,j} \\ b_{2,j} \\ b_{3,j} \end{bmatrix} \leftarrow \begin{bmatrix} 02 & 03 & 01 & 01 \\ 01 & 02 & 03 & 01 \\ 01 & 01 & 02 & 03 \\ 03 & 01 & 01 & 02 \end{bmatrix} \cdot \begin{bmatrix} b_{0,j} \\ b_{1,j} \\ b_{2,j} \\ b_{3,j} \end{bmatrix}, \tag{11.3}$$

with multiplication and addition carried out over $\mathbb{F}_{2^8}$. For multiplication by '02' (respectively x) the function xtime() has already been defined; multiplication by '03' (respectively $x + 1$) has already been handled similarly (cf. page 247).

For inverting the MixColumns transformation every column $(b_{i,j})$ of a block is multiplied by the polynomial $r(x) := r_3 x^3 + r_2 x^2 + r_1 x + r_0$ with coefficients

Table 11-12. ShiftRows for blocks of length 192 bits ($\boldsymbol{L_b} = 6$)

Before ShiftRows						After ShiftRows					
0	4	8	12	16	20	0	4	8	12	16	20
1	5	9	13	17	21	5	9	13	17	21	1
2	6	10	14	18	22	10	14	18	22	2	6
3	7	11	15	19	23	15	19	23	3	7	11

Table 11-13. ShiftRows for blocks of length 256 bits ($\boldsymbol{L_b} = 8$)

Before ShiftRows								After ShiftRows							
0	4	8	12	16	20	24	28	0	4	8	12	16	20	24	28
1	5	9	13	17	21	25	29	5	9	13	17	21	25	29	1
2	6	10	14	18	22	26	30	14	18	22	26	30	2	6	10
3	7	11	15	19	23	27	31	19	23	27	31	3	7	11	15

Table 11-14. Distances of line rotations in ShiftRows

L_b	$c_{L_b,1}$	$c_{L_b,2}$	$c_{L_b,3}$
4	1	2	3
6	1	2	3
8	1	3	4

$r_0(x) = x^3 + x^2 + x, r_1(x) = x^3 + 1, r_2(x) = x^3 + x^2 + 1$, and $r_3(x) = x^3 + x + 1$ and reduced modulo $M(x) := x^4 + 1$. The corresponding matrix is

$$\begin{bmatrix} \text{'0E'} & \text{'0B'} & \text{'0D'} & \text{'09'} \\ \text{'09'} & \text{'0E'} & \text{'0B'} & \text{'0D'} \\ \text{'0D'} & \text{'09'} & \text{'0E'} & \text{'0B'} \\ \text{'0B'} & \text{'0D'} & \text{'09'} & \text{'0E'} \end{bmatrix}. \tag{11.4}$$

11.7 The AddRoundKey Step

The last step of a round carries out an XOR of the round key with the block:

$$(b_{0,j}, b_{1,j}, b_{2,j}, b_{3,j}) \leftarrow (b_{0,j}, b_{1,j}, b_{2,j}, b_{3,j}) \oplus (k_{0,j}, k_{1,j}, k_{2,j}, k_{3,j}),$$

for $j = 0, \ldots, L_b - 1$. In this way, every bit of the result of a round is made dependent on every key bit.

11.8 Encryption as a Complete Process

Encryption with Rijndael is encapsulated in the following pseudocode according to [DaRi], Sections 4.2–4.4. The arguments are passed as pointers to fields of bytes or 4-byte words. The interpretation of the fields, variables, and functions employed is provided in Tables 11-15 through 11-17.

Table 11-15. Interpretation of variables

Variable	Interpretation
Nk	length L_k of the secret user key in 4-byte words
Nb	block length L_b in 4-byte words
Nr	round number L_r according to the table above

Table 11-16. Interpretation of fields

Variables	Size in bytes	Interpretation
CipherKey	4*Nk	secret user key
ExpandedKey	4*Nb * (Nr+1)	field of 4-byte words to hold the round key
Rcon	$\lceil$4*Nb * (Nr+1)/Nk$\rceil$	field of 4-byte words as constant $c(j) := (\mathrm{rc}(j), 0, 0, 0)^a$
State	4*Nb	field for input and output of plain text and encrypted blocks
RoundKey	4*Nb	round key, segment of ExpandedKey

a. It suffices to store the constants $rc(j)$ in a field of size $\lceil$Nb * (Nr+1)/Nk$\rceil \leq 30$ bytes. If the field begins with 0, this byte is unoccupied, since the index j begins with 1. It then is then 31 bytes long.

Table 11-17. Interpretation of functions

Function	Interpretation
KeyExpansion	generation of round key
RotBytes	left rotation of a 4-byte word by 1 byte: (abcd) $\longrightarrow$ (bcda)
SubBytes	S-box substitution S of all bytes of the passed field
Round	regular round
FinalRound	last round without MixColumns
ShiftRows	ShiftRows transformation
MixColumns	MixColumns transformation
AddRoundKey	addition of a round key

Key generation:

```
KeyExpansion (byte CipherKey, word ExpandedKey)
{
  for (i = 0; i < Nk; i++)
    ExpandedKey[i] = (CipherKey[4*i], CipherKey[4*i + 1],
      CipherKey[4*i + 2], CipherKey[4*i + 3]);
  for (i = Nk; i < Nb * (Nr + 1); i++)
  {
    temp = ExpandedKey[i - 1];
    if (i % Nk == 0)
      temp = SubBytes (RotBytes (temp)) ^ Rcon[i/Nk];
    else if ((Nk == 8) && (i % Nk == 4))
      temp = SubBytes (temp);
    ExpandedKey[i] = ExpandedKey[i - Nk] ^ temp;
  }
}
```

Round functions:

```
Round (word State, word RoundKey)
{
  SubBytes (State);
  ShiftRows (State);
  MixColumns (State);
  AddRoundKey (State, RoundKey)
}
FinalRound (word State, word RoundKey)
{
  SubBytes (State);
  ShiftRows (State);
  AddRoundKey (State, RoundKey)
}
```

Entire operation for encrypting a block:

```
Rijndael (byte State, byte CipherKey)
{
  KeyExpansion (CipherKey, ExpandedKey);
  AddRoundKey (State, ExpandedKey);
  for (i = 1; i < Nr; i++)
    Round (State, ExpandedKey + Nb*i);
  FinalRound (State, ExpandedKey + Nb*Nr);
}
```

There exists the possibility of preparing the round key outside of the function `Rijndael` and to pass the key schedule `ExpandedKey` instead of the user key `CipherKey`. This is advantageous when it is necessary in the encryption of texts that are longer than a block to make several calls to `Rijndael` with the same user key.

```
Rijndael (byte State, byte ExpandedKey)
{
  AddRoundKey (State, ExpandedKey);
  for (i = 1; i < Nr; i++)
    Round (State, ExpandedKey + Nb*i);
  FinalRound (State, ExpandedKey + Nb*Nr);
}
```

Especially for 32-bit processors it is advantageous to precompute the round transformation and to store the results in tables. By replacing the permutation and matrix operations by accesses to tables, a great deal of CPU time is saved, yielding improved results for encryption, and, as we shall see, for decryption as well. With the help of four tables each of 256 4-byte words of the form

$$
T_0[w] := \begin{bmatrix} S[w] \bullet \text{`02'} \\ S[w] \\ S[w] \\ S[w] \bullet \text{`03'} \end{bmatrix}, \quad
T_1[w] := \begin{bmatrix} S[w] \bullet \text{`03'} \\ S[w] \bullet \text{`02'} \\ S[w] \\ S[w] \end{bmatrix},
$$

$$
T_2[w] := \begin{bmatrix} S[w] \\ S[w] \bullet \text{`03'} \\ S[w] \bullet \text{`02'} \\ S[w] \end{bmatrix}, \quad
T_3[w] := \begin{bmatrix} S[w] \\ S[w] \\ S[w] \bullet \text{`03'} \\ S[w] \bullet \text{`02'} \end{bmatrix}
$$

$$(11.5)$$

(for $w = 0, \ldots, 255$, $S(w)$ denotes, as above, the S-box replacement), the transformation of a block $b = (b_{0,j}, b_{1,j}, b_{2,j}, b_{3,j})$, $j = 0, \ldots, L_b - 1$, can be determined quickly for each round by the substitution

$$
b_j := (b_{0,j}, b_{1,j}, b_{2,j}, b_{3,j}) \leftarrow T_0[b_{0,j}] \oplus T_1[b_{1,d(1,j)}] \oplus T_2[b_{2,d(2,j)}]
$$
$$
\oplus T_3[b_{3,d(3,j)}] \oplus k_j,
$$

with $d(i,j) := j + c_{L_b,i} \bmod L_b$ (cf. `ShiftRows`, Table 11-14) and $k_j = (k_{0,j}, k_{1,j}, k_{2,j}, k_{3,j})$ as the jth column of the round key.

For the derivation of this result, see [DaRi], Section 5.2.1. In the last round the `MixColumns` transformation is omitted, and thus the result is determined by

$$
b_j \leftarrow \left(S(b_{0,j}), S(b_{1,d(1,j)}), S(b_{2,d(2,j)}), S(b_{3,d(3,j)}) \right) \oplus k_j.
$$

Clearly, it is also possible to use a table of 256 4-byte words, in which

$$
b_j \leftarrow T_0[b_{0,j}] \oplus r\left(T_0[b_{1,d(1,j)}] \oplus r\left(T_0[b_{2,d(2,j)}] \oplus r\left(T_0[b_{3,d(3,j)}]\right)\right)\right) \oplus k_j,
$$

with a right rotation $r(a, b, c, d) = (d, a, b, c)$ by one byte. For environments with limited memory this can be a useful compromise, the price being only a slightly increased calculation time for the three rotations.

11.9 Decryption

For Rijndael decryption one runs the encryption process in reverse order with the inverse transformations. We have already considered the inverses of the transformations SubBytes, ShiftRows, and MixColumns, which in the following are represented in pseudocode by the functions InvSubBytes, InvShiftRows, and InvMixColumns. The inverted S-box, the distances for inversion, the ShiftRows transformation, and the inverted matrix for the inversion of the MixColumns transformation are given on pages 251–252. The inverse round functions are the following:

```
InvFinalRound (word State, word RoundKey)
{
  AddRoundKey (State, RoundKey);
  InvShiftRows (State);
  InvSubBytes (State);
}
InvRound (word State, word RoundKey)
{
  AddRoundKey (State, RoundKey);
  InvMixColumns (State);
  InvShiftRows (State);
  InvSubBytes (State);
}
```

The entire operation for decryption of a block is as follows:

```
InvRijndael (byte State, byte CipherKey)
{
  KeyExpansion (CipherKey, ExpandedKey);
  InvFinalRound (State, ExpandedKey + Nb*Nr);
  for (i = Nr - 1; i > 0; i--)
    InvRound (State, ExpandedKey + Nb*i);
  AddRoundKey (State, ExpandedKey);
}
```

The algebraic structure of Rijndael makes it possible to arrange the transformations for encryption in such a way that here, too, tables can be employed. Here one must note that the substitution S and the InvShiftRows transformation commute, so that within a round their order can be switched. Because of the homomorphism property $f(x + y) = f(x) + f(y)$ of linear transformations the InvMixColumns transformation and addition of the round key can be exchanged when InvMixColumns was used previously on the round key. Within a round the following course is taken:

```
InvFinalRound (word State, word RoundKey)
{
  AddRoundKey (State, RoundKey);
  InvSubBytes (State);
  InvShiftRows (State);
}

InvRound (word State, word RoundKey)
{
  InvMixColumns (State);
  AddRoundKey (State, InvMixColumns (RoundKey));
  InvSubBytes (State);
  InvShiftRows (State);
}
```

Without changing the sequence of transformations over both functions ordered one after the other, they can be redefined as follows:

```
AddRoundKey (State, RoundKey);

InvRound (word State, word RoundKey)
{
  InvSubBytes (State);
  InvShiftRows (State);
  InvMixColumns (State);
  AddRoundKey (State, InvMixColumns (RoundKey));
}

InvFinalRound (word State, word RoundKey)
{
  InvSubBytes (State);
  InvShiftRows (State);
  AddRoundKey (State, RoundKey);
}
```

With this is created the analogous structure to that for encryption. For reasons of efficiency the application of InvMixColumns to the round key in InvRound() is postponed until the key expansion, where the first and last round keys of InvMixColumns are left untouched. The "inverse" round keys are generated with

```
InvKeyExpansion (byte CipherKey, word InvEpandedKey)
{
  KeyExpansion (CipherKey, InvExpandedKey);
  for (i = 1; i < Nr; i++)
    InvMixColumns (InvExpandedKey + Nb*i);
}
```

The entire decryption operation of a block is now as follows:

```
InvRijndael (byte State, byte CipherKey)
{
  InvKeyExpansion (CipherKey, InvExpandedKey);
  AddRoundKey (State, InvExpandedKey + Nb*Nr);
  for (i = Nr - 1; i > 0; i--)
    InvRound (State, InvExpandedKey + Nb*i);
  InvFinalRound (State, InvExpandedKey);
}
```

In analogy to encryption, tables can be precomputed for this form of decryption. With

$$
\mathrm{T_0}^{-1}[w] := \begin{bmatrix} S^{-1}[w] \bullet \text{`0E'} \\ S^{-1}[w] \bullet \text{`09'} \\ S^{-1}[w] \bullet \text{`0D'} \\ S^{-1}[w] \bullet \text{`0B'} \end{bmatrix}, \quad
\mathrm{T_1}^{-1}[w] := \begin{bmatrix} S^{-1}[w] \bullet \text{`0B'} \\ S^{-1}[w] \bullet \text{`0E'} \\ S^{-1}[w] \bullet \text{`09'} \\ S^{-1}[w] \bullet \text{`0D'} \end{bmatrix},
$$

$$
\mathrm{T_2}^{-1}[w] := \begin{bmatrix} S^{-1}[w] \bullet \text{`0D'} \\ S^{-1}[w] \bullet \text{`0B'} \\ S^{-1}[w] \bullet \text{`0E'} \\ S^{-1}[w] \bullet \text{`09'} \end{bmatrix}, \quad
\mathrm{T_3}^{-1}[w] := \begin{bmatrix} S^{-1}[w] \bullet \text{`09'} \\ S^{-1}[w] \bullet \text{`0D'} \\ S^{-1}[w] \bullet \text{`0B'} \\ S^{-1}[w] \bullet \text{`0E'} \end{bmatrix}
$$

$$(11.6)$$

(for $w = 0, \ldots, 255$, $S^{-1}(w)$ denotes the inverse S-box replacement) the result of an inverse round operation on a block $b = (b_{0,j}, b_{1,j}, b_{2,j}, b_{3,j})$, $j = 0, \ldots, L_b - 1$, can be determined by

$$
b_j \leftarrow \mathrm{T_0^{-1}} [b_{0,j}] \oplus \mathrm{T_1^{-1}} \left[b_{1,d^{-1}(1,j)} \right] \oplus \mathrm{T_2^{-1}} \left[b_{2,d^{-1}(2,j)} \right] \oplus \mathrm{T_3^{-1}} \left[b_{3,d^{-1}(3,j)} \right] \\
\oplus k_j^{-1}
$$

for $j = 0, \ldots, L_b - 1$ with $d^{-1}(i, j) := j - c_{L_b, i} \bmod L_b$ (cf. page 250) and the jth column k_j^{-1} the "inverse" round key.

Again in the last round the MixColumns transformation is omitted, and thus the result of the last round is given by

$$
b_j \leftarrow \left(S^{-1}(b_{0,j}), S^{-1}\left(b_{1,d^{-1}(1,j)}\right), S^{-1}\left(b_{2,d^{-1}(2,j)}\right), S^{-1}\left(b_{3,d^{-1}(3,j)}\right) \right) \\
\oplus k_j^{-1}
$$

for $j = 0, \ldots, L_b - 1$.

To save memory one can also make do in decryption with a table of only 256 4-byte words, in which

$$
b_j \leftarrow T_0^{-1}[b_{0,j}] \oplus r\left(T_0^{-1}\left[b_{1,d^{-1}(1,j)}\right] \right. \\
\left. \oplus r\left(T_0^{-1}\left[b_{2,d^{-1}(2,j)}\right] \oplus r\left(T_0^{-1}\left[b_{3,d^{-1}(3,j)}\right] \right) \right) \right) \oplus k_j^{-1},
$$

with a right rotation $r(a, b, c, d) = (d, a, b, c)$ of one byte.

11.10 Performance

Implementations for various platforms have verified the superior performance of Rijndael. The bandwidth suffices for realizations for small 8-bit controllers with small amounts of memory and key generation on the fly up through current 32-bit processors. For purposes of comparison, Table 11-18 provides encryption rates for the candidates RC6, Rijndael, and Twofish, as well as for the older 8051 controller and the Advanced Risc Machine (ARM) as a modern 32-bit chip card controller.

Table 11-18. Comparative Rijndael performance in bytes per second, after [Koeu]

	8051 (3.57 MHz)	ARM (28.56 MHz)
RC6	165	151 260
Rijndael	3005	311 492
Twofish	525	56 289

Because of the more complex `InvMixColumns` operation, the times for decryption and encryption can diverge, depending on the implementation, though this effect can be completely compensated by using the tables described previously. Of course, the times depend on, in addition to the key length, the block length and the number of rounds (see Table 11-4). For comparison, on a Pentium III/200 MHz, throughput of about 8 MByte per second for a key of length 128 bits, about 7 Mbyte per second for 192-bit keys, and about 6 MByte per second for 256-bit keys for blocks of length 128 bits is achievable in both directions. On the same platform, the DES in C can encrypt and decrypt about 3.8 MByte per second (see [Gldm], `http://fp.gladman.plus.com`).

11.11 Modes of Operation

The classical operating modes Electronic Code Book (ECB), Cipher Block Chaining (CBC), Cipher Feedback (CFB), and Output Feedback (OFB) for block ciphers were updated by NIST for use with AES and provided with appropriate test vectors (see [FI81, N38A]). Consideration of additional operating modes, which had begun already in the framework of standardization of AES and which relates to the use of modes of operation in Internet communication, has resulted in the following operating modes:

- **Counter Mode (CTR):** A block keystream is generated and joined to the plain text blocks using XOR.

- **CCM Mode:** To ensure the reliability and integrity of a message, the counter mode is combined with a message authentication code (MAC) based on cipher block chaining (see [N38C]).

- **RMAC:** Using a randomized message authentication code, which is still in development, the validity of a message can be checked with respect to both its content and its source (see [N38B]).

For further details, investigations into security and cryptanalysis, computational times, and current information on AES and Rijndael the reader is referred to the literature cited above as well as the Internet sites of NIST and Vincent Rijmen, which in turn contain many links to further sources of information:

```
http://csrc.nist.gov/CryptoToolkit/tkencryption.html
http://csrc.nist.gov/CryptoToolkit/modes
http://www.esat.kuleuven.ac.be/~rijmen/rijndael
```

In the downloadable source code to this book there is an implementation of AES in the file `aes.c`, which can be used to deepen an understanding of the procedure and to do some experimentation.

CHAPTER 12

Large Random Numbers

Mathematics is full of pseudorandomness—plenty enough to supply all would-be creators for all time.

—D. R. Hofstadter, *Gödel, Escher, Bach*

Anyone who considers arithmetical methods of producing random digits is, of course, in a state of sin.

—John von Neumann,

SEQUENCES OF "RANDOM" NUMERICAL VALUES are used in many statistical procedures, in numerical mathematics, in physics, and also in number-theoretic applications to replace statistical observations or to automate the input of variable quantities. Random numbers are used:

- to select random samples from a larger set,

- in cryptography to generate keys and in running security protocols,

- as initial values in procedures to generate prime numbers,

- to test computer programs (a topic to which we shall return),

- for fun,

as well as in many additional applications. In computer simulations of natural phenomena random numbers can be used to represent measured values, thereby representing a natural process (*Monte Carlo methods*). Random numbers are useful even when numbers are required that can be selected arbitrarily. Before we set out in this chapter to produce some functions for the generation of *large* random numbers, which will be required, in particular, for cryptographic applications, we should take care of some methodological preparations.

There are many sources of random numbers, but we should be sure to differentiate between *genuine random numbers*, which arise as the result of random experiments, and *pseudorandom numbers*, which are generated algorithmically. Genuine random numbers arise from such processes as the tossing of coins or dice, spinning a (fair) roulette wheel, observing processes of radioactive decay with the aid of suitable measuring equipment, and evaluating the output of electronic components. In contrast to these, pseudorandom numbers are computed by algorithms, generated with the aid of *pseudorandom number generators*, which are deterministic, in that they depend only on an initial state and initial value (seed), and therefore are both predictable and reproducible. Pseudorandom numbers thus do not arise *randomly* in the strict sense of the word. The reason that this situation can frequently be ignored is that we are in possession of algorithms that are able to produce pseudorandom numbers of "high quality," where we shall have to explain what we mean by this term.

The first thing that we establish is that in fact, it makes no sense to talk about a single number being "random," but that mathematical requirements for randomness are always satisfied by *sequences* of numbers. Knuth speaks of a *sequence of independent random numbers with a particular distribution*, in which every number is produced *randomly and independently of all other numbers of the sequence*, and every number assumes a value within a certain range of values with a certain probability (see [Knut], Section 3.1). We use the terms "random" and "independent" here to mean that the events leading to the selection of concrete numbers are too complex in their formation and interaction to be detected by statistical or other tests.

This ideal is theoretically unachievable by generating numbers using deterministic procedures. Yet the goal of many different algorithmic techniques is to approach this ideal as closely as possible. The logical structure of deterministic random number generators can be described by a quintuple $(S, R, \phi, \psi, P_{\text{start}})$, where S denotes the finite set of internal states of the generator, R is the set of possible output values, $\phi : S \rightarrow S$ is the state function, $\psi : S \rightarrow R$ is the output function, and P_{start} is a probability measure for the distribution of the initial state s_0. After initialization, at each step $n \geq 1$, first the new state $s_n := \phi(s_{n-1})$ is computed, and from this state, the output value $r_n := \psi(s_n)$ (see [BSI2]). For the evaluation of the random number generators that we are considering here, we begin with the assumption that the start state is uniformly distributed in the set S, and this is indicated with the notation μ_S (for P_{start}). In the next chapter we will be concerned with testing the FLINT/C functions. For this, we will be using large random numbers that do not yet need to satisfy any of the demands of cryptographic security.

Therefore, we first select from the many possibilities at hand a proven and frequently used procedure for generating pseudorandom numbers (for the sake of brevity we shall frequently drop the "pseudo" and speak simply of random numbers, random sequences, and random number generators) and spend some time with the method of *linear congruences*. Beginning with an initial value X_0 the elements of a sequence are generated by the linear recursion

$$X_{i+1} = (X_i a + b) \bmod m. \tag{12.1}$$

This procedure was developed in 1951 by D. Lehmer, and it has enjoyed considerable popularity since that time, since despite their simplicity, linear congruences can produce random sequences with excellent statistical properties, where their quality, as one might expect, depends on the choice of parameters a, b, and m. In [Knut] it is shown that linear congruences with carefully chosen parameters can pass through the hoops of statistical tests with flying colors, but that on the other hand, a *random* selection of parameters almost always leads to a poor generator. The moral is this: Be careful in your choice of parameters!

The choice of m as a power of two has at once the advantage that forming the residue modulo m can be accomplished with a mathematical AND. An accompanying disadvantage is that the least-significant binary digits of numbers thus generated demonstrate less random behavior than the most-significant digits, and thus one must be careful in working with such numbers. In general, one must look out for poor random properties of such numbers formed from sequential values of a linear congruence generator modulo a prime divisor of the modulus m, so that the choice of m as a prime number should also be considered, since in this case individual binary digits are no worse than any others.

The choice of a and m has influence on the periodic behavior of the sequence: Since only finitely many, namely at most m, distinct sequence values can appear, the sequence begins to repeat at the latest with the generation of the $(m+1)$st number. That is, the sequence is periodic. (One says also that the sequence enters a period or a *cycle*.) The entry point into a cycle need not be the initial value X_0, but can be some later value X_μ. The numbers $X_0, X_1, X_2, \ldots, X_{\mu-1}$ are called the nonrecurring elements. We may thus indicate the periodic behavior of the sequence as shown in Figure 12-1.

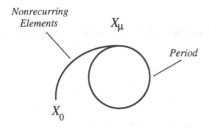

Figure 12-1. Periodic behavior of a pseudorandom sequence

Since the regular repetition of numbers in short cycles represents poor random behavior according to all reasonable criteria, we must strive to maximize the length of the cycles or indeed to find generators that possess only cycles of maximum length. We can establish criteria by which a linear congruence sequence with parameters a, b, and m possesses exactly the maximal period length. Namely, the following conditions should be fulfilled:

(i) $\gcd(b, m) = 1$.

(ii) For all primes p one has $p \mid m \Rightarrow p \mid (a - 1)$.

(iii) $4 \mid m \Rightarrow 4 \mid (a - 1)$.

For a proof and additional details see [Knut], Section 3.2.1.2.

As an example of parameters that fulfill these criteria let us consider the linear congruence that the ISO-C standard recommends as exemplary for the function rand():

$$X_{i+1} = (X_i \cdot 1103515245 + 12345) \bmod m, \tag{12.2}$$

where $m = 2^k$, with k determined by $2^k - 1$ being the largest number representable by the type unsigned int. The number X_{i+1} is not returned as the value of rand(), but rather $X_{i+1}/2^{16} \bmod (\text{RAND\_MAX} + 1)$, so that the function rand() generates all values between 0 and RAND_MAX. The macro RAND_MAX is defined in stdio.h and should have a value of at least 32267 (see [Pla1], p. 337). Here the recommendation of Knuth to do without the least-significant binary digits in the case of power-of-two moduli has apparently been taken into account. We easily determine that the above requirements (i)–(iii) are satisfied and that therefore a sequence produced by this generator possesses the maximum period length 2^k.

Whether this happens to be the case for a particular implementation of the C library, whose source code is usually unavailable,[1] can be tested under favorable circumstances with the aid of the following algorithm by R. P. Brent. The Brent algorithm determines the period length λ of a sequence that is computed by the recursion $X_{i+1} = F(X_i)$ on a set of values D using the generating function $F : D \rightarrow D$ and an initial value $X_0 \in D$. One needs at most $2 \cdot \max\{\mu, \lambda\}$ calculations of the function F (cf.[HKW], 4.2).

Algorithm of Brent for determining the period length λ of a sequence generated by $X_0, X_{i+1} = F(X_i)$

1. Set $y \leftarrow X_0, r \leftarrow 1$, and $k \leftarrow 0$.

2. Set $x \leftarrow y, j \leftarrow k$, and $r \leftarrow r + r$.

3. Set $k \leftarrow k + 1$ and $y \leftarrow F(y)$; repeat this step until $x = y$ or $k \geq r$.

4. If $x \neq y$, go to step 2. Otherwise, output $\lambda = k - j$.

This process is successful only if in step 3 one actually sees the actual sequence values $F(y)$ and not, as in the above ISO recommendation, only their most-significant parts.

We turn first to the actual subject of this chapter and supply ourselves with functions for generating random numbers in CLINT integer format. As our starting

---

[1] The GNU-C library, of the Free Software Foundation, and the EMX-C library, by Eberhard Mattes, are excellent exceptions. The rand() function of the EMX library uses the parameters $a = 69069$, $b = 5$, and $m = 2^{32}$. The multiplier $a = 69069$ suggested by G. Marsaglia produces, together with the modulus $m = 2^{32}$, good statistical results and a maximal period length (see [Knut], pp. 102–104).

point for the generation of prime numbers, we would like to be able to create large numbers with a specified number of binary digits; for these, the highest bit should be set to 1, and the remaining bits should be randomly generated.

12.1 A Simple Random Number Generator

First we construct a linear congruence generator from whose sequential values we will take the digits of a CLINT random number. The parameters $a = 6364136223846793005$ and $m = 2^{64}$ for our generator are taken from the table with results of the spectral test in Knuth ([Knut], pages 102–104). The sequence $X_{i+1} = (X_i \cdot a + 1) \bmod m$ thus generated possesses a maximal period length $\lambda = m$ as well as good statistical properties, as we conclude from the test results presented in the table. The generator is implemented in the following function rand64_l(). On each call to rand64_l() the next number in the sequence is generated and then stored in the global CLINT object SEED64, declared as static. The parameter a is stored in the global variable A64. The function returns a pointer to SEED64.

Function:	linear congruence generator with period length 2^{64}
Syntax:	clint * rand64_l (void);
Return:	pointer to SEED64 with calculated random number

```
clint *
rand64_l (void)
{
  mul_l (SEED64, A64, SEED64);
  inc_l (SEED64);
```

> The reduction modulo 2^{64} proceeds simply by setting the length field of SEED64 and costs almost no computational time.

```
  SETDIGITS_L (SEED64, MIN (DIGITS_L (SEED64), 4));
  return ((clint *)SEED64);
}
```

Next, we require a function for setting the initial values for rand64_l(). This function is called seed64_l(), and it accepts a CLINT object as input, from which it takes at most four of the most-significant digits as initial values in SEED64. The previous value of SEED64 is copied into the static CLINT object BUFF64, and a pointer to BUFF64 is returned.

Function:	set an initial value for rand64_l()
Syntax:	clint * seed64_l (CLINT seed_l);
Input:	seed_l (initial value)
Return:	pointer to BUFF64 with previous value of SEED64

The next function returns random numbers of type ULONG. All numbers are generated with a call to rand64_l(), where the most-significant digits of SEED64 are used to build a number of the requested type.

Function:	generation of a random number of type unsigned long
Syntax:	unsigned long ulrand64_l (void);
Return:	random number of type unsigned long

```
ULONG
ulrand64_l (void)
{
  ULONG val;
  USHORT l;
  rand64_l();
  l = DIGITS_L (SEED64);
  switch (l)
    {
      case 4:
      case 3:
      case 2:
        val = (ULONG)SEED64[l-1];
        val += ((ULONG)SEED64[l] << BITPERDGT);
        break;
      case 1:
        val = (ULONG)SEED64[l];
        break;
      default:
        val = 0;
    }
  return val;
}
```

The FLINT/C package contains the additional functions ucrand64_l(void) and usrand64_l(void), which generate random numbers of types UCHAR and USHORT, respectively. However, we shall not discuss them here. We now present the function rand_l(), which generates large random numbers of CLINT type, with the number of binary digits to be specified.

Function:	generation of a random number of type CLINT
Syntax:	void rand_l (CLINT r_l, int l);
Input:	l (number of binary digits of the number to be generated)
Output:	r_l (random number in the interval $2^{l-1} \leq r\_l \leq 2^l - 1$)

```
void
rand_l (CLINT r_l, int l)
{
  USHORT i, j, ls, lr;
```

The requested number of binary digits l is first bounded by the maximum permitted value for CLINT objects. Then the number ls of required USHORT digits and the position lr of the most-significant binary digit of the most-significant USHORT are determined.

```
l = MIN (l, CLINTMAXBIT);
ls = (USHORT)l >> LDBITPERDGT;
lr = (USHORT)l & (BITPERDGT - 1UL);
```

Now the digits of r_l are generated by successive calls to the function usrand64_l(). The least-significant binary digits of SEED64 are therefore not used for the construction of CLINT digits.

```
for (i = 1; i <= ls; i++)
  {
    r_l[i] = usrand64_l ();
  }
```

Now follows the precise manufacture of r_l by setting the most-significant bit in position lr − 1 of the (ls + 1)st USHORT digit to 1 and the most-significant bits to 0. If lr == 0, then the most-significant bit of the USHORT digit ls is set to 1.

```
  if (lr > 0)
    {
      r_l[++ls] = usrand64_l ();
      j = 1U << (lr - 1); /* j <- 2 ^ (lr - 1) */
      r_l[ls] = (r_l[ls] | j) & ((j << 1) - 1);
    }
  else
    {
      r_l[ls] |= BASEDIV2;
    }
  SETDIGITS_L (r_l, ls);
}
```

12.2 Cryptographic Random Number Generators

We now come to the cryptographic number generators that can be used for
sensitive purposes based on their properties, on the assumption that they have
been properly implemented and secret start values are used (more on this later).
We will first construct the BBS generator, then a random number generator
based on the symmetric algorithm AES, and then another that rests on a chain
of the cryptographic hash functions RIPEMD-160 and SHA-1. With the use of
AES, we build on the previous chapter; with hash functions, whose properties are
collected in Chapter 17, we are somewhat anticipating things.

   We will realize random number generators in such a way that they are
reentrant, so that they can be simultaneously and independently used by several
functions without their interfering with one another. That this is a good idea will
become immediately clear when one considers how a function calls a random
number generator whose internal state has just been deleted by another function.
In this case, the second function will not obtain useful results. This scenario is
heightened when the functions are executed in parallel processes or threads.

   For example, if cryptographic keys are generated within a process or thread,
and during this process the status of the random number generator being used
is deleted by another process (that is, set to zero), then the random number
generator will thereafter no longer produce reliable values, which could lead to
sharply reduced quality of the keys produced by the affected process.

   A way out of this problem is provided by the reentrant property, which
we achieve by storing the internal states of the random number generators in
separate buffers, which are managed individually and used exclusively by the
calling functions.

12.2.1 The Generation of Start Values

For the derivation of start values for cryptographic random number generators, so-called entropy sources are required, which while observable, are neither predictable nor able to be influenced. Every sequence of pseudorandom numbers that proceeds deterministically is at most as secure as its start value. An attacker who knows or can guess the start value of a pseudorandom sequence thereby knows the entire random sequence or the keys or passwords derived from it. The notion of entropy is borrowed from physics, where it is used as a measure of disorder in closed systems. The idea that good start values are achieved from the observation of the greatest possible disorder seems to be more intuitive and compelling than to speak of the "randomness of start values."

For our purposes, we will use primarily artificial sources of entropy, in particular, certain system statistics such as the number of clock ticks for certain processes, measures of external events such as mouse movements or the times between keyboard events or mouse clicks by users.

Such parameters are best combined with one another in a mixture, such as through the use of hash functions.

Functions for obtaining entropy are also offered by various operating systems, for example, by Linux and by the Win32 CryptoAPI under Windows. The Win32 CryptoAPI offers the function CryptGenRandom(), which takes entropy from a variety of sources available to the operating system. Here it is necessary to bind the link library ADVAPI32.LIB in order to use the Win32 DLL ADVAPI32.DLL (see [HoLe]).

Linux and FreeBSD offer entropy via the virtual devices /dev/random and /dev/urandom. The associated driver manages a 512-byte *entropy pool*, which is filled with the results of a variety of continuously monitored unpredictable events. The most productive source of these random events is the keyboard: The last digit of the microsecond-precise time measurement between two keyboard events can be neither predicted nor reproduced. Further sources are times associated with mouse movements, hardware interrupts, and block devices from the kernel. When the entropy pool is queried, 64-byte blocks from the pool are processed sequentially with the hash function SHA-1, and the result of this operation is played back into the pool. The hash function is then applied again to the first 64 bytes of the pool, and the result is finally returned to the calling function as a random value. The process is repeated as often as necessary until the required number of bytes is returned, and read access is terminated. The device file /dev/random always outputs only as many bits as corresponds to the available entropy in the pool. If the requests exceed this amount, then the virtual device is blocked, and it returns additional random bytes only after a sufficient number of events have occurred that can be observed for the production of entropy.

In contrast to /dev/random, the device file /dev/urandom returns values continuously even when the entropy pool is exhausted. In this case, the device returns random values determined in the manner described previously (see [Tso]).

The following function uses, depending on platform and availability, both sources for generating start values. Under Windows, in addition, the 64 result bytes of the WIN32 function QueryPerformanceCounter() are used for collecting entropy. Moreover, the system time is queried, and optionally, a character string of the calling function is accepted so that a user entry, such as input from the keyboard, can be considered in the generation of the start value. The values thus obtained are once more compressed with the hash function RIPEMD-160 to a 20-byte result, which is returned in this form and also as a large integer in CLINT format.

Function:	Generation of entropy for the initialization of pseudorandom number generators. In addition to an optional user-defined character string, entropy bytes are read from system-specific sources: For Win32: Value from QueryPerformanceCounter (64 byte), values from CryptGenRandom. For Linux: Entropy is read from /dev/urandom if this source is available. Altogether, LenRndStr + AddEntropy bytes go into the result. This is output as a CLINT integer. Additionally, a hash value is generated from the entropy data.
Syntax:	int GetEntropy_l (CLINT Seed_l, char *Hashres, int AddEntropy, char *RndStr, int LenRndStr);
Input:	AddEntropy (number of entropy bytes to be generated) RndStr (optional user-defined string, NULL is possible) LenRndStr (length of RndStr in bytes)
Output:	Seed_l (entropy as CLINT integer. If Seed_l == NULL, output is suppressed) Hashres (entropy as RIPEMD-160 hash value, length 20 bytes If Hashres == NULL, output suppressed)
Return:	0 if all O.K. $n > 0$ if n is less than the required number of entropy bytes that could be read E_CLINT_MAL in case of error in memory location

```
int
GetEntropy_l (CLINT Seed_l, UCHAR *Hashres, int AddEntropy,
              char *RndStr, int LenRndStr)
{
 unsigned i, j, nextfree = 0;
 unsigned MissingEntropy = MAX(AddEntropy, sizeof (time_t));
 UCHAR *Seedbytes;
 int BytesRead;
 int LenSeedbytes = LenRndStr + MissingEntropy +
                    sizeof (time_t) + 2*sizeof (ULONG);
 RMDSTAT hws;
 time_t SeedTime;
 FILE *fp;
#if defined _WIN32 && defined _MSC_VER
 LARGE_INTEGER PCountBuff;
 HCRYPTPROV hProvider = 0;
#endif /* defined _WIN32 && defined _MSC_VER? */
 if ((Seedbytes = (UCHAR*)malloc(LenSeedbytes)) == NULL)
  {
   return E_CLINT_MAL;
  }
 if (RndStr != NULL && LenRndStr > 0)
  {
   memcpy (Seedbytes, RndStr, LenRndStr);
   nextfree = LenRndStr;
  }
```

Bring system time into the buffer Seedbytes.

```
SeedTime = (time_t)time(NULL);
for (i = 0; i < sizeof(time_t); i++)
 {
  j = i << 3;
  Seedbytes[nextfree+i] = (UCHAR)((SeedTime >> j) & (time_t)0xff);
 }
nextfree += sizeof (time_t);
MissingEntropy -= sizeof (time_t);
```

Entropy from WIN32 API (link to ADVAPI32.LIB is required.

```
#if defined _WIN32 && defined _MSC_VER
 if (MissingEntropy)
  {
```

Chain with 64-bit value from `QueryPerformanceCounter()`

```
QueryPerformanceCounter (&PCountBuff);
for (i = 0; i < sizeof (DWORD); i++)
 {
   j = i << 3;
   Seedbytes[nextfree + i] =
    (char)((PCountBuff.HighPart >> j) & (DWORD)0xff);
   Seedbytes[nextfree + sizeof (DWORD) + i] =
    (char)((PCountBuff.LowPart >> j) & (DWORD)0xff);
 }
nextfree += 2*sizeof (DWORD);
MissingEntropy -= 2*sizeof (DWORD);
}
```

Chain with values from `CryptGenRandom():`

```
if (CryptAcquireContext(&hProvider, NULL, NULL, PROV_RSA_FULL,
                        CRYPT_VERIFYCONTEXT))
 {
  if (CryptGenRandom (hProvider, MissingEntropy, &Seedbytes[nextfree]))
   {
     nextfree += MissingEntropy;
     MissingEntropy = 0;
   }
 }
if (hProvider)
 {
  CryptReleaseContext (hProvider, 0);
 }
#endif /* defined _WIN32 && _MSC_VER */
```

Fetch entropy from /dev/urandom if this source is available.

```
if ((fp = fopen("/dev/urandom", "r")) != NULL)
 {
  BytesRead = fread(&Seedbytes[nextfree], sizeof (UCHAR), MissingEntropy, fp);
  nextfree += BytesRead;
  MissingEntropy -= BytesRead;
  fclose (fp);
 }
```

> Hash the chained entropy values.

```
if (Hashres != NULL)
 {
  ripeinit (&hws);
  ripefinish (Hashres, &hws, Seedbytes, nextfree);
 }
```

> Seed as an integer in `CLINT` format.

```
if (Seed_l != NULL)
 {
  byte2clint_l (Seed_l, Seedbytes, nextfree);
 }
```

> Overwrite and deallocate seed.

```
SeedTime = 0;
local_memset (Seedbytes, 0, LenSeedbytes);
local_memset (&hws, 0, sizeof (hws));

free (Seedbytes);

return MissingEntropy;
}
```

For an extensive discussion and ideas for obtaining start values, see [Gut1], [Gut2], [East], [Matt].[2]

12.2.2 *The BBS Random Number Generator*

A random number generator that has been well researched with regard to its cryptographic properties is the BBS bit generator of L. Blum, M. Blum, and M. Shub, which is based on results of complexity theory. We would like now to describe the process and then implement it, although without getting into the theoretical details, for which see [Blum] or [HKW], Chapter IV and Section VI.5.

We require two prime numbers p, q congruent to 3 modulo 4, which we multiply together to obtain a modulus n, as well as a number X that is relatively

---

[2] For highly sensitive applications, the generation of start values or even entire random sequences of *genuine* random numbers using suitable hardware components is always to be preferred.

prime to n. From $X_0 := X^2 \pmod{n}$, we obtain the start value X_0 for a sequence of integers that we calculate by successive squaring modulo n:

$$X_{i+1} = X_i^2 \bmod n. \tag{12.3}$$

As random numbers we remove from each value X_i the least-significant bit. We may thus make a formal description of the generator: The state set is denoted by $S := \{0, 1, \ldots, n-1\}$, the random values are defined by $R := \{0, 1\}$, the state transitions are described by the function $\phi : S \rightarrow S, \phi(x) = x^2 \bmod n$, and the output function is $\psi : S \rightarrow R$, with $\psi(x) := x \pmod 2$.

A random sequence constructed of binary digits thus obtained can be considered secure in the cryptographic sense: The ability to predict previous or future binary digits from a portion of those that have already been calculated is possible only if the factors p and q of the modulus are known. If these are kept secret, then according to current knowledge, the modulus n must be factored for one to be able to predict further bits of a BBS random sequence with probability greater than $\frac{1}{2}$ or to reconstruct unknown parts of the sequence. The security of the BBS generator thus rests on the same principle as the RSA procedure. The cost of such derived trust in the quality of the BBS generator lies in the expense of generating random bits; for each bit, the squaring of a number modulo a large integer is required, which is reflected in a large amount of computation time for long sequences. This is of little consequence, however, in the development of shorter sequences of random bits, such as for the creation of a single cryptographic key. In such a case, the sole criterion is security, and in evaluating security, one must take into account the procedure for obtaining start values. Since the BBS generator is also a deterministic procedure, "fresh chance" can be included only as described in the previous section via suitably obtained start values.

With the aid of the function prime_l, prime numbers $p \equiv q \equiv 3 \pmod 4$ are determined, both with approximately the same number of binary digits (this results in the modulus being as difficult as possible to factor, and the security of the BBS generator depends on this), and the modulus $n = pq$ is created.[3]

Beginning with the start value X_0, the next numbers in the sequence $X_{i+1} = X_i \pmod n$ are computed using the function SwitchRandBBS_l(), which outputs as random bit the least-significant bit of X_{i+1}. The value X_{i+1} is stored in a buffer as the current state of the generator, which is managed by the calling function. We will return to the question of how this buffer is to be initialized with a suitable start value with the first call to SwitchRandBBS_l(). But first let us implement the function.

---

[3] Several such moduli of various lengths are contained in the FLINT/C package, though without the associated factors, which are known only to the author ;-).

Function:	deterministic random number generator, after Blum–Blum–Shub
Syntax:	`int` `SwitchRandBBS_l (STATEBBS *rstate);`
Input:	rstate (pointer to state memory)
Output:	rstate (pointer to updated state memory)
Return:	value from $\{0, 1\}$

```
int
SwitchRandBBS_l (STATEBBS *rstate)
{
```

Continue the generator with modular squaring.

```
 msqr_l (rstate->XBBS, rstate->XBBS, rstate->MODBBS);
```

Output the least-significant bit of rstate->XBBS.

```
 return (*LSDPTR_L (rstate->XBBS) & 1);
}
```

The initialization of the BBS generator is accomplished with the help of the function InitRandBBS_l(), which in turn calls two additional functions: The function GetEntropy_l generates a start value seed_l, from which using the second function, seedBBS_l(), the initial state of the generator is calculated. The place where fresh chance comes into play in GetEntropy_l and how a start value is processed have already been discussed in the previous section.

Function:	initialization of the Blum–Blum–Shub pseudorandom number generator including obtaining entropy

Syntax:	`int`
	`InitRandBBS_l (STATEBBS *rstate, char * UsrStr,`
	`                int LenUsrStr, int AddEntropy);`

Input:	rstate (pointer to state memory) UsrStr (pointer to user character string) LenUsrStr (length of the user string in bytes) AddEntropy (number of additional requested entropy bytes)
Output:	rstate (pointer to initialized state memory)
Return:	0 if all O.K. $n > 0$: number of requested but not generated bytes

```
int
InitRandBBS_l (STATEBBS *rstate, char *UsrStr, int LenUsrStr, int AddEntropy)
{
  CLINT Seed_l;
  int MissingEntropy;
```

Generation of the requested entropy and from that the start value

```
  MissingEntropy = GetEntropy_l (Seed_l, NULL, AddEntropy, UsrStr, LenUsrStr);
```

Generation of the internal start state

```
  SeedBBS_l (rstate, Seed_l);
```

Deletion of the start value by overwriting

```
  local_memset (Seed_l, 0, sizeof (CLINT));
  return MissingEntropy;
}
```

The actual initialization of the generator is accomplished by the function seedBBS_l:

Function:	set initial values for randbit_l() and randBBS_l()
Syntax:	int seedBBS_l (STATEBBS *rstate, CLINT seed_l);
Input:	rstate (pointer to state memory)
	seed_l (initial value)
Output:	rstate (pointer to initialized state memory)
Return:	E_CLINT_OK if all O.K.
	E_CLINT_RCP: start value and modulus not relatively prime

```
int
seedBBS_l (STATEBBS *rstate CLINT seed_l)
{
  CLINT g_l;
  str2clint_l (rstate->MODBBS, (char *)MODBBSSTR, 16);
  gcd_l (rstate->MODBBS, seed_l, g_l);
  if (!EQONE_L (g_l))
    {
      return E_CLINT_RCP;
    }

  msqr_l (seed_l, rstate->XBBS, rstate->MODBBS);
```

Set the flag: PRNG is initialized.

```
  rstate->RadBBSInit = 1;

  return E_CLINT_OK;
}
```

Random numbers of type UCHAR are generated by the function bRandBBS_l(), the analogue of the function ucrand64_l():

Function:	generation of a random number of type UCHAR
Syntax:	UCHAR bRandBBS_l (STATEBBS *rstate);
Input:	rstate (pointer to initialized state memory)
Ouput:	rstate (pointer to updated state memory)
Return:	random number of type UCHAR

```
UCHAR
bRandBBS_l (STATEBBS *rstate)
{
  int i;

  UCHAR r = SwitchRandBBS_l (rstate);
  for (i = 1; i < (sizeof (UCHAR) << 3); i++)
    {
      r = (r << 1) + SwitchRandBBS_l (rstate);
    }
  return r;
}
```

For completeness, we should mention the functions sRandBBS_l() and
lRandBBS_l(), which generate random numbers of types USHORT and ULONG.

We still lack the function RandBBS_l, which generates random numbers r_l
with exactly l binary digits r_l in the interval $2^{l-1} \leq r\_l \leq 2^l - 1$. Since
this corresponds to a great extent to the function rand_l(), we shall omit an
extensive description, instead presenting only the function header. Of course,
these functions are contained in the FLINT/C package. To delete state buffers, the
function PurgeRandBBS_l() is available.

Function:	generation of a random number of type CLINT
Syntax:	int
	RandBBS_l (CLINT r_l, STATEBBS *rstate, int l);
Input:	rstate (internal state of the pseudorandom number generator)
	l (number of binary digits of the number to be generated
Ouput:	r_l (random number in the interval $2^{l-1} \leq r\_l \leq 2^l - 1$)
Return:	E_CLINT_OK if all OK
	E_CLINT_RIN if generator is not initialized

Function:	deletion of the internal state of RandBBS
Syntax:	`void`
	`PurgeRandBBS_l (STATEBBS *rstate);`
Input:	`rstate` (internal state of the pseudorandom number generator)
Ouput:	`rstate` (internal state of the generator, deleted by overwriting)

12.2.3 The AES Generator

An additional possibility for constructing random number generators is offered by symmetric block encryption systems, whose statistical and cryptographic properties have been shown to be well suited to the generation of pseudorandom numbers. We can clarify this with the help of the Advanced Encryption Standard, which as representative of modern block encryption systems stands out in relation to security and speed.[4]

With the code space K, the space D of clear text blocks, and the set $C := \{0, \ldots, c - 1\}$ for a constant c, state sets are defined by RandAES via $S := K \times D \times C$. The state function is described by

$$\phi : S \to S, \quad \phi(k, x, i) := \big(\xi(k, x, i), \mathrm{AES}_k(x), i + 1 \ (\mathrm{mod} \ c)\big), \qquad (12.4)$$

with

$$\xi(k, x, i) := \begin{cases} k & \text{if } i \not\equiv 0 \ (\mathrm{mod} \ c), \\ k \oplus \mathrm{AES}_k(x) & \text{if } i \equiv 0 \ (\mathrm{mod} \ c), \end{cases}$$

and the output function via

$$\psi : S \to R, \quad \psi(k, x, i) := x / 2^{8 \cdot (23 - (i \, \mathrm{mod} \, 16))} \mod 2^8. \qquad (12.5)$$

The constant c specifies how frequently the key is updated, to prevent a conclusion from being drawn about one state from the previous state. The price for more security is the time it takes to initialize the key. The most secure, but slowest, variant of the generator is obtained with $c = 1$.

The output of the generator is varied using the counter i in such a way that in sequential steps, various byte positions are selected from the output values.

The initialization of the AES-based pseudorandom number generator RandAES is accomplished via the function `InitRandAES_l`:

---

[4] AES is used in an extended form with a block length of 192 bits. The standard requires 128 bits, while the underlying algorithm Rijndael is designed for block lengths of 256 bits.

Function: initialization of the AES pseudorandom number generator
and production of entropy

Syntax:
```
int
InitRandAES_l (STATEAES *rstate, char *UsrStr,
                    int LenUsrStr, int AddEntropy, int update);
```

Input: rstate (pointer to state memory)
UsrStr (pointer to user character string)
LenUsrStr (length of user string in bytes)
AddEntropy (number of additional requested entropy bytes)
update (frequency of the AES key update)

Ouput: rstate (pointer to initialized state memory)

Return: 0 if all O.K.
$n > 0$: number of requested but not generated entropy bytes

```
int
InitRandAES_l (STATEAES *rstate, char *UsrStr, int LenUsrStr,
              int AddEntropy, int update)
{
  int MissingEntropy, i;
```

Generation of the start value. In `MissingEntropy` is stored how many of the
requested entropy bytes were unavailable.

```
  MissingEntropy = GetEntropy_l (NULL, rstate->XAES, AddEntropy,
                          UsrStr, LenUsrStr);
```

Initialization of AES.

```
  for (i = 0; i < 32; i++)
    {
      rstate->RandAESKey[i] ^= RandAESKey[i];
    }
  AESInit_l (&rstate->RandAESWorksp, AES_ECB, 192, NULL,
      &rstate->RandAESSched, rstate->RandAESKey, 256, AES_ENC);
```

First state change, creation of start state

```
AESCrypt_1 (rstate->XAES, &rstate->RandAESWorksp,
            &rstate->RandAESSched, rstate->XAES, 24);
```

Set frequency of key update as parameter

```
rstate->UpdateKeyAES = update;
```

Initialization of the step counter

```
rstate->RoundAES = 1;
```

Set the initialization flag.

```
rstate->RandAESInit = 1;

return MissingEntropy;
}
```

The state function `SwitchRandAES_1()` is realized as follows:

Function:	Deterministic random number generator based on the Advanced Encryption Standard (AES)
Syntax:	int SwitchRandAES_1 (StateAES *rstate);
Input:	rstate (pointer to state memory)
Ouput:	rstate (pointer to updated state memory)
Return:	random value of length one byte

```
UCHAR
SwitchRandAES_1 (STATEAES *rstate)
{
  int i;
  UCHAR rbyte;
```

State change via application of the function

$$\phi : S \rightarrow S, \quad \phi(k, x, i) := \big(\xi(k, x, i), \mathrm{AES}_k(x), i + 1 \bmod c\big).$$

The content of the buffer rstate->XAES corresponds to the function argument x.

```
AESCrypt_l (rstate->XAES, &rstate->RandAESWorksp,
            &rstate->RandAESSched, rstate->XAES, 24);
```

Generation of a random value via application of the function

$$\psi : S \to S, \quad \psi(k, x, i) := x/2^{8 \cdot (23 - (i \bmod 16))} \bmod 2^8$$

```
rbyte = rstate->XAES[(rstate->RoundAES)++ & 15];
```

Key update if the parameter is set and the prescribed number of rounds is reached

---

```
if (rstate->UpdateKeyAES)
  {
    if (0 == (rstate->RoundAES % rstate->UpdateKeyAES))
      {
        for (i = 0; i < 32; i++)
          {
            rstate->RandAESKey[i] ^= rstate->XAES[i];
          }
        AESInit_l (&rstate->RandAESWorksp, AES_ECB, 192, NULL,
            &rstate->RandAESSched, rstate->RandAESKey, 256, AES_ENC);
      }
  }
return rbyte;
}
```

Random values r_l in the interval $2^{l-1} \le \text{r\_l} \le 2^l - 1$ are specified with the function RandAES_l(), whose function header is given here:

Function:	generation of a random number of type CLINT
Syntax:	int RandAES_1 (CLINT r_l, STATEAES *rstate, int l);
Input:	rstate (internal state of the pseudorandom number generator) l (number of binary digits of the number to be generated)
Ouput:	r_l (random number in the interval $2^{l-1} \le \text{r\_l} \le 2^l - 1$)
Return:	E_CLINT_OK if all O.K. E_CLING_RIN if the generator is not initialized

Additionally, in `random.h` are defined the macros `bRandAES_l()`, `sRandAES_l()`, and `lRandAES_l()`, each of which expects an initialized state buffer as argument, and they generate random numbers of types `UCHAR`, `USHORT`, and `ULONG` from these buffers.

The deletion of the generator takes place in analogy to RandBBS with the following function:

Function:	deletion of the internal state of RandAES
Syntax:	`void` `PurgeRandAES_1 (STATEAES *rstate);`
Input:	rstate (internal state of the pseudorandom number generator)
Ouput:	rstate (internal state of the pseudorandom number generator, deleted by overwriting)

12.2.4 The RMDSHA-1 Generator

The following pseudorandom number generator will be built from the hash functions SHA-1 and RIPEMD-160. Both functions can be calculated extremely quickly, which leads to a generator with excellent performance.

With the definitions $D := \{0, \ldots, 2^{160} - 1\}$, $C := \{0, \ldots, c - 1\}$, $S := D \times C$, and $R := \{0, \ldots, 2^8 - 1\}$ for input values, counters, states, and output values, the state function is described by

$$\phi : S \to S, \quad \phi(x, i) := \big(\text{RIPEMD-160}(x), i + 1 \bmod c\big), \tag{12.6}$$

and the output function determined by

$$\psi : S \to R, \quad \psi(x, i) := \text{SHA-1}(x) / 2^{8 \cdot (19 - (i \bmod 16))} \bmod 2^8. \tag{12.7}$$

As in the case of RandAES, the output is varied with the help of the counter i in such a way that in successive steps, varying byte positions are selected as output values. The initialization of the generator takes place via the function `InitRandRMDSHA1_1()`:

Function:	initialization of the RIPEMD-160/SHA-1 pseudorandom number generator together with entropy creation
Syntax:	int InitRandRMDSHA1_l (STATERMDSHA1 *rstate, char * UsrStr, int LenUsrStr, int AddEntropy);
Input:	rstate (pointer to state memory) UsrStr (pointer to user character string) LenUsrStr (length of the user character string in bytes) AddEntropy (number of additional requested entropy bytes)
Output:	rstate (pointer to initialized state memory)
Return:	0 if all O.K. $n > 0$: number of requested but not generated entropy bytes

```
int
InitRandRMDSHA1_l (STATERMDSHA1 *rstate, char *UsrStr,
                   int LenUsrStr, int AddEntropy)
{
  int MissingEntropy;
```

Generation of start value. In MissingEntropy is stored the number of requested entropy bytes that were not available.

```
  MissingEntropy = GetEntropy_l (NULL, rstate->XRMDSHA1, AddEntropy,
                                 UsrStr, LenUsrStr);
```

First state transition, creation of start state.

```
  ripemd160_l (rstate->XRMDSHA1, rstate->XRMDSHA1, 20);
```

Initialization of the step counter i.

```
  rstate->RoundRMDSHA1 = 1;
```

Set the initialization flag.

```
rstate->RandRMDSHA1Init = 1;

return MissingEntropy;
}
```

The state function `SwitchRandRMDSHA1_1()` outputs a random byte each time it is called:

Function:	Deterministic random number generator based on the hash functions SHA-1 and RIPEMD-160
Syntax:	int SwitchRandRMDSHA1_1 (STATERMDSHA1 *rstate);
Input:	rstate (pointer to state memory)
Output:	rstate (pointer to updated state memory)
Return:	random value of length one byte

```
UCHAR
SwitchRandRMDSHA1_1 (STATERMDSHA1 *rstate)
{
  UCHAR rbyte;
```

Generation of a random value by application of the function

$$\psi : S \to R, \quad \psi(x, i) := \text{SHA-1}(x)/2^{8 \cdot (19 - (i \bmod 16))} \bmod 2^8.$$

```
  sha1_1 (rstate->SRMDSHA1, rstate->XRMDSHA1, 20);
  rbyte = rstate->SRMDSHA1[(rstate->RoundRMDSHA1)++ & 15];
```

State change via application of the function

$$\phi : S \to S, \quad \phi(x, i) := \left(\text{RIPEMD-160}(x), i + 1 \bmod 2^{32} \right).$$

```
  ripemd160_1 (rstate->XRMDSHA1, rstate->XRMDSHA1, 20);

  return rbyte;
}
```

Random numbers r_1 in the interval $2^{l-1} \le r\_1 \le 2^l - 1$ are generated via the function `RandRMDHSA1_1()`, whose function header is given here:

Function:	Generation of a random number of type `CLINT`
Syntax:	`int` `RandRMDSAH1_l (CLINT r_l, STATERMDSHA1 *rstate, int l);`
Input:	rstate (internal state of the pseudorandom number generator) l (number of binary digits of the number to be generated)
Output:	r_l (random number in the interval $2^{l-1} \leq r\_l \leq 2^l - 1$)
Return:	`E_CLINT_OK` if all O.K. `E_CLINT_RIN` if the generator is uninitialized

For this generator as well there are associated macros `bRandRMDSHA1_l()`, `sRandRMDSHA1_l()`, and `lRandRMDSHA1_l()` in the module `random.h`, which expect as argument the appropriate initialized buffer from which random integers of types `UCHAR`, `USHORT`, and `ULONG` are generated.

Finally, for sensitive applications, one needs a function for deleting the internal state of the random number generator:

Function:	deletion of the internal state of RandRMDSHA-1
Syntax:	`void` `PurgeRandSHA_l (STATERMDSHA1 *rstate);`
Input:	rstate (internal state of the pseudorandom number generator)
Ouput:	rstate (internal state of the generator, deleted by overwriting)

12.3 Quality Testing

For investigating the quality of random number generators, a large number of theoretical and empirical tests have been developed that are suitable for detecting the structural properties of sequences of random numbers.

Depending on the area of application, in addition to the statistical requirements on such sequences, one must also consider that random sequences that are to be used in cryptographic applications must not be predictable without the knowledge of secret information or reproducible from a small number of representatives, so as to keep attackers from being able to reconstruct a cryptographic key or sequence of keys derived from the sequence.

As an example, the German Institute for Security in Information Technology has specified in [BSI2] functionality classes and quality criteria for evaluating deterministic random number generators. The specification establishes four classes of increasing security:

K1: A sequence of random vectors composed of random numbers should with high probability contain no identical consecutive elements. Statistical properties of the generated random numbers are unimportant. The length of the random vectors and the probability of error depend on the application.

K2: The generated random numbers should be indistinguishable from true random numbers based on statistical tests. The tests to be applied are the monobit test, poker test, runs and longruns tests from [BSI2] and [FIPS], as well as the additional statistical test of autocorrelation. Altogether, what is checked is how well a given sequence of bits (or a part of such a sequence) satisfies the following conditions:

- Zeros and ones appear equally often.
- After a sequence of n zeros (respectively ones), the next bit will be a one (zero) with probability one-half.
- A given output contains no information about the next output.

K3: It should be impossible for all practical purposes for an attacker to be able to calculate or guess from a known sequence of generated random numbers any previous or future random numbers or an inner state of the generator.

K4: It should be impossible for all practical purposes for an attacker to calculate or guess from an inner state of the generator previous random numbers or states.

12.3.1 Chi-Squared Test

As motivation for dealing with tests for evaluation of property K2, we look first at the *chi-squared test* (also written "χ^2 test"), which with the Kolmogorov–Smirnov test is among the most important tests of goodness of fit. The chi-squared test gives information on how well an empirically obtained probability distribution corresponds to a theoretically expected distribution. The chi-squared test computes the statistic

$$\chi^2 = \sum_{i=1}^{t} \frac{(H(X_i) - n \operatorname{pr}(X_i))^2}{n \operatorname{pr}(X_i)}, \tag{12.8}$$

where for t distinct events X_i we designate $H(X_i)$ the observed frequency of the event X_i, $\operatorname{pr}(X_i)$ the probability for the occurrence of X_i, and n the number of observations. For the case to which these distributions correspond, the statistic χ^2, viewed as a random variable, has the expected value $E(\chi^2) = t - 1$. The threshold values that lead to the rejection of the test hypothesis of equality of the distributions for given error probabilities can be read from tables of the chi-squared distribution for $t - 1$ degrees of freedom (cf. [Bos1], Section 4.1).

The chi-squared test is employed in connection with many empirical tests to measure their results for correspondence with the theoretically calculated test distributions. The test is particularly simple to apply for sequences of uniformly distributed (which is our test hypothesis!) random numbers X_i in a range of values $W = \{0, \ldots, \omega - 1\}$: We assume that each of the numbers in W is taken with the same probability $p = 1/\omega$ and thus expect that among n random numbers X_i each number from W appears approximately n/ω times (where we assume $n > \omega$). However, this should not be *exactly* the case, because the probability P_k that among n random numbers X_i a specific value $w \in W$ appears k times is given by

$$P_k = \binom{n}{k} p^k (1 - p)^{n-k} = \frac{n!}{k! (n-k)!} p^k (1 - p)^{n-k}. \tag{12.9}$$

This *binomial distribution* indeed has the largest values for $k \approx n/\omega$, but the probabilities $P_0 = (1 - p)^n$ and $P_n = p^n$ are not equal to zero. Under the assumption of random behavior we therefore expect to observe in the sequence of the X_i frequencies h_w of individual values $w \in W$ according to the binomial distribution. Whether this actually occurs is established by the chi-squared test in calculating

$$\chi^2 = \sum_{i=0}^{\omega-1} \frac{(h_j - n/\omega)^2}{n/\omega} = \frac{\omega}{n} \sum_{i=0}^{\omega-1} h_i^2 - n. \tag{12.10}$$

The test is repeated for several random samples (partial sequences of X_i). A rough approximation to the chi-squared distribution allows us to deduce that in most cases the test result χ^2 must lie in the interval $\left[\omega - 2\sqrt{\omega}, \omega + 2\sqrt{\omega}\right]$. Otherwise, the given sequence would attest to a lack of randomness. Based on this, the probability of an error, namely, that an actually "good" random sequence is declared "bad" based on the result of the chi-squared test, is about two percent. It is in this sense that the error probability of 10^{-6} that results from the given bounds is to be interpreted in the following tests. The bounds are set such that a "halfway reasonable" probability generator would almost always pass the test, so that known attacks against cryptographic algorithms based on statistical weaknesses in random number generators would fail (see [BSI2], page 7).[5]

The linear congruence generator in the ISO-C standard that we considered above passes this simple test, as do the pseudorandom number generators that we shall implement below for the FLINT/C package.

---

[5] Take note that the test is valid only for a sufficiently large number of samples: This number must be at least $n = 5\omega$ (see [Bos2], Section 6.1), with an even larger number to be preferred.

12.3.2 Monobit Test

For a random sequence of 2500 bytes, or 20 000 bits, a test is made whether approximately the same number of zeros and ones occurs. The test is passed with error probability 10^{-6} if the number of ones (that is, set bits) in a sequence of 20 000 bits lies in the interval $[9\,654, 10\,346]$ (see [BSI2] and [FIPS]).

12.3.3 Poker Test

The poker test is a special case of the chi-squared test with $\omega = 16$ and $n = 5000$. A generated sequence of random numbers is divided into segments of four bits, and the frequencies of the sixteen possible sequences of zeros and ones are counted.

For an execution of the test, a sequence of 20 000 bits is divided into 5000 segments of four bits each. The frequencies h_i, $0 \leq i \leq 15$, of the sixteen four-bit arrangements are counted. For the test to be passed, the value

$$X = \frac{16}{5000} \sum_{i=0}^{15} h_i^2 - 5000 \tag{12.11}$$

must lie, according to the specifications in [BSI2] and [FIPS], in the interval $[1.03, 57.40]$, which corresponds to an error probability of 10^{-6}. Measured values outside the previously mentioned interval $\left[\omega - 2\sqrt{\omega}, \omega + 2\sqrt{\omega}\right] = [8, 24]$, on the other hand, are rejected with the higher error probability 0.02.

12.3.4 Runs Test

A *run* is a sequence of identical bits (zeros or ones). The test counts the frequencies of runs of various lengths and checks for deviations from expected values. In a sequence of 20 000 bits, all runs of the same type (length and bit value, e.g., runs of 2 ones) are counted. The test is passed if the numbers lie in the intervals shown in Table 12-1 (error probability of 10^{-6}).

12.3.5 Longruns Test

As an extension of the runs test, the longruns test checks whether there exists a sequence of identical bits longer than a given length. The test is passed if there is no run of length 34 or longer in a sequence of 20 000 bits.

Table 12-1. Tolerance intervals for runs of various lengths, after [BSI2] and [FIPS]

Run Length	Interval
1	[2267,2733]
2	[1079,1421]
3	[502,748]
4	[233,402]
5	[90,223]
6	[90,233]

12.3.6 Autocorrelation Test

The autocorrelation test provides information about possible existing dependencies within a generated bit sequence. For a sequence of 10 000 bits, $b_1, \ldots, b_{10000}$, and for t in the range $1 \leq t \leq 5000$, the values

$$Z_t = \sum_{i=1}^{5000} b_i \oplus b_{i+1} \qquad (12.12)$$

are computed. The test is passed with probability of error 10^{-6} if all the Z_t lie in the interval $[2327, 2673]$ (see [BSI2] and [FIPS]).

12.3.7 Quality of the FLINT/C Random Number Generators

To demonstrate the properties K2, the required statistical tests for the output width of 8 bits for the random number generators presented here were carried out. In 2313 individual tests, over 20 000 random bits were calculated. All test results lay within the required bounds. The average values were calculated, and they are presented in Table 12-2. Therefore, the generators presented here can be placed in class K2.

Class K3 requires that it be impossible for an attacker to determine predecessors or successors of a given subsequence $r_i, r_{i+1}, \ldots, r_{i+j}$, nor to determine any internal state. For the generator RandAES, this would be equivalent to serious attack possibilities against the encryption procedure AES, which would lead to being able to take ciphered text and produce bits of clear text or of a key. No such attacks are known. Furthermore, the AES is considered a high-strength cryptographic mechanism, so that the generator can be placed in class K3.

If the parameter c is set to the value 1, then in each round, a new key $k_i := \xi(k_{i-1}, x, i-1) = k_{i-1} \oplus \text{AES}_{k_{i-1}}(x)$ is established. Due to this operation, it is impossible to determine a previous internal state (or key) s_{i-j}

Table 12-2. Test results of the FLINT/C random number generators

Test	Rand64	RandRMDSHA-1	RandBBS	RandAES	Tolerance Interval
Monobit	9997.29	10000.11	9999.15	9998.66	$[9654, 10346]$
Poker	15.11	14.70	15.19	15.01	$[1.03, 57.40]$
Runs length 1	2499.55	2501.69	2500.02	2499.86	$[2267, 2733]$
Runs length 2	1250.29	1249.31	1249.38	1249.48	$[1079, 1421]$
Runs length 3	625.05	624.95	625.07	625.22	$[502, 748]$
Runs length 4	312.16	312.32	312.87	312.59	$[233, 402]$
Runs length 5	156.29	156.22	156.15	156.11	$[90, 223]$
Runs length 6	156.36	156.34	156.23	156.41	$[90, 233]$
Longruns	0.00	0.00	0.00	0.00	$[0, 0]$
Autocorrelation	2500.79	2500.06	2501.00	2500.10	$[2327, 2673]$

from knowledge of the internal state s_i, and therefore, with knowledge of the internal state of RandAES, it is even impossible to determine from a subsequence any predecessors of that subsequence. For $c = 1$, then, RandAES can be placed in class K4.

The argumentation for RandRMDSHA1 is similar. Because of the unidirectional properties of SHA-1, one cannot draw conclusions about the internal state of the generator from a subsequence, and therefore, no predecessors or successors can be determined. This ensures membership in class K3. Because of the same property in RIPEMD-160, no previous states can be derived from an internal state of the generator, without which again no predecessors can be determined. Thus the random number generator RandRMDSHA-1 can be placed in class K4.

For RandBBS an argument has already been presented that supports placing the generator in class K4.

An extensive overview of this field can be found in [Knut]. In particular, a comprehensive presentation of the theoretical evaluation of random number generators is provided in [Nied]. Ideas for constructing random number generators presented in this chapter have been taken from [Sali], as well as the type of representation of the test results in Table 12-2. Some pragmatic ideas for testing random sequences are contained in [FIPS].

12.4 More Complex Functions

In this section we will prepare several functions for generating random numbers and random prime numbers with additional boundary conditions that are not specialized to a specific random number generator. Rather, the choice of the generator to use is supported by a parameter. Here it is necessary to pass the appropriate state memory as parameter. The structure

```
struct InternalStatePRNG
{
  STATERMDSHA1 StateRMDSHA1;
  STATEAES StateAES;
  STATEBBS StateBBS;
  int Generator;
};
```

extended by setting

```
typedef struct InternalStatePRNG STATEPRNG;
```

contains the state memory of the individual random number generators previously presented as well as the status variable Generator, which specifies for which random number generator the structure was initialized.

With this definition, the functions InitRand_l(), Rand_l(), lRand_l(), sRand_l(), bRand_l(), and PurgeRand_l() were created. With InitRand_l() a generator is initialized that is then used for subsequent calls of the random functions. The random functions themselves require as parameter a pointer to the initialized structure STATEPRNG.

Function:	Initialization of a yet to be specified random generator with generation of entropy

Syntax:	`int`
	`InitRand_l (STATEPRNG *xrstate, char *UsrStr,`
	`int LenUsrStr, int AddEntropy, int Generator);`

Input:	UsrStr (byte vector for initializing the pseudorandom number generator)
	LenUsrStr (length of UsrStr in bytes)
	AddEntropy (number of requested entropy bytes)
	Generator (pseudorandom number generator to be initialized:
	        FLINT_RND64
	        FLINT_RNDRMDSHA1
	        FLINT_RNDAES
	        FLINT_RNDBBS)

Output:	xrstate (new internal state of the pseudorandom number generator)
Return:	0: OK $n > 0$: number of requested but not generated entropy bytes $n < 0$: specified generator does not exist; RND64 was initialized by default, or $\lvert n \rvert$ requested but not generated entropy bytes

```
int
InitRand_l (STATEPRNG *xrstate, char *UsrStr, int LenUsrStr,
            int AddEntropy, int Generator)
{
  int error;
  switch (Generator)
    {
      case FLINT_RNDBBS:
        error = InitRandBBS_l (&xrstate->StateBBS, (char*)UsrStr,
                               LenUsrStr, AddEntropy);
        xrstate->Generator = FLINT_RNDBBS;
        break;
      case FLINT_RNDRMDSHA1:
        error = InitRandRMDSHA1_l (&xrstate->StateRMDSHA1, (char*)UsrStr,
                                   LenUsrStr, AddEntropy);
        xrstate->Generator = FLINT_RNDRMDSHA1;
        break;
      case FLINT_RNDAES:
        error = InitRandAES_l (&xrstate->StateAES, (char*)UsrStr,
                               LenUsrStr, AddEntropy, 10);
        xrstate->Generator = FLINT_RNDAES;
        break;
      case FLINT_RND64:
        error = InitRand64_l ((char*)UsrStr, LenUsrStr, AddEntropy);
        xrstate->Generator = FLINT_RND64;
        break;
      default:
        InitRand64_l ((char*)UsrStr, LenUsrStr, AddEntropy);
        xrstate->Generator = FLINT_RND64;
        error = -AddEntropy;
    }
  return error;
}
```

Function:	Generation of a pseudorandom number r_l of type CLINT with $2^{l-1} \leq r\_l < 2^l$ using the FLINT/C pseudorandom number generators, previous initialization via call to the initialization function InitRand_l with suitable parameters is required
Syntax:	int Rand_l (CLINT r_l, STATEPRNG *xrstate, int l;)
Input:	xrstate (initialized internal state of the pseudorandom number generator) rmin_l (lower limit for r_l) rmax_l (upper limit for r_l)
Output:	r_l (pseudorandom number) xrstate (new internal state of the pseudorandom number generator)
Return:	E_CLINT_OK if all O.K. E_CLINT_RGE if pmin_l > pmax_l E_CLINT_RNG error in specification of generator in xrstate E_CLINT_RIN if specified random number generator uninitialized or nonexistent

```
int
Rand_l (CLINT r_l, STATEPRNG *xrstate, int l)
{
  int error = E_CLINT_OK;

  switch (xrstate->Generator)
    {
      case FLINT_RNDBBS:
        error = RandBBS_l (r_l, &xrstate->StateBBS,
                          MIN (l, (int)CLINTMAXBIT));
        break;
      case FLINT_RNDAES:
        error = RandAES_l (r_l, &xrstate->StateAES,
                          MIN (l, (int)CLINTMAXBIT));
        break;
```

```
    case FLINT_RNDRMDSHA1:
      error = RandRMDSHA1_l (r_l, &xrstate->StateRMDSHA1,
                                  MIN (l, (int)CLINTMAXBIT));
      break;
    case FLINT_RND64:
      rand_l (r_l, MIN (l, (int)CLINTMAXBIT));
      break;
    default:
      rand_l (r_l, MIN (l, (int)CLINTMAXBIT));
      error = E_CLINT_RIN;
    }
  return error;
}
```

The remaining random functions should be executed only with their associated signatures.

Function:	generation of a pseudorandom number of types UCHAR, USHORT, ULONG; previous initialization via call to initialization function InitRand_l with suitable parameters necessary
Syntax:	UCHAR bRand_l (STATEPRNG *xrstate); USHORT sRand_l (STATEPRNG *xrstate); ULONG lRand_l (STATEPRNG *xrstate);
Input:	xrstate (initialized internal state of pseudorandom number generator)
Output:	xrstate (new internal state of pseudorandom number generator)
Return:	pseudorandom number of type UCHAR, USHORT, ULONG.

With the following function, the internal state of a random number generator is deleted:

Function:	deletion of the internal state of a pseudorandom number generator
Syntax:	`int` `PurgeRand_l (STATEPRNG *xrstate);`
Input:	xrstate (internal state of the pseudorandom number generator)
Output:	xrstate (internal state, deleted by overwriting)
Return:	`E_CLINT_OK` if all OK `E_CLINT_RIN` if no FLINT/C generator is specified in xrstate

There follow some interesting functions with whose help we can determine large random prime numbers. We begin with the search for random numbers that lie within a prescribed interval $[r_{min}, r_{max}]$. This is a generalization of our function `Rand_l()`.

Function:	determination of a pseudorandom number r_l of type `CLINT` with `rmin_l` $\leq$ `r_l` $\leq$ `rmax_l` using the FLINT/C pseudorandom number generators; previous initialization by calling initialization function `InitRand_l` with suitable parameters required

Syntax:	`int`
	`RandlMinMax_l (CLINT r_l, STATEPRNG *xrstate,`
	`                  CLINT rmin_l,CLINT rmax_l);`

Input:	xrstate (Initialized internal state of a pseudorandom number generator) rmin_l (lower bound for r_l) rmax_l (upper bound for r_l)
Output:	r_l (random number) xrstate (new internal state of generator)
Return:	`E_CLINT_OK` if all O.K. `E_CLINT_RGE` if rmin_l > rmax_l `E_CLINT_RNG` if error in specifying generator in xrstate `E_CLINT_RIN` if random number generator uninitialized

```
int
RandMinMax_l (CLINT r_l, STATEPRNG *xrstate, CLINT rmin_l, CLINT rmax_l)
{
  CLINT t_l;
  int error = E_CLINT_OK;
  USHORT l = ld_l (rmax_l);
```

Plausibility: Is $rmin\_l \leq rmax\_l$?

```
  if (GT_L (rmin_l, rmax_l))
    {
      return E_CLINT_RGE;
    }
```

Form auxiliary variable $t\_l := rmax\_l - rmin\_l + 1$.

```
  sub_l (rmax_l, rmin_l, t_l);
  inc_l (t_l);
```

Search for random number less than or equal to $2^{\lfloor ld(rmax\_l) \rfloor}$.

```
  switch (xrstate->Generator)
    {
      case FLINT_RNDAES:
        error = RandAES_l (r_l, &xrstate->StateAES,
                           MIN (l, (int)CLINTMAXBIT));
        break;
      case FLINT_RNDRMDSHA1:
        error = RandRMDSHA1_l (r_l, &xrstate->StateRMDSHA1,
                               MIN (l, (int)CLINTMAXBIT));
        break;
      case FLINT_RNDBBS:
        error = RandBBS_l (r_l, &xrstate->StateBBS,
                           MIN (l, (int)CLINTMAXBIT));
        break;
```

```
    case FLINT_RND64:
      rand_l (r_l, MIN (1, (int)CLINTMAXBIT));
      error = rand_l (r_l, MIN (1, (int)CLINTMAXBIT));
      break;
    default:
      return E_CLINT_RNG;
  }

if (E_CLINT_OK != error)
  {
    return error;
  }
```

Calculate `r_l mod t_l + rmin_l`.

```
mod_l (r_l, t_l, r_l);
add_l (r_l, rmin_l, r_l);

return error;
}
```

With the help of the function `RandMinMax_l()`, we can begin our search for prime numbers p that lie within the interval $[r_{min}, r_{max}]$ and that satisfy the additional condition that $p - 1$ is relatively prime to a specified number f. We search for these numbers with the following algorithm and associated function `FindPrimeMinMaxGcd_l()`:

Algorithm for determining a random prime number p with $r_{min} \leq p \leq r_{max}$ that satisfies the additional condition $\gcd(p - 1, f) = 1$, after [IEEE]

1. Set $k_{min} \leftarrow \lceil (r_{min} - 1)/2 \rceil$ and $k_{max} \leftarrow \lfloor (r_{max} - 1)/2 \rfloor$.

2. Generate randomly an integer k satisfying $k_{min} \leq k \leq k_{max}$.

3. Set $p \leftarrow 2k + 1$.

4. Compute $d \leftarrow \gcd(p - 1, f)$.

5. If $d = 1$, test p for primality. If p is prime, set $d \leftarrow \gcd(p - 1, f)$. Otherwise, go to step 2.

Function:	Determine a prime p_l of type CLINT with rmin_l $\leq$ p_l $\leq$ rmax_l and $\gcd(\text{p\_l} - 1, \text{f\_l}) = 1$ using the FLINT/C pseudorandom number generators; previous initialization required via call to the initialization function InitRand_l with suitable parameters.
Syntax:	int FindPrimeMinMaxGcd_l (CLINT p_l, STATEPRNG *xrstate, CLINT rmin_l, CLINT rmax_l, CLINT f_l);
Input:	xrstate (initialized internal state of a pseudorandom number generator) rmin_l (lower bound for p_l) rmax_l (upper bound for p_l) f_l (integer that should be relatively prime to p_l −1)
Output:	p_l (random, probabilistically determined prime number) xrstate (new internal state of the pseudorandom number generator)
Return:	E_CLINT_OK if all OK E_CLINT_RGE if rmin_l > rmax_l or f_l is even, or if no prime number can be found satisfying the given boundary conditions E_CLINT_RNG if error in specifying the generator in xrstate E_CLINT_RIN if pseudorandom number generator uninitialized

```
int
FindPrimeMinMaxGcd_l (CLINT p_l, STATEPRNG *xrstate, CLINT rmin_l,
                      CLINT rmax_l, CLINT f_l)
{
  CLINT t_l, rmin1_l, g_l;
  CLINT Pi_rmin_l, Pi_rmax_l, NoofCandidates_l, junk_l;
  int error;
```

Check whether f_l is odd.

```
  if (ISEVEN_L (f_l))
    {
      return E_CLINT_RGE;
    }
```

> Estimate the number of prime numbers in the interval [rmin_l, rmax_l], and store the result in NoofCandidates_l.

```
udiv_l (rmin_l, ld_l (rmin_l), Pi_rmin_l, junk_l);
udiv_l (rmax_l, ld_l (rmax_l), Pi_rmax_l, junk_l);
sub_l (Pi_rmax_l, Pi_rmin_l, NoofCandidates_l);
```

> Set rmin_l ← $\lceil (\text{rmin\_l} - 1)/2 \rceil$.

```
dec_l (rmin_l);
div_l (rmin_l, two_l, rmin_l, junk_l);
if (GTZ_L (junk_l))
  {
    inc_l (rmin_l);
  }
```

> Set rmax_l ← $\lfloor (\text{rmax\_l} - 1)/2 \rfloor$.

```
dec_l (rmax_l);
shr_l (rmax_l);
do
  {
```

> Test the breakoff condition for whether number of prime candidates has been reduced to zero. If this is the case, then no prime will be found within the given boundary conditions. This is indicated by the error code E_CLINT_RGE.

```
      if (EQZ_L (NoofCandidates_l))
        {
          return (E_CLINT_RGE);
        }
```

> Determination of a random number.

```
      if (E_CLINT_OK != (error = RandMinMax_l (p_l, xrstate, rmin_l, rmax_l)))
        {
          return error;
```

```
        }
```

> Set the prime number candidate $p\_l \leftarrow 2*p\_l + 1$; thus p_l is odd.

```
        shl_l (p_l);
        inc_l (p_l);

        cpy_l (rmin1_l, p_l);
        dec_l (rmin1_l);
        gcd_l (rmin1_l, f_l, g_l);

        dec_l (NoofCandidates_l);
     }
  while (!(EQONE_L (g_l) && ISPRIME_L (p_l)));

  return error;
}
```

The following two functions are by-products, so to speak, of the previous function. We first generate pseudorandom prime numbers with a specified number of binary digits and with the additional property of being relatively prime to a specified integer. For this we use the function FindPrimeMinMaxGcd_l():

Function:	Determination of a pseudorandom prime number p_1 of type CLINT with $2^{l-1} \leq p\_1 < 2^l$ and $\gcd(p\_1 - 1, f\_1) = 1$ using the FLINT/C pseudorandom number generators; required is previous initialization via a call to the function InitRand_1 with suitable parameters
Syntax:	int FindPrime_1 (CLINT p_1, STATEPRNG *xrstate, USHORT 1, CLINT f_1);
Input:	xrstate (initialized internal state of a pseudorandom number generator) 1 (number of binary digits of p_1) f_1 (number that should be relatively prime to p_1 −1
Output:	p_1 (probabilistically determined prime number) xrstate (new internal state of pseudorandom number generator)
Return:	E_CLINT_OK if all OK E_CLINT_RNG if error in specifying the generator in xrstate E_CLINT_RGE if l = 0 or f_1 odd E_CLINT_RIN if random number generator is uninitialized

```
int
FindPrimeGcd_1 (CLINT p_1, STATEPRNG *xrstate, USHORT 1, CLINT f_1)
{
  CLINT pmin_1;
    clint pmax_1[CLINTMAXSHORT + 1];    int error;
  if (0 == 1)
    {
      return E_CLINT_RGE;
    }
  SETZERO_L (pmin_1);
  SETZERO_L (pmax_1);
  setbit_1 (pmin_1, 1 - 1);
  setbit_1 (pmax_1, 1);
  dec_1 (pmax_1);
  error = FindPrimeMinMaxGcd_1 (p_1, xrstate, pmin_1, pmax_1, f_1);
  return error;
}
```

In the last step we wish to avoid the condition of relative primality by passing one as a parameter in the call FindPrimeGcd_1 (p_1, xrstate, 1, one_1):

<table>
<tr><td>**Function:**</td><td>Determination of a pseudorandom prime number p_l of type CLINT with $2^{l-1} \leq p\_l < 2^l$ using the FLINT/C pseudorandom number generators; previous initialization via a call to the appropriate initialization function is required</td></tr>
<tr><td>**Syntax:**</td><td>int
FindPrime_l (CLINT p_l, STATEPRNG *xrstate, USHORT l);</td></tr>
<tr><td>**Input:**</td><td>xrstate (initialized internal state of a pseudorandom number generator)
l (number of binary digits of p_l)</td></tr>
<tr><td>**Output:**</td><td>p_l (probabilistically determined prime number)
xrstate (new internal state of the pseudorandom number generator)</td></tr>
<tr><td>**Return:**</td><td>E_CLINT_OK if all OK
E_CLINT_RNG if error in specifying the generator in xrstate
E_CLINT_RGE if l = 0
E_CLINT_RIN if random number generator uninitialized</td></tr>
</table>

```
int
FindPrime_l (CLINT p_l, STATEPRNG *xrstate, USHORT l)
{
  return (FindPrimeGcd_l (p_l, xrstate, l, one_l));
}
```

Strategies for Testing LINT

Don't blame the Compiler.
—David A. Spuler: *C++ and C Debugging, Testing, and Code Reliability*

IN THE PREVIOUS CHAPTERS WE have encountered here and there hints for testing individual functions. Without meaningful tests to ensure the quality of our package, all of our work would be for naught, for on what else are we to base our confidence in the reliability of our functions? Therefore, we are now going to give our full attention to this important topic, and to this end we ask two questions that every software developer should ask:

1. How can we be certain that our software functions behave according to their specifications, which in our case means first of all that they are mathematically correct?

2. How can we achieve stability and reliability in the functioning of our software?

Although these two questions are closely related, they are actually concerned with two different problem areas. A function can be mathematically incorrect, for example if the underlying algorithm has been incorrectly implemented, yet it can reliably and stably reproduce this error and consistently give the same false output for a given input. On the other hand, functions that apparently return correct results can be plagued by other sorts of errors, for example an overflow of the length of a vector or the use of incorrectly initialized variables, leading to undefined behavior that remains undetected due to favorable (or should we rather say unfavorable?) test conditions.

We thus must be concerned with both of these aspects and institute development and test methods that can provide us sufficient trust in both the correctness and reliability of our programs. There are numerous publications that discuss the significance and consequences of these wide-ranging requirements for the entire software development process and delve deeply into the issues of software quality. Considered attention to this topic has found expression not least in the international trend to institute the ISO 9000 standard in software production. In this regard one no longer speaks merely of "testing" or "quality assurance," but instead one hears talk of "quality management" or "total quality management," which in part are simply the result of effective marketing, but which nonetheless cast the issue in the proper light, namely, to consider the process of software creation in its multifaceted entirety and thereby improve it. The frequently employed expression "software engineering" cannot blind us to the fact that this process, as it relates to predictability and precision, as a rule can scarcely compete with the classical discipline of engineering.

The comparison may be characterized aptly by the following joke: A mechanical engineer, an electrical engineer, and a software engineer have decided to take an automobile trip together. They seat themselves in the car, but it refuses to start. The mechanical engineer says at once, "The problem is with the motor. The injection nozzle is clogged." "Nonsense," retorts the electrical engineer. "The electronics are to blame. The ignition system has certainly failed." Whereupon the software engineer makes the following suggestion: "Let's all get out of the car and climb back in. Perhaps then it will start."

Without pursuing the further conversations and adventures of the three intrepid engineers, let us proceed to consider some of the options that were implemented in the creation and testing of the FLINT/C package. Above all, the following references were consulted, which do not exhaust the reader with abstract considerations and guidelines but get down to concrete assistance in solving concrete problems, without in the process losing sight of the big picture.[1] Each of these books contains numerous references to further important literature on this topic:

- [Dene] is a standard work that deals with the entire process of software development. The book contains many methodological pointers based on the practical experience of the author as well as many clear and useful examples. The theme of testing is attacked again and again in connection with the various phases of programming and system integration, where the conceptual and methodological fundamentals are discussed together with the practical point of view, all in conjunction with a thoroughly worked out example project.

- [Harb] contains a complete description of the programming language C and the C standard library, and it gives many valuable pointers and comments on the prescriptions of the ISO standard. This is an indispensable reference work to be consulted at every turn.

- [Hatt] goes into great detail on the creation of security-critical software systems in C. Typical experience and sources of error are demonstrated

---

[1] The titles named here represent the author's personal, subjective selection. There are many other books and publications that could as well have been listed here but that have been omitted for lack of space and time.

by means of concrete examples and statistics—and C certainly offers many opportunities for error. There is also comprehensive methodological advice, which if heeded would lead to increased trust in software products.

- [Lind] is an excellent and humorous book, which reveals a deep understanding of the C programming language. Moreover, the author knows how to transmit this understanding to the reader. Many of the topics considered could be supplied the subtitle, "Did you know that . . . ?" and only a very few readers could honestly—hand on heart—reply in the affirmative.

- [Magu] deals with the design of subsystems and is therefore of particular interest to us. Here are discussed the interpretation of interfaces and the principles of dealing with functions with input parameters. The differences between risky and defensive programming are elucidated as well. The effective use of *assertions* (see page 153) as testing aids and for the avoidance of undefined program states is a further strong point of this book.

- [Murp] contains a host of testing tools that can be put to use in testing programs with little effort and that yield immediate useful results. Among its other features the book offers libraries on an accompanying diskette for the implementation of assertions, testing the processing of dynamic memory objects, and reporting the degree of coverage of tests, which were also used for testing the FLINT/C functions.

- [Spul] offers a broad view of methods and tools for testing programs in the C and C++ languages and gives numerous pointers for their effective use. The book contains an extensive overview of programming errors typical in C and C++ and discusses techniques for recognizing and eliminating them.

13.1 Static Analysis

The methodological approaches to testing can be divided into two categories: *static testing* and *dynamic testing*. In the first category are to be found code inspection, whereby the source code is carefully examined and inspected line by line for such problems as deviations from specifications (in our case these are the selected algorithms), errors in reasoning, inaccuracies with respect to the arrangement of code lines or the style guide, doubtful constructions, and the presence of unnecessary code sequences.

Code inspection is supported by the use of analytic tools, such as the well-known Unix lint tools, that largely automate this laborious task. Originally, one of the main applications of lint was to compensate for earlier existing deficits in C in consistency checking of parameters that were passed to functions in separately compiled modules. Meanwhile, there have appeared more convenient products than the classical lint, products that are capable of discovering an enormous bandwidth of potential problems in program code, represented only in small part by syntax errors that definitively prevent a compiler from effecting a translation of the code. A few examples of the problem domains that can be uncovered by static analysis are as follows:

- syntax errors,

- missing or inconsistent function prototypes,

- inconsistencies in the passing of parameters to functions,

- references to or joining of incompatible types,

- use of uninitialized variables,

- nonportable constructs,

- unusual or implausible use of particular language constructs,

- unreachable code sequences,

An imperative condition for stringent type-checking by automated tools is the use of function prototypes. With the help of prototypes an ISO-conforming C compiler is capable of checking, across all modules, the types of arguments passed to functions and detecting inconsistencies. Many compilers can also be set to analyze the source code, as they recognize many problems when the appropriate warning levels are turned on. The C/C++ compiler gcc of the GNU project of the Free Software Foundation, for example, possesses above-average analysis functions, which can be activated with the options -Wall -ansi and -pedantic.[2]

For static testing in setting up the FLINT/C functions, in addition to tests being performed on a number of different compilers (see page 8), there were employed primarily the products PC-lint from Gimpel Software (version 7.5; see [Gimp]) and Splint from the Secure Programming Group at the University of Virginia (version 3.1.1; see [Evan]).[3]

PC-lint has proved itself to be a very useful tool for testing both C and C++ programs. It knows about approximately two thousand separate problems and uses mechanisms that in a limited way derive from the code the values loaded into automatic variables at run time and include this in the diagnosis. In this way many problems, such as exceeding the limits of vectors, that are usually, if at all, detected only at run time (which is to say during testing, it is to be hoped, and not afterwards) can be uncovered already during static analysis.

---

[2] The compiler is included in the various Linux distributions and can also be obtained from http://www.leo.org.

[3] Splint is the successor to the tool LCLint, which was developed in cooperation with the Massachusetts Institute of Technology and Digital Equipment Corporation (DEC). Splint can be found at the address http://splint.cs.virginia.edu/.

In addition to these tools, the freely obtainable Splint has been adapted to run under Linux. Splint distinguishes four modes (weak, standard, check, strict), each connected with certain presets, and which carry out tests of varying degrees of rigorousness. In addition to the typical lint functions, Splint offers possibilities to test programs for the presence of particular specifications, which are inserted as specially formatted comments in the source code. In this way boundary conditions for the implementation of functions and their invocation can be formulated and their conformity to specifications checked, and there are additional possible semantic controls.

For programs not equipped with supplementary specifications the mode set with the option -weak is recommended as standard. However, according to the manual a special reward will be presented to the first person who can produce a "real program" that produces no errors with Splint in -strict mode. As a precondition for using these two tools in a reasonable manner it proved to be useful in testing the FLINT/C functions to test precisely which options are used and to create corresponding profile files so as to configure the tools for individual use.

After extensive revisions of the FLINT/C code, at the end of the test phase neither of the two products produced any warnings that on close examination could be considered serious. With this goes the hope that we have come a long way in fulfilling the conditions set above for the quality of the FLINT/C functions.

13.2 Run-Time Tests

The goal of run-time tests should be to prove that a building block of a piece of software fulfills its specifications. To give the tests sufficient expressive power so as to justify the expense of time and money that goes into their development and execution, we must make of them the same demands that we do of scientific experiments: They must be completely *documented*, and their results must be *reproducible* and *able to be checked* by outsiders. It is useful to distinguish between testing individual modules and integrated system tests, though here the boundaries are fluid (see [Dene], Section 16.1).

To achieve this goal in testing modules the test cases must be so constructed that functions can be exhaustively tested to the extent possible, or in other words, that as large a *coverage* as possible be achieved of the functions being tested. To establish test coverage various metrics can be employed. For example, for *C0 coverage* what is measured is the portion of instructions of a function or module that are actually run through, or, concretely, which instructions are not run through. There are more powerful measurements than C0 coverage, which take note of the portion of branches that are taken (*C1 coverage*), or even the portion of paths of a function that are run through. The last of these is a considerably more complex measure then the first two.

In each case the goal is to achieve maximal coverage with test cases that completely check the behavior of the interface of the software. This covers two aspects that are only loosely connected one with the other: A test driver that runs through all the branches of a function can still leave errors undetected. On the other hand, one can construct cases in which all the properties of a function are tested, even though some branches of the function are not considered. The quality of a test can thus be measured in at least two dimensions.

If to achieve a high degree of test coverage it does not suffice to establish the test cases based simply on knowledge of the specification, which leads to so-called *black box tests*, it is necessary to take into consideration the details of the implementation in the construction of test cases, a modus operandi that leads to so-called *white box tests*. An example where we have created test cases for a special branch of a function based only on the specification is the division algorithm on page 53: To test step 5 the special test data on page 65 were specified, which have the effect that the associated code is executed. On the other hand, the necessity of special test data for division by smaller divisors becomes clear only when one considers that this process is passed off to a special part of the function div_l(). What is involved here is an implementation detail that cannot be derived from the algorithm.

In practice, one usually ends up with a mixture of black box and white box methods, which in [Dene] are aptly called *gray box tests*. However, it can never be expected that one hundred percent coverage is to be achieved, as the following considerations demonstrate: Let us assume that we are generating prime numbers with the Miller–Rabin test with a large number of iterations (50, say) and a corresponding low probability of error $\left(\frac{1}{4}\right)^{-50} \approx 10^{-30}$ (cf. Section 10.5) and then testing the prime numbers that are found with a further, definitive, primality test. Since the flow of control leads to one or the other branch of the program, depending on the outcome of this second test, we have no practically relevant chance to reach the branch that is followed exclusively after a negative test outcome. However, the probability that the doubtful branch will be executed when the program is actually used is just as irrelevant, so that possibly one can more easily live with doing without this aspect of the test than to alter the code semantically in order to create the test possibility artificially. In practice, there are thus always situations to be expected that require the abandonment of the goal of one hundred percent test coverage, however that is measured.

The testing of the arithmetic functions in the FLINT/C package, which is carried out primarily from a mathematical viewpoint, is quite a challenge. How can we establish whether addition, multiplication, division, or even exponentiation of large numbers produces the correct results? Pocket calculators can generally compute only on an order of magnitude equivalent to that of the standard arithmetic functions of the C compiler, and so both of these are of limited value in testing.

To be sure, one has the option of employing as a test vehicle another arithmetic software package by creating the necessary interface and transformations of the number formats and letting the functions compete against each other. However, there are two strikes against such an approach: First, this is not sporting, and second, one must ask oneself why one should have faith in someone else's implementation, about which one knows considerably less than about one's own product. We shall therefore seek other possibilities for testing and to this end employ mathematical structures and laws that embody sufficient redundancy to be able to recognize computational errors in the software. Discovered errors can then be attacked with the aid of additional test output and modern symbolic debuggers.

We shall therefore follow selectively a black box approach, and in the rest of this chapter we shall hope to work out a serviceable test plan for the run-time tests that follows essentially the actual course of testing that was used on the FLINT/C functions. In this process we had the goal of achieving high C1 coverage, although no measurements in this regard were employed.

The list of properties of the FLINT/C functions to be tested is not especially long, but it is not without substance. In particular, we must convince ourselves of the following:

- All calculational results are generated correctly over the entire range of definition of all functions.

- In particular, all input values for which special code sequences are supplied within a function are correctly processed.

- Overflow and underflow are correctly handled. That is, all arithmetic operations are carried out modulo $N_{max} + 1$.

- Leading zeros are accepted without influencing the result.

- Function calls in accumulator mode with identical memory objects as arguments, such as, add_l(n_l, n_l, n_l), return correct results.

- All divisions by zero are recognized and generate the appropriate error message.

There are many individual test functions necessary for the processing of this list, functions that call the FLINT/C operations to be tested and check their results. The test functions are collected in test modules and themselves individually tested before they are set loose on the FLINT/C functions. For testing the test functions the same criteria and the same means for static analysis are employed as for the FLINT/C functions, and furthermore, the test functions should be run through at least on a spot-check basis with the help of a symbolic debugger in single-step mode in order to check whether they test the right thing. In order to determine whether the test functions truly respond properly to errors, it is helpful deliberately to build errors into the arithmetic functions that lead to false results (and then after the test phase to remove these errors without a trace!).

Since we cannot test every value in the range of definition for CLINT objects, we need, in addition to fixed preset test values, randomly generated input values that are uniformly distributed across the range of definition $[0, N_{\max}]$. To this end we use our function rand_l(r_l, bitlen), where we select the number of binary digits to be set in the variable bitlen with the help of the function usrand64_l() modulo $(\mathrm{MAX}_2 + 1)$ randomly from the interval $[0, \mathrm{MAX}_2]$. The first pass at testing must be the functions for generating pseudorandom numbers, which were discussed in Chapter 12, where among other things we employ the chi-squared test described there for testing the statistical quality of the functions usrand64_l() and usrandBBS_l(). Additionally, we must convince ourselves that the functions rand_l() and randBBS_l() properly generate the CLINT number format and return numbers of precisely the predetermined length. This test is also required for all other functions that output CLINT objects. For recognizing erroneous formats of CLINT arguments we have the function vcheck_l(), which is therefore to be placed at the beginning of the sequence of tests.

A further condition for most of the tests is the possibility of determining the equality or inequality and size comparison of integers represented by CLINT objects. We must also test the functions ld_l(), equ_l(), mequ_l(), and cmp_l(). This can be accomplished with the use of both predefined and random numbers, where all cases—equality as well as inequality with the corresponding size relations—are to be tested.

The input of predefined values proceeds optimally, depending on the purpose, by means of the function str2clint_l() or as an unsigned type with the conversion function u2clint_l() or ul2clint_l(). The function xclint2str_l(), complementary to str2clint_l(), is used for the generation of test output. These functions are therefore the next to appear on our list of functions to be tested. For the testing of string functions we exploit their complementarity and check whether executing one function after the other produces the original character string or, for the other order, the output value in CLINT format. We shall return to this principle repeatedly below.

All that now remains to test are the dynamic registers and their control mechanisms from Chapter 9, which in general we would like to include in the test functions. The use of registers as dynamically allocated memory supports us in our efforts to test the FLINT/C functions, where we additionally implement a debug library for the malloc() functions for allocation of memory. A typical function in such a package, of which there are to be found both public-domain and commercial products (cf. [Spul], Chapter 11), is checking for maintenance of the bounds of dynamically allocated memory. With access to the CLINT registers we can keep close tabs on our FLINT/C functions: Every penetration of the border into foreign memory territory will be reported.

A typical mechanism that enables this redirects calls to malloc() to a special test function that receives the memory requests, in turn calls malloc(), and thereby allocates a somewhat greater amount of memory than is actually requested. The block of memory is registered in an internal data structure, and a frame of a few bytes is constructed "right" and "left" of the memory originally requested, which is filled with a redundant pattern such as alternating binary zeros and ones. Then a pointer is returned to the free memory within the frame. A call to free() now in turn goes first to the debug shell of this function. Before the allocated block is released a check is made as to whether the frame has been left unharmed or whether the pattern has been destroyed by overwriting, in which case an appropriate message is generated and the memory is stricken from the registration list. Only then is the function free() actually called. At the end of the application one can check using the internal registration list whether, or which, areas of memory were not released. The orchestrating of the code for rerouting the calls to malloc() and free() to their debug shells is accomplished with macros that are usually defined in #include files.

For the test of the FLINT/C functions the *ResTrack* package from [Murp] is employed. This enables the detection, in certain cases, of subtle instances of exceeding the vector bounds of CLINT variables, which otherwise might have remained undetected during testing.

We have now completed the basic preparations and consider next the functions for basic calculation (cf. Chapter 4)

> add_l(), sub_l(), mul_l(), sqr_l(), div_l(), mod_l(), inc_l(),
> dec_l(), shl_l(), shr_l(), shift_l(),

including the kernel functions

> add(), sub(), mult(), umul(), sqr(),

the mixed arithmetic functions with a USHORT argument

> uadd_l(), usub_l(), umul_l(), udiv_l(), umod_l(), mod2_l(),

and finally the functions for modular arithmetic (cf. Chapters 5 and 6)

> madd_l(), msub_l(), mmul_l(), msqr_l(),

and the exponentiation function

> *mexp*_l().

The calculational rules that we shall employ in testing these functions arise from the group laws of the integers, which have been introduced already in Chapter 5 for the residue class rings $\mathbb{Z}_n$. The applicable rules for the natural numbers are again collected here, where we find an opportunity for testing wherever an equal sign stands between two expressions (see Table 13-1).

Table 13-1. Group law for the integers to help in testing

	Addition	Multiplication
Identity	$a + 0 = a$	$a \cdot 1 = a$
Commutative Law	$a + b = b + a$	$a \cdot b = b \cdot a$
Associative Law	$(a + b) + c = a + (b + c)$	$(a \cdot b) \cdot c = a \cdot (b \cdot c)$

Addition and multiplication can be tested one against the other by making use of the definition

$$ka := \sum_{j=1}^{k} a,$$

at least for small values of k. Further relations amenable to testing are the distributive law and the first binomial formula:

Distributive law : $\qquad a \cdot (b + c) = a \cdot b + a \cdot c,$

Binomial formula : $\qquad (a + b)^2 = a^2 + 2ab + b^2.$

The cancellation laws for addition and multiplication provide the following test possibilities for addition and subtraction, as well as for multiplication and division:

$$a + b = c \Rightarrow c - a = b \text{ and } c - b = a$$

and

$$a \cdot b = c \Rightarrow c \div a = b \text{ and } c \div b = a.$$

Division with remainder can be tested against multiplication and addition by using the division function to compute, for a dividend a and divisor b, first the quotient q and remainder r. Then multiplication and addition are brought into play to test whether

$$a = b \cdot q + r.$$

For testing modular exponentiation against multiplication for small k we fall back on the definition:

$$a^k := \prod_{i=1}^{k} a.$$

From here we can move on to the exponentiation laws (cf. Chapter 1)

$$a^{rs} = (a^r)^s,$$
$$a^{r+s} = a^r \cdot a^s,$$

which are likewise a basis for testing exponentiation in relation to multiplication and addition.

In addition to these and other tests based on the rules of arithmetic calculation we make use of special test routines that check the remaining points of our above list, in particular the behavior of the functions on the boundaries of the intervals of definition of CLINT objects or in other special situations, which for certain functions are particularly critical. Some of these tests are contained in the FLINT/C test suite, which is included in the downloadable source code. The test suite contains the modules listed in Table 13-2.

Table 13-2. FLINT/C test functions

Module Name	Content of Test
testrand.c	linear congruences, pseudorandom number generator
testbbs.c	Blum–Blum–Shub pseudorandom number generator
testreg.c	register management
testbas.c	basic functions cpy_l(), ld_l(), equ_l(), mequ_l(), cmp_l(), u2clint_l(), ul2clint_l(), str2clint_l(), xclint2str_l()
testadd.c	addition, including inc_l()
testsub.c	subtraction, including dec_l()
testmul.c	multiplication
testkar.c	Karatsuba multiplication
testsqr.c	squaring
testdiv.c	division with remainder
testmadd.c	modular addition
testmsub.c	modular subtraction
testmmul.c	modular multiplication
testmsqr.c	modular squaring
testmexp.c	modular exponentiation
testset.c	bit access functions
testshft.c	shift operations
testbool.c	Boolean operations
testiroo.c	integer square root
testgcd.c	greatest common divisor and least common multiple

We shall return to the tests of our number-theoretic functions at the end of Part 2, where they are presented as exercises for the especially interested reader (see Chapter 18).

Part II

Arithmetic in C++ with the Class LINT

The use of anatomic finds as ornamentation in the construction of objects is widespread in different geographical areas and in different ethno-anthropological groups. The human find, usually the bone, becomes a functional part in the construction of objects. The bone seems to lose, at least in part, its actual anatomic identity, in that it is worked and manipulated so that it becomes an integral part of an object thus acquiring a symbolic meaning which goes beyond its bodily essence.

— Sign at the National Museum of Anthropology and Ethnology, Florence, Italy

CHAPTER 14

Let C++ Simplify
Your Life

Our life is frittered away by detail . . . Simplify, simplify.
—H. D. Thoreau, *Walden*

THE PROGRAMMING LANGUAGE C++, UNDER development since 1979 by Bjarne Stroustrup[1] at Bell Laboratories, is an extension of C that promises to dominate the field of software development. C++ supports the principles of object-oriented programming, which is based on the tenet that programs, or, better, processes, comprise a set of objects that interact exclusively through their interfaces. That is, they exchange information or accept certain external commands and process them as a task. In this the *methods* by which an object carries out a task are an internal affair "decided upon" autonomously by the object alone. The data structures and functions that represent the internal state of an object and effect transitions between states are the private affair of the object and should not be detectable from the outside. This principle, known as *information hiding*, assists software developers in concentrating on the tasks that an object has to fulfill within the framework of a program without having to worry about implementation details. (Another way of saying this is that the focus is on "what," not on "how.")

The structural designs for what goes on in the "internal affairs" of objects, containing complete information on the organization of data structures and functions, are the *classes*. With these the external interface of an object is established, and this is decisive for the suite of behaviors that an object can perform. Since all objects of a class reflect the same structural design, they also

---

[1] The following, from Bjarne Stroustrup's Internet home page (http://www.research.att.com/~bs/), may help to answer the question, How do you pronounce "Bjarne Stroustrup"?: "It can be difficult for non-Scandinavians. The best suggestion I have heard yet was 'start by saying it a few times in Norwegian, then stuff a potato down your throat and do it again' :-). Both of my names are pronounced with two syllables: Bjar-ne Strou-strup. Neither the B nor the J in my first name are stressed and the NE is rather weak so maybe Be-ar-neh or By-ar-ne would give an idea. The first U in my second name really should have been a V making the first syllable end far down the throat: Strov-strup. The second U is a bit like the OO in OOP, but still short; maybe Strov-stroop will give an idea."

possess the same interface. But once they have been created (computer scientists say that classes are *instantiated* by objects), they lead independent lives. Their internal states are changed independently of one another and they execute different tasks corresponding to their respective roles in the program.

Object-oriented programming propagates the use of classes as the building blocks of larger structures, which can again be classes or groups of classes, into complete programs, just as houses or automobiles are constructed of prefabricated modules. In the ideal case programs can be cobbled together from libraries of preexisting classes without the necessity for the creation of a significant amount of new code, at least not on the order of magnitude as is typical in conventional program development. As a result it is easier to orient program development to reflect the actual situation, to model directly the actual processes, and thereby to achieve successive refinement until the result is a collection of objects of particular classes and their interrelations, in which the underlying real-world model can still be recognized.

Such a way of proceeding is well known to us from many aspects of our lives, for we do not generally operate directly with raw materials if we wish to build something, but we use, rather, completed modules about whose construction or inner workings we have no detailed knowledge, nor the necessity of such knowledge. By standing on the shoulders of those who built before us, it becomes possible for us to create more and more complex structures with a manageable amount of effort. In the creation of software this natural state of affairs has not previously found its true expression, as software developers turn again and again to the raw materials themselves: Programs are constructed out of atomic elements of a programming language (this constructive process is commonly called *coding*). The use of run-time libraries such as the C standard library does not improve this situation to any great degree, since the functions contained in such libraries are too primitive to permit a direct connection to a more complex application.

Every programmer knows that data structures and functions that provide acceptable solutions for particular problems only seldom can be used for similar but different tasks without modification. The result is a reduction in the advantage of being able to rely on fully tested and trusted components, since any alteration contains the risk of new errors—as much in the design as in programming. (One is reminded of the notification in manuals that accompany various consumer products: "Any alteration by other than an authorized service provider voids the warranty.")

In order that the reusability of software in the form of prefabricated building blocks not founder on the rocks of insufficient flexibility, the concept of *inheritance*, among a number of other concepts, has been developed. This makes it possible to modify classes to meet new requirements without actually altering them. Instead, the necessary changes are packaged in an extension layer.

The objects that thus arise take on, in addition to their new properties, all the properties of the old objects. One might say that they *inherit* these properties. The principle of *information hiding* remains intact. The chances of error are greatly reduced, and productivity is increased. It is like a dream come true.

As an object-oriented programming language C++ possesses the requisite mechanisms for the support of these principles of abstraction.[2] These, however, represent only a potential, but not a guarantee, of being used in the sense of object-oriented programming. To the contrary, the switch from conventional to object-oriented software development requires a considerable intellectual retooling. This is particularly apparent in two respects: On the one hand, the developer who has hitherto achieved good results is forced to devote considerably more attention to the modeling and design phases than what was usually required in traditional methods of software development. On the other hand, in the development and testing of new classes the greatest care is required to obtain error-free building blocks, since they will go on to be used in a great variety of future applications. Information hiding can also mean *bug hiding*, since it defeats the purpose of the idea of object-oriented programming if the user of a class must become familiar with its inner workings in order to find a bug. The result is that errors contained in a class implementation are inherited together with the class, so that all subclasses will be infected with the same "hereditary disease." On the other hand, the analysis of errors that occur with the objects of a class can be restricted to the implementation of the class, which can greatly reduce the scope of the search for the error.

All in all, we must say that while there are strong trends in the direction of using C++ and Java as programming languages, nonetheless, the principles of object-oriented programming beyond an understanding of the essentially complex elements of these languages are multifaceted, and it will be a long time before they are used as a standard method of software development. However, in the meantime, there are powerful and robust tools available that strongly support the development process, from modeling up through the generation of executable code.

Thus the title of this chapter refers not to object-oriented programming and the use of C++ in general, but to the mechanisms offered therein and their significance for our project. These enable the formulation of arithmetic operations with large numbers in a way that is so natural that it is as if they belonged to the standard operations of the programming language. In the following sections, therefore, we will not be presenting an introduction to C++, but a discussion of the development of classes that represent large natural numbers and that export functions to work with these numbers as abstract

---

[2] C++ is not the only object-oriented language. Others are Simula (the precursor of all object-oriented languages), Smalltalk, Eiffel, Oberon, and Java.

methods.[3] The (few) details of the data structures will be hidden both from the user and the client of the class, as will the implementation of the numerous arithmetic and number-theoretic functions. However, before we can use the classes they must be developed, and in this regard we shall have to get our hands dirty with the internal details. Nonetheless, it will surprise no one that we are not going to begin from scratch, but rather make use of the implementation work that we accomplished in the first part of the book and formulate the arithmetic class as an abstract layer, or shell, around our C library.

We shall give the name LINT (Large INTegers) to our class. It will contain data structures and functions as components with the attribute *public*, which determine the possibilities for external access. Access to the structures of the class declared as *private*, on the other hand, can be accomplished only with functions that have been declared either a *member* or *friend* of the class. Member functions of the class LINT can access the functions and data elements of LINT objects by name and are required for servicing the external interface, for processing instructions to the class, and serving as fundamental routines and auxiliary functions for managing and processing internal data structures. Member functions of the class LINT always possess a LINT object as implied left argument, which does not appear in its parameter list. Friend functions of the class do not belong to the class, but they can nonetheless access the internal structure of the class. Unlike the member functions, the friend functions do not possess an implicit argument.

Objects are generated as instances of a class by means of *constructors*, which complete the allocation of memory, the initialization of data, and other management tasks before an object is ready for action. We shall require several such constructors in order to generate our LINT objects from various contexts. Complementary to the constructors we have *destructors*, which serve the purpose of removing objects that are no longer needed and releasing the resources that have been bound to them.

The elements of C++ that we shall particularly use for our class development are the following:

- the *overloading* of operators and functions;

- the improved possibilities, vis à vis C, for input and output.

The following sections are devoted to the application of these two principles in the framework of our LINT class. To give the reader an idea of the form that the LINT class will assume, we show a small segment of its declaration:

---

3   The reader is referred to several works in the standard literature for an introduction to C++ and discussions about it, namely [ElSt], [Str1], [Str2], [Deit], [Lipp], just to name a few of the more important titles. In particular, [ElSt] was taken as the basis for the standardization by the ISO.

```
class LINT
{
  public:
    LINT (void); // constructor
    ~LINT (); // destructor

    const LINT& operator= (const LINT&);
    const LINT& operator+= (const LINT&);
    const LINT& operator-= (const LINT&);
    const LINT& operator*= (const LINT&);
    const LINT& operator/= (const LINT&);
    const LINT& operator    LINT gcd (const LINT&);
    LINT lcm (const LINT&);
    int jacobi (const LINT&);

    friend const LINT operator + (const LINT&, const LINT&);
    friend const LINT operator - (const LINT&, const LINT&);
    friend const LINT operator * (const LINT&, const LINT&);
    friend const LINT operator / (const LINT&, const LINT&);
    friend const LINT operator
    friend LINT mexp (const LINT&, const LINT&, const LINT&);
    friend LINT mexp (const USHORT, const LINT&, const LINT&);
    friend LINT mexp (const LINT&, USHORT, const LINT&);
    friend LINT gcd (const LINT&, const LINT&);
    friend LINT lcm (const LINT&, const LINT&);
    friend int jacobi (const LINT&, const LINT&);

  private:
    clint *n_l;
    int status;
};
```

One may recognize the typical subdivision into two blocks: First the public block is declared with a constructor, a destructor, arithmetic operators, and member functions as well as the friend functions of the class. A short block of private data elements is joined to the public interface, identified by the label *private*. It is an aid to clarity and is considered good style to place the public interface before the private block and to use the labels "public" and "private" only once each within a class declaration.

The list of operators appearing in the section of the class declaration shown here is by no means complete. It is missing some arithmetic functions that cannot be represented as operators as well as most of the number-theoretic functions, which we know already as C functions. Furthermore, the announced constructors are as little represented as the functions for input and output of LINT objects.

In the following parameter lists of the operators and functions the address operator & appears, which has the effect that objects of the class LINT are passed not by value, but by reference, that is, as pointers to the object. The same holds for the return value of LINT objects. This use of & is unknown in C. On close inspection, however, one recognizes that only certain of the member functions return a pointer to a LINT object, while most of the others return their results by value. The basic rule that determines which of these two methods is followed is this: Functions that alter one or more of the arguments passed to them can return this result as a reference, while other functions, those that do not alter their arguments, return their results by value. As we proceed we shall see which method goes with which of the LINT functions.

Classes in C++ are an extension of the complex data type struct in C, and access to an element x of a class is accomplished syntactically in the same way as access to an element of a structure, that is, by A.x, where A denotes an object and x an element of the class.

One should note that in the parameter list of a member function an argument is less completely named than in a like-named friend function, as the following example illustrates:

```
friend LINT gcd (const LINT&, const LINT&);
```

versus

```
LINT LINT::gcd (const LINT&);
```

Since the function gcd() as a member function of the class LINT belongs to an object A of type LINT, a call to gcd() must be in the form A.gcd(b) without A appearing in the parameter list of gcd(). In contrast, the friend function gcd() belongs to no object and thus possesses no implicit argument.

We shall fill in the above sketch of our LINT class in the following chapters and work out many of the details, so that eventually we shall have a complete implementation of the LINT class. The reader who is also interested in a general discussion of C++ is referred to the standard references [Deit], [ElSt], [Lipp], and especially [Mey1] and [Mey2].

14.1 Not a Public Affair: The Representation of Numbers in LINT

> And if my ways are not as theirs
> Let them mind their own affairs.
> —A. E. Housman, *Last Poems* IX

The representation of large numbers that has been chosen for our class is an extension of the representation presented in Part I for the C language. We take from there the arrangement of the digits of a natural number as a vector of clint values, where more-significant digits occupy the places of higher index (cf. Chapter 2). The memory required for this is automatically allocated when an object is generated. This is carried out by the constructors, which are invoked either explicitly by the program or implicitly by the compiler using the allocation function new(). In the class declaration we therefore require a variable of type clint *n_l, to which is associated within one of the constructor functions a pointer to the memory allocated there.

The variable status is used to keep track of various states that can be taken by LINT objects. For example, with status, an overflow or underflow (cf. page 20) can be reported if such an event occurs as a result of operations on LINT objects that would result in the status variable being assigned the value E_LINT_OFL or E_LINT_UFL. Furthermore, we would like to determine whether a LINT object has been initialized, that is, whether any numerical value at all has been assigned to it, before it is used in a numerical expression on the right side of the equal sign. If a LINT object does not possess a numerical value, then status contains the value E_LINT_INV, which all functions must check before an operation is executed. We shall organize our LINT functions and operators in such a way that an error message results if the value of a LINT object, and consequently the value of an expression, is undefined.

The variable status is, strictly speaking, not an element of our numerical representation. It serves rather for reporting and handling error states. The types and mechanisms of error handling are discussed in detail in Chapter 16.

The class LINT defines the following two elements for representing numbers and storing the states of objects:

```
clint* n_l;
int status;
```

Since we are dealing here with private elements, access to these class elements is possible only by means of member or friend functions or operators. In particular, there is no possibility of direct access to the individual digits of a number represented by a LINT object.

14.2 Constructors

Constructors are functions for the generation of objects of a particular class. For the LINT class this can occur with or without initialization, where in the latter case an object is created and the required memory for the storage of the number is allocated, but no value is assigned to the object. The constructor required for this takes no argument and thus takes on the role of the *default* constructor of the class LINT (cf. [Str1], Section 10.4.2). The following default constructor LINT(void) in flintpp.cpp creates a LINT object without assigning it a value:

```
LINT::LINT (void)
  {
    n_l = new CLINT;
    if (NULL == n_l)
      {
        panic (E_LINT_NHP, "constructor 1", 0, __LINE__);
      }
    status = E_LINT_INV;
  }
```

If a newly generated object is also to be initialized with a numerical value, then a suitable constructor must be invoked to generate a LINT object and then assign to it a predefined argument as the value. Depending on the type of argument various overloaded constructors must be provided. The class LINT contains the constructor functions as shown in Table 14-1.

We would now like to consider a further example for the LINT construction of the function LINT (const char*), which generates a LINT object and associates to it a value taken from a character string with ASCII digits. A prefix can be given to the digits contained in the string that contains information about the base of the numerical representation. If a character string is prefixed with 0x or 0X, then hexadecimal digits from the domains $\{0,1,\ldots,9\}$ and $\{a,b,\ldots,f\}$, respectively $\{A,B,\ldots,F\}$, are expected. If the prefix is 0b or 0B, then binary digits from the set $\{0,1\}$ are expected. If there is no prefix at all, then the digits are interpreted as decimal digits. The constructor employs the function str2clint_l() to transform the character string into an object of type CLINT, from which then in the second step a LINT object is created:

```
LINT:: LINT (const char* str)
  n_l = new CLINT;
  if (NULL == n_l) // error with new?
    {
      panic (E_LINT _NHP, "constructor 4", 0, __LINE__);
    }
  if (strncmp (str, "0x", 2) == 0 || strncmp (str, "0X", 2) == 0)
    {
      int error = str2clint_l (n_l, (char*)str+2, 16);
    }
  else
```

```
  {
    if (strncmp (str, "0b", 2) == 0 || strncmp (str, "0B", 2) == 0)
      {
        error = str2clint_l (n_l, (char*)str+2, 2);
      }
    else
      {
        error = str2clint_l (n_l, (char*)str, 10);
      }
  }
switch (error)     {
    case E_CLINT_OK:
      status = E_LINT_OK;
      break;
    case E_CLINT_NPT:
      status = E_LINT_INV;
      panic (E_LINT_NPT, "constructor 4", 1, __LINE__);
      break;
    case E_CLINT_OFL:
      status = E_LINT_OFL;
      panic (E_LINT_OFL, "constructor 4", 1, __LINE__);
      break;
    default:
      status = E_LINT_INV;
      panic (E_LINT_ERR, "constructor 4", error, __LINE__);
  }
}
```

Constructors make possible the initialization of LINT objects among themselves as well as LINT objects with standard types, constants, and character strings, as the following examples demonstrate:

```
LINT a;
LINT one (1);
int i = 2147483647;
LINT b (i);
LINT c (one);
LINT d ("0x123456789abcdef0");
```

The constructor functions are called explicitly to generate objects of type LINT from the specified arguments. The LINT constructor, which, for example, changes unsigned long values into LINT objects, is embodied in the following function:

```
LINT::LINT (USHORT ul)
{
  n_l = new CLINT;
  if (NULL == n_l)
    {
      panic (E_LINT_NHP, "constructor 11", 0, __LINE__);
    }
  ul2clint_l (n_l, ul);
  status = E_LINT_OK;
}
```

Table 14-1. **LINT** *constructors*

Constructor	Semantics: Generation of a LINT Object
LINT (void);	without initialization (default constructor)
LINT (const char* const, char);	from a character string, with the basis of the numerical representation given in the second argument
LINT (const UCHAR*, int)	from a byte vector with the length given in the second argument
LINT (const char*);	from a character string, optionally with prefix 0X for hex numbers or 0B for binary digits
LINT (const LINT&);	from another LINT object (copy constructor)
LINT (int);	from a value of type char, short, or integer
LINT (long int);	from a value of type long integer
LINT (UCHAR);	from a value of type UCHAR
LINT (USHORT);	from a value of type USHORT
LINT (unsigned int);	from a value of type unsigned integer
LINT (ULONG);	from a value of type ULONG
LINT (const CLINT);	from a CLINT object

Now we must provide a destructor function to go with the constructors of the class LINT, which enable the release of objects and, in particular, the memory bound to them. To be sure, the compiler would gladly make a default destructor available to us, but this would release only the memory that the elements of a LINT object possess. The additional memory allocated by the constructors would not be released, and memory leakage would result. The following short destructor fulfills the important tasks of releasing memory occupied by LINT objects:

```
~LINT()
  {
    delete [] n_l;
  }
```

14.3 Overloaded Operators

The *overloading* of operators represents a powerful mechanism that makes it possible to define functions with the same name but with different parameter lists, functions that can then carry out differing operations. The compiler uses the specified parameter list to determine which function is actually meant. To make this possible C++ employs strong type-checking, which tolerates no ambiguity or inconsistency.

The overloading of operator functions makes it possible to use the "normal" way of expressing a sum c = a + b with LINT objects a, b, and c instead of having to invoke a function like, for example, add_l(a_l, b_l, c_l). This enables the seamless integration of our class into the programming language and significantly improves the readability of programs. For this example it is necessary to overload both the operator "+" and the assignment "=".

There are only a few operators in C++ that cannot be overloaded. Even the operator "[ ]", which is used for access to vectors, can be overloaded, for example by a function that simultaneously checks whether the access to a vector oversteps the vector's bounds. However, please note that the overloading of operators opens the door to all possible mischief. To be sure, the effect of the operators of C++ on the standard data types cannot be altered; nor can the predefined precedence order of the operators (cf. [Str1], Section 6.2) be changed or new operators "created." But for individual classes it is fully possible to define operator functions that have nothing in common with what one traditionally has associated with the operator as it is normally employed. In the interest of maintainability of programs one is well advised to stick close to the meaning of the standard operators in C++ when overloading operators if one is to avoid unnecessary confusion.

One should note in the above outline of the LINT class that certain operators have been implemented as friend functions and others as member functions. The reason for this is that we would like, for example, to use "+" or "*" as two-position operators that can not only process two equivalent LINT objects but accept alternatively one LINT object and one of the built-in C++ integer types, and moreover, accept the arguments in either order, since addition is commutative. To this end we require the above-described constructors, which create LINT objects of out integer types. Mixed expressions such as in

```
LINT a, b, c;
int number;
```

```
// Initialize a, b, and number and calculate something or other
// ...

c = number * (a + b / 2)
```

are thus possible. The compiler takes care of calling the appropriate constructor functions automatically and sees to it that the transformation of the integer type number and the constant 2 into LINT objects takes place at run time, before the operators + and * are invoked. We thereby obtain the greatest possible flexibility in the application of the operators, with the restriction that expressions containing objects of type LINT are themselves of type LINT and can thereafter be assigned only to objects of type LINT.

Before we get ourselves involved in the details of the individual operators, we would like to give an overview of the operators defined by the class LINT, for which the reader is referred to Tables 14-2 through 14-5,

Table 14-2. LINT arithmetic operators

+	addition
++	increment (prefix and postfix operators)
-	subtraction
--	decrement (prefix and postfix operators)
*	multiplication
/	division (quotient)
%	remainder

Table 14-3. LINT bitwise operators

&	bitwise AND
|	bitwise OR
^	bitwise exclusive OR (XOR)
<<	shift left
>>	shift right

We now would like to deal with the implementation of the operator functions "*", "=", "*=", and "==", which may serve as examples of the implementation of the LINT operators. First, with the help of the operator "*=" we see how multiplication of LINT objects is carried out by the C function mul_l(). The operator is implemented as a friend function, to which both factors associated

Table 14-4. LINT *logical operators*

==	equality
!=	inequality
<, <=	less than, less than or equal to
>, >=	greater than, greater than or equal to

Table 14-5. LINT *assignment operators*

=	simple assignment
+=	assignment after addition
-=	assignment after subtraction
*=	assignment after multiplication
/=	assignment after division
%=	assignment after remainder
&=	assignment after bitwise AND
|=	assignment after bitwise OR
^=	assignment after bitwise XOR
<<=	assignment after left shift
>>=	assignment after right shift

with the operation are passed as references. Since the operator functions do not change their arguments, the references are declared as const:

```
const LINT operator* (const LINT& lm, const LINT& ln)
{
LINT prd;
  int error;
```

The first step is to query the operator function as to whether the arguments lm and ln passed by reference have been initialized. If this is not the case for both arguments, then error handling goes into effect, and the member function panic(), declared as static, is called (cf. Chapter 15).

```
  if (lm.status == E_LINT_INV)
    LINT::panic (E_LINT_VAL, "*", 1, __LINE__);
  if (ln.status == E_LINT_INV)
    LINT::panic (E_LINT_VAL, "*", 2, __LINE__);
```

> The C function mul_l() is called, to which are passed as arguments the vectors lm.n_l, ln.n_l as factors, as well as prd.n_l for storing the product.

```
error = mul_l (lm.n_l, ln.n_l, prd.n_l);
```

> The evaluation of the error code stored in error distinguishes three cases: If error == 0, then all is right with the world, and the object prd can be marked as initialized. This takes place by setting the variable prd.status to a value unequal to E_LINT_INV, which in normal cases (error == 0) is E_LINT_OK. If an overflow occurred with mul_l(), then error contains the value E_CLINT_OFL. Since the vector prd.n_l contains in this case a valid CLINT integer, the status variable prd.status is simply set to E_LINT_OFL, though without a call to error handling. If error has neither of these two values after the call to mul_l(), then something has gone awry in these functions without our being able to identify more precisely what error has occurred. Therefore, the function panic() is called for further error handling.

```
switch (error)
  {
    case 0:
      prd.status = E_LINT_OK;
      break;
    case E_CLINT_OFL:
      prd.status = E_LINT_OFL;
      break;
    default:
      lint::panic (E_LINT_ERR, "*", error, __LINE__);
  }
```

> If the error cannot be repaired by panic(), there would be no point in returning to this location. The mechanism for error recognition leads here to a defined termination, which in principle is better than continuing the program in an undefined state. As a final step we have the elementwise return of the product prd.

```
    return prd;
  }
```

Since the object prd exists only within the context of the function, the compiler makes sure that a temporary object is created automatically, which represents the value of prd outside the function. This temporary object is generated with the aid of the *copy* constructor LINT(const LINT&) (cf. page 328) and exists until the expression within which the operator was used has been processed, that is, until the closing semicolon has been reached. Due to the declaration of the function value as const such nonsensical constructs as (a * b) = c; will not get past the compiler. The goal is to treat LINT objects in exactly the same way as the built-in integer types.

We can extend the operator functions by the following detail: If the factors to be multiplied are equal, then the multiplication can be replaced by squaring, so that the advantage in efficiency associated with this changeover can be utilized automatically (cf. Section 4.2.2). However, since in general it costs an elementwise comparison of the arguments to determine whether they are equal, which is too expensive for us, we shall be satisfied with a compromise: Squaring will be brought into play only if both factors refer to one and the same object. Thus we test whether ln and lm point to the same object and in this case execute the squaring function instead of multiplication. Here is the relevant code:

```
if (&lm == &ln)
  {
    error = sqr_l (lm.n_l, prd.n_l);
  }
else
  {
    error = mul_l (lm.n_l, ln.n_l, prd.n_l);
  }
```

This falling back on the functions implemented in C from Part I is a model for all of the remaining functions of the class LINT, which is formed like a shell around the kernel of C functions and protects it from the user of the class.

Before we turn our attention to the more complex assignment operator "*=", it seems a good idea to take a closer look at the simple assignment operator "=". Already in Part I we established that assignment of objects requires particular attention (cf. Chapter 8). Therefore, just as in the C implementation we had to pay heed that in assigning one CLINT object to another the content and not the address of the object was assigned, we must likewise for our LINT class define a special version of the assignment operator "=" that does more than simply copy elements of the class: For the same reasons as were introduced in Chapter 8 we must therefore take care that it is not the address of the numerical vector n_l that is copied, but the digits of the numerical representation pointed to by n_l.

Once one has understood the fundamental necessity for proceeding thus, the implementation is no longer particularly complicated. The operator "=" is implemented as a member function, which returns as a result of the assignment a reference to the implicit left argument. Of course, we use internally the C function cpy_l() to move digits from one object into the other. For executing the assignment a = b the compiler calls the operator function "=" in the context of a, where a takes over the role of an implicit argument that is not given in the parameter list of the operator function. Within the member function reference to the elements of the implicit argument is made simply by naming them without context. Furthermore, a reference to the implicit object can be made via the special pointer this, as in the following implementation of the operator "=":

```
const LINT& LINT::operator= (const LINT& ln)
{
  if (ln.status == E_LINT_INV)
    panic (E_LINT_VAL "=", 2 __LINE__);
```

> First, a check is made as to whether the references to the right and left arguments are identical, since in this case copying is unnecessary. Otherwise, the digits of the numerical representation of ln are copied into those of the implied left argument *this, just as the value of status, and with *this the reference to the implicit argument is returned.

```
    if (&ln != this)
      {
        cpy_l (n_l, ln.n_l);
        status = ln.status;
      }
    return *this;
  }
```

One might ask whether the assignment operator must necessarily return any value at all, since after LINT::operator =(const LINT&) is called the intended assignment appears to have been accomplished. However, the answer to the question is clear if one recalls that expressions of the form

```
f (a = b);
```

are allowed. According to the semantics of C++, such an expression would result in a call to the function f with the result of the assignment a = b as argument. Thus is it imperative that the assignment operator return the assigned value as result, and for reasons of efficiency this is done by reference. A special case of such an expression is

```
a = b = c;
```

where the assignment operator is called two times, one after the other. At the second call the result of the first assignment b = c is assigned to a.

In contrast to the operator "*", the operator "*=" changes the leftmost of the two passed factors by overwriting it with the value of the product. The meaning of the expression a *= b as an abbreviated form of a = a * b should, of course, remain true for LINT objects. Therefore, the operator "*=" can, like the operator

"=", be set up as a member function that for the reasons given above returns a reference to the result:

```
const LINT& LINT::operator*= (const LINT& ln)
{
    int error;
    if (status == E_LINT_INV)
      panic (E_LINT_VAL, "*=", 0, __LINE__);
    if (ln.(status == E_LINT_INV)
      panic (E_LINT_VAL, "*=", 1, __LINE__);

    if (&ln == this)
      error = sqr_l (n_l, n_l);
    else
      error = mul_l (n_l, ln.n_l, n_l);

    switch (error)
      {
        case 0:
          status = E_LINT_OK;
          break;
        case E_CLINT_OFL:
          status = E_LINT_OFL;
          break;
        default:
          panic (E_LINT_ERR, "*=", error, __LINE__);
      }
  return *this;
  }
```

As our last example of a LINT operator we shall describe the function "==", which tests for the equality of two LINT objects: As result the value 1 is returned in the case of equality, and otherwise 0. The operator == also illustrates the implementation of other logical operators.

```
const int operator == (const LINT& lm, const LINT& ln)
{
  if (lm.(status == E_LINT_INV)
    LINT::panic (E_LINT_VAL, "==", 1, __LINE__);
  if (ln.(status == E_LINT_INV)
    LINT::panic (E_LINT_VAL, "==", 2, __LINE__);

  if (&ln == &lm)
    return 1;
  else
    return equ_l (lm.n_l, ln.n_l);
}
```

The LINT Public Interface: Members and Friends

Please accept my resignation. I don't want to belong to any club that will accept me as a member.

—Groucho Marx

Every time I paint a portrait I lose a friend
—John Singer Sargent

IN ADDITION TO THE CONSTRUCTOR functions and operators already discussed, there exist further LINT functions that make the C functions developed in Part I available to LINT objects. In the following discussion we make a rough separation of the functions into the categories "arithmetic" and "number-theoretic." The implementation of the functions will be discussed together with examples; otherwise, we shall restrict ourselves to a table of information needed for their proper use. We shall give more extensive treatment in the following sections to the functions for the formatted output of LINT objects, for which we shall make use of the properties of the *stream* classes contained in the C++ standard library. Possible applications, in particular for formatted output of objects of user-defined classes, are given rather short shrift in many C++ textbooks, and we are going to take the opportunity to explicate the construction of the functions needed to output our LINT objects.

15.1 Arithmetic

The following member functions implement the fundamental arithmetic operations as well as modular operations for calculation in residue class rings over the integers as accumulator operations: The object to which a called function belongs contains the function result as implicit argument after its termination. Accumulator functions are efficient, since they operate to the greatest extent without internal auxiliary objects and thus save unnecessary assignments and calls to constructors.

For the cases in which a free assignment of the results of calculations is unavoidable, or in which the automatic overwriting of the implicit argument of the member functions with the result is not desired, the member functions were extended by means of like-named analogous friend functions together with additional friend functions. These are not discussed further here, but are recorded in Appendix B. The treatment of possible error situations in LINT functions that can arise from the use of CLINT functions will be discussed in full in Chapter 16.

Before we list the public member functions, we consider first as an example of their implementation the functions

```
LINT& LINT::mexp (const LINT& e, const LINT& m );
```

and

```
LINT& LINT::mexp (USHORT e, const LINT& m);
```

for exponentiation, an operation for which C++, alas, offers no operator. The functions mexp() were constructed in such a way that the functions used are, according to the type of the operands, the C functions mexpk_l(), mexpkm_l(), umexp_l(), and umexpm_l(), optimized for this purpose (with the corresponding arithmetic friend functions we are likewise dealing with the exponentiation functions wmexp_l() and wmexpm_l() with USHORT base).

Function:	Modular exponentiation with automatic use of Montgomery exponentiation if the modulus is odd.
Syntax:	const LINT& LINT::mexp (const LINT& e, const LINT& m);
Input:	implicit argument (base) e (exponent) m (modulus)
Return:	pointer to the remainder
Example:	a.mexp (e, m);

```
const LINT& LINT::mexp (const LINT& e, const LINT& m)
{
  int error;
  if (status == E_LINT_INV) panic (E_LINT_VAL, "mexp", 0, __LINE__);
```

```
      if (status == E_LINT_INV) panic (E_LINT_VAL, "mexp", 1, __LINE__);
      if (status == E_LINT_INV) panic (E_LINT_VAL, "mexp", 2, __LINE__);

      err = mexp_l (n_l, e.n_l, n_l, m.n_l);
      /* mexp_l() uses mexpk_l() or mexpkm_l() */
      switch (error)
        {
          case 0:
            status = E_LINT_OK;
            break;
          case E_CLINT_DBZ:
            panic (E_LINT_DBZ, "mexp", 2, __LINE__);
            break;
          default:
            panic (E_LINT_ERR, "mexp", error, __LINE__);
        }

    return *this;
}
```

Function:	Modular exponentiation
Syntax:	const LINT& LINT::mexp (USHORT e, const LINT& m);
Example:	a.mexp (e, m);

```
const LINT& LINT::mexp (USHORT e, const LINT& m)
{
  int err;
  if (status == E_LINT_INV) panic (E_LINT_VAL, "mexp", 0, __LINE__);
  if (status == E_LINT_INV) panic (E_LINT_VAL, "mexp", 1, __LINE__);

  err = umexp_l (n_l, e, n_l, m.n_l);

  switch (err)
    {
      // Code as above with mexp (const LINT& e, const LINT& m)
    }
  return *this;
}
```

We now present a collection of additional arithmetic and number-theoretic member functions.

Function:	addition
Syntax:	`const LINT&` `LINT::add(const LINT& s);`
Input:	implicit argument (summand) s (summand)
Return:	pointer to the sum
Example:	`a.add (s);` executes the operation a `+=` s;

Function:	subtraction
Syntax:	`const LINT&` `LINT::sub (const LINT& s);`
Input:	implicit argument (minuend) s (subtrahend)
Return:	pointer to the difference
Example:	`a.sub (s);` executes the operation a `-=` s;

Function:	multiplication
Syntax:	`const LINT&` `LINT::mul (const LINT& s);`
Input:	implicit argument (factor) s (factor)
Return:	pointer to the product
Example:	`a.mul (s);` executes the operation a `*=` s;

Function:	squaring
Syntax:	`const LINT&` `LINT::sqr (void);`
Input:	implicit argument (factor)
Return:	pointer to the implicit argument, which contains the square
Example:	`a.sqr ();` executes the operation `a *= a;`

Function:	division with remainder
Syntax:	`const LINT&` `LINT::divr(const LINT& d, LINT& r);`
Input:	implicit argument (dividend) d (divisor)
Output	r (remainder of the division modulo d)
Return:	pointer to the implicit argument, which contains the quotient
Example:	`a.divr (d, r);` executes the operation `a /= d; r = a % d;`

Function:	residue
Syntax:	`const LINT&` `LINT::mod(const LINT& d);`
Input:	implicit argument (dividend) d (divisor)
Return:	pointer to the implicit argument, which contains the remainder of the division modulo d
Example:	`a.mod (d);` executes the operation `a %= d;`

Function:	residue modulo a power of 2
Syntax:	`const LINT&` `LINT::mod2 (USHORT e)`
Input:	implicit argument (dividend) e (exponent of the power of 2 divisor)
Return:	pointer to the implicit argument, which contains the remainder of the division modulo 2^e
Example:	`a.mod 2(e);` executes the operation `a %= d;`, where `d = ` 2^e
Note:	`mod2` cannot be created by overloading the previously presented function `mod()`, since `mod()` also accepts a `USHORT` argument, which is changed automatically into a `LINT` object by means of the appropriate constructor. Since it cannot be determined from the arguments which function is meant, `mod2()` is given its own name.

Function:	test for equality modulo `m`
Syntax:	`int` `LINT::mequ (const LINT& b, const LINT& m);`
Input:	implicit argument `a` second argument `b` modulus `m`
Return:	1 if $a \equiv b \bmod m$, 0 otherwise
Example:	`if (a.mequ (b, m)) // ...`

Function:	modular addition
Syntax:	`const LINT&` `LINT::madd(const LINT& s, const LINT& m);`
Input:	implicit argument (summand) `s` (summand) `m` (modulus)
Return:	pointer to the implicit argument, which contains the sum modulo `m`
Example:	`a.madd (s, m);`

Function:	modular subtraction
Syntax:	`const LINT& LINT::msub(const LINT& s,` `const LINT& m);`
Input:	implicit argument (minuend) `s` (subtrahend) `m` (modulus)
Return:	pointer to the implicit argument, which contains the difference modulo `m`
Example:	`a.msub (s, m);`

Function:	modular multiplication
Syntax:	`const LINT& LINT::mmul (const LINT& s,` `const LINT& m);`
Input:	implicit argument (factor) `s` (factor) `m` (modulus)
Return:	pointer to the implicit argument, which contains the product modulo `m`
Example:	`a.mmul (s, m);`

Function:	modular squaring
Syntax:	`const LINT& LINT::msqr (const LINT& m);`
Input:	implicit argument (factor)
	`m` (modulus)
Return:	pointer to the implicit argument, which contains the square modulo `m`
Example:	`a.msqr (m);`

Function:	modular exponentiation with exponent a power of 2
Syntax:	`const LINT& LINT::mexp2 (USHORT e,`
	`const LINT& m);`
Input:	implicit argument (base)
	`e` (power to which 2 is to be raised)
	`m` (modulus)
Return:	pointer to the implicit argument, which contains the power modulo `m`
Example:	`a.mexp2 (e, m);`

Function:	modular exponentiation (2^k-ary method, Montgomery reduction)
Syntax:	`const LINT& LINT::mexpkm (const LINT& e,`
	`const LINT& m);`
Input:	implicit argument (base)
	`e` (exponent)
	`m` (odd modulus)
Return:	pointer to the implicit argument, which contains the power modulo `m`
Example:	`a.mexpkm (e, m);`

Function:	modular exponentiation (2^5-ary method, Montgomery reduction)
Syntax:	`const LINT& LINT::mexp5m (const LINT& e,` `const LINT& m);`
Input:	implicit argument (base) e (exponent) m (odd modulus)
Return:	pointer to the implicit argument, which contains the power modulo m
Example:	`a.mexp5m (e, m);`

Function:	left/right shift
Syntax:	`const LINT& LINT::shift (int noofbits);`
Input:	implicit argument (multiplicand/dividend) `(+/-)` `noofbits` (number of bit positions to be shifted)
Return:	pointer to the implicit argument, which contains the result of the shift operation
Example:	`a.shift (512);` executes the operation a `<<= 512;`

Function:	test for divisibility by 2 of a LINT object
Syntax:	`int` `LINT::iseven (void);`
Input:	test candidate a as implicit argument
Return:	1 if a is odd, 0 otherwise
Example:	`if(a.iseven ()) // ...`

Function:	set a binary digit of a LINT object to 1
Syntax:	const LINT& LINT::setbit (unsigned int pos);
Input:	implicit argument a position pos of the bit to be set (counted from 0)
Return:	pointer to a with the set bit at position pos
Example:	a.setbit (512);

Function:	test a binary digit of a LINT object
Syntax:	int LINT::testbit (unsigned int pos);
Input:	implicit argument a position pos of the bit to be tested (counted from 0)
Return:	1 if the bit at position pos is set, 0 otherwise
Example:	if(a.testbit (512)) // ...

Function:	set a binary digit of a LINT object to 0
Syntax:	const LINT& LINT::clearbit (unsigned int pos);
Input:	implicit argument a position pos of the bit to be cleared (counted from 0)
Return:	pointer to a with the cleared bit at position pos
Example:	a.clearbit (512);

Function:	exchange values of two LINT objects
Syntax:	`const LINT&` `LINT::fswap (LINT& b);`
Input:	implicit argument a position b (the value to be swapped for a)
Return:	pointer to the implicit argument with the value b
Example:	`a.fswap (b);` exchanges the values a and b

15.2 Number Theory

In contrast to the arithmetic functions, the following number-theoretic member functions do not overwrite the implicit first argument with the result. The reason for this is that with more complex functions it has been shown in practice not to be practical to overwrite, as is the case with simple arithmetic functions. The results of the following functions are thus returned as values rather than as pointers.

Function:	calculate the greatest integer less than or equal to the base-2 logarithm of a LINT object
Syntax:	`unsigned int` `LINT::ld (void);`
Input:	implicit argument a
Return:	integer part of the base-2 logarithm of a
Example:	`i = a.ld ();`

Function:	calculate the greatest common divisor of two LINT objects
Syntax:	LINT LINT::gcd (const LINT& b);
Input:	implicit argument a second argument b
Return:	gcd (a, b) of the input values
Example:	c = a.gcd (b);

Function:	calculate the multiplicative inverse modulo n
Syntax:	LINT LINT::inv (const LINT& n);
Input:	implicit argument a modulus n
Return:	multiplicative inverse of a modulo n (if the result is equal to zero, then $\gcd(a, n) > 1$ and the inverse does not exist)
Example:	c = a.inv (n);

Function:	calculate the greatest common divisor of a and b as well as its representation g = ua+vb as a linear combination of a and b

Syntax:	LINT
	LINT::xgcd(const LINT& b,
	                    LINT& u, int& sign_u,
	                    LINT& v, int& sign_v);

Input:	implicit argument a, second argument b
Output:	Factor u of the representation of gcd (a, b) sign of u in sign_u factor v of the representation of gcd (a, b) sign of v in sign_v
Return:	$\gcd(a, b)$ of the input values
Example:	g = a.xgcd (b, u, sign_u, v, sign_v);

Function:	calculate the least common multiple (lcm) of two LINT objects
Syntax:	LINT LINT::lcm (const LINT& b);
Input:	implicit argument a factor b
Return:	lcm(a, b) of the input values
Example:	c = a.lcm (b);

Function:	solution of a system of linear congruences $x \equiv a \bmod m, x \equiv b \bmod n$,
Syntax:	LINT LINT::chinrem(const LINT& m, const LINT& b, const LINT& n);
Input:	implicit argument a, modulus m, argument b, modulus n
Return:	solution x of the congruence system if all is ok (Get_Warning_Status() == E_LINT_ERR indicates that an overflow has occurred or that the congruences have no common solution)
Example:	x = a.chinrem (m, b, n);

The friend function chinrem(int noofeq, LINT** coeff) accepts a vector coeff of pointers to LINT objects, which are passed as coefficients $a_1, m_1, a_2, m_2, a_3, m_3, \ldots$ of a system of linear congruences with "arbitrarily" many equations $x \equiv a_i \bmod m_i, i = 1, \ldots,$ noofeq (see Appendix B).

Function:	calculation of the Jacobi symbol of two LINT objects
Syntax:	int LINT::jacobi (const LINT& b);
Input:	implicit argument a, second argument b
Return:	Jacobi symbol of the input values
Example:	i = a.jacobi (b);

Function:	calculation of the integer part of the square root of a LINT object
Syntax:	LINT LINT::introot (void);
Input:	implicit argument a
Return:	integer part of the square root of the input value
Example:	c = a.root ();

Function:	calculation of the integer part of the *b*th root of a LINT object
Syntax:	LINT LINT::introot (const USHORT b);
Input:	implicit argument a, root exponent b
Return:	integer part of the *b*th root of the input value
Example:	c = a.root (b);

Function:	calculation of the square root modulo a prime p of a LINT object
Syntax:	LINT LINT::root (const LINT& p);
Input:	implicit argument a, prime modulus $p > 2$
Return:	square root of a if a is a quadratic residue modulo p otherwise 0 (Get_Warning_Status() == E_LINT_ERR indicates that a is not a quadratic residue modulo p)
Example:	c = a.root (p);

Function:	calculation of the square root of a LINT object modulo a prime product p · q
Syntax:	`LINT` `LINT::root (const LINT& p, const LINT& q);`
Input:	implicit argument a prime modulus $p > 2$, prime modulus $q > 2$
Return:	square root of a if a is a quadratic residue modulo pq otherwise 0 (`Get_Warning_Status() == E_LINT_ERR` indicates that a is not a quadratic residue modulo p*q)
Example:	`c = a.root (p, q);`

Function:	test of whether a LINT object is a square
Syntax:	`int` `LINT::issqr(void);`,
Input:	test candidate a as implicit argument
Return:	square root of a if a is a square otherwise 0 if a `==` 0 or a not a square
Example:	`if(0 == (r = a.issqr ()))  // ...`

Function:	probabilistic primality test of a LINT object
Syntax:	`int` `LINT::isprime (int nsp, int rnds);`
Input:	test candidate p as implicit argument nsp (number of primes for the division test; default is 302) rnds (number of passes through test; default is zero for automatic optimization via the function `prime_l()`)
Return:	1 if p is a "probable" prime 0 otherwise
Example:	`if(p.isprime ())  // ...`

Function:	calculate the two-part of a `LINT` object
Syntax:	`int` `LINT::twofact (LINT& b);`
Input:	implicit argument a
Output:	b (odd part of a)
Return:	exponent of the even part of a
Example:	`e = a.twofact (b);`

15.3 Stream I/O of LINT Objects

The classes contained in the C++ standard library such as `istream` and `ostream` are abstractions of input and output devices derived from the base class `ios`. The class `iostream` is in turn derived from `istream` and `ostream`, and it enables both writing and reading of its objects.[1] Input and output take place with the help of the *insert* and *extract* operators "<<" and ">>" (cf. [Teal], Chapter 8). These arise through overloading the shift operators, for example in the form

```
ostream& ostream::operator<< (int i);
istream& istream::operator>> (int& i);
```

in which they enable output, respectively input, of integer values through expressions of the form

```
cout << i;
cin >> i;
```

As special objects of the classes `ostream` and `istream`, `cout` and `cin` represent the same abstract files as the objects `stdout` and `stdin` of the standard C library.

   The use of the stream operators "<<" and ">>" for input and output makes it unnecessary to consider particular properties of the hardware in use. In and of itself this is nothing new, for the C function `printf()` behaves the same way: A `printf()` instruction should always, regardless of platform, lead to the same result. However, above and beyond the altered syntax, which is oriented to the metaphorical image of the insertion of objects into a stream, the advantages of the C++ implementation of streams lie in the strict type checking, which in the case of `printf()` is possible only to a limited degree, and in its extensibility. In particular, we make use of the latter property by overloading the *insert* and *extract*

---

[1]   We use this name of the stream classes as a synonym for the terms now used in the C++ standard library, with which the class names known up to now are prefixed with `basic_`. The justification for this comes from the standard library itself, where the class names known hitherto are provided with corresponding `typedef`s (cf. [KSch], Chapter 12).

operators so that they support input and output of LINT objects. To this end the class LINT defines the following *stream* operators:

```
friend ostream& operator<< (ostream& s, const LINT& ln);
friend fstream& operator<< (fstream& s, const LINT& ln);
friend ofstream& operator<< (ofstream& s, const LINT& ln);
friend fstream& operator>> (fstream& s, LINT& ln);
friend ifstream& operator>> (ifstream& s, LINT& ln);
```

A simple formulation of the overloaded insert operators for the output of LINT objects might look something like the following:

```
#include <iostream.h>

ostream& operator<< (ostream& s, const LINT& ln)
{
  if (ln.status == E_LINT_INV)
    LINT::panic (E_LINT_VAL, "ostream operator <<", 0, __LINE__);
  s << xclint2str (ln.n_l, 16, 0) << endl;
  s << ld (ln) << " bit" << endl;
  return s;
}
```

The operator << thus defined outputs the digits of a LINT object as hexadecimal values and adds the binary length of the number in a separate line. In the next section we shall consider the possibilities of improving the appearance of the output of LINT objects with the aid of formatting functions, and we shall also use manipulators to make the output customizable.

15.3.1 *Formatted Output of* LINT *Objects*

In this section we shall make use of the base class ios of the C++ standard library and of its member functions to define our own LINT-specific formatting functions for the purpose of controlling the output format of LINT objects. Furthermore, we shall create manipulators that will make the customization of the output format for LINT objects as simple as it is for the standard types defined in C++.

The crucial point in the creation of formatted output of LINT objects is the possibility of setting formatting specifications that will be handled by the insert operator. To this end we shall consider the mechanism provided for the class ios (for details see [Teal], Chapter 6, and [Pla2], Chapter 6), whose member function xalloc() in the objects of the classes derived from ios allocates a status variable of type long and returns an index to this status variable also of type long. We store this index in the long variable flagsindex. By means of this index the member function ios::iword() can be used to access reading and writing to the allocated status variable (cf. [Pla2], page 125).

To ensure that this takes place before a `LINT` object is output, we define, in the file `flintpp.h`, the class `LintInit` as follows:

```
class LintInit
  {
    public:
      LintInit (void);
  };

  LintInit::LintInit (void)
  {
    // get index to long status variable in class ios
    LINT::flagsindex = ios::xalloc();
    // set the default status in cout and in cerr
    cout.iword (LINT::flagsindex) =
    cerr.iword (LINT::flagsindex) =
      LINT::lintshowlength|LINT::linthex|LINT::lintshowbase;
  }
```

The class `LintInit` has as its only element the constructor `LintInit::LintInit()`. Furthermore, in the class `LINT` we define a member datum `setup` of type `LintInit`, which is initialized via the constructor `LintInit::LintInit()`. The call to `xalloc()` takes place within this initialization, and the status variable thereby allocated is given the established standard output format for `LINT` objects. In the following we shall show a section of the `LINT` class declaration, which contains the declaration of `LintInit()` as a *friend* of `LINT`, the declaration of the variables `flagsindex` and `setup`, and various status values as `enum` types:

```
class LINT
  {
    public:
      // ...
      enum {
        lintdec = 0x10,
        lintoct = 0x20,
        linthex = 0x40,
        lintshowbase = 0x80,
        lintuppercase = 0x100,
        lintbin = 0x200,
        lintshowlength = 0x400
      };
      // ...
      friend LintInit::LintInit (void);
```

```
    // ...
  private:
    // ...
    static long flagsindex;
    static LintInit setup;
    // ...
};
```

Setting the variable setup as static has the effect that this variable exists only once for all LINT objects and thus the associated constructor LintInit() is called only once.

We would like now to pause for a moment and consider what all this effort nets us. Setting the output format could just as well be managed via a status variable, which as a member of LINT would be much simpler to deal with. The decisive advantage of the method that we have chosen is that the output format can be set for each output stream separately and independently of the others (cf. [Pla2], page 125), which could not be accomplished with an internal LINT status variable. This is done through the power of the class ios, whose mechanisms we employ for such purposes.

Now that the preliminaries have been taken care of, we can define the status functions as member functions of LINT. These are displayed in Table 15-1.

We shall consider as an example of the implementation of the status functions the function LINT::setf(), which returns the current value of the status variable as a long with reference to an output stream:

```
long LINT::setf (ostream& s, long flag)
  {
  long t = s.iword (flagsindex);
  // the flags for the basis of the numerical representation
  // are mutually exclusive
  if (flag & LINT::lintdec)
    {
    s.iword (flagsindex) = (t & ~LINT::linthex & ~LINT::lintoct
              & ~LINT::lintbin) | LINT::lintdec;
    flag ^= LINT::lintdec;
    }
  if (flag & LINT::linthex)
    {
    s.iword (flagsindex) = (t & ~LINT::lintdec & ~LINT::lintoct
              & ~LINT::lintbin) | LINT::linthex;
    flag ^= LINT::linthex;
    }
  if (flag & LINT::lintoct)
    {
```

```
        s.iword (flagsindex) = (t & ~LINT::lintdec & ~LINT::linthex
                    & ~LINT::lintbin) | LINT::lintoct;
      flag ^= LINT::lintoct;
      }
  if (flag & LINT::lintbin)
    {
      s.iword (flagsindex) = (t & ~LINT::lintdec & ~LINT::lintoct
                  & ~LINT::linthex) | LINT::lintbin;
      flag ^= LINT::lintbin;
      }
  // all remaining flags are mutually compatible
  s.iword (flagsindex) |= flag;
  return t;
  }
```

Table 15-1. LINT *status functions and their effects*

Status Function	Explanation
static long LINT::flags (void);	read the status variable with reference to cout
static long LINT::flags (ostream&);	read the status variable with reference to an arbitrary output stream
static long LINT::setf (long);	set individual bits of the status variable with reference to cout and return the previous value
static long LINT::setf (ostream&, long);	set individual bits of the status variable with reference to an arbitrary output stream and return the previous value
static long LINT::unsetf (long);	restore individual bits of the status variable with reference with reference to cout and return the previous value
static long LINT::unsetf (ostream&, long);	restore individual bits of the status variable with reference to an arbitrary output stream and return the previous value
static long LINT::restoref (long);	set the status variable with reference to cout with a value and return the previous value
static long LINT::restoref (ostream&, long);	set the status variable with reference to an arbitrary output stream with a value and return the previous value

With the help of these and the remaining functions of Table 15-1 we can determine the output formats in the following. First, the standard output format represents the value of a LINT object as a hexadecimal number in a character string, where the output fills as many lines on the screen as required by the number of digits of the LINT object. In an additional line the number of digits of the LINT object is displayed flush left. The following additional modes for output of a LINT object have been implemented:

1. **Base for the representation of digits**
   The standard base for the representation of digits of LINT objects is 16, and for the representation of the length it is 10. This default for LINT objects can be set for the standard output stream cout to a specified base by a call to

   ```
   LINT::setf (LINT::base);
   ```

   and to

   ```
   LINT::setf (ostream, LINT::base);
   ```

   for an arbitrary output stream. Here base can assume any one of the values

   ```
   linthex, lintdec, lintoct, lintbin,
   ```

   which denote the corresponding output format. A call to LINT::setf(lintdec), for example sets the output format to decimal digits. The base for the representation of the length can be set with the function

   ```
   ios::setf (ios::iosbase);
   ```

   with iosbase = hex, dec, oct.

2. **Display of the prefix for the numerical representation**
   The default is for a LINT object to be displayed with a prefix indicating how it is represented. A call to

   ```
   LINT::unsetf(LINT::lintshowbase);
   LINT::unsetf (ostream, LINT::lintshowbase);
   ```

   changes this setting.

3. **Display of hexadecimal digits in uppercase letters**
   The default is the display of hexadecimal digits and the display of the prefix 0x for a hexadecimal representation in lowercase letters a b c d e f. However, a call to

   ```
   LINT::setf (LINT::lintuppercase);
   LINT::setf (ostream, LINT::lintuppercase);
   ```

   changes this, so that the prefix 0X and uppercase letters A B C D E F are displayed.

4. **Display of the length of a LINT object**

   The default is the display of the binary length of a LINT objects. This can be changed by a call to

   ```
   LINT::unsetf (LINT::lintshowlength);
   LINT::unsetf (ostream, LINT::lintshowlength);
   ```

   so that the length is not displayed.

5. **Restoring the status variable for the numerical representation**

   The status variable for the formatting of a LINT object can be restored to a previous value oldflags by a call to the two functions

   ```
   LINT::unsetf (ostream, LINT::flags(ostream));
   LINT::setf (ostream, oldflags);
   ```

   Calls to these two functions are collected in the overloaded function restoref():

   ```
   LINT::restoref (flag);
   LINT::restoref (ostream, flag);
   ```

   Flags can be combined, as in the call

   ```
   LINT::setf (LINT::bin | LINT::showbase);
   ```

This, however, is permitted only for flags that are not mutually exclusive.

The output function that finally generates the requested representational format for LINT objects is an extension of the operator ostream& operator <<(ostream& s, LINT ln) already sketched above, which evaluates the status variables of the output stream and generates the appropriate output. For this the operator uses the auxiliary function lint2str() contained in flintpp.cpp, which in turn calls the function xclint2str_l() to represent the numerical value of a LINT object in a character string:

```
ostream& operator << (ostream& s, const LINT& ln)
  {
    USHORT base = 16;
    long flags = LINT::flags (s);
    char* formatted_lint;

    if (ln.status == E_LINT_INV)
      LINT::panic (E_LINT_VAL, "ostream operator<<", 0, __LINE__);

    if (flags & LINT::linthex)
      {
        base = 16;
      }
    else
```

```
      {
        if (flags & LINT::lintdec)
          {
            base = 10;
          }
      else
          {
            if (flags & LINT::lintoct)
              {
                base = 8;
              }
            else
              {
                if (flags & LINT::lintbin)
                  {
                      base = 2;
                  }
              }
          }
      }
  if (flags & LINT::lintshowbase)
    {
      formatted_lint = lint2str (ln, base, 1);
    }
  else
    {
      formatted_lint = lint2str (ln, base, 0);
    }

  if (flags & LINT::lintuppercase)
    {
      strupr_l (formatted_lint);
    }

  s << formatted_lint << flush;

  if (flags & LINT::lintshowlength)
    {
      long _flags = s.flags (); // get current status
      s.setf (ios::dec);// set flag for decimal display
      s << endl << ld (ln) << " bit" << endl;
      s.setf (_flags); // restore previous status
    }

    return s;
}
```

15.3.2 *Manipulators*

Building on the previous mechanisms, we would like in this section to obtain more convenient possibilities for controlling the output format for LINT objects. To this end we use *manipulators*, which are placed directly into the output stream and thus display the same effects as occur in calling the above status functions. Manipulators are addresses of functions for which there exist special *insert* operators that on their part accept a pointer to a function as argument. As an example we consider the following function:

```
ostream& LintHex (ostream& s)
{
  LINT::setf (s, LINT::linthex);
  return s;
}
```

This function calls the status function setf(s, LINT::linthex) in the context of the specified output stream ostream& s and thereby effects the output of LINT objects as hexadecimal numbers. The name LintHex of the function without parentheses is viewed as a pointer to the function (cf. [Lipp], page 202) and can be set in an output stream as a manipulator with the help of the *insert* operator

```
ostream& ostream::operator<< (ostream& (*pf)(ostream&))
{
  return (*pf)(*this);
}
```

defined in the class ostream:

```
LINT a ("0x123456789abcdef0");
cout << LintHex << a;

ostream s;
s << LintDec << a;
```

The LINT manipulator functions operate according to the same pattern as the standard manipulators in the C++ library, for example dec, hex, oct, flush, and endl: The insert operator << simply calls the manipulator function LintHex() or LintDec() at the appropriate place. The manipulators ensure that the status flags belonging to the output streams cout, respectively s, are set. The overloaded operator<< for the output of LINT objects takes over the representation of the LINT object a in the requested form.

The format settings for the output of LINT objects can all be carried out with the help of the manipulators presented in Table 15-2.

Table 15-2. LINT *manipulators and their effects*

Manipulator	Effect: Form of the Output of LINT Values
LintBin	as binary numbers
LintDec	as decimal numbers
LintHex	as hexadecimal numbers
LintOct	as octal numbers
LintLwr	with lowercase letters a, b, c, d, e, f for hexadecimal representation
LintUpr	with uppercase letters A, B, C, D, E, F for hexadecimal representation
LintShowbase	with prefix for the numerical representation (0x or 0X for hexadecimal, 0b for binary)
LintNobase	without prefix for numerical representation
LintShowlength	indicating the number of digits
LintNolength	without indicating the number of digits

In addition to the manipulators of Table 15-2, which require no argument, the manipulators

```
LINT_omanip<int> SetLintFlags (int flags)
```

and

```
LINT_omanip<int> ResetLintFlags (int flags)
```

are available, which can be used as alternatives to the status functions LINT::setf() and LINT::unsetf():

```
cout << SetLintFlags (LINT::flag) << ...; // turn on
cout << ResetLintFlags (LINT::flag) << ...; // turn off
```

For the implementation of these manipulators the reader is referred to the sources (flintpp.h and flintpp.cpp) in connection with the explanation of the *template* class omanip<T> in [Pla2], Chapter 10. The LINT flags are shown once again in Table 15-3.

Table 15-3. LINT *flags for output formatting and their effects*

Flag	Value
lintdec	0x010
lintoct	0x020
linthex	0x040
lintshowbase	0x080
lintuppercase	0x100
lintbin	0x200
lintshowlength	0x400

We shall now clarify the use of the format functions and manipulators by means of the following example:

```
#include "flintpp.h"
#include <iostream.h>
#include <iomanip.h>

main()
{
  LINT n ("0x0123456789abcdef"); // LINT number with base 16
  long deflags = LINT::flags(); // store flags

  cout << "Default representation: " << n << endl;

  LINT::setf (LINT::linthex | LINT::lintuppercase);
  cout << "hex representation with uppercase letters: " << n << endl;
  cout << LintLwr << "hex representation with lowercase letters: " << n << endl;
  cout << LintDec << "decimal representation: " << n << endl;
  cout << LintBin << "binary representation: " << n << endl;
  cout << LintNobase << LintHex;
  cout << "representation without prefix: " << n << endl;
  cerr << "Default representation Stream cerr: " << n << endl;

  LINT::restoref (deflags);
  cout << "default representation: " << n << endl;

  return;
}
```

15.3.3 *File I/O for* LINT *Objects*

Functions for the output of LINT objects to files and functions for reading them are unavoidable for practical applications. The input and output classes of the

C++ standard library contain member functions that permit the setting of objects into an input or output stream for file operations, so we are fortunate in that we can use the same syntax as we used above. The operators needed for output to files are similar to those of the last section, where, however, we can do without the formatting.

We define the two operators

```
friend ofstream& operator<< (ofstream& s, const LINT& ln);

friend fstream& operator<< (fstream& s, const LINT& ln);
```

for output streams of the class ofstream and for streams of the class fstream, which supports both directions, that is, both input and output. Since the class ofstream is derived from the class ostream, we can use its member function ostream::write() to write unformatted data to a file. Since only the digits of a LINT object that are actually used are stored, we can deal sparingly with the storage space of the data medium. Here the USHORT digits of the LINT object are actually written as a sequence of UCHAR values. To ensure that this always occurs in the correct order, independent of the numerical representation scheme of a particular platform, an auxiliary function is defined that writes a USHORT value as a sequence of two UCHAR types. This function neutralizes the platform-specific ordering of the digits to base 256 in memory and thereby allows data that were written on one computer type to be read on another that possibly orders the digits of a number differently or perhaps interprets them differently when they are read from mass storage. Relevant examples in this connection are the *little-endian* and *big-endian* architectures of various processors, which in the former case order consecutive increasing memory addresses in increasing order, and in the latter case do so in decreasing order.[2]

```
template <class T>
  int write_ind_ushort (T& s, clint src)
  {
    UCHAR buff[sizeof(clint)];
    unsigned i, j;
    for (i = 0, j = 0; i < sizeof(clint); i++, j = i << 3)
      {
        buff[i] = (UCHAR)((src & (0xff << j)) >> j);
      }
    s.write (buff, sizeof(clint));
```

---

[2] Two bytes B_i and B_{i+1} with addresses i and $i + 1$ are interpreted in the little-endian representation as USHORT value $w = 2^8 B_{i+1} + B_i$ and in the big-endian representation as $w = 2^8 B_i + B_{i+1}$. The analogous situation holds for the interpretation of ULONG values.

```
    if (!s)
      {
        return -1;
      }
    else
      {
        return 0;
      }
  }
```

The function write_ind_ushort() returns in the case of error the value −1, while it returns 0 if the operation is successful. It is implemented as a *template*, so that it can be used with both ofstream objects and fstream objects. The function read_ind_ushort() is created as its counterpart:

```
  template <class T>
  int read_ind_ushort (T& s, clint *dest)
  {
    UCHAR buff[sizeof(clint)];
    unsigned i;     s.read (buff, sizeof(clint));

    if (!s)
      {
        return -1;
      }
    else
      {
        *dest = 0;
        for (i = 0; i < sizeof(clint); i++)
          {
            *dest |= ((clint)buff[i]) << (i << 3);
          }
        return 0;
      }
  }
```

The output operators now use this neutral format to write from a LINT object to a file. To elucidate the situation we shall present the implementation of the operator for the class ofstream.

```
ofstream& operator<< (ofstream& s, const LINT& ln)
  {
    if (ln.status == E_LINT_INV)
      LINT::panic (E_LINT_VAL, "ofstream operator<<", 0, __LINE__);
```

```
    for (int i = 0; i <= DIGITS_L (ln.n_l); i++)
      {
        if (write_ind_ushort (s, ln.n_l[i]))
          {
            LINT::panic (E_LINT_EOF, "ofstream operator<<", 0, __LINE__);
          }
      }
    return s;
}
```

Before a LINT object is written to a file, the file must be opened for writing, for which one could use the constructor

```
ofstream::ofstream (const char *, openmode)
```

or the member function

```
ofstream::open (const char *, openmode)
```

In each case the ios flag ios::binary must be set, as in the following example:

```
LINT r ("0x0123456789abcdef");
// ...
ofstream fout ("test.io", ios::out | ios::binary);
fout << r << r*r;
// ...
fout.close();
```

The importation of a LINT object from a file is effected in a complementary way, with analogous operators, to that of output of a LINT object to a file.

```
friend ifstream& operator >> (ifstream& s, LINT& ln);
friend fstream& operator >> (fstream& s, LINT& ln);
```

Both operators first read a single value, which specifies the number of digits of the stored LINT object. Then the corresponding number of digits are read in. The USHORT values are read according to the above description under the action of the function read_ind_ushort():

```
ifstream& operator>> (ifstream& s, LINT& ln)
{
  if (read_ind_ushort (s, ln.n_l))
    {
```

```
          LINT::panic (E_LINT_EOF, "ifstream operator>>", 0, __LINE__);
      }
    if (DIGITS_L (ln.n_l) < CLINTMAXSHORT)
      {
        for (int i = 1; i <= DIGITS_L (ln.n_l); i++)
          {
            if (read_ind_ushort (s, &ln.n_l[i]))
              {
                LINT::panic (E_LINT_EOF, "ifstream operator>>", 0, __LINE__);
              }
          }
      }


    // No paranoia! Check the imported value!
    if (vcheck_l (ln.n_l) == 0)
      {
        ln.status = E_LINT_OK;
      }
    else
      {
        ln.status = E_LINT_INV;
      }
  return s;
  }
```

To open a file from which the LINT object is to be read it is again necessary to set the ios flag ios::binary:

```
LINT r, s;
// ...
ifstream fin;
fin.open ("test.io", ios::in | ios::binary);
fin >> r >> s;
// ...
fin.close();
```

In the importation of LINT objects the *insert* operator >> checks whether the values read represent the numerical representation of a valid LINT object. If this is not the case, the member datum status is set to E_LINT_INV, and the specified target object is thereby marked as "uninitialized." On the next operation on this object the LINT error handler is invoked, which is what we shall study in more detail in the next chapter.

CHAPTER 16

Error Handling

O hateful error, melancholy's child!
—Shakespeare, *Julius Caesar*

16.1 (Don't) Panic ...

The C++ functions presented in the foregoing chapters embody mechanisms for analyzing whether during the execution of a called C function an error or other situation has occurred that requires a particular response or at least a warning. The functions test whether the passed variables have been initialized and evaluate the return value of the called C functions:

```
LINT f (LINT arg1, LINT arg2)
{
  LINT result;
  int err;
  if (arg1.status == E_LINT_INV)
    LINT::panic (E_LINT_VAL, "f", 1, __LINE__);
  if (arg2.status == E_LINT_INV)
    LINT::panic (E_LINT_VAL, "f", 2, __LINE__);
  // Call C function to execute operation; error code is stored in err
  err = f_l (arg1.n_l, arg2.n_l, result.n_l);
  switch (err)
    {
      case 0:
        result.status = E_LINT_OK;
        break;
      case E_CLINT_OFL:
        result.status = E_LINT_OFL;
        break;
      case E_CLINT_UFL:
        result.status = E_LINT_UFL;
        break;
      default:
        LINT::panic (E_LINT_ERR, "f", err, __LINE__);
    }
  return result;
}
```

If the variable status contains the value E_LINT_OK, then this is the optimal case. In less happy situations, in which overflow or underflow has occurred in a C function, the variable status is set to the appropriate value E_LINT_OFL or E_LINT_UFL. Since our C functions already react to an overflow or underflow with a reduction modulo $N_{max} + 1$ (cf. page 20), in such cases the functions terminate normally. The value of the variable status can then be queried with the member function

```
LINT_ERRORS LINT::Get_Warning_Status (void);
```

Furthermore, we have seen that the LINT functions always call a function with the well-chosen name panic() when the situation gets too hot to handle. The task of this member function is first of all to output error messages, so that the user of the program is made aware that something has gone awry, and secondly to ensure a controlled termination of the program. The LINT error messages are output via the stream cerr, and they contain information about the nature of the error that has occurred, about the function that has detected the error, and about the arguments that have triggered the error. In order that panic() be able to output all of this information, such information arriving from the calling function must be delivered, as in the following example:

```
LINT::panic (E_LINT_DBZ, "%", 2, __LINE__);
```

Here it is announced that a division by zero in the operator "%" has appeared in the line specified by the ANSI macro __LINE__, caused by the operator's argument number 2. The arguments are indicated as follows: 0 always denotes the implicit argument of a member function, and all other arguments are numbered from left to right, beginning with 1. The LINT error routine panic() outputs error messages of the following type:

Example 1: Use of an uninitialized LINT object as argument.

```
critical run-time error detected by class LINT:
Argument 0 in Operator *= uninitialized, line 1997
ABNORMAL TERMINATION
```

Example 2: Division by a LINT object with the value 0.

```
critical run-time error detected by class LINT:
Division by zero, operator/function/, line 2000
ABNORMAL TERMINATION
```

The functions and operators of the LINT class recognize the situations listed in Table 16-1.

Table 16-1. LINT *function error codes*

Code	Value	Explanation
E_LINT_OK	0x0000	everything ok
E_LINT_EOF	0x0010	file I/O error in the stream operator << or >>
E_LINT_DBZ	0x0020	division by zero
E_LINT_NHP	0x0040	Heap error: new returns the NULL pointer
E_LINT_OFL	0x0080	overflow in function or operator
E_LINT_UFL	0x0100	underflow in function or operator
E_LINT_VAL	0x0200	an argument of a function is uninitialized or has an illegal value
E_LINT_BOR	0x0400	incorrect base passed as argument to a constructor
E_LINT_MOD	0x0800	even modulus in mexpkm()
E_LINT_NPT	0x1000	NULL pointer passed as argument
E_LINT_RIN	0x2000	call to an uninitialized pseudorandom number generator

16.2   User-Defined Error Handling

As a rule, it is necessary to adapt error handling to particular requirements. The LINT class offers support in this regard in that the LINT error function panic() can be replaced by user-defined functions. Additionally, the following function is called, which takes as argument a pointer to a function:

```
void
LINT::Set_LINT_Error_Handler (void (*Error_Handler)
      (LINT_ERRORS, const char*, int, int, const, char*))
{
  LINT_User_Error_Handler = Error_Handler;
}
```

The variable LINT_User_Error_Handler is defined and initialized in flintpp.cpp as

```
static void (*LINT_User_Error_Handler)
(LINT_ERRORS, const char*, int, int, const char*) = NULL;
```

If this pointer has a value other than NULL, then the specified function is called instead of panic(), and it contains the same information as panic() would have. With respect to the implementation of a user-defined error-handling routine one has a great deal of freedom. But one must realize that the errors reported by the class LINT usually signal program errors, which are irreparable at run time. It would make no sense to return to the program segment in which such an error has occurred, and in general, in such cases the only reasonable course of action is to terminate the program.

The return to the LINT error routine panic() is effected by a call to

```
LINT::Set_LINT_Error_Handler(NULL);
```

The following example demonstrates the integration of a user-defined function for error handling:

```
#include "flintpp.h"
void my_error_handler (LINT_ERRORS err, const char* func,
                       int arg, int line, const char* file)
{
  //... Code
}
main()
{
  // activation of the user-defined error handler:
  LINT::Set_LINT_Error_Handler (my_error_handler);

  // ... Code

  // reactivate the LINT error handler:
  LINT::Set_LINT_Error_Handler (NULL);

  // ... Code
}
```

16.3 LINT Exceptions

The *exception* mechanism of C++ is an instrument that is easier to utilize and thereby more effective for error handling than the methods offered by C. The error routine LINT::panic() described previously is limited to the output of error messages and the controlled termination of a program. In general, we are less interested in the division function in which a division by zero has occurred than the function that has called the division and thereby precipitated the error, information that LINT::panic() does not contain and thus cannot pass along. In particular, it is impossible with LINT::panic() to return to this function in order to remove an error there or to react in a way specific to the function. Such possibilities, on the other hand, are offered by the exception mechanism of C++, and we would like here to create the conditions that will make this mechanism usable for the LINT class.

Exceptions in C++ are based principally on three types of constructs: the try block, the catch block, and the instruction throw, by means of which a function signals an error. The first, the catch block, has the function of a local error-handling routine for the try block: Errors that occur within a try block and are announced by means of throw will be caught by the catch block, which follows the try block. Further instructions of the try block are then ignored. The type of error is indicated by the value of the throw instruction as parameter of the accompanying expression.

The connection between try and catch blocks can be sketched as follows:

```
try
  {
    ... // If an error is signaled within an operation with
    ... // throw, then it can be
    ... // caught by the following catch block.
  }
  ...
catch (argument)
  {
    ... // here follows the error handling routine.
  }
```

If an error does not occur directly within a try block but in a function that is called from there, then this function is terminated, and control is returned to the calling function until, by following the chain of calls in reverse order, a function within a try block is reached. From there control is passed to the appropriate catch block. If no try block is found, then the generic error routine appended by the compiler is called, which then terminates the program, usually with some nonspecific output.

It is clear what the errors are in the LINT class, and it would be a simple possibility to call throw with the error codes, which are provided to the panic() routine by the LINT functions and operators. However, the following solution offers a bit more comfort: We define an abstract base class

```
class LINT_Error
{
  public:
    char* function, *module;
    int argno, lineno;
    virtual void debug_print (void) const = 0; // pure virtual
    virtual ~LINT_Error() {function = 0; module = 0;};
};
```

as well as classes of the following type that build on it:

```
// division by zero
class LINT_DivByZero : public LINT_Error
{
  public:
    LINT_DivByZero (const char* func, int line, const char* file);
    void debug_print (void) const;
};

LINT_DivByZero::LINT_DivByZero (const char* func, int line, const char* file)
{
  module = file;
  function = func;
  lineno = line;
  argno = 0;
}
void LINT_DivByZero::debug_print (void) const
{
  cerr << "LINT-Exception:" << endl;
  cerr << "division by zero in function "
       << function << endl;
  cerr << "module: " << module << ", line: "
       << lineno << endl;
}
```

For every type of error there exists such a class that like the example shown here can be used with

```
throw LINT_DivByZero(function, line);
```

to report this particular error. Among others, the following subclasses of the base class LINT_Error are defined:

```
class LINT_Base : public LINT_Error // invalid basis
{ ... };
class LINT_DivByZero : public LINT_Error // division by zero
{ ... };
class LINT_EMod : public LINT_Error // even modulus for mexpkm
{ ... };
class LINT_File : public LINT_Error // error with file I/O
{ ... };
class LINT_Heap : public LINT_Error // heap error with new
{ ... };
```

```
class LINT_Init : public LINT_Error // function argument illegal or uninitialized
{ ... };

class LINT_Nullptr : public LINT_Error // null pointer passed as argument
{ ... };

class LINT_OFL : public LINT_Error // overflow in function
{ ... };

class LINT_UFL : public LINT_Error // underflow in function
{ ... };
```

With this we are in a position, on the one hand, to catch LINT errors without distinguishing specifically which error has occurred by inserting a catch block

```
catch (LINT_Error const &err) // notice: LINT_Error is abstract
  {
    // ...
    err.debug_print();
    // ...
  }
```

after a try block, while on the other hand we can carry on a goal-directed search for an individual error by specifying the appropriate error class as argument in the catch instruction.

One should note that as an abstract base class LINT_Error is not instantiatable as an object, for which reason the argument err can be passed only by reference and not by value. Although all the LINT functions have been equipped with the panic() instruction for error handling, the use of exceptions does not mean that we must alter all the functions. Rather, we integrate the appropriate throw instructions into the panic() routine, where they are called in conjunction with the error that has been reported. Control is then transferred to the catch block, which belongs to the try block of the calling function. The following code segment of the function panic() clarifies the modus operandi:

```
void LINT::panic (LINT_ERRORS error, const char* func,
                  int arg, int line, const char* file)
{
  if (LINT_User_Error_Handler)
    {
      LINT_User_Error_Handler (error, func, arg, line, file);
    }
```

```
    else
      {
        cerr << "critical run-time error detected by the
                          class LINT:\n";
        switch (error)
          {
            case E_LINT_DBZ:
                cerr << "division by zero, function " << func;
                cerr << ", line " << line << ", module " << file << endl;
#ifdef LINT_EX
                throw LINT_DivByZero (func, line, file);
#endif
                break;
                // ...
          }
      }
  }
```

The behavior that results in the case of an error can be completely controlled by user-defined routines for error handling without the necessity of intervention into the LINT implementation. Moreover, the exception handling can be completely turned off, which is necessary when this mechanism is not supported by a C++ compiler that is to be used. In the case of the present panic() function the exceptions must be turned on explicitly via the definition of the macro LINT_EX, such as with the compiler option -DLINT_EX. Some compilers require the specification of additional options for exception handling to be activated.

To close, we present a small demonstration of the LINT exceptions:

```
#include "flintpp.h"
main(void)
{
  LINT a = 1, b = 0;
  try
    {
      b = a / b;// error: division by 0
    }
  catch (LINT_DivByZero error) // error handling for division by 0
    {
      error.debug_print ();
      cerr << "division by zero in the module" << __FILE__
          << ", line " << __LINE__;
    }
}
```

Translated with GNU gcc by a call to

```
gcc -fhandle-exceptions -DLINT_EX divex.cpp flintpp.cpp flint.c -lstdc++
```

the program produces, in addition to the error message of the function panic(), the following output:

```
LINT-Exception:
division by zero in operator/function /
module: flintpp.cpp, line: 402
division by zero in module divex.cpp, line 17
```

The significant difference between this and standard error handling without exceptions is that we discover by means of the catch routine where the error was actually caused, namely in line 17 of the module divex.cpp, even though it was discovered somewhere else entirely, namely in the module flintpp.cpp. For debugging large programs this is an extremely helpful source of information.

CHAPTER 17

An Application Example: The RSA Cryptosystem

> The next question was the obvious one, "Can this be done with ordinary
> encipherment? Can we produce a secure encrypted message, readable by the
> authorised recipient without any prior secret exchange of the key etc?" . . . I
> published the existence theorem in 1970.
>
> —J. H. Ellis, "The Story of Non-Secret Encryption"

AS WE APPROACH THE END of our story we would like to investigate the possibility of
testing what we have labored over chapter by chapter against a realistic and current example, one that clearly demonstrates the connection between the theme
of cryptographic application and the deployment of our programmed functions.
We shall make a brief excursion into the principle of asymmetric cryptosystems
and then turn our attention to the RSA algorithm as the classic example of such a
system, which was published in 1978 by its inventors/discoverers, Ronald Rivest,
Adi Shamir, and Leonard Adleman (see [Rive], [Elli]), and which by now has been
implemented worldwide.[1] The RSA algorithm is patented in the United States
of America, but the patent expired on 20 September 2000. Against the free use
of the RSA algorithm stood the claims of RSA Security, who possessed rights
to the trade name "RSA," which triggered vehement discussion in connection
with work on the standard P1363 [IEEE], with in some cases rather grotesque
results, for example, the suggestion of rechristening the RSA procedure "biprime
cryptography." There have also appeared less serious suggestions, such as FRA
(former RSA algorithm), RAL (Ron, Adi, Leonard), and QRZ (RSA − 1). Upon expiry
of their patent RSA Security weighed in with its opinion:

> Clearly, the terms "RSA algorithm," "RSA public-key algorithm,"
> "RSA cryptosystem," and "RSA public-key cryptosystem" are well
> established in standards and open academic literature. RSA Security
> does not intend to prohibit the use of these terms by individuals
> or organizations that are implementing the RSA algorithm ("RSA-
> Security—Behind the Patent," September 2000).[2]

---

[1] According to http://www.rsasecurity.com by 1999 over three hundred million products
containing RSA functions had been sold.

[2] http://www.rsasecurity.com/solutions/developers/total-solution/faq.html.

17.1 Asymmetric Cryptosystems

The fundamental idea behind asymmetric cryptosystems was published in 1976 by Whitfield Diffie and Martin Hellman in the groundbreaking article "New Directions in Cryptography" (see [Diff]). Asymmetric cryptosystems, in contrast to symmetric algorithms, do not use a secret key employed both for encryption and decryption of a message, but a pair of keys for each participant consisting of a public key E for encryption and a different, secret, key D for decryption. If the keys are applied to a message M one after another in sequence, then the following relation must hold:

$$D\left(E\left(M\right)\right) = M. \tag{17.1}$$

One might picture this arrangement as a lock that can be closed with one key but for which one needs a second key to unlock it.

For the sake of security of such a procedure it is necessary that a secret key D not be able to be derived from the public key E, or that such a derivation be infeasible on the basis of time and cost constraints.

In contrast to symmetric systems, asymmetric systems enable certain simplifications in working with keys, since only the public key of a participant A need be transmitted to a communication partner B for the latter to be in a position to encrypt a message that only participant A, as possessor of the secret key, can decrypt. This principle contributes decisively to the openness of communication: For two partners to communicate securely it suffices to agree on an asymmetric encryption procedure and exchange public keys. No secret key information needs to be transmitted. However, before our euphoria gets out of hand we should note that in general, one cannot avoid some form of key management even for asymmetric cryptosystems. As a participant in a supposedly secure communication one would like to be certain that the public keys of other participants are *authentic*, so that an attacker, with the nefarious goal of intercepting secret information, cannot undetected interpose him- or herself and give out *his* or *her* key as the public key under the guise of its being that of the trusted partner. To ensure the authenticity of public keys there have appeared surprisingly complex procedures, and in fact, there are already laws on the books that govern such matters. We shall go into this in more detail below.

The principle of asymmetric cryptosystems has even more far-reaching consequences: It permits the generation of *digital signatures* in which the function of the key is turned on its head. To generate a digital signature a message is "encrypted" with a secret key, and the result of this operation is transmitted together with the message. Now anyone who knows the associated public key can "decrypt" the "encrypted" message and compare the result with the original message. Only the possessor of the secret key can generate a digital signature that can withstand such a comparison. We note that in the case of digital signatures the terms "encryption" and "decryption" are not quite the correct ones, so that we shall speak rather of "generation" and "verification" of a digital signature.

A requirement for the implementation of an asymmetric encryption system for the generation of digital signatures is that the association of $D(M)$ and M can be reliably verified. The possibility of such a verification exists if the mathematical operations of encryption and decryption are commutative, that is, if their execution one after the other leads to the same, original, result regardless of the order in which they are applied:

$$D(E(M)) = E(D(M)) = M. \tag{17.2}$$

By application of the public key E to $D(M)$ it can be checked in this case whether $D(M)$ is valid as a digital signature applied to the message M.

The principle of digital signatures has attained its present importance in two important directions:

- The laws on digital and electronic signatures in Europe and the United States create a basis for the future use of digital signatures in legal transactions.

- The increasing use of the Internet for electronic commerce has generated a strong demand for digital signatures for identification and authentication of those taking part in commercial transactions, for authenticating digital information, and for ensuring the security of financial transactions.

It is interesting to observe that the use of the terms "electronic signature" and "digital signature" bring into focus the two different approaches to signature laws: For an electronic signature all means of identification used by one party, such as electronic characters, letters, symbols, and images, are employed to authenticate a document. A digital signature, on the other hand, is realized as an electronic authentication procedure based on information-technological processes that is employed to verify the integrity and authenticity of a transmitted text. Confusion arises because these two terms are frequently used interchangeably, thus mixing up two different technical processes (see, for example, [Mied]).

While the laws on electronic signatures in general leave open just what algorithms will be used for the implementation of digital signatures, most protocols being discussed or already implemented for identification, authentication, and authorization in the area of electronic transactions over the Internet are based on the RSA algorithm, which suggests that it will continue to dominate the field. The generation of digital signatures by means of the RSA algorithm is thus a particularly current example of the application of our FLINT/C functions.

The author is aware that the following paragraphs represent a painfully brief introduction to an enormously significant cryptographic principle. Nevertheless, such brevity seems to be justified by the large number of extensive publications on this topic. The reader wishing to know more is referred to [Beut], [Fumy],

[Salo], and [Stin] as introductory sources, to the more comprehensive works [MOV] and [Schn], and to the more mathematically oriented monographs [Kobl], [Kran], and [HKW].

17.2 The RSA Algorithm

All that is merely probable is probably false.

—René Descartes

We shall now present a brief outline of the mathematical properties of the RSA algorithm, and we shall see how the RSA procedure can be implemented both as an asymmetric cryptosystem and an asymmetric signature scheme. Following the mathematical principles of the RSA algorithm we shall develop C++ classes with RSA functions for encryption and decryption as well as for the generation and authentication of digital signatures. In this way we shall clarify the possibilities offered for the implementation of the methods of our LINT class.

The most important aspect of the RSA algorithm is the pair of keys, which have a particular mathematical form: An RSA key pair consists of three basic components: the modulus n, the public key component e (encryption), and the secret key component d (decryption). The pairs $\langle e, n \rangle$ and $\langle d, n \rangle$ then form a public and private key.

We first generate the modulus n as the product $n = pq$ of two prime numbers p and q. If $\phi(n) = (p-1)(q-1)$ denotes the Euler phi function (cf. page 177), then for a given n the public key component e can be chosen such that $e < \phi(n)$ and $\gcd(e, \phi(n)) = 1$. The secret component d corresponding to n and e is obtained by calculating the inverse $d = e^{-1} \bmod \phi(n)$ (cf. Section 10.2).

We illustrate this principle with the help of a small example: We choose $p = 7$ and $q = 11$. Then we have $n = 77$ and $\phi(n) = 2^2 \cdot 3 \cdot 5 = 60$. Due to the condition $\gcd(e, \phi(n)) = 1$, the least possible value for the key component e is 7, from which we derive the value $d = 43$ for the key component d, since $7 \cdot 43 \equiv 301 \equiv 1 \bmod 60$. With these values we can apply the RSA algorithm to a toy example, in which we calculate, say, that the "message" 5 is encrypted to $5^7 \bmod 77 = 47$ and the decryption $47^{43} \bmod 77 = 5$ restores the original message.

Equipped now with such keys (we shall soon discuss what constitutes a realistic size for the various key components) and appropriate software, communication partners can securely exchange information with each other. To demonstrate the procedure we consider the process by which a participant Ms. A sends an RSA-encoded message to a communication partner Mr. B:

1. B generates his RSA key with components n_B, d_B, and e_B. He then gives the public key $\langle e_B, n_B \rangle$ to A.

2. Now A would like to send an encrypted message M to B ($0 \leq M < n_B$). Since A has received from B his public key $\langle e_B, n_B \rangle$, A calculates

$$C = M^{e_B} \bmod n_B$$

and sends the encrypted value C to B.

3. After B has obtained the encrypted message C from A, then B decodes this message by calculating

$$C = M^{d_B} \bmod n_B$$

using his secret key $\langle d_B, n_B \rangle$. Now B possesses the plain text M of the message.

It is not difficult to see why this works. Because $d \cdot e \equiv 1 \bmod \phi(n)$, there exists an integer k such that $d \cdot e = 1 + k \cdot \phi(n)$. We thus obtain

$$C^d \equiv M^{de} \equiv M^{1+k \cdot \phi(n)} \equiv M \cdot \left(M^{\phi(n)} \right)^k \equiv M \bmod n, \qquad (17.3)$$

where we have made use of the theorem of Euler quoted on page 177, from which we deduce that $M^{\phi(n)} \equiv 1 \bmod n$ if $\gcd(M, n) = 1$. For the more theoretically interesting case that $\gcd(M, n) > 1$, equation (17.3) holds as well: For relatively prime p and q, we have the isomorphism $\mathbb{Z} \simeq \mathbb{Z}_p \times Z_q$. Since $ve \equiv 1 \bmod \gcd(p - 1, q - 1)$, it follows that $M^{ve} = M$ in $\mathbb{Z}_p$ and in Z_q (obviously for $M = 0$ as well), and therefore also in Z_n.

An alternative to key generation is the use of *univeral exponents* $\lambda :=$ $\mathrm{lcm}(p - 1, q - 1)$ instead of $\phi(n)$. The basis for this is the following theorem of Carmichael: Let $\lambda(\ )$ denote the Carmichael function, defined by $\lambda(n) :=$ $\mathrm{lcm}\left(\lambda\left(2^{a_0} \right), \phi\left(p_1^{a_1} \right), \ldots, \phi\left(p_r^{a_r} \right) \right)$ for all $n = 2^{a_0} \phi\left(p_1^{a_1} \right) \cdots \phi\left(p_r^{a_r} \right)$, where the p_i are distinct prime numbers and

$$\lambda\left(2^t \right) := \begin{cases} 2^{t-1} & \text{if } t < 3, \\ 2^{t-2} & \text{if } t \geq 3. \end{cases}$$

Then for all $a \in \mathbb{Z}_n^\times$, we have $a^{\lambda(m)} \equiv 1 \bmod n$. For a proof, see page 15 of [Kran]. As above, this can also be extended to the case $\gcd(M, n) = 1$, since from $ev = 1 + k\lambda(n)$ we have $ve \equiv 1 \bmod \gcd(p - 1, q - 1)$, and so in $\mathbb{Z}_p$ and $\mathbb{Z}_q$ we have $M^{ve} = M$. On account of the isomorphism $\mathbb{Z} \simeq \mathbb{Z}_p \times Z_q$, this holds in $\mathbb{Z}_n$ as well. The advantage of using λ lies in a smaller exponent e, since λ is always a proper divisor of $(p - 1)(q - 1)$. In practice, this advantage is negligible, since $\gcd(p - 1, q - 1)$ for random values of p and q is small with high probability.

It is clear that the security of the RSA algorithm depends on the ease of factorability of n. If n can be factored into its components p and q, then the secret key d can be determined from the public key e. Conversely, the factorization of n can be easily accomplished if both key components d and e are known: If $k := de - 1$, then k is a multiple of $\phi(n)$, and therefore we have $k = r \cdot 2^t$ with odd r and $t \geq 1$. For every $g \in \mathbb{Z}_n$ we have $g^k \equiv g^{de-1} \equiv gg^{-1} \equiv 1 \bmod n$, and therefore $g^{k/2}$ is a square root of 1 modulo n, of which there are four: In addition to ± 1 there are the roots $\pm x$ with $x \equiv 1 \bmod p$ and $x \equiv -1 \bmod q$. Thus $p \mid (x - 1)$ and $q \mid (x + 1)$ (cf. Section 10.4.3). By calculating $p = \gcd(x - 1, n)$ one thus obtains the factorization of n (cf. page 212).

Possibilities for attacking the RSA algorithm other than factorization of the modulus are either as expensive as this or rely on the special weaknesses of individual protocols used in implementing the RSA cryptosystem, but do not rely on the RSA algorithm itself. Based on the current state of knowledge the following conditions lead to opportunities to attack the RSA algorithm:

1. **Common modulus**

   The use of a common modulus for several participants leads to an obvious weakness: Based on what we have just said, each participant can use his or her own key components e and d to factorize the common modulus $n = pq$. From a knowledge of the factors p and q as well as the public key components of other participants with the same modulus their secret keys can be calculated.

2. **Small public exponents**

   Since the computational time for the RSA algorithm for a given modulus depends directly on the size of the exponents e and d, it would appear attractive to choose these as small as possible. For example, 3, as the smallest possible exponent, requires only one squaring and one multiplication modulo n, so why not save valuable computing time in this way?

   Let us assume that an attacker was able to capture three encoded messages C_1, C_2, and C_3, each of which encodes the same plain text M, encoded with the keys $\langle 3, n_i \rangle$ of three different recipients:

   $$C_1 = M^3 \bmod n_1, \quad C_2 = M^3 \bmod n_2, \quad C_3 = M^3 \bmod n_3.$$

   It is highly probable that $\gcd(n_i, n_j) = 1$ for $i \neq j$, so that the attacker can use the Chinese remainder theorem (cf. page 203) to find a value C for which

   $$C \equiv M^3 \bmod n_1 n_2 n_3.$$

   Since it is also true that $M^3 < n_1 n_2 n_3$, we have that C is actually equal to M^3, and the attacker can obtain M directly by calculating $\sqrt[3]{C}$. Such assaults, known as broadcast attacks, can always be carried out when the number of cryptograms C_i is greater than the public exponent, and this holds even if the plain texts to be encoded are not identical but are merely linearly dependent on one another, that is, if relations like $M_i = a + b \cdot M_j$ hold (cf. [Bone]). To avoid such an attack it is therefore necessary to choose the public exponents not too small (in no case less than $2^{16} + 1 = 65537$)

and in addition to add random redundancy to broadcast messages before their encryption. This can take place by filling in the message in some appropriate way up to a suitable value less than the modulus. Such a process is called *padding* (cf. page 396 and [Schn], Section 9.1).

3. **Small secret exponents and small intervals between p and q**

   Even more problematic than small public exponents are small secret exponents: M. Wiener [Wien] showed already in 1990 how, given a key $\langle e, n \rangle$ with $e < \phi(n)$, the associated private key component d can be calculated if d is too small. Wiener's result was further sharpened by D. Boneh and G. Durfee [Bone], who showed that d can be computed from $\langle e, n \rangle$ if $d < n^{0.292}$. However, it is conjectured that the result holds as well for $d < n^{0.5}$.

   It is plausible that the modulus n can be easily factored when $p \approx q \approx \sqrt{n}$, by dividing by odd natural numbers close to $\sqrt{n}$. The situation is also dangerous when the difference between p and q is less than $n^{1/4}$, for then the factorization method of Fermat can be applied: To factor n it suffices to produce natural numbers $x, y \notin \{ n - 1, n + 1 \}$ such that $4n = x^2 - y^2$, for then, the factors of n are $\frac{1}{2}(x + y)$ and $\frac{1}{2}(x - y)$. The search for x and y runs over $x = \lceil 2\sqrt{n} \rceil, \lceil 2\sqrt{n} \rceil + 1, \lceil 2\sqrt{n} \rceil + 2, \dots$ until $x^2 - 4n$ is a square (which can be checked with the aid of the function issqr_1). The cost of factorization by this method is $O\left((p - q)^2 / \sqrt{n}\right)$, and it is easy to manage when $|p - q| < cn^{1/4}$, with a constant $c \ll n^{1/4}$.

   Work of B. de Weger, extended with proven methods of attack by Wiener, Boneh, and Durfee, shows how the security of the procedure depends on the sizes of both the secret key and the difference of the prime factors $|p - q|$: Let $|p - q| = n^\beta$ and $d = n^\delta$. The modulus $n = pq$ can be factored efficiently if $2 - 4\beta < \delta < 1 - \sqrt{2\beta - \frac{1}{2}}$ or $\delta < \frac{1}{6}(4\beta + 5) - \frac{1}{3}\sqrt{(4\beta + 5)(4\beta - 1)}$ (see [deWe]).

   As a consequence of his results, de Weger recommends choosing p, q, and d such that $\delta + 2\beta > \frac{7}{4}$. For $\delta \geq \frac{1}{2}$, as suggested in the previous result, β must be chosen to be greater than $\frac{5}{8}$ to follow this suggestion.

   This is in accord with suggestions to be found elsewhere, according to which $0.5 < |\log_2 p - \log_2 q| < 30$ should hold (see [EESSI]).

4. **Encryption of small texts**

   Boneh, Joux, and Nguyen have presented a particularly efficient method with which it is frequently possible to determine, for an arbitrary public key $\langle e, n \rangle$, the plain text $M \leq 2^m$ from the cipher text $C = M^e$. The necessary time for this corresponds to $2 \cdot 2^{m/2}$ modular exponentiations. Additionally, $2^{m/2}m$ bits of memory are required (see[Bon2]). RSA encryption with symmetric keys of length less than 128 bits without additional redundancy must therefore be considered completely insecure (see also the following section).

5. **Weaknesses in implementation**

   In addition to the weaknesses caused by the choice of parameters there is a host of potential implementation problems that can adversely affect the security of the RSA algorithm, as is the case with any encryption procedure. Certainly, the greatest care must be taken with implementations completely in software that are not protected from outside attack by measures implemented in hardware. Reading from memory contents, observation of bus activity or CPU states, can lead to the disclosure of secret key information. At the minimum, all data in main memory that in any way are correlated with the secret components of the RSA algorithm (or any other cryptosystem) should be erased immediately after use with active overwriting (for example, with the function purge_l(), which appears on page 164).

   The functions in the FLINT/C library are already equipped for this purpose. In secure mode local variables and allocated memory are overwritten with zeros before termination of the function and are thereby deleted. Here a certain degree of care is necessary, since the optimization capabilities of the compiler are so highly developed that a simple instruction at the end of a function that can be seen to have no effect on the function's termination might simply be ignored. And there is more: One must take into account that calls to the function memset() in the C standard library are ignored if the compiler cannot recognize any useful purpose in calling it.

   The following example illustrates these effects. The function f_l() uses two automatic variables: CLINT key_l and USHORT secret. At the end of the function, whose contents are of no further interest here, memory should be overwritten by assigning 0 to secret and, respectively, by a call to memset() in the case of key_l. The C code looks like this:

```
int
f_l (CLINT n_l)
{
  CLINT key_l;
  USHORT secret;

  ...
  /* overwrite the variables */
  secret = 0;
  memset (key_l, 0, sizeof (key_l));
  return 0;
}
```

And what does the compiler make of this (Microsoft Visual C/C++ 6.0, compilation with `cl -c -FAs -O2`)?

```
PUBLIC          _f
;          COMDAT _f
_TEXT          SEGMENT
_ key _l$ = -516
_ secret $ = -520
_f          PROC NEAR                                   ; COMDAT

; 5       :      CLINT key _l;
; 6       :      USHORT secret;

    ...
; 18      :      /* overwrite the variables */
; 19      :      secret = 0;
; 20      :      memset (key_l, 0, sizeof (key _l));
; 21      :      return 0;

        xor     eax, eax

; 22 : }

        add     esp, 532                                ; 00000214H
        ret     0
_f          ENDP
_TEXT          ENDS
```

The assembler code generated by the compiler documents that the instructions to delete the variables key_l and secret are passed over without effect. From the point of view of optimization this is a desirable result. Even the *inline* version of the function memset() is simply optimized away. For security-critical applications, however, this strategy is simply too clever.

The active deletion of security-critical variables by overwriting must therefore be implemented in such a way that it is actually carried out. One should note that in this case *assertions* can prevent the checking for effectiveness, since the presence of the assertions forces the compiler to execute the code. When the assertions are turned off, then optimization again goes into effect.

For the FLINT/C package the following function is implemented, which accepts a variable number of arguments and treats them according to their size as standard integer types and sets them to 0, or for other data structures calls memset() and lets it do the overwriting:

```
static void purgevars_l (int noofvars, ...)
{
  va_list ap;
  size_t size;

  va_start (ap, noofvars);
  for (; noofvars > 0; -noofvars)
    {
      switch (size = va_arg (ap, size_t))
        {
          case 1:        *va_arg (ap, char *) = 0;
                  break;
          case 2:        *va_arg (ap, short *) = 0;
                  break;
          case 4:        *va_arg (ap, long *) = 0;
                  break;
          default: memset (va_arg(ap, char *), 0, size);
        }
    }
  va_end (ap);
}
```

The function expects pairs of the form (byte length of the variable, pointer to the variable) as arguments, prefixed in noofvars by the number of such pairs.

As an extension of this function the macro PURGEVARS_L() is defined by

```
#ifdef FLINT_SECURE
#define PURGEVARS_L(X) purgevars_l X
#else
#define PURGEVARS_L(X) (void)0
#endif /* FLINT_SECURE */
```

so that security mode can be turned on and off as required. Deletion of the variables in f() can take place as follows:

```
/* overwrite the variables */
PURGEVARS_L ((2, sizeof (secret), & secret,
            sizeof (key_1), key_1));
```

The compiler cannot ignore the call to this function on the principle of optimization strategy, which could be accomplished only by an extraordinarily effective global optimization. In any case, the effect of such security measures should be checked by means of code inspection:

```
PUBLIC          _f
EXTRN           _purgevars_l:NEAR
;          COMDAT _f
_TEXT           SEGMENT
_key_l$ = -516
_secret$ = -520
_f        PROC NEAR                                    ; COMDAT
; 9 : {
        sub     esp, 520                               ; 00000208H
; 10       :    CLINT key_l;
; 11       :    USHORT secret;
    ...
; 18       :       /* overwrite the variables */
; 19       :       PURGEVARS_L ((2, sizeof (secret), &secret,
                        sizeof (key_l), key_l));
        lea     eax, DWORD PTR _key_l$[esp+532]
        push    eax
        lea     ecx, DWORD PTR _secret$[esp+536]
        push    514                                    ; 00000202H
        push    ecx
        push    2
        push    2
        call    _purgevars_l
; 20       : return 0;
        xor     eax, eax
; 21       : }
        add     esp, 552                               ; 00000228H
        ret     0
_f        ENDP
_TEXT           ENDS
```

As a further protective measure in connection with the implementation
of security-critical applications we should mention a comprehensive
mechanism for error handling that sees to it that even in the case of invalid
arguments or other exceptional situations no sensitive information is
divulged. Likewise, suitable measures should be considered for establishing
the authenticity of the code of a cryptographic application, so that the
insertion of Trojan horses is prevented or at least detected before the code
can be executed. Taking a cue from the story of the Trojan War, *Trojan horse*
is the name given to software that has been altered in such a way that it
apparently functions correctly but has additional undesirable effects such

as the transmittal of secret key information to an attacker via an Internet connection.

To get a grip on such problems, frequently, in practice, for cryptographic operations, "security boxes," or "S-Boxes" for short, are implemented, whose hardware is protected against attack by encapsulation in conjunction with detectors or sensors.

If all these known traps are avoided, then there remains only the risk that the modulus will be factored, and this risk can be effectively eliminated by choosing sufficiently large prime numbers. To be sure, it has not been proved that there is no easier method to break the RSA algorithm than factorization, and there is also no proof that factorization of large integers is truly as difficult a problem as it presently seems to be, but these issues have not adversely affected the practical application of the algorithm to date: The RSA algorithm is the most commonly implemented asymmetric cryptosystem worldwide, and its use in the generation of digital signatures continues to increase.

There are many places in the literature where it is recommended that so-called *strong* primes p and q be used in order to protect the modulus against some of the simpler factorization methods. A prime p is called *strong* in this connection if

(i) $p - 1$ has a large prime divisor r,

(ii) $p + 1$ has a large prime divisor s,

(iii) $r - 1$ has a large prime divisor t.

The importance of strong prime numbers to the security of the RSA algorithm is not everywhere equally emphasized. Recently, there has been an increase in the number of voices that assert that while the use of strong prime numbers is not harmful, it also does not accomplish a great deal (cf. [MOV], Section 8.2.3, Note 8.8, as well as [RegT], Appendix 1.4) or even that they should not be used (see [Schn], Section 11.5). In the program example that follows we shall therefore do without the generation of strong primes. For those who are nonetheless interested, we sketch here a procedure for constructing such primes:

1. The first step in the construction of a strong prime p with ℓ_p binary digits consists in the search for primes s and t satisfying $\log_2(s) \approx \log_2(t) \approx \frac{1}{2}\ell_p - \log_2 \ell_p$. Then we search for a prime r for which $r - 1$ is divisible by t, by testing sequentially numbers of the form $r = k \cdot 2t + 1$, $k = 1, 2, \ldots$, for primality until we encounter a prime number. This almost always occurs in at most $\lfloor 2 \ln 2t \rfloor$ steps (cf. [HKW], page 418).

2. We now invoke the Chinese remainder theorem (see page 203) to calculate a solution of the simultaneous congruences $x \equiv 1 \bmod r$ and

$x \equiv -1 \bmod s$, by setting $x_0 := 1 - 2r^{-1}s \bmod rs$, where r^{-1} is the multiplicative inverse of r modulo s.

3. For our prime number search we use an odd initial value: We generate a random number z with a number of digits close to but less than (sometimes denoted by $\lesssim$) the desired length of p, and set $x_0 \leftarrow x_0 + z + rs - (z \bmod rs)$. If x_0 is even, then we set $x_0 \leftarrow x_0 + rs$. With x_0 in hand we begin our determination of p. We test the values $p = x_0 + k \cdot 2rs$, $k = 0, 1, \ldots$, until the desired number of digits ℓ_p for p is reached and p is prime. If an RSA key is to contain a specified public exponent e, then it is worthwhile to ensure additionally that $\gcd(p - 1, e) = 1$. The above conditions on p have now been completely fulfilled. For the prime number tests we use the Miller–Rabin test implemented in the function prime_l().

Whether or not strong primes are used for keys, in every case it is practical to have available a function that generates primes of a specified length or within a specified interval. A procedure for this that additionally ensures that a prime p thus generated satisfies the further condition $\gcd(p - 1, f) = 1$ for a specified number f is given in [IEEE], page 73. Here is the algorithm in a slightly altered form.

Algorithm to generate a prime p such that $p_{\min} \leq p \leq p_{\max}$

1. Generate a random number p, $p_{\min} \leq p \leq p_{\max}$.

2. If p is even, set $p \leftarrow p + 1$.

3. If $p > p_{\max}$, set $p \leftarrow p_{\min} + p \bmod (p_{\max} + 1)$ and go to step 2.

4. Compute $d := \gcd(p - 1, f)$ (cf. Section 10.1). If $d = 1$, test p for primality (cf. Section 10.5). If p is prime, then output p and terminate the algorithm. Otherwise, set $p \leftarrow p + 2$ and go to step 3.

A realization of this procedure as a C++ function is contained in the FLINT/C package (source file flintpp.cpp).

Function: generation of a prime number p within an interval $[p_{\min}, p_{\max}]$ satisfying the additional condition $\gcd(p-1, f) = 1$, f an odd positive integer

Syntax:
```
LINT
findprime(const LINT& pmin,
const LINT& pmax, const LINT& f);
```

Input: pmin: smallest permissible value
pmax: largest permissible value
f: odd positive integer, which should be relatively prime to $p - 1$

Return: LINT prime p determined by a probabilistic test (cf. Section 10.5) with $\gcd(p-1, f)$

```
LINT findprime (const LINT& pmin, const LINT& pmax, const LINT& f)
{
  if (pmin.status == E_LINT_INV) LINT::panic (E_LINT_VAL, "findprime", 1, __LINE__);
  if (pmax.status == E_LINT_INV) LINT::panic (E_LINT_VAL, "findprime", 2, __LINE__);
  if (pmin > pmax) LINT::panic (E_LINT_VAL, "findprime", 1, __LINE__);
  if (f.status == E_LINT_INV) LINT::panic (E_LINT_VAL, "findprime", 3, __LINE__);

  if (f.iseven()) // 0 < f must be odd
    LINT::panic (E_LINT_VAL, "findprime", 3, __LINE__);

  LINT p = randBBS (pmin, pmax);
  LINT t = pmax - pmin;

  if (p.iseven())
    {
      ++p;
    }

  if (p > pmax)
    {
      p = pmin + p % (t + 1);
    }
  while ((gcd (p - 1, f) != 1) || !p.isprime())
    {
      ++p;
      ++p;

      while (p > pmax)
        {
          p = pmin + p % (t + 1);
```

```
        if (p.iseven())
          {
            ++p;
          }
      }
   }
 return p;
}
```

Additionally, the function findprime() is overloaded so that instead of the interval boundaries p_{min} and p_{max} a binary length can be set.

Function:	generation of a prime number p within the interval $\left[2^{\ell-1}, 2^{\ell} - 1\right]$ satisfying the additional condition $\gcd(p-1, f) = 1$, f an odd positive integer
Syntax:	LINT findprime(USHORT l, const LINT& f);
Input:	l: desired binary length f: odd positive integer, which should be relatively prime to $p - 1$
Return:	LINT prime p with $\gcd(p-1, f)$

With regard to the key length to be chosen, a look at the development worldwide of attempts at factorization is most informative: In April 1996 after months-long cooperative work at universities and research laboratories in the USA and Europe under the direction of A.K. Lenstra[3] the RSA modulus

$$RSA\text{-}130 = 18070820886874048059516561644059055662781025167694013$$
$$49170127021450056662540244048387341112759081$$
$$23033717818879665631820132114880557$$

with 130 decimal places was factored as

---

[3]   Lenstra: Arjen K.: *Factorization of RSA-130 using the Number Field Sieve*, http://dbs.cwi.nl.herman.NFSrecords/RSA-130; see also [Cowi].

$$RSA\text{-}130 = 39685999459597454290161126162883786067576449112810064$$
$$832555157243$$
$$\times\ 45534498646735972188403686897274408864356301263205069600999044599.$$

Then in February 1999, RSA-140 was factored into its two 70-digit factors. This success was accomplished under the direction of Herman J. J. te Riele of CWI in the Netherlands with teams from the Netherlands, Australia, France, Great Britain, and the USA.[4] RSA-130 and RSA-140 came from a list of 42 RSA moduli published in 1991 by the firm RSA Data Security, Inc. as encouragement to the cryptographic research community.[5] The calculations that led to the factorization of RSA-130 and RSA-140 were divided among a large number of workstations and the results collated. The calculational effort to factor RSA-140 was estimated to be 2000 MIPS years[6] (for RSA-130 it was about 1000 MIPS years).

Only a short time later, namely at the end of August 1999, news of the factorization of RSA-155 flashed across the globe. At a cost of about 8000 MIPS years the next number in the list of RSA challenges had been laid to rest, again under the direction of Herman te Riele with international participation. With the factorization of

$$RSA\text{-}155 = 10941738641570527421809707322040357612003732945449205990913842131476349984288934784717997257891267332497625752899781833797076537244027146743531593354333897$$

into the two 78-digit factors

$$RSA\text{-}155 = 1026395928297411057720541965739916759007165678080380668030341933521790711307779$$
$$\times\ 106603488380168454820927220360012878679207958575989291522270608237193062808643$$

the magical threshold of 512 was crossed, a length that for many years had been considered safe for key lengths.

---

[4] E-mail from Herman.te.Riele@cwi.nl in Number Theory Network of 4 February 1999. See also http://www.rsasecurity.com.

[5] http://www.rsasecurity.com.

[6] MIPS = mega instructions per second measures the speed of a computer. A computer works at 1 MIPS if is can execute 700,000 additions and 300,000 multiplications per second.

After the factorization of the next RSA challenge, RSA-160, with the participation of the Gernab Institute for Security in Information Technology (BSI) in Bonn, in April 2003, it was in December 2003 that a consortium of the University of Bonn; the Max Planck Institute for Mathematics, in Bonn; the Institute for experimental Mathematics, in Essen; and the BSI factored the 174-digit number

$$RSA\text{-}576 = 1881988129206079638386972394616504398071635633794173827007633564229888597152346654853190606065047430453173880113033967161996923212057340318795506569962213051687593076502570 59$$

into two 87-digit factors:

$$RSA\text{-}576 = 398075086424064937397125500550386491199064362342526708406385189575946388957261768583317$$
$$\times\ 472772146107435330253622307197304822463291469530209711645985217113052071125636359039752 7.$$

The question of what key length is to be considered adequate for the RSA algorithm is revised each time progress in factorization is made. A. K. Lenstra and Eric R. Verheul [LeVe] provide some concrete advice in this regard in their description of a model for the determination of recommended key lengths for many types of cryptosystems. Beginning with a set of well-founded and conservative assumptions, combined with current findings, they calculate some prognoses as to minimum key lengths to recommend in the future and display them in tabular form. The values shown in Table 17-1, which are valid for asymmetric procedures like RSA, El-Gamal, and Diffie–Hellman, are taken from their results.

Table 17-1. Recommended key lengths according to Lenstra and Verheul

Year	Key Length (in Bits)
2001	990
2005	1149
2010	1369
2015	1613
2020	1881
2025	2174

We may conclude that an RSA key should possess no fewer than 1024 binary digits if it is to provide a comfortable margin of safety for critical applications. We may conclude as well, however, that successes in factorization are gradually approaching this value, and one must keep careful tabs on developments. It is therefore worthwhile to distinguish different application purposes and for sensitive applications to consider using 2048 or more binary digits (cf. [Schn], Chapter 7, and [RegT], Appendix 1.4).[7] With the FLINT/C package we are well equipped to produce such key lengths. We need not be too concerned that the expense of factorization decreases in proportion to the speed of new hardware, since this same hardware allows us to create longer keys as required. The security of the RSA algorithm can thus always be ensured by keeping sufficiently ahead of the progress in factorization.

How many such keys are available? Are there enough so that every man, woman, and child on the planet (and perhaps even their pet cats and dogs) can be provided one or more RSA keys? To this the prime number theorem provides the answer, according to which the number of prime numbers less than an integer x is asymptotically approximated by $x/\ln x$ (cf. page 220): Moduli of length 1024 bits are generated as products of two prime numbers each of length approximately 512 bits. There are about $2^{512}/512$ such primes, that is, about 10^{151}, each pair of which forms a modulus. If we let $N = 10^{151}$, then there are $N(N-1)/2$ such pairs, which comes to about 10^{300} different moduli for which additionally that number again can be chosen for secret key components. This overwhelmingly large number is difficult to grasp, but consider, for example, that the entire visible universe contains "only" about 10^{80} elementary particles (cf. [Saga], Chapter 9). To put it another way, if every person on Earth were given ten new moduli every day, then the process could continue for 10^{287} years without a modulus being reused, and to date Earth has existed "only" a few billion years.

Finally, that an arbitrary text can be represented as a positive integer is obvious: By associating a unique integer to each letter of an alphabet texts can be interpreted in any number of ways as integers. A common example is the numerical representation of characters via ASCII code. An ASCII-encoded text can be turned into a single integer by considering the code value of an individual character as a digit to base 256. The probability that such a process would result in an integer M for which $\gcd(M, n) > 1$, that is, such that M contains as a factor one of the factors p, q, of an RSA key n, is vanishingly small. If M is too large for the modulus n of an RSA key, that is, larger than $n - 1$, then the text can be divided into blocks whose numerical representations $M_1, M_2, M_3, \ldots$ all are less than n. These blocks must then be individually encrypted.

For texts of considerable length this becomes tiresome, and therefore one seldom uses the RSA algorithm for the encryption of long texts. For this purpose

---

[7] It is useful to choose RSA keys of binary length a multiple of 8, in conformity with the convention that such keys should end at the end of a byte.

one may employ symmetric cryptosystems (such as Triple-DES, IDEA, or Rijndael; see Chapter 11 and [Schn], Chapters 12, 13, 14), with which the process goes much more quickly and with equivalent security. For an encrypted transmittal of the necessary key, which must be kept secret with symmetric procedures, the RSA algorithm is perfectly suited.

17.3 Digital RSA Signatures

> "Please, your Majesty," said the Knave, "I didn't write it, and they can't prove that I did: there's no name signed at the end."
>
> —Lewis Carroll, *Alice's Adventures in Wonderland*

To clarify how the RSA algorithm is used for generating digital signatures we consider the following process, by which a participant A sends a message M with her digital signature to a participant B, upon which B checks the validity of the signature.

1. A generates her RSA key with components n_A, d_A, and e_A. She then transmits her public key $\langle e_A, n_A \rangle$ to B.

2. A would now like to send a message M with her signature to B. To this end A generates the redundancy $R = \mu(M)$ with $R < n_A$ using a *redundancy function* μ (see below). Then A calculates the signature

$$S = R^{d_A} \bmod n_A$$

and sends (M, S) to B.

3. B possesses the public key $\langle e_A, n_A \rangle$ of A. After B has received the message M and the signature S from A, then B calculates

$$R = \mu(M),$$
$$R' = S^{e_A} \bmod n_A,$$

with the public key $\langle e_A, n_A \rangle$ of A.

4. B now checks whether $R' = R$. If this is the case, then B accepts the digital signature of A . Otherwise, B rejects it.

Digital signatures that must be checked by a separate transmittal of the signed message M are called *digital signatures with appendix*.

The signature procedures with appendix are used primarily for signing messages of variable lengths whose numerical representation exceeds the modulus, so that $M \geq n$. In principle, one could, as we did above, divide the message into blocks $M_1, M_2, M_3, \ldots$ of suitable lengths $M_i < n$ and encrypt and sign each block separately. However, leaving aside the fact that in such a case a counterfeiting problem arises consisting in the possibility of mixing up the order of the blocks and the signatures belonging to the blocks, there are two further compelling reasons to employ, instead of construction of blocks, the function μ that we named the redundancy function in the paragraph above in which we discussed calculating a digital signature.

The first is that a redundancy function $\mu : \mathfrak{M} \to \mathbb{Z}_n$ maps arbitrary messages M from a message space $\mathfrak{M}$ into the residue class ring $\mathbb{Z}_n$, whereby messages typically are reduced by the application of *hash functions* (cf. page 398) to values $z \lesssim 2^{160}$, which then are linked with predefined sequences of characters. Since the image of M under μ is signed in a single RSA step and hash functions can be calculated quickly by design, the use of such a procedure represents great savings in time over the number of RSA steps required for the individual blocks of M.

The second reason is that the RSA algorithm has an undesirable property for creating signatures: For two messages M_1 and M_2 the multiplicative relation

$$(M_1 M_2)^d \bmod n = \left(M_1^d M_2^d \right) \bmod n \tag{17.4}$$

holds, which supports the counterfeiting of signatures if no measures are taken against it.

On account of this property, called *homomorphism*, of the RSA function it would be possible without the inclusion of redundancy R to have messages digitally signed with a "hidden" signature. To do this one could select a secret message M and a harmless message M_1, from which a further message $M_2 := M M_1 \bmod n_A$ is formed. If one succeeded in getting a person or authority A to digitally sign the messages M_1 and M_2, then one would obtain the signatures $S_1 = M_1^{d_A} \bmod n_A$ and $S_2 = M_2^{d_A} \bmod n_A$, from which one can create the signature to M by calculating $S_2 S_1^{-1} \bmod n_A$, which was probably not what A had in mind, though nonetheless A may not have noticed this when generating the signatures S_1 and S_2: The message M would in this case be said to have a *hidden* signature.

To be sure, one could counter that with high probability M_2 does not represent a meaningful text and that anyway, A would not be well advised to sign M_1 or M_2 at a stranger's request and without examining the contents with care. Yet one should not rely on such assumptions of reasonableness when it comes to human behavior in order to justify the weaknesses of a cryptographic protocol, especially when such weaknesses can be eliminated, such as in this case by including redundancy. In order to achieve this redundancy, the redundancy function μ must satisfy the property

$$\mu\left(M_1 M_2\right) \neq \mu\left(M_1\right) \mu\left(M_2\right) \tag{17.5}$$

for all $M_1, M_2 \in \mathfrak{M}$ and thus ensure that the signature function itself does not possess the undesirable homomorphism property.

Supplementary to the signature procedures with appendix there are additional methods known that make it possible to extract the signed message from the signature itself, the so-called *digital signatures with message recovery* (cf. [MOV], Chapter 11, [ISO2], and [ISO3]). Digital signatures with message recovery based on the RSA algorithm are particularly suited for short messages with a binary length less than one-half the binary length of the modulus.

However, in every case the security properties of redundancy functions should be carefully examined, such as is demonstrated by the procedure published in 1999 by Coron, Naccache, and Stern for attacking such schemes. The procedure is based on an attacker having access to a large number of RSA signatures attached to messages whose representation as an integer is divisible exclusively by small primes. Based on such a makeup of the messages it is possible under favorable conditions, without knowledge of the signature key, to construct additional signatures to additional messages, which would amount to counterfeiting these signatures (cf. [Coro]). The ISO has reacted to this development: In October 1999 the workgroup SC 27 removed the standard [ISO2] from circulation and published the following announcement:

> Based on various attacks on RSA digital signature schemes . . . , it is the consensus of ISO/IEC JTC 1/SC 27 that IS 9796:1991 no longer provides sufficient security for application-independent digital signatures and is recommended to be withdrawn.[8]

The withdrawn standard refers to digital signatures for which the RSA function is applied directly to a short message. Signatures with appendix, which arise by way of a hash function, are not included.

A widely distributed redundancy scheme for which the attack of Coron, Naccache, and Stern has at best a theoretical significance and represents no real threat is set by the PKCS #1 format of RSA laboratories (cf. [RDS1], [Coro], pages 11–13, and [RDS2]). The PKCS #1 format specifies how a so-called *encryption block* EB should appear as input value to an encryption or signing operation:

$$\mathrm{EB} = 00\|\mathrm{BT}\|\mathrm{PS}_1\| \ldots \|\mathrm{PS}_\ell\|00\|\mathrm{D}_1\| \ldots \|\mathrm{D}_n.$$

At the head, after the introductory 00 byte, is a byte BT that describes the block type (01 for private key operations, that is, signatures; 02 for public key operations, that is, encryption) and then at least eight filler bytes $\mathrm{PS}_1 \ldots \mathrm{PS}_\ell$, $\ell \geq 8$, with the value FF (hex) in the case of signing and nonzero random values in the case of encryption. There follows 00 as separator byte, and then come finally the data bytes $\mathrm{D}_1 \ldots \mathrm{D}_n$: the payload, so to speak. The number ℓ of filler bytes PS_i depends on the size of the modulus m and the number n of data bytes: If k is defined by

$$2^{8(k-1)} \leq m < 2^{8k}, \tag{17.6}$$

---

[8]   ISO/IEC JTC 1/SC27: *Recommendation on the withdrawal of IS 9796:1991*, 6 October 1991.

then

$$\ell = k - 3 - n, \tag{17.7}$$

and for the number n of data bytes, it follows that

$$n \leq k - 11. \tag{17.8}$$

The minimum number $8 \leq \ell$ of filler bytes is required for encryption for reasons of security. It is thus possible to prevent an attacker from attaching a catalog of encrypted messages to a public key and comparing the result with a given encrypted text to determine the plain text without knowing the associated secret key.[9]

In particular, when one and the same message is encrypted with several keys, it is important that the PS_i be random numbers that are determined anew for each encryption operation.

In the signing case the data bytes D_i are typically constructed from an identifier for a hash function H and the value $H(M)$ of this hash function (called the *hash value*), which represents the text M to be signed. The resulting data structure is called the *DigestInfo*. The number of data bytes depends in this case on the constant length of the hash value, independent of the length of the text. This is particularly advantageous when M is much longer than $H(M)$. We shall not go into the precise process for the construction of the data structure *DigestInfo*, but simply assume that the data bytes correspond to the value $H(M)$ (but see in this connection [RDS1]).

From the cryptographic point of view there are several fundamental requirements to place on hash functions so as not to diminish the security of a redundancy scheme based on such a function and thereby call the entire signing procedure into question. When we consider the use of hash and redundancy functions in connection with digital signatures and the possibilities for manipulating them that might arise, we observe the following:

In accordance with our considerations thus far, we start with the assumption that a digital signature with appendix relates to a redundancy $R = \mu(M)$ whose principal component is the hash value of the text to be signed. Two texts M and M' for which $H(M) = H(M')$, and consequently $\mu(M) = \mu(M')$, possess the same signature $S = R^d = \mu(M)^d = \mu(M')^d \bmod n$. The recipient of a signature to the text M could now conclude that the signature actually refers to the text M', which in general would be contrary to the intent of the sender. Likewise, the sender could assume actually to have signed the text M'. The point here is that texts $M \neq M'$ with $H(M) = H(M')$ always exist, due to the fact

---

[9] We have already mentioned the attack of Boneh, Joux, and Nguyen.

that infinitely many texts are mapped to finitely many hash values. This is the price to be paid for the convenience of hash values of fixed length.[10]

Since we must also assume the existence of texts that possess identical signatures in relation to a particular hash or redundancy function (where we assume that the same signature key has been used), then it is crucial that such texts not be easy to find or to construct.

In sum, a hash function should be easy to compute, but this should not be the case for the inverse mapping. That is, given a value H of a hash function it should not be easy to find a preimage that is mapped to H. Functions with this property are called *one-way functions*. Furthermore, a hash function must be *collision-free*, meaning that it must not be easy to find two different preimages of a given hash value. Until the present, these properties were satisfied by hash functions such as the widely used functions RIPEMD-160 (cf. [DoBP]) and the Secure Hash Algorithm SHA-1 (cf. [ISO1]). It now appears, however, that for digital signatures in the near term (according to NIST and [RegT] from 2010 on), lengths of hash values of 256 bits and greater will be required.

In recent months, reports of the discovery of collisions have provoked a discussion about a requirement to migrate to new hash algorithms. In 2004, results were published related to the hash functions MD4, MD5, HAVAL128, RIPEMD, SHA-0,[11] and a weak variant of SHA-1 with a reduced number of passes (see [WFLY]). In the meantime, while all of these algorithms have come to be considered broken, and in particular are considered unsuitable for use in creating digital signatures, a similar development for SHA-1 seems to be in store, with uncertainty reigning while the drama runs its course. Even if reports on this issue in February 2005, whose sensational publication seems to have been more for serving the interests of those bearing the tidings than of the situation itself, have not led to the outright rejection of the algorithm, the noose seems to be tightening. However, a panicked reaction based on vague suppositions should be rejected, given its worldwide use and the significance of SHA-1 for countless applications.

Given the many different uses to which SHA-1 is being put, it is not very productive to debate what measures may need to be taken before the possible consequences of new methods of attack for individual application areas and thereby the actions to be taken are carefully analyzed. A closer look will show that in most cases, no rush to action is required, and instead, the measures already taken in the mid and long terms should suffice. New hash functions will be needed that will meet security needs for the foreseeable future, given what is known about the newest methods of attack, and these new functions should

---

[10] In the language of mathematics we would say that hash functions $H : \mathfrak{M} \rightarrow \mathbb{Z}_n$ that map texts of arbitrary length to values in $\mathbb{Z}_n$ are not *injective*.

[11] This was an earlier version of SHA-1 from 1993, which in 1995 was replaced by SHA-1, which was designed to overcome specific weaknesses.

not be finding themselves in the headlines every half year. Whether the answer already exists in SHA-224, SHA-256, SHA-384, or SHA-512 (see [F180]) needs to be investigated. An increase in the block length may not suffice to compensate for possible weaknesses in the functional building blocks of a hash algorithm. It is always possible that methods of attack will be developed whose effect is independent of the block length, as has been discussed in relation to the hash algorithms that we have mentioned.

How one finds suitable algorithms has been demonstrated by the European Union in the development of RIPEMD in connection with the RIPE project,[12] and in the USA with the competition for the development of the AES. Within the framework of a public international competition, new candidates for hash algorithms with the greatest possible transparency can be put to the test and the most suitable algorithms adopted. The only disadvantage of such a process is that it costs time: In the case of AES it was about three years from the announcement of the competition until a victor was crowned, and four years altogether before the standard was published in 2001. Given this experience, until 2010 is enough time for the development and standardization of new hash functions, although the migration to a new algorithm (or, better, two or three of them) will take time.

Whether in specific applications a switch to other transitional algorithms might be necessary, and what consequences might be thereby associated, can be evaluated only on a case by case basis.

We shall not go into further detail on this topic, which is very important to cryptography. The interested reader is referred to [Pren] or [MOV], Chapter 9, as well as the literature cited therein, above all literature on the current state of affairs. Algorithms for transforming texts or hash values into natural numbers can be found in [IEEE], Chapter 12: "Encoding Methods" (we already have available the corresponding functions clint2byte_l() and byte2clint_l(); cf. page 152). Implementations of RIPEMD-160, SHA-1, and SHA-256 can be found in ripemd.c, sha1.c, and sha256.c in the downloadable source code.

In thinking about the signature protocol described above we are immediately confronted with the following question: How can B know whether he is in possession of the *authentic* public key of A? Without such certainty B cannot trust the signature, even if it can be verified as described above. This becomes critical when A and B do not know each other personally or when there has been no personal exchange of public keys, which is the normal case in communication over the Internet.

To make it possible for B nonetheless to trust in the authenticity of A's digital signature, A can present her communication partner a *certificate* from a *certification authority* that attests to the authenticity of A's public key. An informal

---

[12] RIPEMD has been further developed to RIPEMD160 [DoBP]. Although RIPEMD160 has meanwhile been rejected in favor of SHA-1, this algorithm in its current state remains unbroken.

"receipt," which one may believe or not, is, of course, inadequate. A certificate is rather a data set that has been formatted according to some standard[13] that among other things speaks to the identity of A as well as her public key and that itself has been digitally signed by the certification authority.

The genuineness of a participant's key can be verified with the help of the information contained in the certificate. Applications that support such verification in software already exist. The future multiplicity of such applications, whose technical and organizational basis will be based on so-called *public key infrastructures* (PKI), can today only be guessed at. Concrete uses are emerging in the digital signing of e-mail, the validation of commercial transactions, e-commerce and m-commerce, electronic banking, document management, and administrative procedures (see Figure 17-1).

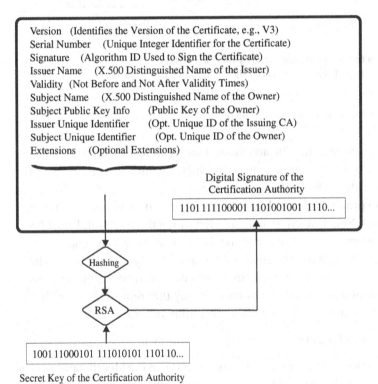

Version   (Identifies the Version of the Certificate, e.g., V3)
Serial Number   (Unique Integer Identifier for the Certificate)
Signature   (Algorithm ID Used to Sign the Certificate)
Issuer Name   (X.500 Distinguished Name of the Issuer)
Validity (Not Before and Not After Validity Times)
Subject Name   (X.500 Distinguished Name of the Owner)
Subject Public Key Info   (Public Key of the Owner)
Issuer Unique Identifier   (Opt. Unique ID of the Issuing CA)
Subject Unique Identifier   (Opt. Unique ID of the Owner)
Extensions   (Optional Extensions)

Digital Signature of the
Certification Authority

1101 111100001 1101001001 1110...

Hashing

RSA

1001 11000101 111010101 1101 10...

Secret Key of the Certification Authority

Figure 17-1. Example of the construction of a certificate

On the assumption that B knows the public key of the certification authority, B can now verify the certificate presented by A and thereafter A's signature to become convinced of the authenticity of the information.

---

[13] Widely used is ISO 9594-8, which is equivalent to the ITU-T (formerly CCITT) recommendation X.509v3.

The example presented in Figure 17-2, which shows a client's digitally signed bank statement together with the certificate of the bank presented by a certification authority, demonstrates this process.

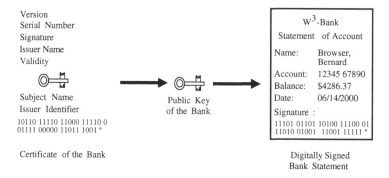

Certificate of the Bank   Digitally Signed Bank Statement

B verifies the certificate presented by the bank and uses the public key of the bank to verify the digital signature of the bank

Figure 17-2. Certification of a digital signature

Such a bank statement has the advantage that it can reach the client over any electronic transmittal path, such as e-mail, in which it would be further encrypted to protect the confidentiality of the information.

However, the problem of trust has not been hereby miraculously cleared up, but merely shifted: Now B need no longer believe directly in the validity of A's key (in the above example that of the bank), but in exchange must check the genuineness of the certificate presented by A. For certainty to be attained, the validity of certificates must be verified anew for every occurrence, either from the source that issued the certificate or an authority that represents it. Such a procedure can succeed only if the following conditions are met:

- the public key of the certification authority is known;

- the certification authority takes the greatest care in the identification of the receivers of certificates and in the protection of their private certification keys.

To achieve the first of these desiderata the public key of the certification authority can be certified by an additional, higher, authority, and so forth, resulting in a hierarchy of certification authorities and certificates. However, verification along such a hierarchy assumes that the public key of the highest certification authority, the *root certification authority*, is known and can be accepted as authentic. Trust in this key must thus be established by other means through suitable technical or organizational measures.

The second condition holds, of course, for all authorities of a certification hierarchy. A certification authority, in the sense of granting legal force to a signature, must establish the organizational and technical processes for which detailed requirements have been set in law or associated implementing orders.

At the end of 1999, a European Union directive was adopted that established a framework for the use of electronic signatures in Europe (cf. [EU99]). The guideline was enacted to avoid conflicting regulations among the individual member states. In decisive points, it requires regulations that deviate from SigG in its original 1997 version, in which it joins the "technical-legal approach," which is also followed by the SigG of 1997, with the "market-economy approach" to form a "hybrid approach." The technical-legal approach is represented by "advanced" and "qualified electronic signatures," and the market-economy approach by "electronic signatures."

In the area of the market-economy approach, no technical requirements are made on the "electronic." For qualified electronic signatures, the technical and organizational requirements are regulated, which contributes to the actual security of these signatures, as the basis for legal consequences being able to be linked to qualified electronic signatures.

Important components of the regulations for guaranteeing the actual security are, in addition to the liability of certification service providers, the requirements for technical security of the components used and the security requirements for the facilities and processes of the certification service providers, as well as their supervision.

A corresponding revision of the German signature law was concluded in the first quarter of 2001 (see [SigG]), in which the guidelines of the EU were implemented. The significant change with respect to the old version of the law is the acceptance of "qualified electronic signatures," which now are permitted as a substitute for written signatures and as admissible evidence in court.

The goal of this law is to create basic conditions for qualified electronic signatures. The use of electronic signatures is optional, though certain regulations could require them in specific instances. In particular, regulations could be established regarding the use of qualified electronic signatures in the work of public institutions.

We now leave this interesting topic, which can pursued further in [Bies], [Glad], [Adam], [Mied], and [Fegh], and turn our attention, finally, to the implementation of C++ classes that provide for encryption and the generation of digital signatures.

17.4 RSA Classes in C++

In this section we develop a C++ class RSAkey that contains the functions

- RSAkey::RSAkey() for RSA key generation;

- RSAkey::export() for exporting public keys;

- RSAkey::decrypt() for decryption;

- RSAkey::sign() for digital signing using the hash function RIPEMD-160;

as well as a class RSApub for the storage and application of public keys only with the functions

- RSApub::RSApub() for importing a public key from an object of the class RSAkey;

- RSApub::crypt() for encrypting a text;

- RSApub::authenticate() for authenticating a digital signature.

The idea is not merely to look at cryptographic keys as numbers with particular cryptographic properties, but to consider them as objects that bring with themselves the methods for their application and make them available to the outside world but that nonetheless restrictively prevent unmediated access to private key data. Objects of the class RSAkey thus contain, after the generation of a key, a public and a private RSA key component as private elements, as well as the public functions for encryption and signing. Alternatively, the constructor functions enable the generation of keys

- with fixed length and internal initialization of the BBS random number generator;

- with adjustable length and internal initialization of the BBS random number generator;

- with adjustable length and passing of a LINT initialization value for the BBS random number generator via the calling program.

Objects of the class RSApub contain only the public key, which they must import from an RSAkey object, and the public functions for encryption and verification of a signature. To generate an object of the RSApub class, then, an initialized RSAkey object must already exist. In contrast to objects of type RSAkey, RSApub objects are considered unreliable and can be more freely handled than RSAkey objects, which in serious applications may be transmitted or stored in data media only in encrypted form or protected by special hardware measures.

Before we realize these example classes we would like to set ourselves some boundary conditions that will limit the implementation cost at something appropriate for what is merely an example: For the sake of simplicity, input values for RSA encryption will be accepted only if they are smaller than the modulus; a subdivision of longer texts into blocks will not occur. Furthermore, we shall leave aside the more costly functional and security-related features that would be necessary in a full-fledged implementation of the RSA classes (see in this regard the pointer on page 384).

However, we do not wish to do without an effective possibility of speeding up the calculations for decryption or signing. By application of the Chinese remainder theorem (see page 203) the RSA operations with the secret key d can be made about four times as fast as with the usual method of calculating a single power: Given a secret key $\langle d, n \rangle$ with $n = pq$ we form $d_p := d \bmod (p - 1)$ and $d_q := d \bmod (q - 1)$ and employ the extended Euclidean algorithm to compute the representation $1 = rp + sq$, from which we extract the value r as the multiplicative inverse of p modulo q (cf. Section 10.2). We then employ the components p, q, d_p, d_q, r to calculate $c = m^d \bmod n$ as follows:

1. Calculate $a_1 \leftarrow m^{d_p} \bmod p$ and $a_2 \leftarrow m^{d_q} \bmod q$.

2. Calculate $c \leftarrow a_1 + p\left((a_2 - a_1) r \bmod q\right)$.

After step 1 we have $a_1 \equiv m^{d_p} \equiv m^d \bmod p$ and $a_2 \equiv m^{d_q} \equiv m^d \bmod q$. To see this, just use the little theorem of Fermat (cf. page 177), according to which $m^{p-1} \equiv 1 \bmod p$, respectively $m^{q-1} \equiv 1 \bmod q$. From $d = \ell(p - 1) + d_p$ with integral ℓ it follows that

$$m^d \equiv m^{\ell(p-1)+d_p} \equiv \left(m^{p-1}\right)^{\ell} m^{d_p} \equiv m^{d_p} \bmod p, \qquad (17.9)$$

and analogously, we have the same for $m^d \bmod q$. An application of the Garner algorithm (see page 207) with $m_1 := p$, $m_2 := q$, and $r := 2$ shows us at once that c in step 2 represents the desired solution. Rapid decryption is implemented in the auxiliary function RSAkey::fastdecrypt(). All exponents modulo $p, q,$ or n are calculated via Montgomery exponentiation with the LINT function (cf. page 344).

```
// Selection from the include file rsakey.h

...

#include "flintpp.h"
#include "ripemd.h"

#define BLOCKTYPE_SIGN 01
#define BLOCKTYPE_ENCR 02

// The RSA key structure with all key components
typedef struct
{
    LINT pubexp, prvexp, mod, p, q, ep, eq, r;
    USHORT bitlen_mod;// binary length of modulus
    USHORT bytelen_mod; // length of modulus in bytes
} KEYSTRUCT;
```

```
// the structure with the public key components
typedef struct
{
    LINT pubexp, mod;
    USHORT bitlen_mod;// binary length of the modulus
    USHORT bytelen_mod; // length of modulus in bytes
} PKEYSTRUCT;

class RSAkey
{
  public:
    inline RSAkey (void) {};
    RSAkey (int);
    RSAkey (int, const LINT&);
    PKEYSTRUCT export_public (void) const;
    UCHAR* decrypt (const LINT&, int*);
    LINT sign (const UCHAR*, int);

  private:
    KEYSTRUCT key;

    // auxiliary functions
    int makekey (int, const LINT& = 1);
    int testkey (void);
    LINT fastdecrypt (const LINT&);
};

class RSApub
{
  public:
    inline RSApub (void) {};
    RSApub (const RSAkey&);
    LINT crypt (const UCHAR*, int);
    int verify (const UCHAR*,ž int, const LINT&);

  private:
    PKEYSTRUCT pkey;
};

// selection from module rsakey.cpp
...
#include "rsakey.h"

//////////////////////////////////////////////////////////////////////
// member functions of the class RSAkey

// constructor generates RSA keys of specified binary length
RSAkey::RSAkey (int bitlen)
{
```

```
  int done;
  seedBBS ((unsigned long)time (NULL));
  do
    {
      done = RSAkey::makekey (bitlen);
    }
  while (!done);
}

// constructor, generates RSA keys of specified binary length to the
// optional public exponent PubExp. The initialization of random number
// generator randBBS() is carried out with the specified LINT argument rnd.
// If PubExp == 1 or it is absent, then the public exponent is chosen
// randomly. If PubExp is even, then an error status is generated
// via makekey(), which can be caught by try() and catch() if
// error handling is activated using Exceptions.
RSAkey::RSAkey (int bitlen, const LINT& rand, const LINT& PubExp)
{
  int done;
  seedBBS (rand);
  do
    {
      done = RSAkey::makekey (bitlen, PubExp);
    }
  while (!done);
}

// export function for public key components
PKEYSTRUCT RSAkey::export_public (void) const
{
  PKEYSTRUCT pktmp;
  pktmp.pubexp = key.pubexp;
  pktmp.mod = key.mod;
  pktmp.bitlen_mod = key.bitlen_mod;
  pktmp.bytelen_mod = key.bytelen_mod;
  return pktmp;
}

// RSA decryption
UCHAR* RSAkey::decrypt (const LINT& Ciph, int* LenMess)
{
  UCHAR* EB = lint2byte (fastdecrypt (Ciph), LenEB);
  UCHAR* Mess = NULL;
  // Parse decrypted encryption block, PKCS#1 formatted
  if (BLOCKTYPE_ENCR != parse_pkcs1 (Mess, EB, LenEB, key.bytelen_mod))
    {
```

```
        // wrong block type or incorrect format
        return (UCHAR*)NULL;
      }
    else
      {
        return Mess; // return pointer to message
      }
}
  // RSA signing
  LINT RSAkey::sign (const UCHAR* Mess, int LenMess)
  {
    int LenEncryptionBlock = key.bytelen_mod - 1;
    UCHAR HashRes[RMDVER>>3];
    UCHAR* EncryptionBlock = new UCHAR[LenEncryptionBlock];

    ripemd160 (HashRes, (UCHAR*)Mess, (ULONG)LenMess);

    if (NULL == format_pkcs1 (EncryptionBlock, LenEncryptionBLock,
                              BLOCKTYPE_SIGN, HashRes, RMDVER >> 3))
      {
        delete [] EncryptionBlock;
        return LINT (0);// error in formatting: message too long
      }

    // change encryption block into LINT number (constructor 3)
    LINT m = LINT (EncryptionBlock, LenEncryptionBlock);
    delete [] EncryptionBlock;

    return fastdecrypt (m);
  }

  ///////////////////////////////////////////////////////////////////////
  // private auxiliary functions of the class RSAkey

  // ... among other things: RSA key generation according to IEEE P1363, Annex A
  // If parameter PubExp == 1 or is absent, a public exponent
  // of length half the modulus is determined randomly.
  int RSAkey::makekey (int length, const LINT& PubExp)
  {
    // generate prime p such that 2 ^ (m - r - 1) <= p < 2 ^ (m - r), where
    // m = |_(length + 1)/2_| and r random in interval 2 <= r < 15
    USHORT m = ((length + 1) >> 1) - 2 - usrandBBS_l () % 13;
    key.p = findprime (m, PubExp);

    // determine interval bounds qmin and qmax for prime q
    // set qmin = |_(2 ^ (length - 1))/p + 1_|
    LINT qmin = LINT(0).setbit (length - 1)/key.p + 1;
    // set qmax = |_(2 ^ length - 1)/p)_|
    LINT qmax = (((LINT(0).setbit (length - 1) - 1) << 1) + 1)/key.p;
```

```
  // generate prime q > p with length qmin <= q <= qmax
  key.q = findprime (qmin, qmax, PubExp);

  // generate modulus mod = p*q such that 2 ^ (length - 1) <= mod < 2 ^ length
  key.mod = key.p * key.q;

  // calculate Euler phi function
  LINT phi_n = key.mod - key.p - key.q + 1;

  // generate public exponent if not specified in PubExp
  if (1 == PubExp)
    {
      key.pubexp = randBBS (length/2) | 1; // half the length of the modulus
      while (gcd (key.pubexp, phi_n) != 1)
        {
          ++key.pubexp;
          ++key.pubexp;
        }
    }
  else
    {
      key.pubexp = PubExp;
    }
  // generate secret exponent
  key.prvexp = key.pubexp.inv (phi_n);

  // generate secret components for rapid decryption
  key.ep = key.prvexp % (key.p - 1);
  key.eq = key.prvexp % (key.q - 1);
  key.r = inv (key.p, key.q);
  return testkey();
}

// test function for RSA-key
int RSAkey::testkey (void)
{
  LINT mess = randBBS (ld (key.mod) >> 1);
  return (mess == fastdecrypt (mexpkm (mess, key.pubexp, key.mod)));
}

// rapid RSA decryption
LINT RSAkey::fastdecrypt (const LINT& mess)
{
  LINT m, w;
  m = mexpkm (mess, key.ep, key.p);
  w = mexpkm (mess, key.eq, key.q);
  w.msub (m, key.q);
  w = w.mmul (key.r, key.q) * key.p;
```

```
    return (w + m);
}

////////////////////////////////////////////////////////////////////////
// member functions of the class RSApub

// constructor RSApub()
RSApub::RSApub (const RSAkey& k)
{
  pkey = k.export();// import public key from k
}

// RSA encryption
LINT RSApub::crypt (const UCHAR* Mess, int LenMess)
{
  int LenEncryptionBlock = key.bytelen_mod - 1;
  UCHAR* EncryptionBlock = new UCHAR[LenEncryptionBlock];

  // format encryption block according to PKCS #1
  if (NULL == format_pkcs1 (EncryptionBlock, LenEncryptionBlock,
                            BLOCKTYPE_ENCR, Mess, (ULONG)LenMess))
    {
      delete [] EncryptionBlock;
      return LINT (0); // formatting error: message too long
    }
  // transform encryption block into LINT number (constructor 3)
  LINT m = LINT (EncryptionBlock, LenEncryptionBlock);
  delete [] EncryptionBlock;

  return (mexpkm (m, pkey.pubexp, pkey.mod));
}

// verification of RSA signature
int RSApub::verify (const UCHAR* Mess, int LenMess, const LINT& Signature)
{
  int length, BlockType verification = 0;
  UCHAR m H1[RMDVER>>3];
  UCHAR* H2 = NULL;
  UCHAR* EB = lint2byte (mexpkm (Signature, pkey.pubexp, pkey.mod), &length);
  ripemd160 (H1 (UCHAR*)Mess, (ULONG)LenMess);

  // take data from decrypted PKCS #1 encryption block
  BlockType = parse_pkcs1 (H2, EB, &length, pkey.bytelen_mod);

  if ((BlockType == 0 || BlockType == 1) && // Block Type Signature
      (HashRes2 > NULL) && (length == (RMDVER >> 3)))
    {
      verification = !memcmp ((char *)H1, (char *)H2, RMDVER >> 3);
    }
```

```
    return verification;
}
```

The class implementations RSAkey and RSApub contain in addition the following operators, which are not discussed further here:

```
RSAkey& operator= (const RSAkey&);

friend int operator== (const RSAkey&, const RSAkey&);
friend int operator!= (const RSAkey&, const RSAkey&);
friend fstream& operator<< (fstream&, const RSAkey&);
friend fstream& operator>> (fstream&, RSAkey&);
```

and

```
RSApub& operator= (const RSApub&);

friend int operator== (const RSApub&, const RSApub&);
friend int operator!= (const RSApub&, const RSApub&);
friend fstream& operator<< (fstream&, const RSApub&);
friend fstream& operator>> (fstream&, RSApub&);
```

These are for elementwise allocation, tests for equality and inequality, as well as reading and writing of keys to and from mass storage. However, one must note that the private key components are stored in plain text, just as the public key is. For a real application the secret keys must be stored in encrypted form and in a secure environment.

There are also the member functions

```
RSAkey::purge (void),
RSApub::purge (void),
```

which delete keys by overwriting their LINT components with zeros. The formatting of message blocks for encryption or signing corresponding to the PKCS #1 specification is taken over by the function

```
UCHAR* format_pkcs1 (const UCHAR* EB, int LenEB,
UCHAR BlockType, const UCHAR* Data, int LenData);
```

The analysis of decrypted message blocks for verifying the format and for the extraction of useful data is handled by the function

```
int parse_pkcs1 (UCHAR*& PayLoad, const UCHAR* EB, int* LenData);
```

The classes RSAkey and RSApub are extendable in a number of ways. For example, one could imagine a constructor that accepts a public key as parameter and generates a suitable modulus and secret key. For a practical implementation the inclusion of additional hash functions may be necessary. Message blocking is also required. The list of worthwhile extensions is long, and a full discussion would break the bounds and the binding of this book.

An example test application of the classes RSAkey and RSApub is to be found in the module rsademo.cpp contained in the FLINT/C package. The program is translated with

```
gcc -O2 -DFLINT_ASM -o rsademo rsademo.cpp rsakey.cpp
    flintpp.cpp randompp.cpp flint.c aes.c ripemd.c sha256.c entropy.c random.c
    -lflint -lstdc++
```

if one implements, for example, the GNU C/C++ compiler gcc under Linux and uses the assembler functions in libflint.a.

CHAPTER 18

Do It Yourself: Test LINT

90% of the time is spent in 10% of the code.
—Robert Sedgewick, *Algorithms*

WE HAVE ALREADY DISCUSSED THE topic of testing in Chapter 13, where we subjected the basic arithmetic functions of the first part of the book to extensive static and dynamic tests. We now require a similar treatment for the validation of the C++ class LINT, and furthermore, we still must provide tests of the number-theoretic C functions.

The approach of the static tests can be carried over directly to the LINT class, where the tool PC-lint (see [Gimp]) used for the static analysis of C functions will stand us here in good stead as well, since we can use it for checking the syntactic correctness and (within certain bounds) the semantic plausibility of the LINT class and its elements.

We are also interested in the functional aspects of our class implementation: We must demonstrate that the methods contained in LINT return correct results. The process that we used earlier, where the results of equivalent or mutually inverse operations were used to establish correctness, can also, of course, be used on C++ functions. In the following example this process is embodied in the function testdist(), which links addition and multiplication by way of the distributive law. Even here one can see how much less syntactic complication is needed in comparison with the test functions in C. The test function consists principally of two lines of code!

```
#include <stdio.h>
#include <stdlib.h>
#include "flintpp.h"

void report_error (LINT&, LINT&, LINT&, int);
void testdist (int);

#define MAXTESTLEN CLINTMAXBIT
#define CLINTRNDLN (ulrand64_l()% (MAXTESTLEN + 1))
```

```
main()
{
  testdist (1000000);
}
void testdist (int nooftests)
{
  LINT a;
  LINT b;
  LINT c;
  int i;

  for (i = 1; i < nooftests; i++)
    {
      a = randl (CLINTRNDLN);
      b = randl (CLINTRNDLN);
      c = randl (CLINTRNDLN);

      // test of + and * by application of the distributive law
      if ((a + b)*c != (a*c + b*c))
        report_error (a, b, c, __LINE__);
    }
}
void report_error (LINT& a, LINT& b, LINT& c, int line)
{
  LINT d = (a + b) * c;
  LINT e = a * c + b * c;
  cerr << "error in distributive law before line " << line << endl;
  cerr << "a = " << a << endl;
  cerr << "b = " << b << endl;
  cerr << "(a + b) * c = " << d << endl;
  cerr << "a * c + b * c = " << e << endl;
  abort();
}
```

We now leave it to the reader as an exercise to test all the LINT operators in this or a similar manner. For orientation, one may look at the test routines for the C functions. However, there are some new aspects to consider, such as the prefix and postfix operators ++ and --, as well as the fact that == is also an operator that must be tested. Here are some additional program notes:

- Tests of the error routine panic() with all defined errors, with and without *exceptions*;

- Tests of the I/O functions, stream operators, and manipulators;

- Tests of the arithmetic and number-theoretic functions.

The number-theoretic functions can be tested according to the same principles as the arithmetic functions. To examine the function to be tested one is well advised to use inverse functions, equivalent functions, or different implementations of the same function that are as independent as possible from one another. We have examples of each of these variants:

- If the Jacobi symbol indicates that an element of a finite ring is a square, this can be verified by calculating the square root. Conversely, a calculated square root can be verified as such by a simple modular squaring.

- The function inv() for calculating the multiplicative inverse i of an integer a modulo n can be tested with the condition $ai \equiv 1 \bmod n$.

- For calculating the greatest common divisor of two integers one may make use of the two FLINT/C functions gcd_l() and xgcd_l(), where the latter returns the representation of the greatest common divisor as a linear combination of the arguments. The results can be compared one with the other, and the linear combination can be constructed, which in turn must agree with the greatest common divisor.

- Redundance is also to be found in the relation between the greatest common divisor and the least common multiple: For integers a, b one has the relation

$$\operatorname{lcm}(a, b) = \frac{|ab|}{\gcd(a, b)},$$

a fruitful relation that can also easily be checked. Additional useful formulas that relate the greatest common divisor and least common multiple are presented in Section 10.1.

- Finally, the RSA procedure can be invoked for testing the primality test: If p or q is not prime, then $\phi(n) \neq (p-1)(q-1)$. The RSA procedure will work correctly only if the Fermat test for p and q states that p and q are probably prime. Thus some mutually inverse RSA operations and a comparison of the decrypted messages with the original messages will certainly reveal whether the primality test has been implemented correctly.

There are thus sufficiently many and varied approaches to effective testing of the LINT functions. The reader is encouraged to develop and implement at least one such test for each LINT function. It is highly effective both as a test and as an exercise and will develop in the user of the LINT class familiarity with how the class works and the uses to which it might be put.

CHAPTER 19

Approaches for
Further Extensions

ALTHOUGH WE NOW HAVE AT our disposal a software package with a well-founded and well-rounded suite of functions, we confront now the question of in what directions our work might be continued. There are possibilities for work in the areas of functionality and performance.

With regard to functionality, one can imagine the application of the basic functions in FLINT/C to areas that have been only touched upon or not even mentioned at all, such as factorization or elliptic curves, which have properties that have led to increasing interest in them for application to cryptography. The interested reader can find detailed explications in [Bres], [Kobl], and [Mene], but also in the standard works [Cohe], [Schn], and [MOV], which we have cited frequently and which contain many references to the literature.

A second area for development is that of measures for improving throughput, first and foremost the increase in digit length from 16 to 32 bits ($B = 2^{32}$), as well as through the use of assembler functions and, for platforms that support it, the C/C++ implementation.

The work in development and testing for this last approach could be carried out independent of platform, such as with the help of the GNU compiler gcc, using the gcc type `unsigned long long`: The type `CLINT` would be defined by `typedef ULONG CLINT[CLINTMAXLONG];`. Furthermore, certain constants would have to be adjusted that relate to the base of the internal representation of integers.

In the functions of the FLINT/C package all explicit *casts* and other references to USHORT must be replaced by ULONG and those to ULONG by `unsigned long long` (or after a suitable `typedef` by, say, ULLONG. A few functions that make assumptions about the length of a digit in the data type used must be ported. After an extensive test and debugging phase including static syntax checking (cf. Chapter 13) the FLINT/C package would then be ready for CPUs with 64-bit word length.

The inclusion of assembler functions also makes it possible to operate with digits of 32 bits and results of 64 bits, and to do so on processors that themselves have only a 32-bit word length but that nonetheless support a 64-bit result of an arithmetic operation.

Since with the use of assembler functions we are abandoning our previous strategy of independence of special platforms, it is useful to implement such functions in a narrowly targeted way. We must therefore identify those FLINT/C functions that would most profit in speedup from assembler support. It is not difficult to determine which are the functions in question. They are those arithmetic functions with quadratic run-time behavior: multiplication, squaring, and division. Since the basic operations occupy the principal portion of time taken up by most of the number-theoretic functions, time improvements in those functions would be linear, without directly changing the implementation of the algorithms. To benefit from such a potential, for the FLINT/C package the functions

```
mult(), umul(), sqr(),  div_l(),
```

are implemented in 80x86 assembler. The functions `mult()`, `umul()`, and `sqr()` form the respective kernels of the functions `mult_l()`, `umul_l()`, and `sqr_l()` (see page 72). The functions support arguments up to length 4096 binary digits, which is 256 ($= \text{MAX}_B$) digits of a `CLINT` number, and results of double that length. The assembler functions are, like the corresponding C functions, implemented according to the algorithms given in Chapter 4, where access to the CPU register allows processing of 32-bit arguments and 64-bit results with the arithmetic machine commands (cf. Chapter 2).

The modules `mult.asm`, `mult.s`, `umul.asm`, `umul.s`, `sqr.asm`, `sqr.s`, as well as `div.asm` and `div.s`, are contained in the FLINT/C package as assembler code. They can be assembled using Microsoft MASM (call: `ml /Cx /c /Gd <filename>`), Watcom WASM,[1] or GNU GAS, and these replace the corresponding C functions when the module `flint.c` is translated with `-DFLINT_ASM`.[2] The calculation times given again in Appendix D permit a direct comparison of some of the important functions with and without assembler support.

Montgomery exponentiation (see Chapter 6) offers additional savings potential, and also the two auxiliary functions `mulmon_l()` and `sqrmon_l()` (cf. page 111) can be implemented profitably as assembler functions with 32-bit digits. A starting point for this is offered by the modules `mul.asm` and `sqr.asm`. As the interested reader can see, there is a very large sandbox out there to play in.

For now, this is all we know.

—Jon Hiseman, *Colosseum*

---

[1] Depending on the compiler used the indicators `mult`, `umul`, `sqr`, and `div_l` of the assembler procedures are to be provided with underscores (`_mult`, `_umul`, `_sqr`, and `_div_l`), since WASM does not generate them.

[2] With the modules `mult.asm`, `sqr.asm`, `umul.asm`, and `div.asm` this functions on 80x86 compatible platforms. For other platforms one must carry out the corresponding implementations.

Part III

Appendices

And all the little girls cried, "Boohoo,
we want to have our appendix out too!"
—Ludwig Bemelmans, *Madeline*

APPENDIX A

Directory of C Functions

A.1 Input/Output, Assignment, Conversions, Comparisons

int byte2clint_l (CLINT n_l, char *bytes, int len);	conversion of a byte vector to CLINT (after IEEE, P1363, 5.5.1)
UCHAR* clint2byte_l (CLINT n_l, int *len);	convert CLINT to a byte vector (according to IEEE, P1363, 5.5.1)
int cmp_l (CLINT a_l, CLINT b_l);	size comparison of a_l and b_l
int cpy_l (CLINT dest_l, CLINT src_l);	assignment of src_l to dest_l
int equ_l (CLINT a_l, CLINT b_l);	test of equality of a_l and b_l
void fswap_l (CLINT a_l, CLINT b_l);	exchange of a_l and b_l
clint* setmax_l (CLINT n_l);	set n_l to the largest CLINT integer representable by the number N_{max}
int str2clint_l (CLINT n_l, char *N, USHORT b);	convert a character string to the base b to CLINT
void u2clint_l (CLINT num_l, USHORT ul);	convert USHORT to CLINT
void ul2clint_l (CLINT num_l, ULONG ul);	convert ULONG to CLINT

`unsigned int` `vcheck_l (CLINT n_l);`	CLINT format check
`char*` `verstr_l ();`	output the version of the FLINT/C library in a character string, with identifiers 'a' for assembler support and 's' for FLINT/C security mode

`char*`
`xclint2str_l (CLINT n_l,`
`    USHORT base, int showbase);`
	convert from CLINT into a character string to the base base, with or without prefix

A.2 Basic Calculations

`int`
`add_l (CLINT a_l, CLINT b_l,`
`    CLINT s_l)`
	addition: sum of a_l and b_l, output in s_l

`int` `dec_l (CLINT a_l)`	decrement a_l

`int`
`div_l (CLINT a_l, CLINT b_l,`
`    CLINT q_l, CLINT r_l)`
	division with remainder: division of a_l by b_l, quotient in q_l, remainder in r_l

`int` `inc_l (CLINT a_l)`	increment a_l

`int`
`mul_l (CLINT a_l, CLINT b_l,`
`    CLINT p_l)`
	multiplication: product of a_l and b_l, output in p_l

`int` `sqr_l (CLINT a_l, CLINT p_l)`	square a_l, output in p_l

`int`
`sub_l (CLINT a_l, CLINT b_l,`
`    CLINT s_l)`
	subtraction: difference of a_l and b_l, output in s_l

int uadd_l (CLINT a_l, USHORT b, CLINT s_l)	mixed addition: sum of a_l and b, output in s_l
int udiv_l (CLINT a_l, USHORT b, CLINT q_l, CLINT r_l)	mixed division with remainder: division of a_l by b, quotient in q_l, remainder in r_l
int umul_l (CLINT a_l, USHORT b, CLINT p_l)	mixed multiplication: product of a_l and b, output in p_l
int usub_l (CLINT a_l, USHORT b, CLINT c_l)	mixed subtraction: difference of a_l and b, output in s_l

A.3 Modular Arithmetic

int madd_l (CLINT a_l, CLINT b_l, CLINT c_l, CLINT m_l);	modular addition: addition of a_l and b_l modulo m_l, output in c_l
int mequ_l (CLINT a_l, CLINT b_l, CLINT m_l);	test for equality of a_l and b_l modulo m_l
int mexp_l (CLINT bas_l, CLINT e_l, CLINT p_l,CLINT m_l);	modular exponentiation, auto- matic use of mexpkm_l() if modu- lus odd, otherwise mexpk_l()
int mexp2_l (CLINT bas_l, USHORT e, CLINT p_l, CLINT m_l);	modular exponentiation, expo- nent e a power of 2
int mexp5_l (CLINT bas_l, CLINT exp_l, CLINT p_l,CLINT m_l);	modular exponentiation, 2^5-ary method

`int`
`mexp5m_l (CLINT bas_l, CLINT exp_l,`
    `CLINT p_l, CLINT m_l);`
	Montgomery exponentiation, 2^5-ary method, odd modulus

`int`
`mexpk_l (CLINT bas_l, CLINT exp_l,`
    `CLINT p_l, CLINT m_l);`
	modular exponentiation, 2^k-ary method, dynamic memory with `malloc()`

`int`
`mexpkm_l (CLINT bas_l, CLINT exp_l,`
    `CLINT p_l, CLINT m_l);`
	Montgomery exponentiation, 2^k-ary method with odd modulus

`int`
`mmul_l (CLINT a_l, CLINT b_l,`
    `CLINT c_l, CLINT m_l);`
	modular multiplication: multiplication of a_l and b_l mod m_l, output in c_l

`int`
`mod_l (CLINT d_l, CLINT n_l,`
    `CLINT r_l);`
	residue of d_l mod n_l, output in r_l

`int`
`mod2_l (CLINT d_l, ULONG k,`
    `CLINT r_l);`
	residue of d_l mod 2^k

`int`
`msqr_l (CLINT a_l, CLINT c_l,`
    `CLINT m_l);`
	modular squaring of a_l mod n_l, square in p_l

`int`
`msub_l (CLINT a_l, CLINT b_l,`
    `CLINT c_l, CLINT m_l);`
	modular subtraction: subtraction of a_l and b_l mod m_l, output in c_l

`void`
`mulmon_l (CLINT a_l, CLINT b_l,`
    `CLINT n_l, USHORT nprime,`
    `USHORT log B_r, CLINT p_l);`
	modular multiplication of a_l and b_l mod n_l, product in p_l (Montgomery method, $B^{\log B\_r-1} \leq n\_l < B^{\log B\_r}$)

`void`
`sqrmon_l (CLINT a_l, CLINT n_l,`
    `USHORT nprime, USHORT logB_r,`
    `CLINT p_l);`
	modular squaring of a_l mod n_l, square in p_l (Montgomery method, $B^{\log B\_r-1} \leq n\_l < B^{\log B\_r}$)

int
umadd_l (CLINT a_l, USHORT b,
    CLINT c_l, CLINT m_l);

mixed modular addition: addition of a_l and b mod m_l, output in c_l

int
umexp_l (CLINT bas_l, USHORT e,
    CLINT p_l, CLINT m_l);

modular exponentiation, USHORT exponent

int
umexpm_l (CLINT bas_l, USHORT e,
    CLINT p_l, CLINT m_l);

modular exponentiation, odd modulus, USHORT exponent

int
ummul_l (CLINT a_l, USHORT b,
    CLINT p_l, CLINT m_l);

mixed modular multiplication of a_l and b_l mod n_l, product in p_l

USHORT
umod_l (CLINT d_l, USHORT n);

residue of d_l mod n

int
umsub_l (CLINT a_l, USHORT b,
    CLINT c_l, CLINT m_l);

mixed modular subtraction: subtraction of a_l and b mod m_l, output in c_l

int
wmexp_l (USHORT bas, CLINT e_l,
    CLINT p_l, CLINT m_l);

modular exponentiation, USHORT base

int
wmexpm_l (USHORT bas, CLINT e_l,
    CLINT p_l, CLINT m_l);

Montgomery exponentiation, odd modulus, USHORT base

A.4 Bitwise Operations

void
and_l (CLINT a_l, CLINT b_l,
    CLINT c_l)

bitwise AND of a_l and b_l, output in c_l

int
clearbit_l (CLINT a_l,
    unsigned int pos)

test and clear the bit of a_l in position pos

void or_l (CLINT a_l, CLINT b_l, CLINT c_l)	bitwise OR of a_l and b_l, output in c_l
int setbit_l (CLINT a_l, unsigned int pos)	test and set the bit of a_l in position pos
int shift_l (CLINT a_l, long int noofbits)	left/right shift of a_l by noofbits bits
int shl_l (CLINT a_l)	right shift of a_l by 1 bit
int shr_l (CLINT a_l)	left shift of a_l by 1 bit
int testbit_l (CLINT a_l, unsigned int pos)	test the bit of a_l in position pos
void xor_l (CLINT a_l, CLINT b_l, CLINT c_l)	bitwise exclusive OR (XOR) of a_l and b_l, output in c_l

A.5 Number-Theoretic Functions

int chinrem_l (unsigned noofeq, clint** coeff_l, CLINT x_l)	solution of simultaneous linear congruences, output in x_l
void gcd_l (CLINT a_l, CLINT b_l, CLINT g_l)	greatest common divisor of a_l and b_l, output in g_l
int introot_l (CLINT a_l, USHORT b, CLINT r_l)	integer part of bth root of a_l, output in r_l
void inv_l (CLINT a_l, CLINT n_l, CLINT g_l, CLINT i_l)	gcd of a_l and n_l and inverse of a_l mod n_l

unsigned iroot_l (CLINT a_l, CLINT r_l)	integer part of square root of a_l, output in r_l
int jacobi_l (CLINT a_l, CLINT b_l)	Legendre/Jacobi symbol, a_l over b_l
void lcm_l (CLINT a_l, CLINT b_l, CLINT v_l)	least common multiple of a_l and b_l, output in v_l
int prime_l (CLINT n_l, unsigned noofsmallprimes, unsigned iterations)	Miller–Rabin primality test of n_l with division sieve

int
primroot_l (CLINT x_l,
    unsigned noofprimes,
    clint** primes_l)
	determine a primitive root modulo n, output in x_l

int proot_l (CLINT a_l, CLINT p_l, CLINT x_l)	square root of a_l mod p_l, output in x_l
int root_l (CLINT a_l, CLINT p_l, CLINT q_l, CLINT x_l)	square root of a_l mod p_l*q_l, output in x_l
USHORT sieve_l (CLINT a_l, unsigned noofsmallprimes)	division sieve, division of a_l by small primes

void
xgcd_l (CLINT a_l, CLINT b_l,
    CLINT g_l,
    CLINT u_l, int *sign_u,
    CLINT v_l, int *sign_v)
	greatest common divisor of a_l and b_l and representation of gcd in u_l and v_l with sign in sign_u and sign_v

A.6 Generation of Pseudorandom Numbers

UCHAR bRand_l (STATEPRNG *xrstate)	generation of a pseudorandom number of type UCHAR

UCHAR bRandBBS_l (STATEBBS *xrstate)	generation of a pseudorandom number of type UCHAR with the BBS generator
int FindPrime_l (CLINT p_l, STATEPRNG *xrstate, USHORT l)	deterimine a pseudorandom prime p_l of type CLINT with $2^{l-1} \leq p\_l < 2^{l}$

int
FindPrimeGcd_l (CLINT p_l,
    STATEPRNG *xrstate,
    USHORT l, CLINT f_l)
	deterimine a pseudorandom prime p_l of type CLINT with $2^{l-1} \leq p\_l < 2^{l}$ and $\gcd(p\_l - 1, f\_l) = 1$

int
FindPrimeMinMaxGcd_l (CLINT p_l,
    STATEPRNG *xrstate,
    CLINT rmin_l,
    CLINT rmax_l, CLINT f_l)
	deterimine a pseudorandom prime p_l of type CLINT with rmin_l $\leq$ p_l $\leq$ rmax_l and $\gcd(p\_l - 1, f\_l) = 1$

int
GetEntropy_l (CLINT Seed_l,
    char *Hashres,int AddEntropy,
    char *RndStr, int LenRndStr)
	generate entropy for initializing pseudorandom number generator

int
InitRand_l (STATEPRNG *xrstate,
    char *UsrStr, int LenUsrStr,
    int AddEntropy, int Generator)
	initialize a yet to be specified random number generator with generation of entropy

int
InitRandAES_l (STATEAES *rstate,
    char *UsrStr, int LenUsrStr,
    int AddEntropy)
	initialize the AES random number generator with generation of entropy

int
InitRandBBS_l (STATEBBS *rstate,
    char *UsrStr, int LenUsrStr,
    int AddEntropy)
	initialize the Blum–Blum–Shub random number generator with generation of entropy

int
InitRandRMDSHA1_l (
    STATERMDSHA1 *rstate,
    char * UsrStr, int LenUsrStr,
    int AddEntropy)
	initialize the RandRMDSHA-1 random number generator with generation of entropy

ULONG lRand_l (STATEPRNG *xrstate)	generator for random numbers of type ULONG
void PurgeRand_l (STATEPRNG *xrstate)	delete internal state of a pseudo-random generator
void PurgeRandAES_l (STATEAES *rstate)	delete internal state of pseudo-random generator RandAES
void PurgeRandBBS_l (STATEBBS *rstate)	delete internal state of pseudo-random generator RandBBS
void PurgeRandRMDSHA1_l (STATERMDSHA1 *rstate)	delete internal state of pseudorandom generator RandRMDSHA1
int Rand_l (CLINT r_l, STATEPRNG *xrstate, int l)	generation of a pseudorandom number r_l of type CLINT with $2^{l-1} \leq r\_l < 2^l$ using the FLINT/C pseudorandom number generators
void rand_l (CLINT r_l, int l)	CLINT random number with l binary digits, linear congruences
clint* rand64_l (void)	64-bit random number generator
int RandAES_l (CLINT r_l, STATEAES *rstate, int l)	CLINT random numbers with l binary digits via AES random number generator using an individual state buffer
int RandBBS_l (CLINT r_l, STATEBBS *rstate, int l)	CLINT random numbers with l binary digits via BBS random number generator using an individual state buffer
clint* randBBS_l (CLINT r_l, int l)	CLINT random numbers with l binary digits using BBS bit generator
int RandlMinMax_l (CLINT r_l, STATEPRNG *xrstate, CLINT rmin_l, CLINT rmax_l)	determine a CLINT random number r_l with $rmin\_l \leq r\_l \leq rmax\_l$

int RandRMDSHA1_l (CLINT r_l, STATERMDSHA1 *rstate, int l)	CLINT random number with l binary digits via the RMDSHA1 random number generator using an individual state buffer
int randbit_l (void)	BBS bit generator
clint* seed64_l (CLINT seed_l)	initialization of rand64_l() with CLINT value
void seedBBS_l (CLINT seed_l)	initialization of randbit_l() with CLINT value
USHORT sRand_l (STATEPRNG *xrstate)	generate a pseudorandom number of type USHORT
int SwitchRandAES_l (STATEAES *rstate)	deterministic random number generator based on AES
int SwitchRandBBS_l (STATEBBS *rstate)	deterministic random number generator based on BBS
int SwitchRandRMDSHA1_l (STATERMDSHA1 *rstate)	deterministic random number generator based on hash functions SHA-1 and RIPEMD-160
UCHAR ucrand64_l (void)	generator for random numbers of type UCHAR
UCHAR ucrandBBS_l (void)	BBS generator for random number of type UCHAR
ULONG ulrand64_l (void)	generator for random numbers of type ULONG
ULONG ulrandBBS_l (void)	BBS generator for random number of type ULONG
clint* ulseed64_l (ULONG seed)	initialization of rand64_l() with ULONG value

void ulseedBBS_l (ULONG seed)	initialization of randbit_l() with ULONG value
USHORT usrand64_l (void)	generator for random numbers of type USHORT
USHORT usrandBBS_l (void)	BBS generator for random number of type USHORT

A.7 Register Management

clint* create_l (void)	generate a CLINT register
int create_reg_l (void)	generate the CLINT register bank
void free_l (CLINT n_l);	clear a register by overwriting and release memory
void free_reg_l (void)	clear all registers of the register bank by overwriting, then release memory
clint* get_reg_l (unsigned int reg)	generate reference to register reg of the register bank
void purge_l (CLINT n_l)	clear a CLINT object by overwriting
int purge_reg_l (unsigned int reg)	clear a register of the register bank by overwriting
int purgeall_reg_l (void)	clear all registers of the register bank by overwriting
void set_noofregs_l (unsigned int nregs)	set number of registers

Directory of
C++ Functions

B.1 Input/Output, Conversion, Comparison: Member Functions

```
LINT (void);
```
Constructor 1:
an uninitialized LINT object is generated

```
LINT (const char* str,
      int base);
```
Constructor 2:
LINT is constructed from a string of digits to base base

```
LINT (const UCHAR* byte,
      int len);
```
Constructor 3:
LINT is constructed from a byte vector with digits to base 2^8 according to IEEE P1363, significance of bits grows from left to right

```
LINT (const char* str);
```
Constructor 4:
LINT is constructed from an ASCII string with C-Syntax

```
LINT (const LINT&);
```
Constructor 5:
LINT is constructed from LINT (copy constructor)

```
LINT (signed int);
```
Constructor 6:
LINT is constructed from an integer of type int

```
LINT (signed long);
```
Constructor 7:
LINT is constructed from an integer of type long

LINT (unsigned char);	**Constructor 8:** LINT is constructed from an integer of type unsigned char
LINT (USHORT);	**Constructor 9:** LINT is constructed from an integer of type unsigned short
LINT (unsigned int);	**Constructor 10:** LINT is constructed from an integer of type unsigned int
LINT (unsigned long);	**Constructor 11:** LINT is constructed from an integer of type unsigned long
LINT (const CLINT);	**Constructor 12:** LINT is constructed from an integer of type CLINT
inline char* binstr (void) const;	representation of a LINT integer as a binary number
inline char* decstr (void) const;	representation of a LINT integer as decimal number
inline void disp (char* str);	display of a LINT integer with previous output of str
Static long flags (ostream& s);	read static LINT status variable associated with ostream s
static long flags (void);	read static LINT status variable associated with ostream cout
LINT& fswap (LINT& b);	exchange of implicit argument a with argument b
inline char* hexstr (void) const;	representation of a LINT integer as a hexadecimal number
UCHAR* lint2byte (int* len) const;	transformation of a LINT integer into a byte vector, output of length in len, according to IEEE P1363, significance of bytes increasing from left to right

`char*`
`lint2str (USHORT base,`
`    const int showbase = 0) const;`
	representation of a LINT integer as character string to base base, prefix 0x, or 0b if showbase > 0

`inline char*` `octstr (void) const;`	representation of a LINT integer as an octal number
`const LINT&` `operator = (const LINT& b);`	assignment $a \leftarrow b$
`void` `purge (void);`	clear implicit argument a by over-writing
`static long` `restoref (long int flags);`	reset LINT status variable referring to ostream cout to the value in flags

`static long`
`restoref (ostream& s,`
`    long int flags);`
	set the LINT status variable referring to ostream s to the value in flags

`static long` `setf (long int flags);`	set status bits in flags in LINT status variable referring to ostream cout
`static long` `setf (ostream& s, long int flags);`	set status bits of value flags in LINT status variable referring to ostream s
`static long` `unsetf (long int flags);`	unset status bits of flags in LINT status variable referring to ostream cout
`static long` `unsetf (ostream& s, long int flags);`	unset status bits in flags in LINT status variable referring to ostream s

B.2 Input/Output, Conversion, Comparison: Friend Functions

void fswap (LINT& a, LINT& b);	exchange of a and b
UCHAR* lint2byte (const LINT& a, int* len);	transformation of a into a byte vector, output of length in len, according to IEEE P1363, significance of bytes increasing from left to right

char*
lint2str (const LINT& a,
    USHORT base,
    int showbase);
	representation of a as character string to base base, with prefix 0x, or 0b if showbase > 0

ostream& LintBin (ostream& s);	ostream manipulator for binary representation of LINT integers
ostream& LintDec (ostream& s);	ostream manipulator for decimal representation of LINT integers
ostream& LintHex (ostream& s);	ostream manipulator for hex representation of LINT integers
ostream& LintLwr (ostream& s);	ostream manipulator for use of lowercase letters in hex representation of LINT integers
ostream& LintNobase (ostream& s);	ostream manipulator for omission of a prefix 0x or 0b in hex or binary representation of LINT integers
ostream& LintNolength (ostream& s);	manipulator for the omission of binary length in the output LINT integers
ostream& LintOct (ostream& s);	ostream manipulator for the octal representation of LINT integers

ostream& LintShowbase (ostream& s);	ostream manipulator for the display of a prefix 0x (resp. 0b) in hex (resp. binary) representation of LINT integers
ostream& LintShowlength (ostream& s);	ostream manipulator for display of the binary length in the output of LINT integers
ostream& LintUpr (ostream& s);	ostream manipulator for use of uppercase letters in the hex representation of LINT integers
const int operator != (const LINT& a, const LINT& b);	test a != b
const int operator < (const LINT& a, const LINT& b);	comparison a < b
fstream& operator << (fstream& s, const LINT& ln);	overloaded insert operator for writing LINT integers to files, output stream of type fstream
ofstream& operator << (ofstream& s, const LINT& ln);	overloaded insert operator for writing LINT integers to files, output stream of type ofstream
ostream& operator << (ostream& s, const LINT& ln);	overloaded insert operator for output of LINT integers, output stream of type ostream
const int operator <= (const LINT& a, const LINT& b);	comparison a <= b
const int operator == (const LINT& a, const LINT& b);	test a == b
const int operator > (const LINT& a, const LINT& b);	comparison a > b

const int operator >= (const LINT& a, const LINT& b);	comparison a >= b
fstream& operator >> (fstream& s, LINT& ln);	overloaded extract operator for reading LINT integers from files, input/output stream of type fstream
ifstream& operator >> (ifstream& s, LINT& ln);	overloaded extract operator for reading LINT integers from files, input stream of type ifstream
void purge (LINT& a);	clear by overwriting
LINT_omanip<int> ResetLintFlags (int flag);	manipulator to unset status bits of value flag in the LINT status variable
LINT_omanip<int> SetLintFlags (int flag);	manipulator for setting status bits of the value flag in the LINT status variable

B.3 Basic Operations: Member Functions

const LINT& add (const LINT& b);	addition c = a.add (b);
const LINT& divr (const LINT& d, LINT& r);	division with remainder quotient = dividend.div (divisor, remainder);
const LINT& mul (const LINT& b);	multiplication c = a.mul (b);
const LINT operator -- (int);	decrement operator (postfix) a--;
const LINT& operator -- (void);	decrement operator (prefix) --a;

```
const LINT&
operator %= (const LINT& b);
```
remainder and assignment a %= b;

```
const LINT&
operator *= (const LINT& b);
```
multiplication and assignment a *= b;

```
const LINT&
operator /= (const LINT& b);
```
division and assignment a /= b;

```
const LINT
operator ++ (int);
```
increment operator (postfix) a++;

```
const LINT&
operator ++ (void);
```
increment operator (prefix) ++a;

```
const LINT&
operator += (const LINT& b);
```
addition and assignment a += b;

```
const LINT&
operator -= (const LINT& b);
```
subtraction and assignment a -= b;

```
const LINT&
sqr (void);
```
squaring c = a.sqr (b);

```
const LINT&
sub (const LINT& b);
```
subtraction c = a.sub (b);

B.4 Basic Operations: Friend Functions

```
const LINT
add (const LINT& a, const LINT& b);
```
addition c = add (a, b);

```
const LINT
divr (const LINT& a,
    const LINT& b, LINT& r);
```
division with remainder quotient
= div (dividend, divisor,
remainder);

```
const LINT
mul (const LINT& a, const LINT& b);
```
multiplication c = mul (a, b);

```
const LINT                              subtraction c = a - b;
operator - (const LINT& a,
    const LINT& b);

const LINT                              remainder c = a % b;
operator % (const LINT& a,
    const LINT& b);

const LINT                              multiplication c = a * b;
operator * (const LINT& a,
    const LINT& b);

const LINT                              division c = a / b;
operator / (const LINT& a,
    const LINT& b);

const LINT                              addition c = a + b;
operator + (const LINT& a,
    const LINT& b);

const LINT                              squaring b = sqr (a);
sqr (const LINT& a);


const LINT                              subtraction c = sub (a, b);
sub (const LINT& a, const LINT& b);
```

B.5 Modular Arithmetic: Member Functions

```
const LINT&                             modular addition,
madd (const LINT& b, const LINT& m);    c = a.madd (b, m);


int                                     comparison of a and b modulo m if (a.mequ
mequ (LINT& b, const LINT& m)           (b, m)) ...
const;

const LINT&                             modular exponentiation with
mexp (const LINT& e, const LINT& m);    Montgomery reduction for odd
                                        modulus m, c = a.mexp (e, m);
```

`const LINT&` `mexp (USHORT u, const LINT& m);`	modular exponentiation with USHORT exponent, Montgomery reduction for odd modulus m, c = a.mexp (u, m);
`const LINT&` `mexp2 (USHORT u, const LINT& m);`	modular exponentiation with power of two exponent 2^u, c = a.mexp2 (u, m);

`const LINT&`
`mexp5m (const LINT& e,`
`    const LINT& m);`
	modular exponentiation with Montgomery reduction for odd modulus m, c = a.mexp5m (e, m);

`const LINT&`
`mexpkm (const LINT& e,`
`    const LINT& m);`
	modular exponentiation with Montgomery reduction for odd modulus m, c = a.mexpkm (e, m);

`const LINT&`
`mmul (const LINT& b,`
`    const LINT& m);`
	modular multiplication, c = a.mmul (b, m);

`const LINT&` `mod (const LINT& m);`	remainder b = a.mod (m);
`const LINT&` `mod2 (USHORT u);`	remainder modulo power of two 2^u, b = a.mod (u);
`const LINT&` `msqr (const LINT& m);`	modular squaring, c = a.msqr (m);
`const LINT&` `msub (const LINT& b, const LINT& m);`	modular subtraction, c = a.msub(b, m);

B.6 Modular Arithmetic: Friend Functions

LINT
madd (const LINT& a,
    const LINT& b,
    const LINT& m);
	modular addition, c = madd (a, b, m);

int
mequ (const LINT& a,
    const LINT& b,
    const LINT& m);
	comparison of a and b modulo m
	if (mequ (a, b, m)) ...

LINT
mexp (const LINT& a,
    const LINT& e,
    const LINT& m);
	modular exponentiation with Montgomery reduction for odd modulus m, c = mexp (a, e, m);

LINT
mexp (const LINT& a,
    USHORT u,
    const LINT& m);
	modular exponentiation with USHORT exponent, Montgomery reduction for odd modulus m, c = mexp (a, u, m);

LINT
mexp (USHORT u,
    const LINT& e,
    const LINT& m);
	modular exponentiation with USHORT base, Montgomery reduction for odd modulus m, c = mexp (u, e, m);

LINT
mexp2 (const LINT& a,
    USHORT u,
    const LINT& m);
	modular exponentiation with power of two exponent 2^u, c = mexp2 (a, u, m);

LINT
mexp5m (const LINT& a,
    const LINT& e,
    const LINT& m);
	modular exponentiation with Montgomery reduction, only for odd modulus m, c = mexp5m (a, e, m);

LINT
mexpkm (const LINT& a,
    const LINT& b,
    const LINT& m);
	modular exponentiation with Montgomery reduction, only for odd modulus m, c = mexpkm (a, e, m);

LINT
mmul (const LINT& a,
    const LINT& b,
    const LINT& m);
	modular multiplication, c = mmul (a, b, m);

LINT
mod (const LINT& a,
    const LINT& m);

remainder b = mod (a, m);

LINT
mod2 (const LINT& a,
    USHORT u);

remainder modulo power of two
2^u, b = mod (a, u);

LINT
msqr (const LINT& a,
    const LINT& m);

modular squaring, c = msqr (a,
m);

LINT
msub (const LINT& a,
    const LINT& b,
    const LINT& m);

modular subtraction, c =
msub(a, b, m);

B.7 Bitwise Operations: Member Functions

const LINT&
clearbit (const unsigned int i);

clear a bit at position i, a.clearbit (i);

const LINT&
operator &= (const LINT& b);

AND and assignment, a &= b;

const LINT&
operator ^= (const LINT& b);

XOR and assignment, a ^= b;

const LINT&
operator |= (const LINT& b);

OR and assignment, a |= b;

const LINT&
operator <<= (int i);

left shift and assignment, a <<= i;

const LINT&
operator >>= (int i);

right shift and assignment, a >>= i;

```
const LINT&                              set a bit at position i, a.setbit (i);
setbit (unsigned int i);


const LINT&                              shift (left and right) by i bit
shift (int i);                           positions, a.shift (i);


const int                                test a bit at position i, a.testbit (i);
testbit (unsigned int i) const;
```

B.8 Bitwise Operations: Friend Functions

```
const LINT                               AND, c = a & b;
operator & (const LINT& a,
     const LINT& b);

const LINT                               XOR, c = a ^ b;
operator ^ (const LINT& a,
     const LINT& b);

const LINT                               OR, c = a | b;
operator | (const LINT& a,
     const LINT& b);

const LINT                               left shift, b = a << i;
operator << (const LINT& a,
     int i);

const LINT                               right shift, b = a >> i;
operator >> (const LINT& a,
     int i);

const LINT                               shift (left and right) by i bit
shift (const LINT& a, int i);            positions, b = shift (a, i);
```

B.9 Number-Theoretic Member Functions

LINT
chinrem (const LINT& m,
    const LINT& b,
    const LINT& n) const;

return a solution x of the system of simultaneous congruences $x \equiv a \bmod m$ and $x \equiv b \bmod n$, if a solution exists

LINT
gcd (const LINT& b);

return gcd of a and b

LINT
introot (void) const;

return integer part of the bth root of a

LINT
introot (const USHORT b) const;

return integer part of the bth root of a

LINT
inv (const LINT& b) const;

return the multiplicative inverse of a mod b

int
iseven (void) const;

test a for divisibility by 2: true if a even

int
isodd (void) const;

test a for divisibility by 2: true if a odd

int
isprime (int nsp = 302,
    int rnds = 0) const;

test a for primality

LINT
issqr (void) const;

test a for being square

int
jacobi (const LINT& b) const;

return the Jacobi symbol $\left(\frac{a}{b}\right)$

LINT
lcm (const LINT& b) const;

return the least common multiple of a and b

unsigned int
ld (void) const;

return $\lfloor \log_2(a) \rfloor$

`LINT` `root (void) const;`	return the integer part of the square root of a
`LINT` `root (const LINT& p) const;`	return the square root of a modulo an odd prime p

`LINT`
`root (const LINT& p,`
`    const LINT& q) const;`
	return the square root of a modulo p*q, where p and q are odd primes

`int` `twofact (LINT& odd) const;`	return the even part of a, odd contains the odd part of a

`LINT`
`xgcd (const LINT& b,`
`    LINT& u, int& sign_u,`
`    LINT& v, int& sign_v)`
`    const;`
	extended Euclidean algorithm with return of gcd of a and b, u and v contain the absolute values of the factors of the linear combination `g = sign_u*u*a + sign_v*v*b`

B.10 Number-Theoretic Friend Functions

`LINT`
`chinrem (unsigned noofeq,`
`    LINT** coeff);`
	return a solution of a system of simultaneous linear congruences. In coeff is passed a vector of pointers to LINT objects as coefficients a1, m1, a2, m2, a3, m3, ... of the congruence system with noofeq equations $x \equiv a_i \bmod m_i$

`LINT`
`extendprime (const LINT& pmin,`
`const LINT& pmax,`
`    const LINT& a,`
`    const LINT& q,`
`    const LINT& f);`
	return a prime p with $pmin \leq p \leq pmax$, with $p \equiv a \bmod q$ and $\gcd(p-1, f) = 1$, f odd

`LINT`
`extendprime (USHORT l,`
`    const LINT& a,`
`    const LINT& q,`
`    const LINT& f);`
	return a prime p of length l bits, i.e., $2^{l-1} \leq p < 2^l$, with $p \equiv a \bmod q$ and $\gcd(p-1, f) = 1$, f odd

LINT
findprime (const LINT& pmin,
    const LINT& pmax,
    const LINT& f);
	return a prime p with $pmin \leq p \leq$ $pmax$ and $\gcd(p-1, f) = 1$, f odd

LINT findprime (USHORT l);	return a prime p of length l bits, i.e., $2^{l-1} \leq p < 2^l$
LINT findprime (USHORT l, const LINT& f);	return a prime p of length l bits, i.e., $2^{l-1} \leq p < 2^l$ and $\gcd(p-1, f) = 1$, f odd
LINT gcd (const LINT& a, const LINT& b);	return gcd of a and b
LINT introot (const LINT& a);	return the integer part of a
LINT introot (const LINT& a, const USHORT b);	return the integer part of the bth root of a
LINT inv (const LINT& a, const LINT& b);	return the multiplicative inverse of a mod b
int iseven (const LINT& a);	test a for divisibility by 2: true if a even
int isodd (const LINT& a);	test a for divisibility by 2: true if a odd
int isprime (const LINT& p int nsp = 302, int rnds = 0);	test p for primality
LINT issqr (const LINT& a);	test a for being a square

`int`
`jacobi (const LINT& a,`
`    const LINT& b);`
	return the Jacobi symbol $\left(\frac{a}{b}\right)$

`LINT`
`lcm (const LINT& a,`
`    const LINT& b);`
	return the least common multiple of a and b

`unsigned int` `ld (const LINT& a);`	return $\lfloor \log_2(a) \rfloor$

`LINT`
`nextprime (const LINT& a,`
`    const LINT& f);`
	return the smallest prime p above a with $\gcd(p-1, f) = 1$, f odd

`LINT`
`primroot (unsigned noofprimes,`
`    LINT** primes);`
	return a primitive root modulo p. In `noofprimes` is passed the number of distinct prime factors of the group order $p - 1$, in primes a vector of pointers to `LINT` objects, beginning with $p - 1$, then come the prime divisors $p_1, \ldots, p_k$ of the group order $p - 1 = p_1^{e_1} \cdots p_k^{e_k}$ with $k =$ `noofprimes`

`LINT` `root (const LINT& a);`	return the integer part of the square root of a

`LINT`
`root (const LINT& a,`
`    const LINT& p);`
	return the square root of a modulo an odd prime p

`LINT`
`root (const LINT& a,`
`    const LINT& p,`
`    const LINT& q);`
	return the square root of a modulo p*q for p and q odd primes

`LINT`
`strongprime (const LINT& pmin,`
`    const LINT& pmax,`
`    const LINT& f);`
	return a strong prime p with pmin $\leq p \leq$ pmax, $\gcd(p-1, f) = 1$, f odd, default lengths lr, lt, ls of prime divisors r of $p - 1$, t of $r - 1$, s of $p + 1$: lt $\lesssim \frac{1}{4}$, ls $\approx$ lr $\lesssim \frac{1}{2}$ of the binary length of pmin

LINT
strongprime (const LINT& pmin,
    const LINT& pmax,
    USHORT lt,
    USHORT lr,
    USHORT ls,
    const LINT& f);

return a strong prime p with pmin $\leq$ p $\leq$ pmax, $\gcd(p - 1, f) = 1$, f odd, lengths lr, lt, ls of prime divisors r of $p - 1$, t of $r - 1$, s of $p + 1$

LINT
strongprime (USHORT l);

return a strong prime p of length l bits, i.e., $2^{l-1} \leq p < 2^l$

LINT
strongprime (USHORT l,
    const LINT& f);

return a strong prime p of length l bits, i.e., $2^{l-1} \leq p < 2^l$, with $\gcd(p - 1, f) = 1$, f odd

LINT
strongprime (USHORT l,
    USHORT lt,
    USHORT lr,
    USHORT ls,
    LINT& f);

return a strong prime p of length l bits, i.e., $2^{l-1} \leq p < 2^l$, with $\gcd(p - 1, f) = 1$, f odd lt $\lesssim \frac{1}{4}$, ls $\approx$ lr $\lesssim \frac{1}{2}$ of length of p

int
twofact (const LINT& even,
    LINT& odd);

return the even part of a, odd contains the odd part of a

LINT
xgcd (const LINT& a,
    const LINT& b,
    LINT& u, int& sign_u,
    LINT& v, int& sign_v);

extended Euclidean algorithm with return of gcd of a and b, u and v contain the absolute values of the factors of the linear combination g = sign_u*u*a + sign_v*v*b

B.11   Generation of Pseudorandom Numbers

LINT randBBS (const LINT& rmin, const LINT& rmax);	return a LINT random number r with $rmin \leq r \leq rmax$
LINT randBBS (int l);	return a LINT random number of length l bits
LINT randl (const LINT& rmin, const LINT& rmax);	return a LINT random number r with $rmin \leq r \leq rmax$
LINT randl (const int l);	return a LINT random number of length l bits
int seedBBS (const LINT& seed);	initialization of BBS random number generator with initial value seed
void seedl (const LINT& seed);	initialization of the 64-bit ran- dom number generator based on linear congruences with initial value seed

B.12   Miscellaneous Functions

LINT_ERRORS Get_Warning_Status (void);	query error status of a LINT object

static void
Set_LINT_Error_Handler
    (void (*)(LINT_ERRORS err,
    const char*, int, int));
	activation of a user routine for
	handling errors with LINT op-
	erations. The registered routine
	replaces the LINT standard er-
	ror handler panic(); deactivation
	of registration of user routine
	and simultaneous reactivation of
	use routine panic() managed by
	the call Set_LINT_Error_Handler
	(NULL);

APPENDIX C

Macros

C.1 Error Codes and Status Values

E_CLINT_DBZ	−1	division by zero
E_CLINT_OFL	−2	overflow
E_CLINT_UFL	−3	underflow
E_CLINT_MAL	−4	memory allocation error
E_CLINT_NOR	−5	register not available
E_CLINT_BOR	−6	invalid base in str2clint_l()
E_CLINT_MOD	−7	even modulus in Montgomery reduction
E_CLINT_NPT	−8	null pointer passed as argument
E_VCHECK_OFL	1	vcheck_l() warning: number too long
E_VCHECK_LDZ	2	vcheck_l() warning: leading zeros
E_VCHECK_MEM	−1	vcheck_l() error: null pointer

C.2 Additional Constants

BASE	0x10000	base $B = 2^{16}$ of the CLINT number format
BASEMINONE	0xffffU	$B - 1$
DBASEMINONE	0xffffffffUL	$B^2 - 1$
BASEDIV2	0x8000U	$\lfloor B/2 \rfloor$
NOOFREGS	16U	standard number of registers in register bank

BITPERDGT	16UL	number of binary digits per CLINT digit
LDBITPERDGT	4U	logarithm of BITPERDGT to base 2
CLINTMAXDIGIT	256U	maximal number of digits to base B of a CLINT object
CLINTMAXSHORT	(CLINTMAXDIGIT + 1)	USHORTs to be allocated for a CLINT object
CLINTMAXBYTE	(CLINTMAXSHORT << 1)	number of allocated bytes for a CLINT object
CLINTMAXBIT	(CLINTMAXDIGIT << 4)	maximal number of binary digits of a CLINT object
r0_l, ... , r15_l	get_reg_l(0), ... , get_reg_l(15)	pointer to CLINT registers $0, \ldots, 15$
FLINT_VERMAJ		higher version number of the FLINT/C library
FLINT_VERMIN		lower version number of the FLINT/C library
FLINT_VERSION	((FLINT_VERMAJ << 8) + FLINT_VERMIN)	version number of the FLINT/C library
FLINT_SECURE	0x73, 0	identifier 's' or ' ' for the FLINT/C security mode

C.3 Macros with Parameters

ANDMAX_L (a_l)	SETDIGITS_L((a_l), (MIN(DIGITS_L(a_l), (USHORT)CLINTMAXDIGIT)); RMLDZRS_L((a_l))	reduction modulo $(N_{max} + 1)$
ASSIGN_L (a_l, b_l)	cpy_l((a_l), (b_l))	assignment a_l ← b_l
BINSTR_L (n_l)	xclint2str_l((n_l), 2, 0)	conversion of a CLINT object into binary rep- resentation
bRandAES_L (S)	((UCHAR)SwitchRandAES_l((S))	generation of a ran- dom number of type UCHAR
bRandRMDSHA1_L (S)	((UCHAR)SwitchRandAES_l((S))	generation of a ran- dom number of type UCHAR
clint2str_l (n_l, base) CLINT2STR_L (n_l, base).	xclint2str_l((n_l),(base),0)	representation of a CLINT object as char- acter string without prefix
DECDIGITS_L (n_l)	(--*(n_l))	reduce number of digits by 1
DECSTR_L (n)	xclint2str_l((n), 10, 0)	conversion of a CLINT object into decimal representation
DIGITS_L (n_l)	(*(n_l))	read number of digits of n_l to base B
DISP_L (S, A)	printf("%s%s\n%u bit\n\n", (S), HEXSTR_L(A), ld_l(A))	standard output of a CLINT object
EQONE_L (a_l)	(equ_l((a_l), one_l) == 1)	comparison a_l == 1

EQZ_L (a_l)	(equ_l((a_l), nul_l) == 1)	comparison a_l == 0
GE_L (a_l, b_l)	(cmp_l((a_l), (b_l)) > -1)	comparison a_l $\geq$ b_l
GT_L (a_l, b_l)	(cmp_l((a_l), (b_l)) == 1)	comparison a_l $>$ b_l
GTZ_L (a_l)	(cmp_l((a_l), nul_l) == 1)	comparison a_l > 0
HEXSTR_L (n_l)	xclint2str_l((n_l), 16, 0)	conversion of a CLINT object into hex representation
INCDIGITS_L (n_l)	(++*(n_l))	increase number of digits by 1
INITRAND64_LT()	seed64_l((unsigned long) time(NULL)	initialization of random number generator rand64_l() with system clock
INITRANDBBS_LT()	seedBBS_l((unsigned long) time(NULL))	initialization of the random bit generator randbit_l() by means of system clock
ISEVEN_L (n_l)	(DIGITS_L(n_l) == 0 || (DIGITS_L(n_l) > 0 && (*(LSDPTR_L(n_l)) & 1U) == 0))	test whether n_l is odd
ISODD_L (n_l)	(DIGITS_L(n_l) > 0 && (*(LSDPTR_L(n_l)) & 1U) == 1)	test whether n_l is odd
ISPRIME_L (n_l)	prime_l((n_l), 302, 5)	primality test with fixed parameters

LE_L (a_l, b_l)	(cmp_l((a_l), (b_l)) < 1)	comparison a_l $\leq$ b_l
lRandAES_l (S)	(((ULONG)\ SwitchRandAES_l((S)))\ << 24) | ((ULONG)\ SwitchRandAES_l((S)))\ << 16)|((ULONG)\ SwitchRandAES_l((S)))\ << 8) |((ULONG)\ SwitchRandAES_l((S))))	generate a random number of type ULONG
lRandRMDSHA1_l (S)	(((ULONG)\ SwitchRandRMDSHA1_l((S)))\ << 24) | ((ULONG)\ SwitchRandRMDSHA1_l((S)))\ << 16)|((ULONG)\ SwitchRandRMDSHA1_l((S)))\ << 8) |((ULONG)\ SwitchRandRMDSHA1_l((S))))	generate a random number of type ULONG
LSDPTR_L (n_l)	((n_l) + 1)	pointer to least-significant digit of a CLINT object
LT_L (a_l, b_l)	(cmp_l((a_l), (b_l)) == -1)	comparison a_l < b_l
MAX_L (a_l, b_l)	(GT_L((a_l), (b_l)) ? (a_l) : (b_l))	maximum of two CLINT values
MEXP_L (a_l, e_l, p_l, n_l)	mexp5_l((a_l), (e_l), (p_l), (n_l)) mexpkm_l((a_l), (e_l), (p_l), (n_l)) mexp5m_l((a_l), (e_l), (p_l), (n_l))	exponentiation, alternative
MEXP_L (a_l, e_l, p_l, n_l)	mexpk_l((a_l), (e_l), (p_l), (n_l))	exponentiation

MIN_L (a_l, b_l)	(LT_L((a_l), (b_l)) ? (a_l) : (b_l))	minimum of two CLINT values
MSDPTR_L (n_l)	((n_l) + DIGITS_L(n_l))	pointer to most-significant digit of a CLINT object
OCTSTR_L (n_l)	xclint2str_l((n_l), 8, 0)	conversion of a CLINT object into octal representation
RMLDZRS_L (n_l)	while((DIGITS_L(n_l) > 0)&& (*MSDPTR_L(n_l) == 0)) {DECDIGITS_L(n_l);}	remove leading zeros from a CLINT object
SET_L(n_l, ul)	ul2clint_l((n_l), (ul))	assignment n_l ← ULONG ul
SETDIGITS_L (n_l, 1)	(*(n_l) = (USHORT)(1))	set number of digits n_l to 1
SETONE_L (n_l)	u2clint_l((n_l), 1U)	set n_l to 1
SETTWO_L (n_l)	u2clint_l((n_l), 2U)	set n_l to 2
SETZERO_L (n_l)	(*(n_l) = 0)	set n_l to 0
sRandAES_l (S)	(((USHORT)\ SwitchRandAES_l((S))\ << 8) | (USHORT)\ SwitchRandAES_l((S)))	generate a random number of type USHORT

sRandRMDSHA1_l (S)	(((USHORT)\ sRandRMDSHA1_l((S))\ << 8) | (USHORT)\ sRandRMDSHA1_l((S)))	generate a random number of type USHORT
SWAP (a, b)	((a)^=(b),(b)^=(a),(a)^=(b))	exchange
SWAP_L (a_l, b_l)	(xor_l((a_l),(b_l),(a_l)), xor_l((b_l),(a_l),(b_l)), xor_l((a_l),(b_l),(a_l)))	exchange two CLINT values
ZEROCLINT_L (n_l)	memset((A), 0, sizeof(A))	delete a CLINT variable by overwriting

APPENDIX D

Calculation Times

CALCULATION TIMES FOR SEVERAL FLINT/C functions, calculated with a Pentium 3 processor running at 2.4 GHz and 1 Gbyte main memory under Linux with gcc 3.2.2, are given in Tables D-1 and D-2. The times for n operations were measured and then divided by n. Depending on the functions, n ranged between 100 and 5 million. An additional table (Table D-3) shows, for comparison, calculation times that were measured for several functions in the GNU Multi Precision Arithmetic library (GMP, version 4.1.2); cf. page 464.

Table D-1. Calculation times for several C functions (without assembler support)

Binary digits of the arguments; time in seconds

	128	256	512	768	1024	2048	4096
add_l	$1.0 \cdot 10^{-7}$	$1.4 \cdot 10^{-7}$	$2.4 \cdot 10^{-7}$	$3.2 \cdot 10^{-7}$	$4.9 \cdot 10^{-7}$	$7.4 \cdot 10^{-7}$	$1.2 \cdot 10^{-6}$
mul_l	$1.1 \cdot 10^{-6}$	$2.3 \cdot 10^{-6}$	$5.7 \cdot 10^{-6}$	$1.1 \cdot 10^{-5}$	$1.8 \cdot 10^{-5}$	$6.8 \cdot 10^{-5}$	$2.6 \cdot 10^{-4}$
sqr_l	$7.7 \cdot 10^{-7}$	$1.5 \cdot 10^{-6}$	$4.6 \cdot 10^{-6}$	$1.0 \cdot 10^{-5}$	$1.1 \cdot 10^{-5}$	$3.7 \cdot 10^{-5}$	$1.4 \cdot 10^{-4}$
div_l*	$1.1 \cdot 10^{-6}$	$1.9 \cdot 10^{-6}$	$4.6 \cdot 10^{-6}$	$8.5 \cdot 10^{-6}$	$1.7 \cdot 10^{-5}$	$6.3 \cdot 10^{-5}$	$2.4 \cdot 10^{-4}$
mmul_l	$3.2 \cdot 10^{-6}$	$6.8 \cdot 10^{-6}$	$2.2 \cdot 10^{-5}$	$4.6 \cdot 10^{-5}$	$8.1 \cdot 10^{-5}$	$3.1 \cdot 10^{-4}$	$1.2 \cdot 10^{-3}$
msqr_l	$2.9 \cdot 10^{-6}$	$6.3 \cdot 10^{-6}$	$2.1 \cdot 10^{-5}$	$4.2 \cdot 10^{-5}$	$7.4 \cdot 10^{-5}$	$2.8 \cdot 10^{-4}$	$1.1 \cdot 10^{-3}$
mexpk_l	$5.6 \cdot 10^{-4}$	$2.4 \cdot 10^{-3}$	$1.4 \cdot 10^{-2}$	$4.1 \cdot 10^{-2}$	$9.2 \cdot 10^{-2}$	$6.8 \cdot 10^{-1}$	5.2
mexpkm_l	$2.5 \cdot 10^{-4}$	$1.1 \cdot 10^{-3}$	$6.3 \cdot 10^{-3}$	$1.8 \cdot 10^{-2}$	$4.1 \cdot 10^{-2}$	$3.0 \cdot 10^{-1}$	2.2

*For the function div_l the number of digits refers to the dividend, while the divisor has half that number of digits.

One can see clearly the savings that squaring achieves over multiplication. Even the advantage realized by Montgomery exponentiation in mexpkm_l() can been seen, which requires only a little more than half the time needed for exponentiation using mexpk_l(). An RSA step with a 2048-bit key can thereby be computed in half a second, and with application of the Chinese remainder theorem (cf. page 203), in only one-fourth of a second.

Table D-2 demonstrates the difference in time that results from the use of assembler routines. Assembler support results in a speed advantage of about 70% for the modular functions. The gap between multiplication and squaring remains stable at about 50%.

Since the two functions mulmon_l() and sqrmon_l() do not exist as assembler routines, in this comparison the exponentiation function mexpk_l() can catch up significantly to the Montgomery exponentiation mexpm_l(). Both functions are roughly equally fast. There exists here an interesting potential for further improvement in performance (cf. Chapter 19) by means of suitable assembler extensions.

In the comparison between the FLINT/C and GMP functions (see Table D-3) one may see that the GMP multiplication and division are faster by 30% and 40% than the corresponding FLINT/C functions. In comparison with GMP version 2.0.2 in the first edition of this book, the functions for modular exponentiation in both libraries were about the same. Here GMP developers have achieved a speed advantage of a factor of two for the GMP library.

Since the GMP library is the fastest of the available libraries for large-integer arithmetic, we need not feel dissatisfied with this result. Rather, it can serve as an impetus to the reader to plumb the possibilities of the FLINT/C library. What would be required are assembler implementations of Montgomery multiplication and squaring, a further development of the Karatsuba methods for multiplication and squaring and their porting into assembler, and experiments for determining the most advantageous combination of these methods.

Table D-2. Calculation times for several C functions (with 80x86 assembler support)

Binary digits of the arguments; time in seconds

	128	256	512	768	1024	2048	4096
mul_l	$1.5 \cdot 10^{-6}$	$2.2 \cdot 10^{-6}$	$4.6 \cdot 10^{-6}$	$9.1 \cdot 10^{-6}$	$1.4 \cdot 10^{-5}$	$4.9 \cdot 10^{-5}$	$1.9 \cdot 10^{-4}$
sqr_l	$1.2 \cdot 10^{-6}$	$1.8 \cdot 10^{-6}$	$3.6 \cdot 10^{-6}$	$5.8 \cdot 10^{-6}$	$9.1 \cdot 10^{-6}$	$2.8 \cdot 10^{-5}$	$9.9 \cdot 10^{-5}$
div_l*	$9.8 \cdot 10^{-7}$	$9.7 \cdot 10^{-7}$	$2.3 \cdot 10^{-6}$	$3.1 \cdot 10^{-6}$	$5.7 \cdot 10^{-6}$	$2.0 \cdot 10^{-5}$	$7.3 \cdot 10^{-5}$
mmul_l	$2.8 \cdot 10^{-6}$	$4.8 \cdot 10^{-6}$	$1.1 \cdot 10^{-5}$	$2.1 \cdot 10^{-5}$	$3.4 \cdot 10^{-5}$	$1.2 \cdot 10^{-4}$	$4.7 \cdot 10^{-4}$
msqr_l	$2.3 \cdot 10^{-6}$	$4.2 \cdot 10^{-6}$	$9.5 \cdot 10^{-6}$	$1.9 \cdot 10^{-5}$	$2.9 \cdot 10^{-5}$	$1.0 \cdot 10^{-4}$	$3.8 \cdot 10^{-4}$
mexpk_l	$4.1 \cdot 10^{-4}$	$1.3 \cdot 10^{-3}$	$6.1 \cdot 10^{-3}$	$1.7 \cdot 10^{-2}$	$3.6 \cdot 10^{-2}$	$2.5 \cdot 10^{-1}$	1.9
mexpkm_l	$2.8 \cdot 10^{-4}$	$1.1 \cdot 10^{-3}$	$5.9 \cdot 10^{-3}$	$1.7 \cdot 10^{-2}$	$3.7 \cdot 10^{-2}$	$2.7 \cdot 10^{-1}$	2.1

*For the function div_l the number of digits refers to the dividend, while the divisor has half that number of digits.

Table D-3. Calculation times for several GMP functions (with 80x86 assembler support)

Binary digits of the arguments; time in seconds

	128	256	512	768	1024	2048	
mpz_add	$4.3 \cdot 10^{-8}$	$5.4 \cdot 10^{-8}$	$7.8 \cdot 10^{-8}$	$1.0 \cdot 10^{-7}$	$1.4 \cdot 10^{-7}$	$2.2 \cdot 10^{-7}$	$4.1 \cdot 10^{-7}$
mpz_mul	$1.7 \cdot 10^{-7}$	$5.5 \cdot 10^{-7}$	$1.8 \cdot 10^{-6}$	$3.7 \cdot 10^{-6}$	$8.1 \cdot 10^{-6}$	$1.9 \cdot 10^{-5}$	$5.7 \cdot 10^{-5}$
mpz_mod*	$2.1 \cdot 10^{-7}$	$5.1 \cdot 10^{-7}$	$1.2 \cdot 10^{-6}$	$1.8 \cdot 10^{-6}$	$3.9 \cdot 10^{-6}$	$9.4 \cdot 10^{-6}$	$3.1 \cdot 10^{-5}$
mpz_powm	$5.6 \cdot 10^{-5}$	$4.0 \cdot 10^{-4}$	$2.4 \cdot 10^{-3}$	$6.7 \cdot 10^{-3}$	$2.5 \cdot 10^{-2}$	$1.0 \cdot 10^{-1}$	$6.5 \cdot 10^{-1}$

*For the function mpz_mod the number of digits refers to the dividend, while the divisor has half that number of digits.

APPENDIX E
Notation

$\mathbb{N}$	the set of nonnegative integers $0, 1, 2, 3, \ldots$
$\mathbb{N}^+$	the set of positive integers $1, 2, 3, \ldots$
$\mathbb{Z}$	the set of integers $\ldots, -2, -1, 0, 1, 2, 3, \ldots$
$\mathbb{Z}_n$	the residue class ring modulo n over the integers (Chapter 5)
$\mathbb{Z}_n^\times$	reduced residue system modulo n
$\mathbb{F}_{p^n}$	finite field with p^n elements
$\bar{a}$	the residue class $a + n\mathbb{Z}$ in $\mathbb{Z}_n$
$a \approx b$	a approximately equal to b
$a \lesssim b$	a less than and approximately equal to b
$a \leftarrow b$	assignment: the variable a is given the value b
$\lvert a \rvert$	absolute value of a
$a \mid b$	a divides b without remainder
$a \nmid b$	a does not divide b
$a \equiv b \bmod n$	a is congruent to b modulo n, that is, $n \mid (a - b)$
$a \not\equiv b \bmod n$	a is not congruent to b modulo n, that is, $n \nmid (a - b)$
$\gcd(a, b)$	greatest common divisor of a and b (Section 10.1)
$\mathrm{lcm}(a, b)$	least common multiple of a and b (Section 10.1)
$\phi(n)$	Euler phi function (Section 10.2)

$O(\ )$	"Big-Oh." For two real-valued functions f and g with $g(x) \geq 0$ one writes $f = O(g)$ and says "f is big-Oh of g" if there exists a constant C such that $f(x) \leq Cg(x)$ for all x sufficiently large.
$\left(\dfrac{a}{b}\right)$	Jacobi symbol (Section 10.4.1)
$\lfloor x \rfloor$	greatest integer less than or equal to x
$\lceil x \rceil$	least integer greater than or equal to x
P	the set of computational problems that can be solved in polynomial time
NP	the set of computational problems that can be solved nondeterministically in polynomial time
$\log_b x$	logarithm of x to the base b
B	$B = 2^{16}$, the base for the representation of objects of type CLINT
MAX_b	maximal number of digits for a CLINT object to base B
MAX_2	maximal number of digits for a CLINT object to base 2
$N_{\max}$	largest natural number that can be represented by a CLINT object

Arithmetic and Number-Theoretic Packages

IF THERE BE ANY LINGERING doubt in the mind of the reader as to the attractiveness and utility of algorithmic number theory, a glance at the large number of web sites that treat this topic should bring doubt to any such doubt at once, perhaps even by overwriting the reader's cerebral registers. Just punch the search string "number theory" into your favorite Internet search engine, and up pop thousands of entries, a few of which have already been cited in this book. Many of these web sites contain links to available software packages or enable such packages to be downloaded. Such offers encapsulate a large bandwidth of functions for large-integer arithmetic, algebra, group theory, and number theory, demonstrating the efforts of many able and enthusiastic developers.

An extensive list of sources for such software packages can be found on the Number Theory Web Page, managed by Keith Matthews (University of Queensland, Brisbane, Australia). The web site is located at

`http://www.maths.uq.edu.au/~krm/web.html.`

The site also contains links to universities and research institutes as well as pointers to publications on relevant topics. In sum, this site is a veritable treasure trove. The following overview represents a small selection from the list of available software packages:

- **ARIBAS** is an interpreter that executes arithmetic and number-theoretic functions for large integers. ARIBAS implements the algorithms from [Fors] in Pascal. ARIBAS can be obtained as a supplement to that book, by anonymous ftp, from the directory `pub/forster/aribas` under `ftp.mathematik.uni-muenchen.de` or from `http://www.mathematik.uni-muenchen.de/` `forster`.

- **CALC**, by Keith Matthews, is a calculation program for arbitrarily large integers that takes commands on a command line, executes them, and displays the results. CALC makes available about 60 number-theoretic functions. The package is implemented in ANSI C and uses the parser generator YACC or BISON for parsing the command line. CALC can be obtained from `http://www.numbertheory.org/calc/krm_calc.html`.

- **GNU MP**, or **GMP**, from the GNU project, is a portable C library for arithmetic with arbitrarily large integers, as well as rational and real numbers. GMP achieves excellent performance due to the use of assembler code for an impressive array of CPUs. GMP can be obtained via ftp from `www.gnu.org`, `prep.ai.mit.edu`, as well as GNU mirror sites.

- **LiDIA** is one of the software libraries developed at the Technical University Darmstadt for number-theoretic calculations. LiDIA contains an extensive collection of highly optimized functions for calculating in $\mathbb{Z}$, $\mathbb{Q}$, $\mathbb{R}$, $\mathbb{C}$, $\mathbb{F}_{2^n}$, $\mathbb{F}_{p^n}$, as well as for interval arithmetic. Current factorization algorithms are also implemented, such as for lattice base reduction, linear-algebraic algorithms, methods for calculating in number fields, and polynomials. LiDIA supports interfaces to other arithmetic packages, including the GMP package. LiDIA's own interpreted language LC facilitates, through its support of C++, the transition to translated programs. All platforms are supported that permit the use of long file names and for which a suitable C++ compiler is available, such as Linux 2.0.x, Windows NT 4.0, OS/2 Warp 4.0, HPUX-10.20, Sun Solaris 2.5.1/2.6. A port to the Apple Macintosh is also available. LiDIA can be obtained at `http://www.informatik.tu-darmstadt.de/TI/LiDIA`.

- **Numbers**, by Ivo Düntsch, is a library of object files that provide basic number-theoretic functions for numbers with up to 150 decimal digits. The functions, written in Pascal, and the interpreter, contained in the package as well, were developed with the goal of providing students with nontrivial examples and experiments in calculation. The source for Numbers is `http://archives.math.utk.edu/software/msdos/number.theory/num202d/.html`.

- **PARI** is a number-theoretic package by Henri Cohen et al. that implements the algorithms presented in [Cohe]. PARI can be used as an interpreter and as a function library that can be linked to programs. Through the use of assembler code for various platforms (UNIX, Macintosh, PC, and others) a high level of performance is achieved. PARI can be obtained at `www.parigp-home.de`.

References

[Adam] Adams, Carlisle, Steve Lloyd: *Understanding Public Key Infrastructure Concepts, Standards & Deployment*, Macmillan Technical Publishing, Indianapolis, 1999.

[AgKS] Agrawal, Maninda, Neeraj Kayal, Nitin Saxena: PRIMES is in P, *Indian Institute of Technology*, 2003.

[BaSh] Bach, Eric, Jeffrey Shallit: *Algorithmic Number Theory, Vol. 1, Efficient Algorithms*, MIT Press, Cambridge (MA), London, 1996.

[BCGP] Beauchemin, Pierre, Gilles Brassard, Claude Crépeau, Claude Goutier, Carl Pomerance: The generation of random numbers that are probably prime, *Journal of Cryptology*, Vol. 1, No. 1, pp. 53–64, 1988.

[Bern] Daniel J. Bernstein: Proving primality after Agrawal–Kayal–Saxena, Draft paper, http://cr.yp.to/papers.html#aks, 2003.

[Beut] Beutelspacher, Albrecht: *Kryptologie*, 2. Auflage, Vieweg, 1991.

[Bies] Bieser, Wendelin, Heinrich Kersten: *Elektronisch unterschreiben—die digitale Signatur in der Praxis*, 2. Auflage, Hüthig, 1999.

[BiSh] Biham, Eli, Adi Shamir: Differential cryptanalysis of DES-like cryptosystems, *Journal of Cryptology*, Vol. 4, No. 1, 1991, pp. 3–72.

[Blum] Blum, L., M. Blum, M. Shub: A simple unpredictable pseudo-random number generator, *SIAM Journal on Computing*, Vol. 15, No. 2, 1986, pp. 364–383.

[BMBF] Bundesministerium für Bildung, Wissenschaft, Forschung und Technologie: *IUKDG—Informations- und Kommunikationsdienste-Gesetz—Umsetzung und Evaluierung*, Bonn, 1997.

[BMWT] Bundesministerium für Wirtschaft und Technologie: *Entwurf eines Gesetzes über Rahmenbedingungen für elektronische Signaturen—Diskussionsentwurf zur Anhörung und Unterrichtung der beteiligten Fachkreise und Verbände*, April 2000.

[Bone] Boneh, Dan: Twenty years of attacks on the RSA-cryptosystem, *Proc. ECC*, 1998.

[Bon2] Boneh, Dan, Antoine Joux, Phong Q. Nguyen: Why Textbook ElGamal and RSA Encryption are Insecure, *Advances in Cryptology*, ASIACRYPT 2000, Lecture Notes in Computer Science 1976, pp. 30–43, Springer-Verlag, 2000.

[Born] Bornemann, Folkmar: PRIMES Is in P: A Breakthrough for "Everyman," *Notices of the AMS*, May 2003.

[Bos1] Bosch, Karl: *Elementare Einführung in die Wahrscheinlichkeitsrechnung*, Vieweg, 1984.

[Bos2] Bosch, Karl: *Elementare Einführung in die angewandte Statistik*, Vieweg, 1984.

[Boss] Bosselaers, Antoon, René Govaerts, Joos Vandewalle: Comparison of three modular reduction functions, in *Advances in Cryptology*, CRYPTO 93, *Lecture Notes in Computer Science No. 773*, pp. 175–186, Springer-Verlag, New York, 1994.

[Bres] Bressoud, David M.: *Factorization and Primality Testing*, Springer-Verlag, New York, 1989.

[BSI1] Bundesamt für Sicherheit in der Informationstechnik: Geeignete Algorithmen zur Erfüllung der Anforderungen nach §17 Abs. 1 through 3 SigG of 22 May 2001 in association with Anlage 1 Abschnitt I Nr. 2 SigV of 22 November 2001. Published 13 February 2004 in *Bundesanzeiger* Nr. 30, pp. 2537–2538.

[BSI2] Bundesamt für Sicherheit in der Informationstechnik: Anwendungshinweise und Interpretation zum Schema (AIS). Funktionalitätsklassen und Evaluations-methodologie für deterministische Zufallszahlengeneratoren. AIS 20. Version 1. Bonn, 1999.

[Burt] Burthe, R. J., Jr.: Further investigations with the strong probable prime test, *Mathematics of Computation*, Volume 65, pp. 373–381, 1996.

[Bund] Bundschuh, Peter: *Einführung in die Zahlentheorie*, 3. Auflage, Springer-Verlag, Berlin, Heidelberg, 1996.

[BuZi] Burnikel, Christoph, Joachim Ziegler: Fast recursive division, Forschungs-bericht MPI-I-98-1-022, Max-Planck-Institut für Informatik, Saarbrücken, 1998.

[CJRR] Chari, Suresh, Charanjit Jutla, Josyula R. Rao, Pankaj Rohatgi: *A Caution-ary Note Regarding Evaluation of AES Candidates on Smart Cards*, 1999, http://csrc.nist.gov/encryption/aes/round1/conf2/papers/chari.pdf

[Cohe] Cohen, Henri: *A Course in Computational Algebraic Number Theory*, Springer-Verlag, Berlin, Heidelberg, 1993.

[Coro] Coron, Jean-Sebastien, David Naccache, Julien P. Stern: On the security of RSA padding, ed. M. Wiener, in *Advances in Cryptology, CRYPTO '99, Lecture Notes in Computer Science No. 1666*, pp. 1–17, Springer-Verlag, New York, 1999.

[Cowi] Cowie, James, Bruce Dodson, R.-Marije Elkenbracht-Huizing, Arjen K. Lenstra, Peter L. Montgomery, Joerg Zayer: A world wide number field sieve factoring record: on to 512 bits, ed. K. Kim and T. Matsumoto, in *Advances in Cryptology, ASIACRYPT '96, Lecture Notes in Computer Science No. 1163*, pp. 382–394, Springer-Verlag, Berlin 1996.

[CrPa] Crandall, Richard E., Jason S. Papadopoulos: On the implementation of AKS-class primality tests, http://developer.apple.com/hardware/ ve/pdf/aks3.pdf.

[DaLP] Damgard, Ivan, Peter Landrock, Carl Pomerance: Average case error estimates for the strong probable prime test, *Mathematics of Computation*, Volume 61, pp. 177–194, 1993.

[DaRi] Daemen, Joan, Vincent Rijmen: *AES-Proposal: Rijndael*, Doc. Vers. 2.0, September 1999, http://www.nist.gov/encryption/aes

[DR02] Daemen, Joan, Vincent Rijmen: The Design of Rijndael: AES: The Advanced Encryption Standard, Springer-Verlag, Heidelberg, 2002.

[Deit] Deitel, H. M., P. J. Deitel: *C++: How To Program*, Prentice Hall, 1994.

[Dene] Denert, Ernst: *Software-Engineering*, Springer-Verlag, Heidelberg, 1991.

[deWe] De Weger, Benne: Cryptanalysis of RSA with small prime difference, *Cryptology ePrint Archive*, Report 2000/016, 2000.

[Diff] Diffie, Whitfield, Martin E. Hellman: *New Directions in Cryptography*, IEEE Trans. Information Theory, pp. 644–654, Vol. IT-22, 1976.

[DoBP] Dobbertin, Hans, Antoon Bosselaers, Bart Preneel: RIPEMD-160, a strength-ened version of RIPEMD, ed. D. Gollman, in *Fast Software Encryption, Third International Workshop, Lecture Notes in Computer Science No. 1039*, pp. 71–82, Springer-Verlag, Berlin, Heidelberg, 1996.

[DuKa] Dussé, Stephen R., Burton. S. Kaliski: A cryptographic library for the Motorola DSP56000, in *Advances in Cryptology, EUROCRYPT '90, Lecture Notes in Computer Science No. 473*, pp. 230–244, Springer-Verlag, New York, 1990.

[Dunc] Duncan, Ray: *Advanced OS/2-Programming: The Microsoft Guide to the OS/2-Kernel for Assembly Language and C Programmers*, Microsoft Press, Redmond, Washington, 1981.

[East] Eastlake, D., S. Crocker, J. Schiller: *Randomness Recommendations for Security*, RFC1750, 1994.

[Elli] Ellis, J. H.: *The Possibility of Non-Secret Encryption*, 1970, http://www.cesg.gov.uk/htmsite/publications/media/possnse.pdf.

[ElSt] Ellis, Margaret A., Bjarne Stroustrup: *The Annotated C++ Reference Manual*, Addison-Wesley, Reading, MA, 1990.

[Endl] Endl, Kurth, Wolfgang Luh: *Analysis I*, Akademische Verlagsgesellschaft Wiesbaden, 1977.

[Enge] Engel-Flechsig, Stefan, Alexander Roßnagel eds., *Multimedia-Recht*, C. H. Beck, Munich, 1998.

[EESSI] European Electronic Signature Standardization Initiative: *Algorithms and Parameters for Secure Electronic Signatures*, V.1.44 DRAFT, 2001.

[EU99] *Richtlinie 1999/93/EG des Europäischen Parlaments und des Rates vom 13. Dezember 1999 über gemeinschaftliche Rahmenbedingungen für elektronische Signaturen.*

[Evan] Evans, David: *Splint Users Guide*, Version 3.1.1-1, Secure Programming Group University of Virginia Department of Computer Science, June 2003.

[Fegh] Feghhi, Jalal, Jalil Feghhi, Peter Williams: *Digital Certificates: Applied Internet Security*, Addison-Wesley, Reading, MA, 1999.

[Fiat] Fiat, Amos, Adi Shamir: How to prove yourself: practical solutions to identification and signature problems, in *Advances in Cryptology, CRYPTO '86, Lecture Notes in Computer Science No. 263*, pp. 186–194, Springer-Verlag, New York, 1987.

[FIPS] Federal Information Processing Standard Publication 140 - 1: *Security requirements for cryptographic modules*, US Department of Commerce/ National Institute of Standards and Technology (NIST), 1994.

[FI80] National Institute of Standards and Technology: *Secure Hash Algorithm*, Federal Information Processing Standard 180-2, NIST, 2001.

[FI81] National Institute of Standards and Technology: *DES Modes of Operation*, Federal Information Processing Standard 81, NIST, 1980.

[F197] National Institute of Standards and Technology: *ADVANCED ENCRYPTION STANDARD (AES)*, Federal Information Processing Standards Publication 197, November 26, 2001

[Fisc] Fischer, Gerd, Reinhard Sacher: *Einführung in die Algebra*, Teubner, 1974.

[Fors] Forster, Otto: *Algorithmische Zahlenthorie*, Vieweg, Braunschweig,1996.

[Fumy] Fumy, Walter, Hans Peter Rieß: *Kryptographie*, 2. Auflage, Oldenbourg, 1994.

[Gimp] Gimpel Software: *PC-lint, A Diagnostic Facility for C and C++*.

[Glad] Glade, Albert, Helmut Reimer, Bruno Struif, editors: *Digitale Signatur & Sicherheitssensitive Anwendungen*, DuD-Fachbeiträge, Vieweg, 1995.

[Gldm] Gladman, Brian: A Specification for Rijndael, the AES Algorithm, http://fp.gladman.plus.com, 2001.

[GoPa] Goubin, Louis, Jacques Patarin DES and differential power analysis, *Proceedings of CHES'99*, Lecture Notes in Computer Science, No. 1717, Springer-Verlag, 1999.

[Gord] Gordon, J. A.: Strong primes are easy to find, *Advances in Cryptology, Proceedings of Eurocrypt '84*, pp. 216–223, Springer-Verlag, Berlin, Heidelberg, 1985.

[Gut1] Gutmann, Peter: Software generation of Practically Strong Random Numbers, *Usenix Security Symposium*, 1998

[Gut2] Gutmann, Peter: *Random Number Generation*, www.cs.auckland.ac.nz/~pgut001, 2000.

[Halm] Halmos, Paul, R.: *Naive Set Theory*, Springer-Verlag New York, 1987.

[Harb] Harbison, Samuel P, Guy L. Steele, Jr.: *C: A Reference Manual*, 4th Edition, Prentice Hall, Englewood Cliffs, 1995.

[Hatt] Hatton, Les: Safer C: *Developing Software for High-Integrity and Safety-Critical Systems*, McGraw-Hill, London, 1995.

[Heid] Heider, Franz-Peter: *Quadratische Kongruenzen*, unpublished manuscript, Cologne, 1997.

[Henr] Henricson, Mats, Erik Nyquist: *Industrial Strength C++*, Prentice Hall, New Jersey, 1997.

[HeQu] Heise, Werner, Pasquale Quattrocchi: *Informations- und Codierungstheorie*, Springer-Verlag, Berlin, Heidelberg, 1983.

[HKW] Heider, Franz-Peter, Detlef Kraus, Michael Welschenbach: *Mathematische Methoden der Kryptoanalyse*, DuD-Fachbeiträge, Vieweg, Braunschweig, 1985.

[Herk] Herkommer, Mark: *Number Theory: A Programmer's Guide*, McGraw-Hill, 1999.

[HoLe] Howard, Michael, David LeBlanc: *Writing Secure Code*, Microsoft Press, 2002.

[IEEE] IEEE P1363 / D13: *Standard Specifications for Public Key Cryptography*, Draft Version 13, November 1999.

[ISO1] ISO/IEC 10118-3: *Information Technology—Security Techniques—Hash-Functions. Part 3: Dedicated Hash-Functions*, CD, 1996.

[ISO2] ISO/IEC 9796: *Information Technology—Security Techniques—Digital Signature Scheme giving Message Recovery*, 1991.

[ISO3] ISO/IEC 9796-2: *Information Technology—Security Techniques—Digital Signature Scheme Giving Message Recovery, Part 2: Mechanisms Using a Hash-Function*, 1997.

[Koeu] Koeune, F., G. Hachez, J.-J. Quisquater: *Implementation of Four AES Candidates on Two Smart Cards*, UCL Crypto Group, 2000.

[Knut] Knuth, Donald Ervin: *The Art of Computer Programming, Vol. 2: Seminumerical Algorithms*, 3rd Edition, Addison-Wesley, Reading, MA, 1998.

[Kobl] Koblitz, Neal: *A Course in Number Theory and Cryptography*, Springer-Verlag, New York, 2nd Edition 1994.

[Kob2] Koblitz, Neal: *Algebraic Aspects of Cryptography*, Springer-Verlag, Berlin, Heidelberg, 1998.

[KoJJ] Kocher, Paul, Joshua Jaffe, Benjamin Jun: *Introduction to Differential Power Analysis and Related Attacks*, 1998, http://www.cryptography.com/dpa/technical/

[Kran] Kranakis, Evangelos: *Primality and Cryptography*, Wiley-Teubner Series in Computer Science, 1986.

[KSch] Kuhlins, Stefan, Martin Schader: *Die C++-Standardbibliothek*, Springer-Verlag, 1999.

[LeVe] Lenstra, Arjen K., Eric R. Verheul: *Selecting Cryptographic Key Sizes*, 1999, http://www.cryptosavvy.com

[Lind] van der Linden, Peter: *Expert C Programming*, SunSoft/Prentice Hall, Mountain View, CA, 1994.

[Lipp] Lippman, Stanley, B.: *C++ Primer*, 2nd Edition, Addison-Wesley, Reading, MA, 1993.

[Magu] Maguire, Stephen A.: *Writing Solid Code*, Microsoft Press, Redmond, Washington, 1993.

[Matt] Matthews, Tim: *Suggestions for Random Number Generation in Software*, RSA Data Security Engineering Report, December 1995.

[Mene] Menezes, Alfred J.: *Elliptic Curve Public Key Cryptosystems*, Kluwer Academic Publishers, 1993.

[Mey1] Meyers, Scott D.: *Effective C++*, 2nd Edition, Addison-Wesley, Reading, Mass., 1998.

[Mey2] Meyers, Scott D.: *More Effective C++*, 2nd Edition, Addison-Wesley, Reading, Mass., 1998.

[Mied] Miedbrodt, Anja: *Signaturregulierung im Rechtsvergleich, Der Elektronische Rechtsverkehr* 1, Nomos Verlagsgesellschaft Baden-Baden, 2000.

[Mont] Montgomery, Peter L.: Modular multiplication without trial division, *Mathematics of Computation*, pp. 519–521, 44 (170), 1985.

[MOV] Menezes, Alfred J., Paul van Oorschot, Scott A. Vanstone, *Handbook of Applied Cryptography*, CRC Press, 1997.

[Murp] Murphy, Mark L.: *C/C++ Software Quality Tools*, Prentice Hall, New Jersey, 1996.

[N38A] National Institute of Standards and Technology: *Recommendation for Block Cipher Modes of Operation*, NIST Special Publication 800-38A, 2001.

[N38B] National Institute of Standards and Technology: *DRAFT Recommendation for Block Cipher Modes of Operation: The RMAC Authentication Mode*, NIST Special Publication 800-38B, 2002.

[N38C] National Institute of Standards and Technology: *Recommendation for Block Cipher Modes of Operation: The CCM Mode for Authentication and Confidentiality*, NIST Special Publication 800-38C, 2004.

[Nied] Niederreiter, Harald: *Random Number Generation and Quasi-Monte Carlo Methods*, SIAM, Philadelphia, 1992.

[NIST] Nechvatal, James, Elaine Barker, Lawrence Bassham, William Burr, Morris Dworkin, James Foti, Edward Roback: *Report on the Development of the Advanced Encryption Standard*, National Institute of Standards and Technology, 2000.

[Nive] Niven, Ivan, Herbert S. Zuckerman: *Einführung in die Zahlentheorie* vols. I und II, Bibliographisches Institut, Mannheim, 1972.

[Odly] Odlyzko, Andrew: *Discrete Logarithms: The Past and the Future*, AT&T Labs Research, 1999.

[Petz] Petzold, Charles: *Programming Windows: The Microsoft Guide to Writing Applications for Windows 3.1*, Microsoft Press, Redmond, Washington, 1992.

[Pla1] Plauger, P. J.: *The Standard C Library*, Prentice-Hall, Englewood Cliffs, New Jersey, 1992.

[Pla2] Plauger, P. J.: *The Draft Standard C++ Library*, Prentice-Hall, Englewood Cliffs, New Jersey, 1995.

[Pren] Preneel, Bart: *Analysis and Design of Cryptographic Hash Functions*, Dissertation at the Katholieke Universiteit Leuven, 1993.

[Rabi] Rabin, Michael, O.: *Digital Signatures and Public-Key Functions as Intractable as Factorization*, MIT Laboratory for Computer Science, Technical Report, MIT/LCS/TR-212, 1979.

[RDS1] RSA Laboratories: *Public Key Cryptography Standards, PKCS #1: RSA Encryption*, Version 2.1, RSA Security Inc., 2002.

[RDS2] RSA Security, Inc.: *Recent Results on Signature Forgery*, RSA Laboratories Bulletin, 1999, `http://www.rsasecurity.com/`.

[RegT] Regulierungsbehörde für Telekommunikation und Post (RegTP): *Bekanntmachung zur elektronischen Signatur nach dem Signaturgesetz und Signaturverordnung (Übersicht über geeignete Algorithmen)*, January 2, 2005.

[Rein] Reinhold, Arnold: *P=?NP Doesn't Affect Cryptography*, May 1996, `http://world.std.com/_reinhold/p=np.txt`

[Ries] Riesel, Hans: *Prime Numbers and Computer Methods for Factorization*, Birkhäuser, Boston, 1994.

[Rive] Rivest, Ronald, Adi Shamir, Leonard Adleman: A method for obtaining digital signatures, *Communications of the ACM* 21, pp. 120–126, 1978.

[Rose] Rose, H: E.: *A Course in Number Theory*, 2nd Edition, Oxford University Press, Oxford, 1994.

[Saga] Sagan, Carl: *Cosmos*, Random House, New York, 1980.

[Sali] Saliger, Uwe: *Sichere Implementierung und Integration kryptographischer Softwarekomponenten am Beispiel der Zufallszahlengenerierung*, Diplomarbeit an der Universität Bonn, 2002.

[Salo] Salomaa, Arto: *Public-Key Cryptography*, 2nd Edition, Springer-Verlag, Berlin, Heidelberg, 1996.

[Schn] Schneier, Bruce: *Applied Cryptography*, 2nd Edition, John Wiley & Sons, New York, 1996.

[Scho] Schönhage, Arnold: A lower bound on the length of addition chains, *Theoretical Computer Science*, pp. 229–242, Vol. 1, 1975.

[Schr] Schröder, Manfred R.: *Number Theory in Science and Communications*, 3rd edition, Springer-Verlag, Berlin, Heidelberg, 1997.

[SigG] *Gesetz über Rahmenbedingungen für elektronische Signaturen und zur Änderung weiterer Vorschriften*, at `http://www.iid.de/iukdg`, 2001.

[SigV] Verordnung zur elektronischen Signatur (Signaturverordnung, SigV) of 16 November 2001.

[Skal] Skaller, John Maxwell: Multiple precision arithmetic in C, edited by Dale Schumacher, in *Software Solutions in C*, Academic Press, pp. 343–454, 1994.

[Spul] Spuler, David A.: *C++ and C Debugging, Testing and Reliability*, Prentice Hall, New Jersey, 1994.

[Squa] Daemen, Joan, Lars Knudsen, Vincent Rijmen: The block cipher square, *Fast Software Encryption, Lecture Notes in Computer Science No. 1267*, pp. 149–165, Springer-Verlag, 1997.

[Stal] Stallings, William: *Cryptography and Network Security*, 2nd Edition, Prentice Hall, New Jersey, 1999.

[Stin]   Stinson, Douglas R.: *Cryptography—Theory and Practice*, Prentice Hall, New Jersey, 1995.

[Stlm]   Stallman, Richard M.: *Using and Porting GNU CC*, Free Software Foundation.

[Str1]   Stroustrup, Bjarne: *The C++ Programming Language*, 3rd Edition, Addison-Wesley, Reading, MA, 1997.

[Str2]   Stroustrup, Bjarne: *The Design and Evolution of* C++, Addison-Wesley, Reading, MA, 1994.

[Teal]   Teale, Steve: *C++ IOStreams Handbook*, Addison-Wesley, Reading, MA, 1993.

[Tso]   Ts'o, Theodore: `random.c`; Version 1.89, 1999

[WFLY]   Wan, Xiaoyun, Dengguo Feng, Xuejia Lai, HongboYu: *Collisions for Hash Functions MD4, MD5, HAVAL-128 and RIPEMD*, August 2004.

[Wien]   Wiener, Michael: Cryptanalysis of short RSA secret exponents, in *IEEE Transactions on Information Theory*, 36(3): pp. 553–558, 1990.

[Yaco]   Yacobi, Y.: Exponentiating faster with addition chains, *Advances in Cryptology, EUROCRYPT '90, Lecture Notes in Computer Science No. 473*, pp. 222–229, Springer-Verlag, New York, 1990.

[Zieg]   Ziegler, Joachim: personal communication 1998, 1999.

Index